Michelangelo and His Influence

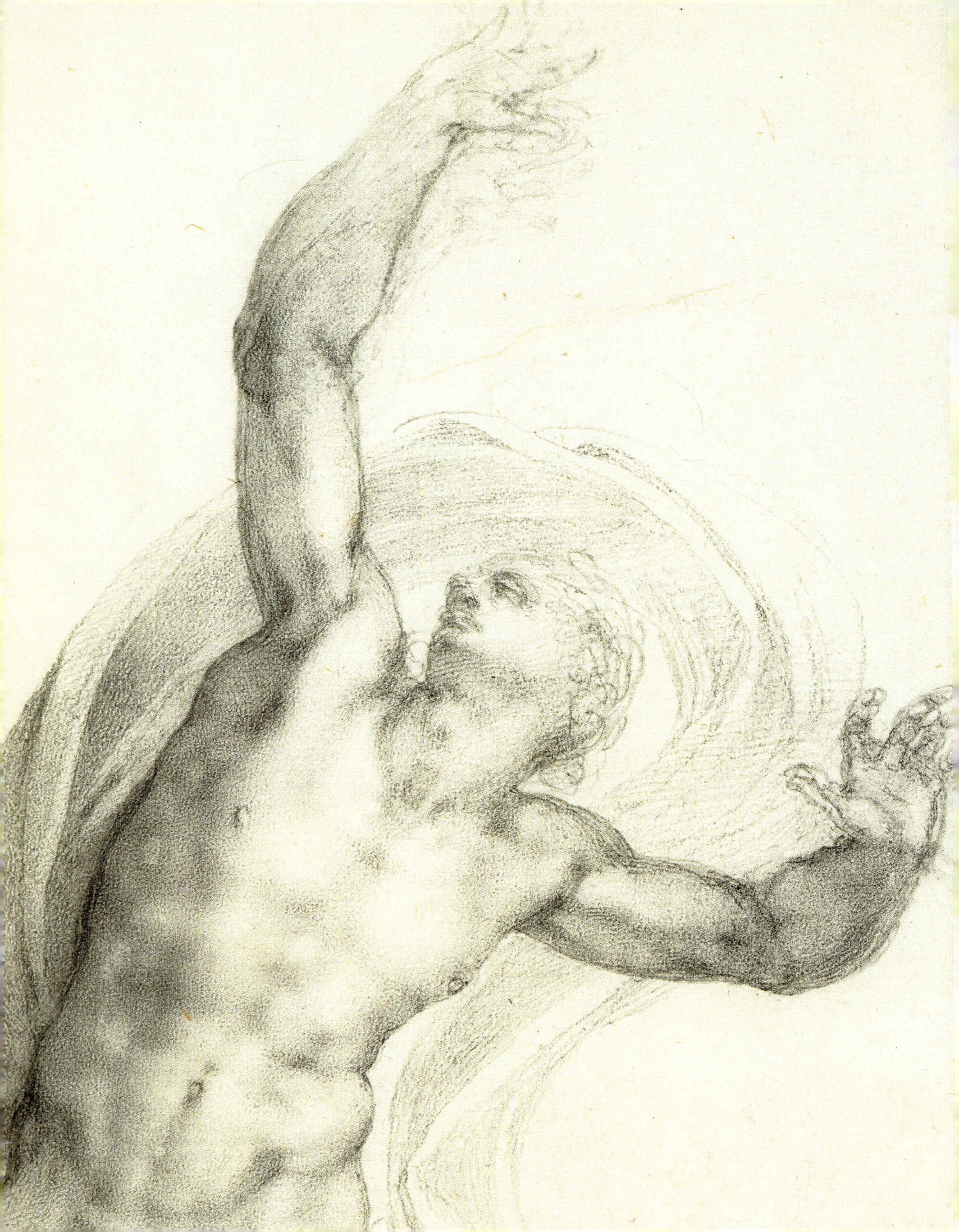

Michelangelo and His Influence

Drawings from Windsor Castle

Paul Joannides

NATIONAL GALLERY OF ART, WASHINGTON
LUND HUMPHRIES PUBLISHERS, LONDON

The exhibition *Michelangelo and His Influence: Drawings from Windsor Castle* was organized by the Royal Library, Windsor Castle, in association with the National Gallery of Art, Washington, the Kimbell Art Museum, Fort Worth, and the Art Institute of Chicago.

NATIONAL GALLERY OF ART, WASHINGTON
27 October 1996–5 January 1997

KIMBELL ART MUSEUM, FORT WORTH
19 January–30 March 1997

THE ART INSTITUTE OF CHICAGO
12 April–22 June 1997

FITZWILLIAM MUSEUM, CAMBRIDGE
7 October–14 December 1997

THE QUEEN'S GALLERY, LONDON
23 January–5 April 1998

© copyright 1996 Board of Trustees, National Gallery of Art, Washington / Lund Humphries Publishers, London

Text by Paul Joannides © 1996 National Gallery of Art, Washington
Preface by Oliver Everett © 1996 Her Majesty Queen Elizabeth II
Text by Martin Clayton © 1996 Her Majesty Queen Elizabeth II

PHOTOGRAPHIC CREDITS
Illustrations from The Royal Collection, Windsor Castle, Royal Library © 1996 Her Majesty Queen Elizabeth II
Other illustrations © 1996 sources as listed

All rights reserved. This book may not be reproduced, in whole or part (beyond the copying permitted by Sections 107 and 108 of the U.S. Copyright Law, and except by reviewers from the public press), without written permission from the publishers.

First published in Great Britain in 1996 by Lund Humphries Publishers Limited,
Park House, 1 Russell Gardens, London NW11 9NN
Trade distribution in the USA by Antique Collectors' Club, Market Street Industrial Park,
Wappingers Falls, New York

Produced by the National Gallery of Art, Washington
Editor-in-Chief, Frances P. Smyth
Edited by Julie Warnement
Designed by Phyllis Hecht
Typeset in Adobe Garamond and Poetica Chancery by Artech Graphics II, Inc., Baltimore, Maryland
Printed in Great Britain by BAS Printers Limited, Over Wallop, Stockbridge, Hampshire,
on 150 gsm Fineblade Smooth

LIBRARY OF CONGRESS CATALOGUING-IN-PUBLICATION DATA
Joannides, Paul.
Michelangelo and his influence : drawings from Windsor Castle / Paul Joannides.
p. cm.
Catalogue of an exhibition held at the National Gallery of Art, Washington, 27 Oct. 1996–5 Jan. 1997; Kimbell Art Museum, Fort Worth, 19 Jan.–30 March 1997; The Art Institute of Chicago, 12 April–22 June 1997.
Includes bibliographical references.
ISBN 0-89468-261-X (paper)
1. Michelangelo Buonarroti, 1475–1564—Exhibitions. 2. Michelangelo Buonarroti, 1475–1564—Influence—Exhibitions. 3. Drawing, Italian—Exhibitions. 4. Drawing, Renaissance—Italy—Exhibitions. 5. Drawing—England—Windsor—Exhibitions. 6. Windsor Castle. Royal Library—Exhibitions. I. Michelangelo Buonarroti, 1475–1564. II. National Gallery of Art (U.S.) III. Kimbell Art Museum. IV. Art Institute of Chicago. V. Title.
NC257.B8A4 1996
741.945—dc20 96-26592
CIP

BRITISH LIBRARY CATALOGUING-IN-PUBLICATION DATA
A catalogue record of this book is available from the British Library
ISBN 0 85331 722 4 (cloth)
ISBN 0 85331 713 5 (paperback)

NOTE TO THE READER
Dimensions are in centimeters, followed by inches within parentheses, with height preceding width.

ILLUSTRATIONS
FRONT COVER: detail of cat. 16; BACK COVER: detail of cat. 7; FRONTISPIECE: detail of cat. 39;
PAGE 6: detail of cat. 51; PAGE 10: detail of cat. 18

Contents

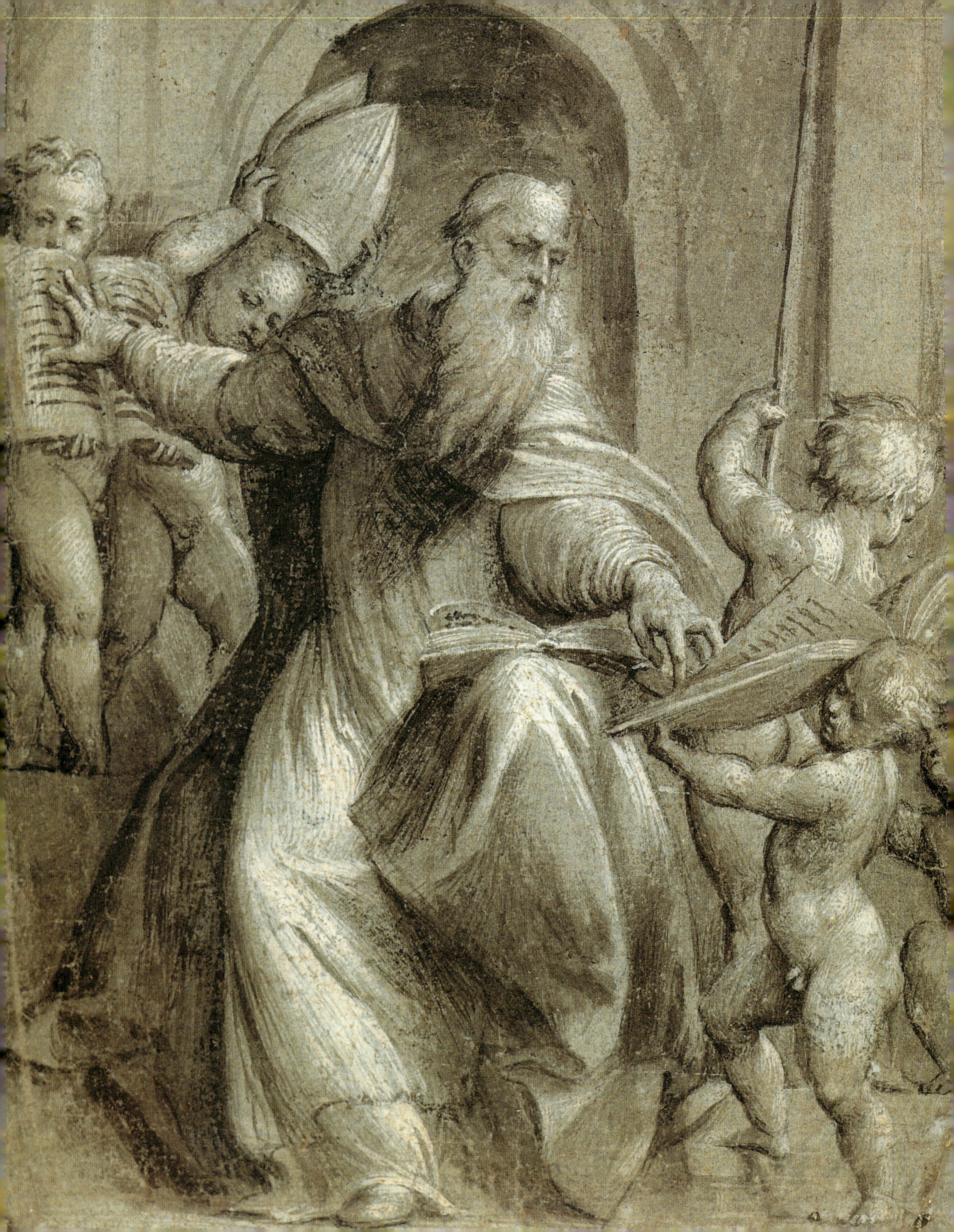

Directors' Foreword

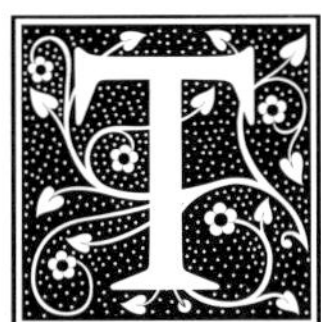

he British Royal Collection includes superlative works of art in numerous areas, but is perhaps most widely known for its old master drawings. The drawings housed in the Royal Library at Windsor Castle have been gathered by many monarchs over more than three centuries. This collection, especially famous for its Italian drawings, includes an unrivaled group of Leonardos and works by the legendary Michelangelo. A number of these drawings have been generously lent to traveling exhibitions in recent years.

The outstanding collection of Michelangelo's drawings shows many aspects of his art and is unusually rich in his rare but highly prized presentation drawings. Thus, the Royal Collection provides a remarkable opportunity to appreciate the variety and power of Michelangelo's draftsmanship. The depth of the Renaissance collection also provides a wide range of drawings by other early Italian masters that reveals their contemporary reaction to Michelangelo's extraordinary art.

For her gracious generosity in lending such a marvelous selection of works, we are most of all indebted to Her Majesty Queen Elizabeth II.

For conceiving this exhibition based on the Royal Collection, we are grateful to Martin Clayton, assistant curator at Windsor Castle, and to Paul Joannides, fellow of Clare Hall and lecturer in history of art at the University of Cambridge. We are especially grateful to Dr. Joannides for sharing his research and extensive knowledge of Michelangelo in this catalogue, and to Mr. Clayton for his essay on provenance.

We deeply appreciate the collegial friendship and help from Oliver Everett, the Librarian at Windsor Castle, and Jane Roberts, curator of the Print Room, as well as Theresa-Mary Morton, curator of exhibitions; they have been wonderful in supporting the exhibition and in arranging the details of the loan.

Our thanks go also to Andrew Robison, Andrew W. Mellon senior curator at the National Gallery of Art, Suzanne Folds McCullagh, curator of earlier prints and drawings at the Art Institute of Chicago, and the undersigned Edmund Pillsbury for their help in developing the selection and in coordinating the exhibition at their respective museums. The exhibition is supported by an indemnity from the Federal Council on the Arts and the Humanities.

EARL A. POWELL
Director
National Gallery of Art

EDMUND P. PILLSBURY
Director
Kimbell Art Museum

JAMES N. WOOD
Director
The Art Institute of Chicago

Preface

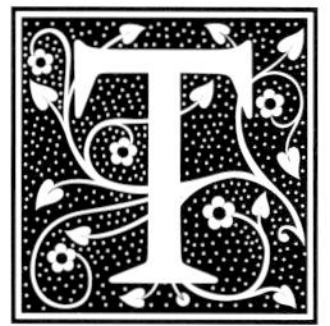

he Royal Library at Windsor Castle houses in its Print Room, the Royal Collection of over thirty thousand drawings and watercolors. Amongst these, Italian drawings of the sixteenth and seventeenth centuries are particularly well represented. Best known are the six hundred drawings by Leonardo da Vinci dating from the late fifteenth and early sixteenth centuries. However, the holdings of works by Michelangelo, Raphael, and their contemporaries also constitute a most important part of the collection.

The Michelangelo drawings at Windsor include some of his most famous works, the presentation drawings, such as the *Fall of Phaeton* (cat. 9a), *Tityus* (cat. 12a), the *Archers* (cat. 16), and the *Three Labors of Hercules* (cat. 18). As A. E. Popham and Johannes Wilde pointed out in the introduction of their catalogue raisonné of the earlier Italian drawings in the Royal Collection (published in 1949), although the drawings by Raphael at Windsor (eighteen) are about equal in number to those by Michelangelo (twenty-two), they are not indispensable to an appreciation of him as a draftsman in the same way as the presentation drawings are in the case of Michelangelo.

From Michelangelo's drawings, and those of his peers, at Windsor it is possible to study many aspects of the history of art of that period. We are particularly grateful to Paul Joannides for having made the fascinating and perceptive study of Michelangelo and his influence that is illustrated in this exhibition and that is contained in this catalogue. It includes fourteen of the seventeen drawings catalogued by Popham and Wilde as autograph, and four of the five drawings of *écorchés* that were subsequently published as Michelangelo's own work. They are here studied alongside other drawings from the collection that relate to Michelangelo's oeuvre.

The Michelangelo drawings in the Royal Collection have never previously been shown in such a manner as here, to illustrate not only Michelangelo's brilliant draftsmanship but also how his work influenced and affected others in the first half of the sixteenth century and beyond.

One of the many points of interest in the Royal Collection is the way in which it represents the artistic tastes and collecting habits of successive kings, queens, and princes. The collection does not comprise an even and comprehensive range of artistic work. It is more of a reflection on the character and interests of its royal collectors over the centuries.

These points are illustrated in the present exhibition. As is suggested in Martin Clayton's note on provenance, some of these Michelangelo drawings may have been collected in the seventeenth century by King Charles II. Other Michelangelo and related drawings shown here were acquired by King George III in the latter part of the eighteenth century. Of all the royal contributors to the Royal Collection of old master drawings, George III must rank first. About half of the present collection was acquired by him. Of the drawings he acquired, Italian old masters were predominant. He bought several large entire collections from Italian sources; and his librarian, Richard Dalton, made a number of visits to Italy on his behalf and brought back rich pickings, probably including Michelangelo's famous presentation drawings.

It has been a great pleasure for us in the Royal Library to work on this exhibition with our colleagues in the National Gallery of Art, Washington; the Kimbell Art Museum, Fort Worth; and the Art Institute of Chicago. The salutary care and attention with which these institutions show their exhibitions not only ensures the safety of these highly important works but also enables a large number of people to see the drawings to their best advantage.

OLIVER EVERETT
Librarian, Windsor Castle

Acknowledgments

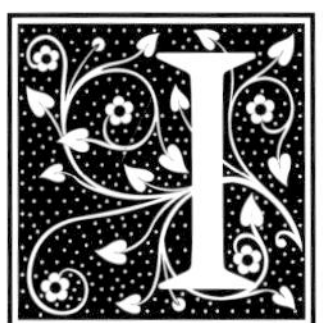n working on this exhibition the compiler has incurred numerous debts. To those curators in the Print Room at Windsor Castle, with whom he worked closely for many months, he would like to express his deepest gratitude: Jane Roberts, whose warmth, firm sense of direction, and clarity of mind made the routine tasks pleasurable and the others delightful; Theresa-Mary Morton, who undertook complicated organizational responsibilities with a *sprezzatura* easier to envy than emulate; Martin Clayton, who sparked the project and collaborated closely on every aspect of it, whose knowledge of the drawings saved the compiler from many solecisms, and whose critical acumen immeasurably improved both ideas and prose—were it not for his reticence, his name would appear more frequently in these pages; and Henrietta Ryan, who though not specifically concerned with this exhibition, was always ready to facilitate its progress. The compiler also owes particular debts of gratitude to two scholars of Michelangelo: William Wallace, who read the introduction and made many helpful suggestions, and Raphael Rosenberg, who did the same with the section devoted to sculpture.

Most of the drawings have been newly examined and restored for the exhibition, and, as a consequence, some new information has been revealed: this is thanks to the painstaking and sensitive work of Alan Donnithorne and Julian Clare.

The choice of exhibits and their ordering benefited greatly from visits to Windsor by the three American curators in whose museums they will be displayed: Suzanne Folds McCullagh from the Art Institute of Chicago, Edmund Pillsbury from the Kimbell Art Museum, Fort Worth, and Andrew Robison from the National Gallery of Art, Washington. They acted both as midwives and collaborators, and this exhibition would be much the poorer without their energy, decision, and critical sensitivity to the works to be displayed.

The compiler is deeply grateful to those at the National Gallery of Art who produced the exhibition catalogue under the leadership of editor-in-chief, Frances Smyth, in particular to Julie Warnement for her very sensitive work on editing, and to Phyllis Hecht for her skillful design.

The compiler also wishes to thank a number of scholars and curators not immediately involved with this exhibition but who, in different ways and to different extents, in some cases indirectly, in some cases unwittingly, provided assistance. If any are surprised to find their names here, it will demonstrate only that their generosity is graced with modesty: Lizzie Boubli, Barbara Brejon de Lavergnée, Emmanuelle Brugerolles, Dominique Cordellier, Philippe Costamagna, Janet Cox-Rearick, Taco Dibbits, Anne V. Lauder, Lucia Monaci-Moran, Catherine Monbeig-Goguel, Elizabeth Pilliod, Pina Ragionieri, William W. Robinson, Rick Scorza, Craig Hugh Smyth, Julien Stock, Bruce Sutherland, and Françoise Viatte.

Some thirty years ago the compiler was introduced to the analysis of artistic invention, transmission, and reception by the teaching of Michael Jaffé, whose own studies of Rubens and circle are exemplary in treating these themes. The channels cut by scholarship sometimes resemble those cut by art, and if in this exhibition the influence of Michelangelo is felt to be pervasive, it is the compiler's hope that that of Michael Jaffé will be equally so in the catalogue.

PAUL JOANNIDES

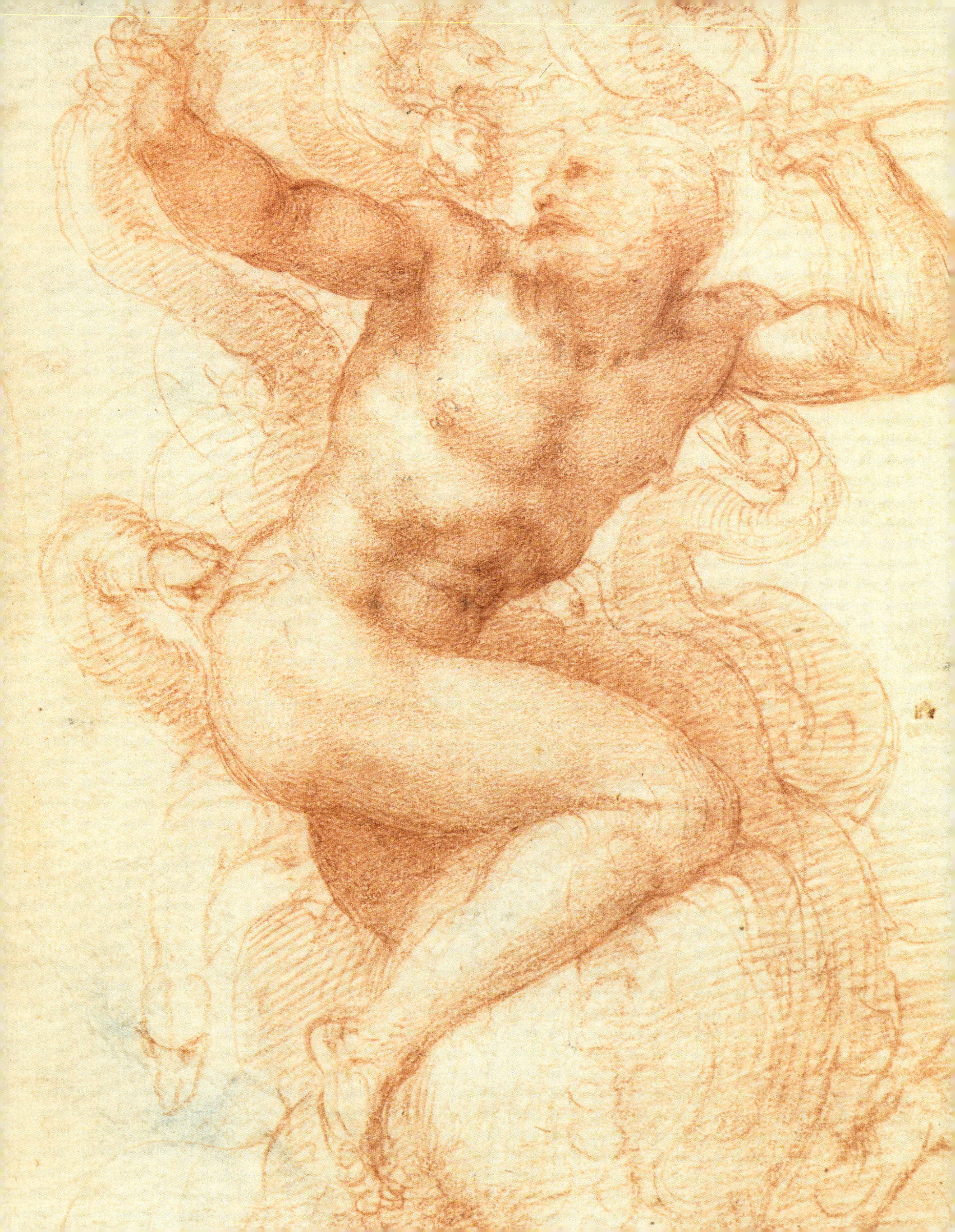

Introduction

Michelangelo's Life and Art

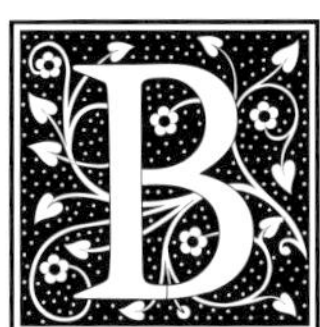

orn in 1475, dying in 1564, recorded in Domenico Ghirlandaio's studio at the age of eleven, described as working on the *Rondanini Pietà* within a few days of his death, Michelangelo is an artist whose active career—more than three-quarters of a century—is one of the most extraordinary in the history of art. It was matched in the sixteenth century only by Titian, and not subsequently until Picasso.

Michelangelo's biography is well known, but its outlines should be recalled. His family was middle class, living on small landholdings and investments, but with memories of better days. One of Michelangelo's ancestors had been a banker, but his father, Ludovico, occupied minor administrative posts in the Florentine government. The family's status was uncertain, above artisan level but well below the ruling circles of Florentine society. It is a characteristic of Michelangelo that throughout his life, he emphasized his family's supposedly noble origins and worked for its elevation.

Michelangelo early displayed a passion for the visual arts. His father opposed this, but Michelangelo's personality was not one to admit restraint and he was taken at ten or eleven into the studio of Ghirlandaio where he worked for two or three years. But Michelangelo became fascinated by sculpture, perhaps from studying the antique in the Medici sculpture garden, and his own efforts attracted the interest of the city's de facto ruler, Lorenzo the Magnificent (1449–1492)—a very distant relative of Michelangelo's—who took him into his household. Michelangelo's association with the Medici was to become a central thread of his life. The young artist fled suddenly in 1494, prompted by a friend's dream prophesying disaster for the Medici, just before Piero, the politically inept son of Lorenzo, was expelled from Florence. Michelangelo returned in 1495, not unsympathetic to the quasi-theocratic government of Savonarola, but soon transferred to Rome. There, before the age of twenty-five, he executed two of his most famous works of sculpture, the *Bacchus* and the Saint Peter's *Pietà*. In 1501 he returned again to Florence, now under moderate but anti-Medicean republican government, in order to execute the great marble *David*. The statue's success was such that the republic deluged Michelangelo with commissions, but not one was finished—setting the pattern for a lifetime of unfinished work—because he was recalled to Rome to work for the new pope, Julius II.

In 1505–1506 Michelangelo began a gigantic tomb for Julius that was to be completed only in drastically reduced form forty years later. The pope soon shelved the project, probably because of its cost. Michelangelo, mortified, fled to Florence, where he remained for several months. But he was compelled to return to the pope's service and, in 1507–1508, made a large bronze statue of Julius for the church of San Petronio in recently reconquered Bologna. It was destroyed only three years later, in 1511. In 1508, back in Rome, Michelangelo was commanded by Julius to fresco the vault of the Sistine Chapel, a task he undertook virtually single-handed and completed to universal acclaim in 1512. He then resumed work on the tomb but was soon diverted once more. The Medici were reinstated in Florence in 1512 and, at the death of Julius in 1513, Giovanni de' Medici, Lorenzo's son, was elected pope as Leo X. In 1516 he commissioned Michelangelo to build a façade for San Lorenzo, the family's church in Florence. Michelangelo hoped to combine this massive task with the execution of a reduced version of the tomb. While in Florence he also continued to supply his friend Sebastiano Luciani, later known as Sebastiano del Piombo, with designs for paintings. This joint effort was intended to combat the overwhelming success of Raphael, their common rival, who was monopolizing papal commissions in Rome. Raphael died prematurely in 1520, and the same year the façade project was postponed, probably because of spiraling costs.

Michelangelo was immediately diverted to another Medici project: the execution of a sepulchral chapel, also in San Lorenzo. This was intended to house a dense complement of sculpted and painted decoration of which only part was ever completed. The death of Leo X in 1521 caused a crisis in Medici finances and slowed the work, but when, in late 1523, his cousin Giulio became pope as Clement VII, the project regained momentum. But work was interrupted by the political turmoil of the Sack of Rome in 1527 and the simultaneous expulsion of the Medici from Florence, in which Michelangelo sided against the family. Following Florence's recapture in 1530 after a siege by the papal forces, Michelangelo was reconciled with Clement VII, but the impetus had gone from his Florentine projects and he spent as much as possible of the next four years in Rome. There he developed a deep friendship for the young Roman aristocrat, Tommaso de' Cavalieri, for whom he made a number of presentation drawings.

Michelangelo's final move to Rome came shortly before Clement's death in 1534. He detested the revived Medici regime and never returned to Florence, although he was compelled to avoid open hostility to its rulers to protect his own and his family's interests. In Rome he hoped to resume work on the Julius Tomb, but was again diverted. The new Pope Paul III prevailed upon him to pursue a project that Clement had initiated: the mural painting of the *Last Judgment* on the altar wall of the Sistine Chapel. This he completed in 1541. During the 1530s he had also begun to extend his work in architecture, replanning one of the most important secular sites in Rome, the Capitol. Michelangelo also developed another important friendship, with the Roman aristocrat, poetess, and religious thinker Vittoria Colonna, who helped deepen Michelangelo's own religious convictions; to her he presented elaborately finished drawings of Christian subjects. Paul III next commanded Michelangelo to paint the Pauline Chapel but, under pressure from the exasperated heirs of Pope Julius, Michelangelo succeeded in limiting his work on this scheme sufficiently to bring the tomb to a compromised conclusion in 1545. On it were included his last finished works of sculpture, the *Rachel* and the *Leah*, as well as the *Moses*, carved many years earlier.

The Pauline Chapel was completed in 1550, shortly after the death of Paul III. Michelangelo continued to make designs for paintings to be executed by others, and he permitted some of his presentation drawings, both secular and sacred, to be reproduced in paintings and engravings, but he executed no more paintings. Neither did he accept further commissions for sculpture: his sculptural activity over the last nineteen years of his life was all for himself. It comprised three *Pietàs*, all unfinished and probably worked on consecutively. They were probably intended for Michelangelo's own tomb. The four-figure group now in Florence certainly was. In public work, Michelangelo's last years were primarily devoted to architecture, above all the rebuilding of Saint Peter's, a task he assumed in 1547 following the death of its architect of the previous quarter century, Antonio da Sangallo the Younger, whom Michelangelo despised. Michelangelo stamped the building irrevocably with his own personality and exerted over it, almost until his death, unparalleled control. He also prepared plans for the church of San Giovanni dei Fiorentini, which remained unexecuted; the conversion of the Baths of Diocletian into the church of Santa Maria degli Angeli; and the construction of the Sforza chapel in Santa Maria Maggiore. Throughout the last thirty years of his life, Michelangelo exercised considerable indirect powers of patronage as artistic and architectural advisor to a succession of popes. His presence dominated the artistic scene in Rome.

In range, quantity, including unfinished works, and quality of output, as a master in painting, sculpture, and architecture as well as a considerable poet, Michelangelo has probably had no equal, let alone a superior. The recognition accorded him, even by those not enamored of his art, was imposed by the irreducible grandeur of his achievements. At the age of thirty he was already referred to by Pietro Soderini, the *gonfaloniere* of Florence, as "unico in Italia, forse etiam in universo" (unique in Italy, perhaps even in the universe). Michelangelo was the single living artist included in the first edition of Giorgio Vasari's *Lives*, in which he was seen as supreme in all three arts, the culmination of an essentially Tuscan development that had begun with Cimabue and

Giotto. This cannot be ascribed wholly to Tuscan chauvinism. The praise of Vasari, a Medici partisan, was particularly significant since Michelangelo, though no longer actively opposing the Medici dukedom by 1550, had as recently as 1544 offered to erect at his own expense an equestrian statue of Francis I in Florence should the king liberate the city from the Medici yoke. Vasari's choice of Michelangelo as the hero of his *Lives*—when a powerful alternative candidate existed in Raphael—gave Michelangelo a certain leverage, rendering it difficult for the Medici duke, Cosimo I, to impose his will on the Florentine artist, who above all others reflected glory on the city and its ruling family.

In Venice, a counterattack on Michelangelo's painting was mounted by Pietro Aretino and Lodovico Dolce, employing the examples of Raphael and Titian to invoke those areas of art in which their heroes excelled. But even here, Michelangelo's sculpture escaped censure: it was agreed that it surpassed even the antique. And later critics who attacked his work, or those painters who took different paths from his, generally acknowledged Michelangelo's commanding presence in one or other of the areas in which he practiced. Furthermore, until his very last years Michelangelo could never be sidelined as a grand old man, because his unceasing self-renewal as an artist both stimulated new developments and re-opened interpretation of his earlier work. It is hardly exaggeration to say that none of the most ambitious art and architecture produced in Italy between 1520 and 1600 escaped some engagement with his work.

As commentators have always insisted, Michelangelo's art is unrelentingly serious and grand, even though, until at least the time of the *Last Judgment*, severity is often tempered by an exquisite and intense aestheticism, from which sensuality is not invariably absent, as can be seen most obviously in his male nudes. But Michelangelo's rarefied and highly strung sense of form is less often appreciated: edges of drapery and precision of contour display the capacity of his line to evoke a purist three-dimensionality, and his abstractly beautiful rhythms both equal and owe a debt to those of Botticelli. But even in his earliest work, Michelangelo's devotion to beauty was not for its own sake. At the court of Lorenzo the Magnificent, he had absorbed a Platonic aesthetic that identified the beautiful with the ideal. This ideal resided largely in the male nude, treated in a manner profoundly influenced by classical sculpture, and traditionally seen as Michelangelo's primary vehicle of expression. The nude's centrality in his work was intimately bound with Michelangelo's own homosexuality, encouraged, perhaps, by that of his poetic and Platonic mentors, such as Politian. But it would be reductive to ascribe it solely to sexuality, for in Michelangelo's work the body is an actor in a drama of the spirit and the spirit remains permanently unsatisfied: Michelangelo's figures are preoccupied by loss, aspiration, or striving. However beautiful, the body in Michelangelo's work remains the *carcere terreno* (the prison of the flesh). Throughout his life Michelangelo seems to have been impelled by religious beliefs that, although increasing in profundity as he grew older, were always intense. That this spirituality was appreciated, even in Venice whence an attack was mounted on the supposed indecency of the *Last Judgment*, is revealed in the famous exchange between Paolo Veronese and an inquisitor in 1573. Veronese had been censured for including irrelevant and trivial figures and actions in a painting of the *Last Supper*. In his defense Veronese maintained that he was accustomed to include decorative elements in accordance with his own taste and that Michelangelo had done the same in the *Last Judgment*. The inquisitor replied, "There is nothing in this painting which is not spiritual."

The testimony of a later artist might also be cited, the response of Jean-François Millet to Michelangelo's drawing, in the Louvre (Inv. 716 / C. 92), for Sebastiano's Ubeda *Pietà*: "But when I saw a drawing of Michelangelo's—a man in a swoon—that was another thing! The expression of the relaxed muscles, the planes and modeling of the figure weighed down by physical suffering, gave me a succession of feelings: I was tormented by pain, I pitied him, I suffered with that very body, those very limbs. I saw that he who had done this was capable, with a single figure, to personify the good and evil of all humanity" (Sensier 1881, 50).

Michelangelo's Early Work as a Guide to His Artistic Range

Michelangelo's artistic and conceptual range can be understood by examining his work up to around 1505. It is impossible to reconstruct this period fully: a high proportion of his sculpture of the 1490s is lost, only one painting probably by him from that decade survives, and very few drawings can securely be dated before 1500. Nevertheless in these two decades are found the main contours of Michelangelo's artistic personality, and consideration of them is revealing. It was then that some of the main themes developed by Michelangelo's autograph drawings in this exhibition were established.

Michelangelo's education was unusually lacking in constraint. After initial training with Ghirlandaio, he was introduced by the Medici household to the most privileged position possible for a young artist, removing him from the necessities of workshop life and providing him freedom to develop under the liberal supervision of Lorenzo's favored sculptor, the former pupil of Donatello, Bertoldo. Michelangelo came into contact with members of Florence's most powerful and prestigious families and with some of the city's, and Italy's, leading intellectuals. Such experiences were a foundation for his later career: they gave him a range of contacts and a social and cultural self-confidence, despite his sometimes *farouche* persona, which few contemporaries could match. His artistic experiences were correspondingly varied and the components of his art many and wide-ranging. A desire for omni-competence, propelled by an innate competitiveness as well as by an intellectual fascination in varieties of expression, induced him to master forms of art with which he is not generally associated. Michelangelo was not an artist who had a "style" in whose terms everything was interpreted. So strong a personality could experiment freely without fear of diluting his identity. An anecdote is emblematic: Ascanio Condivi and Vasari recount that the young Michelangelo would copy drawings by old masters borrowed from friends, artificially age them, and return the copies as originals. From early on, Michelangelo had the forger's capacity for mimicry but, unlike most forgers, this sprang from superabundance of talent.

Ghirlandaio, the most ambitious and technically competent of Florentine fresco painters, was, when Michelangelo joined him, engaged on one of the largest fresco schemes executed in Florence in the fifteenth century, the decoration of the choir of Santa Maria Novella for the Tornabuoni—important Medici allies. From the artist who boasted of his desire to fresco the city's walls, Michelangelo learned a lack of trepidation before large surfaces and the superb technique that has ensured for his own frescoes so remarkable a state of preservation. But in pointed contrast, Michelangelo's earliest work, now lost but recorded by Condivi, was very small: a colored copy after Martin Schongauer's engraving the *Torment of Saint Anthony* (fig. 1). Michelangelo was fascinated by the scaly forms of Schongauer's devils, and studied fishes in the marketplace in order to reproduce their scales. In this the young artist displayed interests worth enumerating: in the miniature; in high levels of finish; in accurate depiction of natural forms; in, broadly, anatomical research. His choice of model is also significant: not Italian or antique but northern European art—to which Michelangelo was more open than he later admitted. Furthermore, Schongauer's image is richly loaded, for Anthony and his devils are airborne and the saint's torment is simultaneously an elevation, like Michelangelo's later *Ganymede* (see cat. 15), which Schongauer's graphic picture prefigures in miniaturist precision.

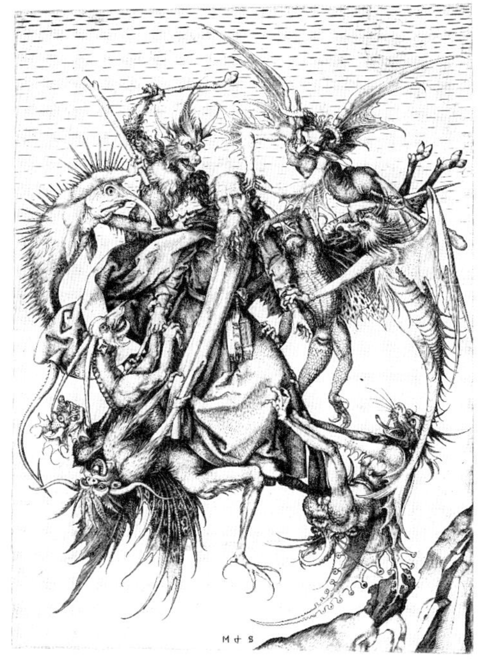

fig. 1. Martin Schongauer, *The Torment of Saint Anthony*, engraving, 31.2 x 23 cm. British Museum, London, Department of Prints and Drawings

Presentation drawings are also indirectly anticipated in Michelangelo's few but significant surviving pen copies after earlier art, specifically after figures from frescoes by Giotto (Musée du Louvre, Paris 706 recto / C. 3 recto) and Masaccio (Staatliche Graphische Sammlung, Munich 2191 recto / C. 4 recto and fig. 2, Graphische Sammlung Albertina, Vienna Sc. R. 150 recto / C. 5 recto), two artists whose work was also studied by Ghirlandaio. Michelangelo's copies are not sketchy but very fully worked, employing a crosshatching that, while learned from Ghirlandaio, far surpasses his in volumetric density and subtlety of surface effect. Indeed, these drawings are more richly elaborated than any known copies by Michelangelo's contemporaries. As well as familiarizing him with the forms and ideas of great Florentine forerunners, to whose work he returned repeatedly throughout his life, they must also have been conceived as demonstration pieces and, perhaps, as gifts: not one has a Casa Buonarroti provenance.

Such interests—in the blocklike forms of early trecento and early quattrocento painting, in the expressive and agonized line of recent northern European art—might seem alien to the artist who sculpted, probably in 1492, a pseudo-classical high relief of the *Battle of the Centaurs* (fig. 3). This establishes his fascination with the male nude, displaying a range of expression from struggle and effort to disabling pain: it looks forward to the cartoon of the *Battle of Cascina*, to the *Flood* and the *Brazen Serpent* on the Sistine vault and, finally, to the *Last Judgment*. The *Centaurs* was in part inspired by a bronze battle relief by Bertoldo, in turn based on a Roman relief in Pisa. But Michelangelo's figures are more individually expressive than those either of Bertoldo or his prototype, and much more fully rounded, like statuettes. The *Centaurs* is the first surviving statement of Michelangelo's interest in antique sculpture, of which the Medici's outstanding collection has yet to be reconstructed. The antique was probably the single most important source of Michelangelo's art and, until the beginning of work on the Sistine ceiling, it was the figure types of the classical period, with their clarity of form and abstracted musculature, which most attracted him. But, the movement and stresses of Hellenistic sculpture became more central during his second Roman sojourn, 1505–1506, when he witnessed the rediscovery of the *Laocoön* and came to appreciate the fragmentary *Torso Belvedere*, which had been known since the 1420s. Both the *Laocoön* (compare fig. 101) and the *Torso* had a fundamental effect on his art. Their inspiration can be traced through the Sistine ceiling, the *Last Judgment* (compare fig. 97) and even the Pauline Chapel frescoes (see pages 184–199), as well as much of the statuary carved for the Julius Tomb between 1516 and 1530, and some of that planned and executed in the New Sacristy (see pages 138–145).

The *Centaurs*, the overture to Michelangelo's many-act engagement with the figural ideals of classical antiquity, also initiated his employment of gridlike composition. Bertoldo had preceded him in this, but Michelangelo's use is more rigorous. It was to remain Michelangelo's preferred system for multifigure compositions and provided, most spectacularly, the structure of the *Last Judgment*. It combined compositional cohesion of a simple but powerful kind with maximal freedom for individual figures—one reason why students of Michelangelo generally copied individual figures and rarely reproduced entire compositions.

Michelangelo left the *Centaurs* unfinished because, he later said, of the death of a great prince, undoubtedly Lorenzo. But even had it been completed in every detail, its breadth of conception and individual strength of forms would seem incompatible with an interest in Schongauer. The *Centaurs* also differs radically from a *Virgin and Child with Angels* (fig. 4) sculpted a little earlier

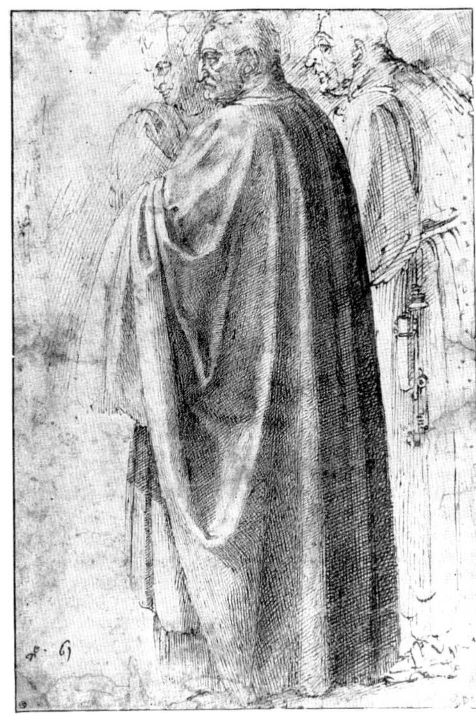

fig. 2. Michelangelo after Masaccio, *Figures from the Sagra*, pen and ink, 29 x 20 cm. Graphische Sammlung Albertina, Vienna

BELOW LEFT: fig. 3. Michelangelo, *The Battle of the Centaurs*, marble, 82 x 91.5 cm. Casa Buonarroti, Florence

BELOW RIGHT: fig. 4. Michelangelo, *The Virgin and Child with Angels*, marble, 57 x 40 cm. Casa Buonarroti, Florence

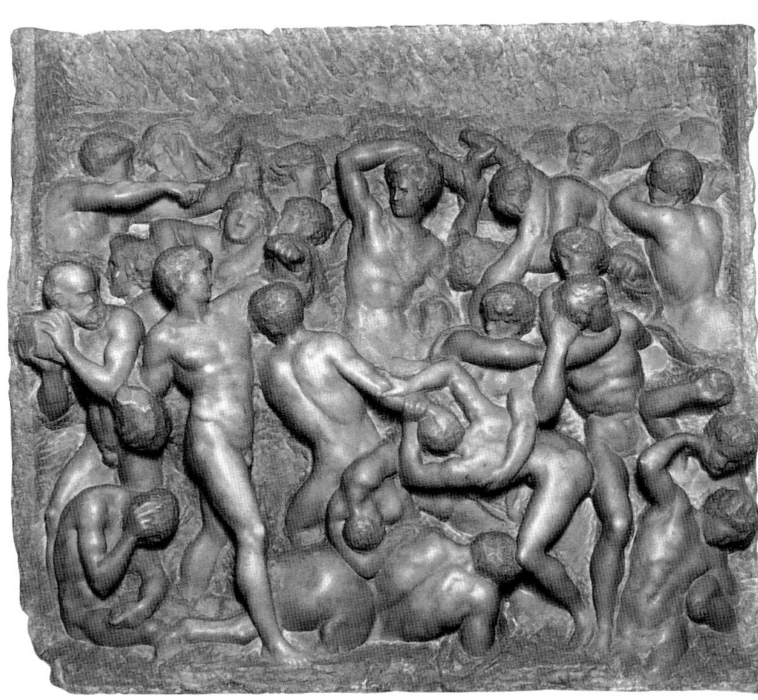

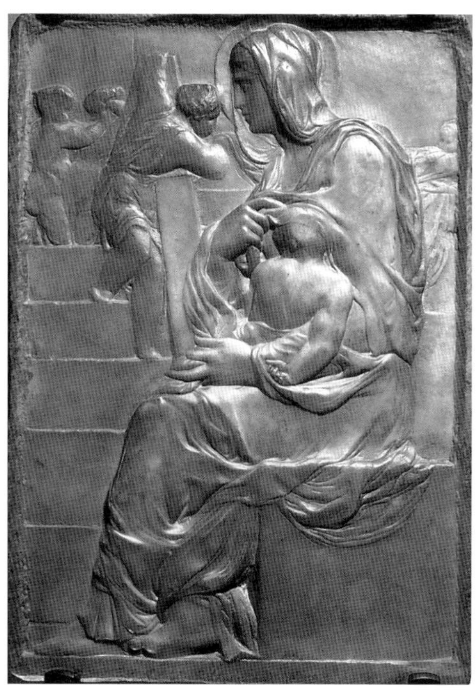

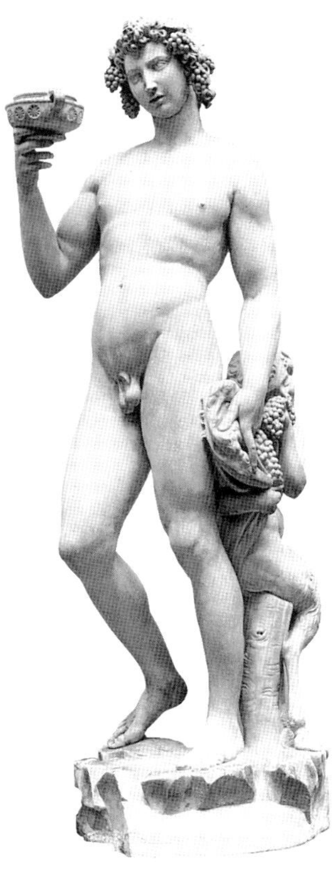

fig. 5. Michelangelo, *Bacchus and a Satyr*, marble, height 203 cm. Museo Nazionale del Bargello, Florence [Fratelli Alinari, 1995]

in very low relief. Technically, this relief invited, as Vasari noted, overt comparison with the art of Donatello and Desiderio da Settignano; formally, in the massiveness of the Virgin, it reflected Michelangelo's study of Giotto and Masaccio; theologically, with the child fallen asleep at the breast, it poignantly communicates the Passion as well as the Virgin's anticipation of the Son's death; psychologically it conveys the separation of mother and child that is a central and tragic part of Michelangelo's treatments of the Madonna.

Probably in 1492, Michelangelo completed a crucified Christ in pigmented wood (fig. 67), reportedly as a gift to the prior of Santo Spirito, who had allowed him to undertake dissections. This was an innovative rendering: a slim, young Christ, whose elegant figure with tapering legs and widespread arms conveys pathos by overall rhythm rather than by energy of local modeling. Poignant and self-contained, designed to be seen at a distance, it seems, despite its anatomical precision, less like sculpture than a silhouetted crucifix of the type painted by Lorenzo Monaco. It became a model for paintings by Mariotto Albertinelli and Jacopo da Pontormo. That Michelangelo's first two religious works of sculpture were a Virgin and child and a crucified Christ is appropriate, for devotion to Christ and devotion to the Virgin—rather than the saints—were the alpha and omega of Michelangelo's religious experience.

The slim Christ seems at the opposite pole to the strong forms of the over-life-size freestanding *Hercules* that Michelangelo carved, on his own initiative, probably in 1493. The statue is lost but, if we can trust a series of probable reductions, his *Hercules* was a powerfully muscled, beardless young man in a contemplative, standing pose, with crossed calves, which provided minimal support (fig. 74). Such divergence between a pictorial Christian image and a more robust classical one is repeated once more in the two great works that Michelangelo carved in Rome in the second half of the 1490s. The *Bacchus and a Satyr* is a freestanding group, designed to be seen throughout 360 degrees, presenting the viewer with a series of surprises and creating disquiet, since it seems unstable (fig. 5). Its starting point is an antique group, of which many examples exist, in which Bacchus and a satyr are placed side by side: the complexity of Michelangelo's *Bacchus*, however, outstrips its antique model technically in its deep undercutting and disrupts it emotionally. As Vasari noted, Bacchus combines the powerful male and the voluptuous female

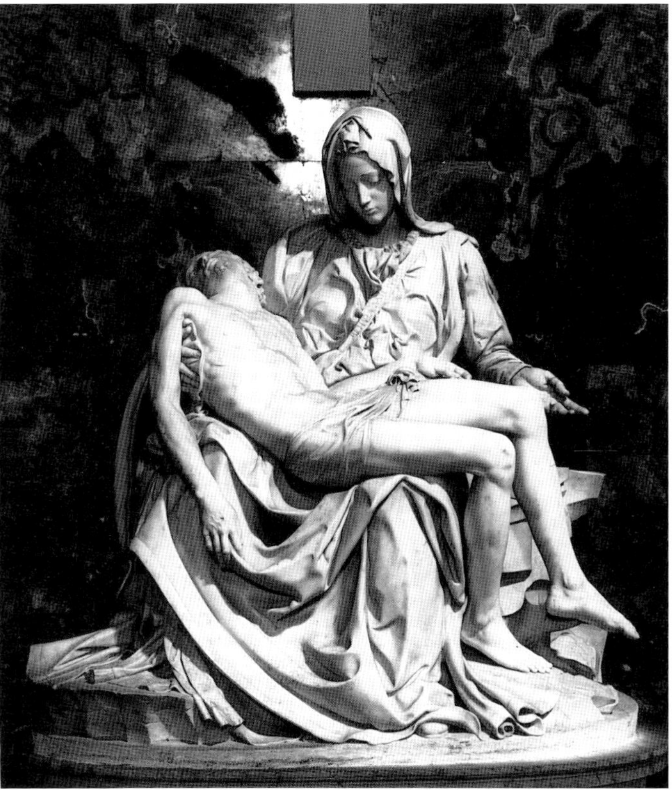

fig. 6. Michelangelo, *Pietà*, marble, height 174 cm. Fabrica di San Pietro in Vaticano

body, and Michelangelo referred to an antique *Venus Genetrix* for aspects of the pose. It is revealing that one of Michelangelo's earliest surviving drawings after the antique, on a sheet in the Musée Condé, Chantilly (29 recto / c. 24), is a copy of an *Apollo Sauroctonous* transformed into a female nude. Whatever psychological inferences may be drawn from these examples of sexual mixing, whatever Platonic dimension they possess, they demonstrate Michelangelo's capacity to separate pose from context and to perceive ranges of possibilities not explicit in his models.

By contrast the *Pietà* is a painting in marble (fig. 6). An infinity of gradations of smoothness and corrugation of surface is deployed to create a play of light and shade as soft as in a painting by Leonardo da Vinci. Indeed, the types of the Virgin and Christ, and some aspects of the drapery are based on sculpture by Leonardo's own master, Verrocchio, who had died in 1488. Michelangelo was already aware of Leonardo's work and both the multiple viewpoint of the *Bacchus* and the play of light and shade in the *Pietà* exemplify Michelangelo's response to the living artist from whom he learned most. Michelangelo and Leonardo were to be placed in direct competition in the Sala del Cinquecento in the Palazzo Vecchio in 1504–1505, but the contrasts between them should not obscure the links: in particular, the profound debts owed by the younger man, which were to emerge repeatedly in his art. Although Michelangelo treated Leonardo with public contempt, he made free use of his forms and ideas with a vigor that reveals how closely he had studied them and how profoundly he understood them.

Michelangelo's Drawings

The crucible in which these different forms of art and different interests were fused was Michelangelo's draftsmanship. His statement to Francisco de Hollanda about drawing was about his own work: "design, which by another name is called drawing . . . is the fount and body of painting and sculpture and architecture and of every other kind of painting and the root of all sciences" (Holroyd 1911, 275). No artist—with the possible exception of Leonardo—was more technically gifted. Michelangelo possessed, until very old age, extraordinary physical dexterity and unsurpassed control of hand movement. The artist who could assault paper with the point of a quill and scrawl down a figure drawing in a few seconds with such velocity that the lines jump from the surface while simultaneously retaining coherence as modeling, could also labor with microscopic precision over graphic pictures whose local subtleties, of texture, modeling, and atmosphere, outstrip the work of any miniaturist. No artist ever showed more awareness of flexibility within forms, of the play of dense modeling against empty areas, of tense and soft contour. None has ever been more acutely aware of the signifying capacity of sinews, muscles, and joints. Michelangelo criticized Albrecht Dürer's study of bodies for showing them stationary and stiff, and the criticism is revealing of Michelangelo, because figures in his work are always in motion, either actual or implicit.

Michelangelo's drawings range widely in style and type. Some of these are exemplified in the Windsor collection, but it is not representative: indeed, no single collection of Michelangelo's drawings, following the large dispersals of the late eighteenth and mid-nineteenth centuries from the Casa Buonarroti, can claim this, although the two collections in Florence (the Casa Buonarroti and the Galleria degli Uffizi) taken together and that in the British Museum come closest.

The range of media and supports employed by Michelangelo was relatively narrow, and he would count, in this respect, among the more conservative of his contemporaries. His main innovation was to take up, in the first decade of the sixteenth century, red chalk, which had been introduced to Florence by Leonardo. Judging from his surviving work, Michelangelo did not employ colored papers or prepared papers; metal-point, whose use was widespread in the Florence of his youth, although largely abandoned by 1520, held no appeal. Michelangelo rarely used both black and red chalk together and never chalks of other colors. Like most artists, he often outlined forms in chalk before working over them in pen, and, occasionally, he corrected pen drawings in chalk as well as vice versa: indeed, the presence of a second medium often indicates a correction. He occasionally combined techniques, chalk and pen, wash and white heightening, but rarely for figure or drapery studies after the first phase of work on the Sistine. Multimedia drawings were employed mostly for architectural *modelli*: façades, ground plans, and architectural-sculptural schemes. In these, the structure is usually indicated by ruled lines, while variations in relief, the substantialities of walls, thicknesses, and relative solidities were conveyed by wash and, sometimes, white heightening (fig. 7). Only in the last few years of his life, when manual control was slipping, and when his architectural and figure drawing underwent a technical convergence, did combinations of chalk, wash, and white become dominant, gradually submerging local form.

This relative purism of his graphic techniques corresponded to Michelangelo's attitudes to sculpture and painting. His idealization of *buon fresco,* which, unlike most of his contemporaries, he rarely retouched, is a part of this, and it was remarked by the conservators who recently cleaned the Sistine ceiling that Michelangelo never took shortcuts and never cheated. The same is true of his panel paintings, as their solid technique testifies. In sculpture he elevated the carved above the molded, although his interest in molded sculpture was far greater than he claimed. As far as possible, he tried to carve figures and groups from single blocks, an ambition that combined a technical virtuosity with an idealistic commitment to marble's integrity. In executing his sculpture, after his earliest period, he tended to minimize employment of devices like the drill in favor of points and chisels. The phrase "truth to materials" would simplify Michelangelo's approach, but some such ethic underlies his work. In drawing, this meant that he endeavored to obtain his desired effects not by additions or approximations, but by the fullest possible exploitation of a single medium. Soft and simplified sketches were made in red chalk as well as studies hatched as sharply as if in metal-point. A sheet at Christ Church, Oxford (figs. 8, 9, 0068 recto and verso / C. 86 recto and verso), contains examples of each type. Black chalk could stroke compositional sketches or single figures onto the paper, produce hard and plastic forms, or create the most sleek evocations of skin texture and musculature. Pen could be used for the most instantaneous of

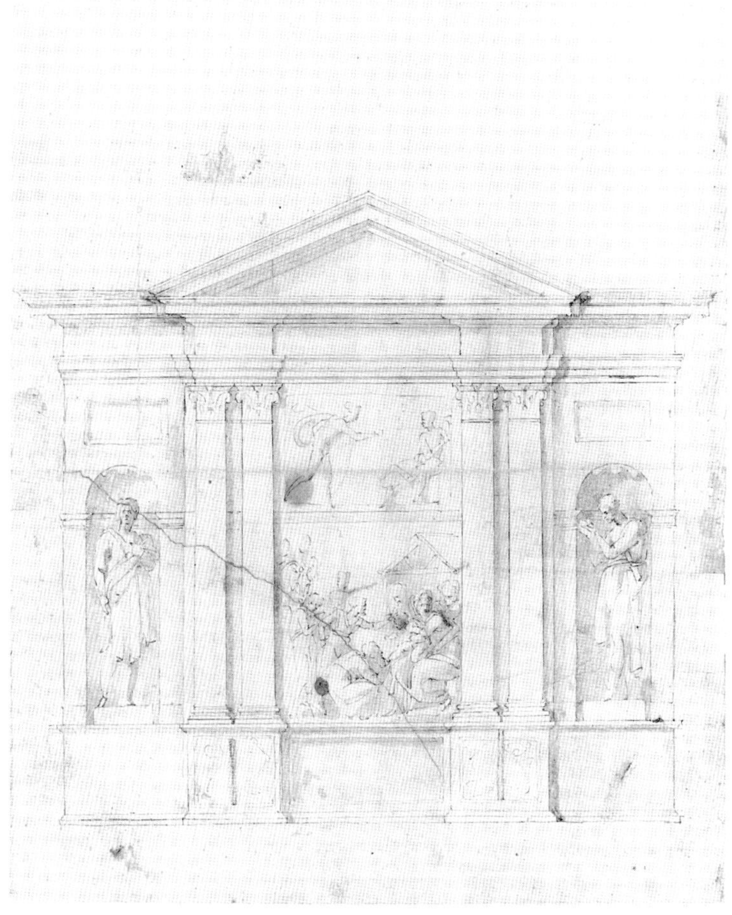

fig. 7. Michelangelo, *Design for an Altar*, pen and ink, and wash with some black chalk, 35 x 29.1 cm. The Governing Body, Christ Church, Oxford

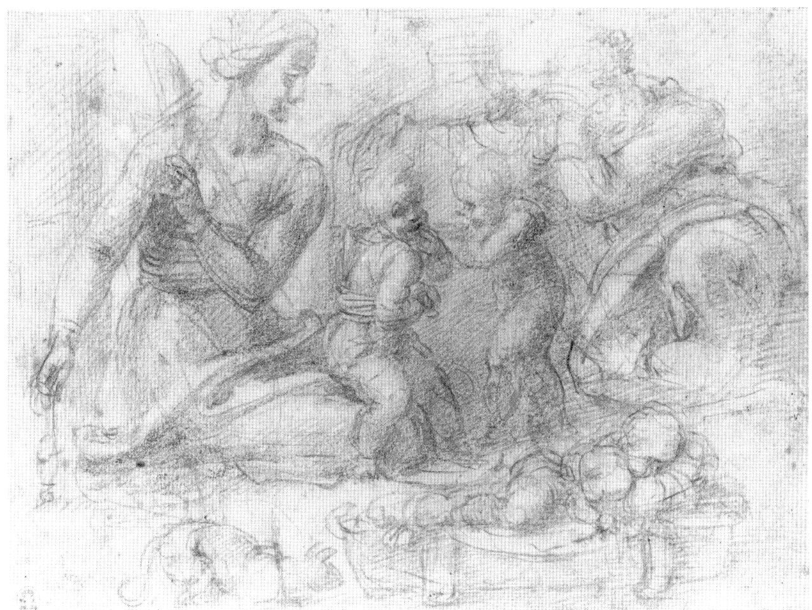

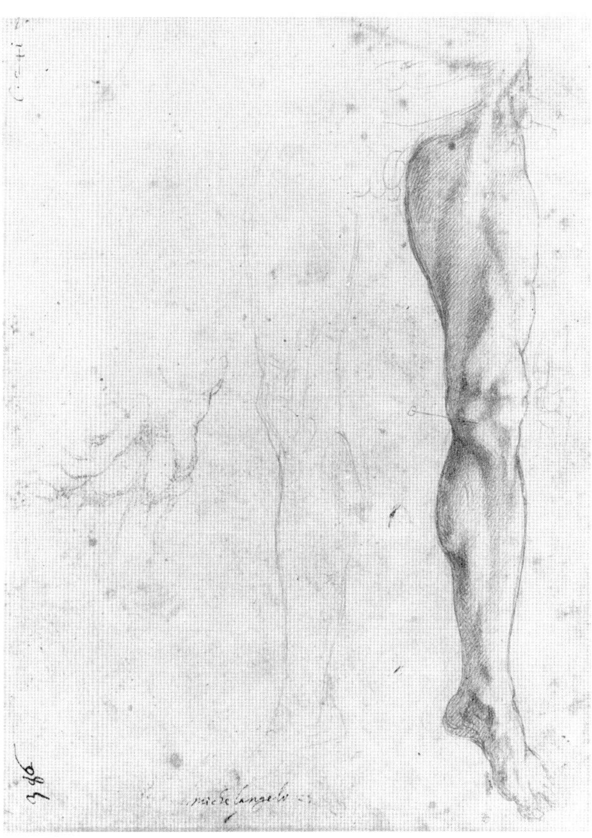

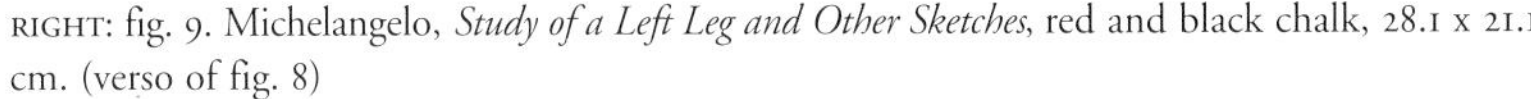

LEFT: fig. 8. Michelangelo, *Holy Family (?)*, red and black chalk, 21.1 x 28.1 cm. The Governing Body, Christ Church, Oxford

RIGHT: fig. 9. Michelangelo, *Study of a Left Leg and Other Sketches*, red and black chalk, 28.1 x 21.1 cm. (verso of fig. 8)

sketches, from jaggedly expressive indications of pose no more than a couple of centimeters high, through fast large drawings, modeled in "bracelet" hatching—curving movements of the pen that seem to run round the form and spring it into three-dimensionality—and swelling broken contours, to the most highly finished crosshatched studies, which rival marble sculpture in density and counterfeit flesh in the subtlety of their surfaces. On occasion, Michelangelo separated contour and modeling. He could evoke a form in three dimensions with a stressed outline or, still more difficult, could model one by crosshatching entirely without contours (Hamburger Kunsthalle 21094 recto / C. 35 recto).

This unparalleled intensity of graphic realization—combined with Michelangelo's comprehensive understanding of the emotional language of the human body, nude and draped—was central to the deployment of such different artistic ideas in his work. Michelangelo's art was probably as indebted to that of earlier periods—and at times to that of his contemporaries—as Raphael's. But whatever the source of an idea, whether an early Netherlandish print, a trecento fresco, a classical sculpture, or a painting or drawing by Leonardo, the plastic conviction of Michelangelo's drawing and his sensitivity to emotional accent transmuted his borrowings—or thefts—into forms entirely individual.

Michelangelo's Effect on Sixteenth-Century Italian Art

Sycophancy, from quite early in his career, was a characteristic of other artists' dealings with Michelangelo. They were overwhelmed by the scale of his projects and the dynamism of their execution, intimidated by his extraordinarily powerful personality and his corrosive wit. But admiration was genuine, for not merely were Michelangelo's achievements of a scale and prominence that could not be ignored, but the animating ideas of his work also provided colossal if dangerous stimulus. It would be a mistake to ascribe their behavior solely to the self-interest of would-be subcontractors, anxious to obtain slices of major projects.

Yet this stimulus was relatively slow to manifest itself. Unlike Raphael, a brilliant organizer who rapidly established teams of pupils and assistants, and rapidly imbued them with his artistic ideas, Michelangelo never, even for his most elaborate and ambitious projects, surrounded himself with assistants; such was his perfectionism that he found it temperamentally arduous to work with others. Only when supervising the carving of architectural or decorative forms was he able to direct assistants with ease. Michelangelo began the Sistine ceiling with the firm intention of working with a group of Florentine artists, but he soon dismissed them and continued alone, aided only by a couple of minor artists, Bernardino Zacchetti and Giovanni Trignoli, whose roles have never been defined with clarity and who, indeed, may have painted no more than nonfigurative elements. None of his very few pupils had any independent career, and this was remarked upon by Vasari within a few years of Michelangelo's death. His most productive direct relations with other artists were with painters and, to a lesser extent, sculptors already formed by the time they met him, such as Giovanni Montorsoli, Sebastiano del Piombo, and Daniele da Volterra. They were intelligent enough and ambitious enough to understand and respond to his ideas.

The dissemination of Michelangelo's artistic forms and ideas was also slow for another reason. Raphael had realized very early the value of prints as a means of circulating his inventions. He formed an association with the most able engraver of his time, Marcantonio Raimondi. Raimondi and his team reproduced a large number of Raphael's works, generally from his *modelli* rather than his finished paintings in order, presumably, that both painting and print could be "published" simultaneously. Raphael also took advantage of the exploitation by Ugo da Carpi of the chiaroscuro mode of woodcut, which was ideal for reproducing *modelli*, and many of his compositions were circulated in this form. In contrast, although Marcantonio had engraved some figures from the *Battle of Cascina* by about 1511 and a couple of details from the Sistine ceiling circa 1512–1513, Michelangelo's work was virtually unavailable in reproduction. It was only in the 1540s that engravings after his work were produced in large numbers, but, for the most part, they fell far below Marcantonio's work in richness of modeling and technical inventiveness. They were explicitly reproductive in a way Marcantonio's were not. Before Michelangelo's death, most of his presentation drawings and some of his Roman sculpture had been reproduced, and the whole of the *Last Judgment* was available from the mid-1540s in the prints of Giorgio Ghisi and Niccolò della Casa. But the Sistine ceiling was not copied as a whole. Purchasers had to content themselves with the series of seventy-three prophets and sibyls, *ignudi* and ancestors issued by Adamo Scultori in the 1550s, which was lively but coarse, and with six prophets and sibyls, together with the ancestors below them, engraved by Ghisi in the 1540s. Once these prints were available, copying naturally expanded, and frequently drawings were made after them rather than the originals. Indeed, a suite of pen copies on yellow-washed paper of the *ignudi* at Windsor (RL 0634–0645 / Popham and Wilde 469–480) and of prophets and sibyls in the Louvre (Inv. 754–762), which seem to belong to a single series, are all derived from the engravings of Adamo Scultori. Probably confected for tourists, such drawings contributed simultaneously to a wider knowledge of Michelangelo's visual ideas and to their coarsening and impoverishment.

To discuss adequately Michelangelo's effect on art in the sixteenth century would require a book. It is one that should be written, for his work was the focus of many of the artistic and spiritual issues that preoccupied the period. In the present context, however, no more than an outline is possible.

Sculpture

Among contemporary sculptors, Michelangelo's example was slow to take effect. One difficulty was that his sculpture developed so rapidly that only the most alert could respond to it. One such was Leonardo. He had made a small graphic critique of Michelangelo's *David* (Windsor RL 12591), which he evidently found too angular. However, when providing Gianfrancesco Rustici with designs for the group of the *Preaching of the Baptist* (1507–1511) (fig. 10) on the Florentine Baptistery, he perceived the possibilities inherent in Michelangelo's unfinished *Saint Matthew*. He saw that its complex pose, with contorted forms and sense of internal struggle, would make an apt model for Rustici's *Scribe* and *Pharisee*. Baccio da Montelupo, who seems to have been on good

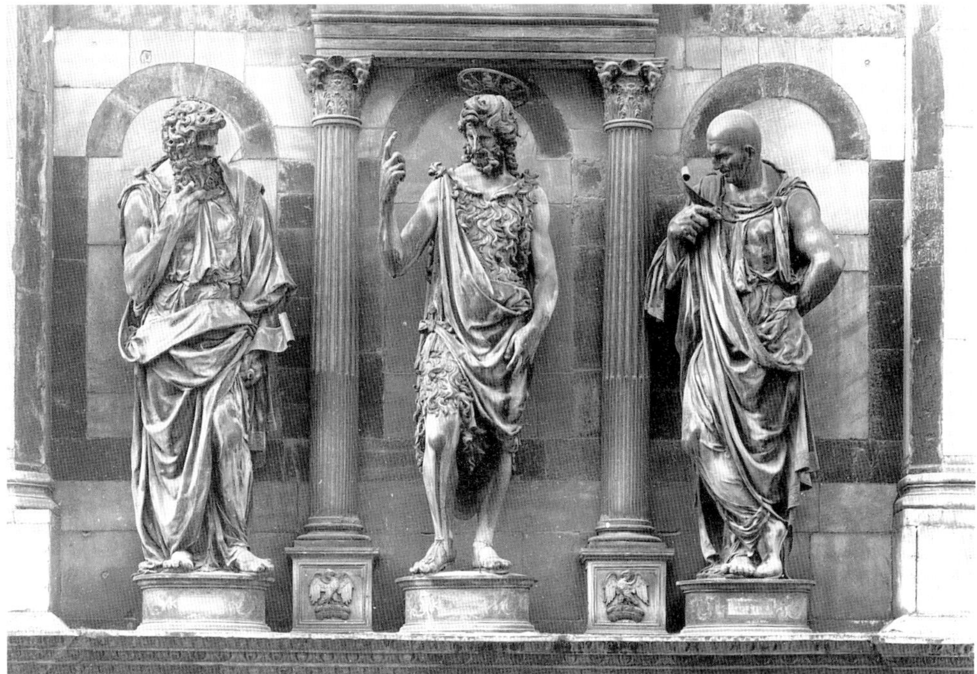

fig. 10. Gianfrancesco Rustici to the Design of Leonardo da Vinci, *The Preaching of the Baptist*, bronze, height 265 cm. The Baptistery, Florence [Fratelli Alinari, 1995]

terms with Michelangelo and whose son worked with him on two occasions, was chosen, presumably on Michelangelo's recommendation, to complete the chasing of Michelangelo's lost bronze *David*. It is not surprising, therefore, that Baccio's *Mars* on the tomb of Benedetto Pesaro in the Venetian church of Santa Maria Gloriosa dei Frari responds to the marble *David*, especially in the effort to elevate the centers of sculptural interest and in the modeling of the torso. Although the *David* challenged other sculptors to attempt the gigantic, as did Baccio Bandinelli and Bartolommeo Ammanati in their companion pieces in the Piazza della Signoria, for the most part its formal qualities were not highly influential. Raphael, who copied and adapted the *David* in a number of drawings, probably made more use of it than any other contemporary. A small model, perhaps made by Michelangelo in preparation for his great marble, known in a cast in wax in the Casa Buonarroti, was much more widely copied than the statue (fig. 11). This is significant, for models in wax and clay are fragile and the proportion of loss in this area of Michelangelo's work is enormous. Vasari said that Michelangelo gave two cases of models to his pupil Antonio Mini when Mini went to France in 1531; yet this intellectual dowry has entirely disappeared. It is rare that we can gain knowledge of lost models by Michelangelo, but one, at least, can plausibly be reconstructed. Around 1504, Michelangelo made several sketches for a standing male figure, almost certainly one of the apostles he had contracted to carve for the Cathedral of Florence. It would have been difficult for another sculptor to make a three-dimensional rendering from this drawing, but, in fact, a version of the figure, included in a large retable in Zaragoza, was carved in the early 1520s by Michelangelo's friend Alonso Berruguete. It seems most probable that Berruguete had either been given a model by Michelangelo or had been allowed to copy one (figs. 12, 13).

Jacopo Sansovino was probably the most important immediate contemporary seriously to approach Michelangelo's sculpture, but he was little concerned with the interior life of the figure or, for the most part, with the expressive nude. His largest debts to Michelangelo—with whom his hopes of collaborating on the façade of San Lorenzo were thwarted—are found in his major Roman sculpture: *Saint James* in San Jacopo dei Spagnoli, of which his friend Leonardo Sellaio wrote to Michelangelo on 29 January 1520, "si dice è delle vostre," and the *Madonna del Parto* (fig. 14) in San Agostino. In the *Saint James*, Jacopo drew inspiration from the grandly draped statues that Michelangelo had devised for the façade. For the *Madonna* he studied the seated figures that Michelangelo had planned for the Julius Tomb—especially the *Moses*, the only one to be exe-

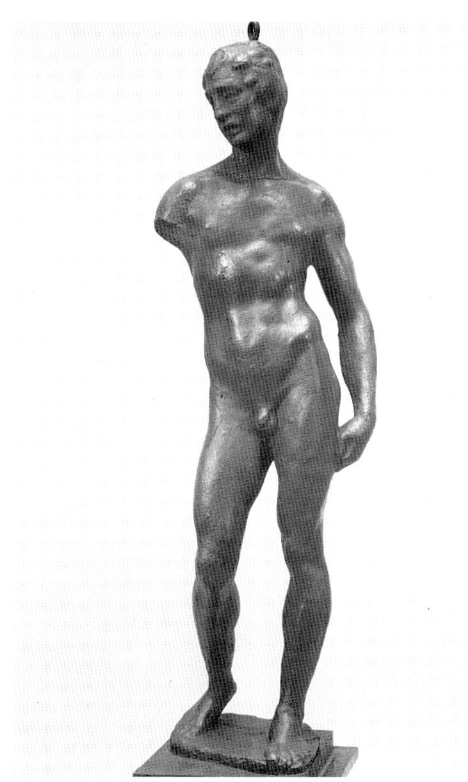

fig. 11. After Michelangelo, *Model for David (?)*, wax, height 49 cm. Casa Buonarroti, Florence

LEFT: fig. 12. Michelangelo, *Sketch for a Standing Apostle*, pen and ink, 20.1 x 7.8 cm. Musée du Louvre, Paris, Département des Arts Graphiques [Photo RMN]

RIGHT: fig. 13. Alonso Berruguete, *Saint John the Evangelist*, pigmented wood, height 95 cm. Museo Nacional de Escultura, Valladolid. [Ministerio de Cultura]

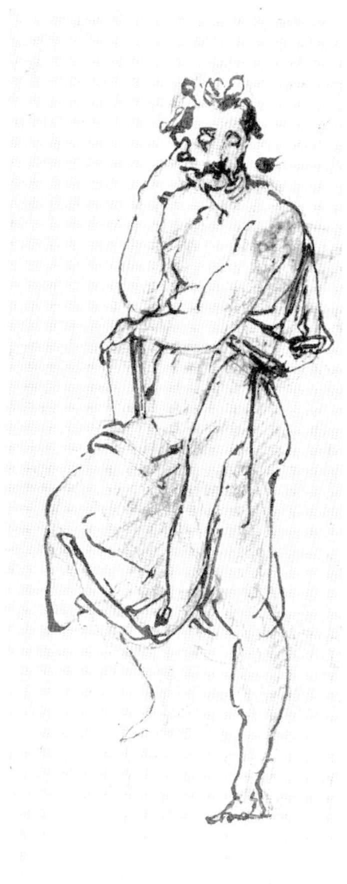

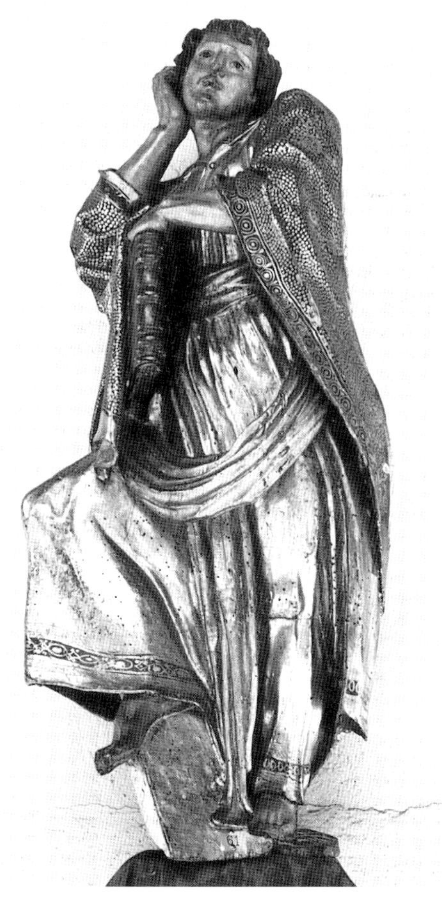

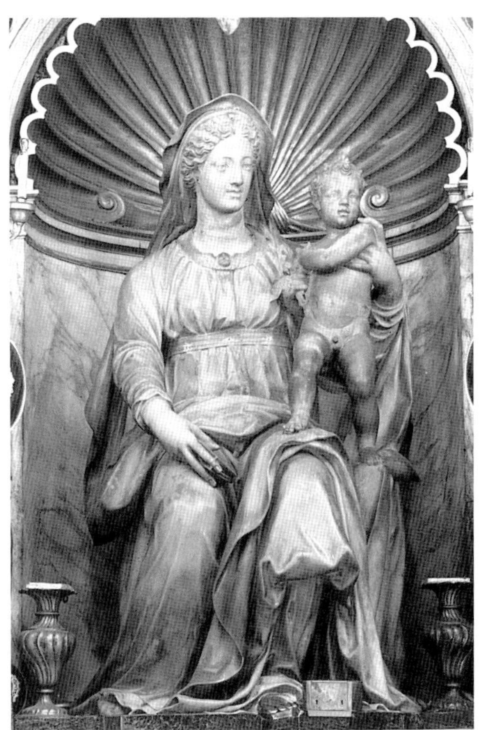

fig. 14. Jacopo Sansovino, *Madonna del Parto*, marble, height 188 cm. San Agostino, Rome [The Conway Library, Courtauld Institute of Art]

cuted—and the related figures of prophets and sibyls on the Sistine vault. In 1525, perhaps to overcome the rift between Michelangelo and Jacopo, it was mooted that the latter should sculpt a double tomb to Michelangelo's design, now lost. Although nothing came of this, Michelangelo's lost drawing may lie behind his later and highly imaginative Venetian tombs. But for the most part Jacopo's figural sculpture in Venice shows little trace of Michelangelo's influence, except in a decorative role in the nude bearded figures he designed for the spandrels of the arches in the Marciana Library.

In the execution of these figures Sansovino was aided for a period by a younger Florentine sculptor, Bartolommeo Ammanati. Probably in 1530 or 1531, Ammanati, together with his friend Nanni di Baccio Bigio, had raided Michelangelo's Via Mozza studio and had stolen some of his drawings and models. These he had been compelled to return, but he must have learned something of Michelangelo's current ideas and methods. His works in the 1530s display many echoes of Michelangelesque schemes. No figure drawings can firmly be attributed either to Sansovino, after his earliest period, or to Ammanati, but one in the present exhibition (cat. 11) may exemplify a type that either might have made in the decade 1540–1550. Surprisingly, however, two of the earliest responses to Michelangelo's *Slave* designs of the mid-1510s occurred in Venice well before Sansovino arrived in 1527. A *Saint Sebastian*, sculpted by Bartolommeo Bergamasco in 1522 for the shrine of San Rocco in the eponymous church, reveals knowledge of the pose of Michelangelo's *Bearded Slave*, now in the Galleria dell'Accademia, Florence. And Titian's *Saint Sebastian*, a panel in his Brescia polyptych, documented as under way in 1520, is based on another *Slave* design, known only from Michelangelo's drawings. There must have been some leakage from Michelangelo's studio, but how this occurred and how his drawings came to be known in Venice is conjectural.

Two sculptors who assisted Michelangelo during the last phase of work in the Medici chapel, Giovanni Montorsoli and Niccolò Tribolo, showed some response to the developing forms of the musculature of Michelangelo's figures and to their increasingly complex design. But, while both made some use of Michelangelesque sculptural forms in their subsequent work, neither can really be said to have exploited in any profound way Michelangelo's ideas. Montorsoli based his powerful *Saint Paul* (fig. 15) of the mid-1530s on Michelangelo's Medici *Dukes,* but his sculpture gradually became dry and linear. Most of Tribolo's later work was scenic in nature, giving him little opportunity to exploit a genuinely Michelangelesque sensibility. However, their companion, Raffaello da Montelupo, by whom a number of pen drawings are known (cats. 3, 10), did copy and adapt some of the master's drawings. He is one of the very few sculptors who can be demonstrated—as opposed to assumed—to have done so. But when he worked again with Michelangelo on the completion of the Julius Tomb in the 1540s, he produced weak figures that betrayed the master's ideas.

Only in the generation of sculptors young enough to have been Michelangelo's grandchildren was there real understanding and penetration of Michelangelo's most dynamic sculptural phase, that of the 1520s and early 1530s. Florentine sculptors like Pierino da Vinci and Vincenzo Danti showed a confidence in dealing with Michelangelo's ideas, when they chose to use them, which suggests that his achievement was no longer felt oppressive. And the greatest of all of them, Giambologna, was able to push Michelangelo's most complex formal ideas beyond Michelangelo's own work. Thus, some of Michelangelo's sculpture of the 1520s, like the *Victory* and the model for *Samson and the Two Philistines,* were the inspiration of Giambologna's experiments with serpentine composition, such as *Florence Triumphant over Pisa* (fig. 16) and the *Rape of the Sabines.*

A comparable response, less dramatic but more profound than Giambologna's and again remarkable in that it occurred in Venice, was exemplified by Alessandro Vittoria, who handled Michelangelesque form with great confidence. Less concerned than Giambologna with serpentine poses and multifigure groups, he had deeper appreciation of the spiritual intensity of Michelangelo's work, in particular in isolated figures (fig. 17). In the intensity of feeling that he communicated, Vittoria was the sculptural equivalent of Tintoretto and stood in similar relation to Michelangelo: both had collections of casts of his work.

These sculptors were looking at Michelangelo's work prior to the *Last Judgment.* The public sculpture he produced after 1540, as visible on the Julius Tomb, had small effect outside Rome. But there it was pervasive, and the predominant solidity, even stolidity, and dryness of Roman

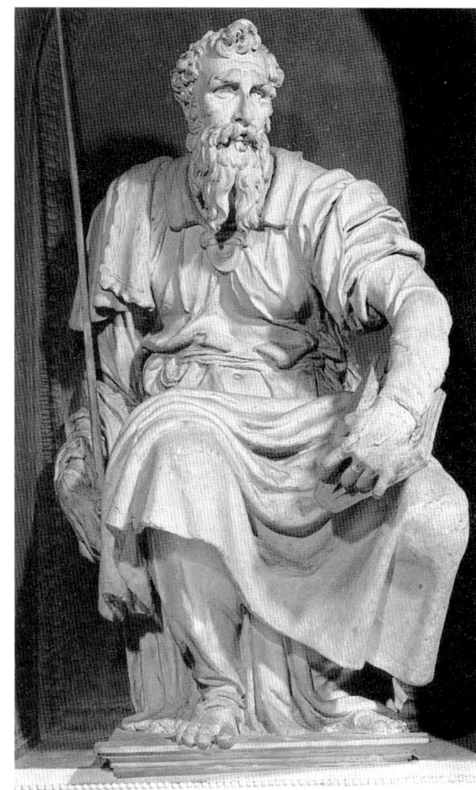

fig. 15. Giovanni Montorsoli, *Saint Paul,* stucco, height 155 cm. Chapel of Saint Luke, Santissima Annunziata, Florence [Fratelli Alinari, 1995]

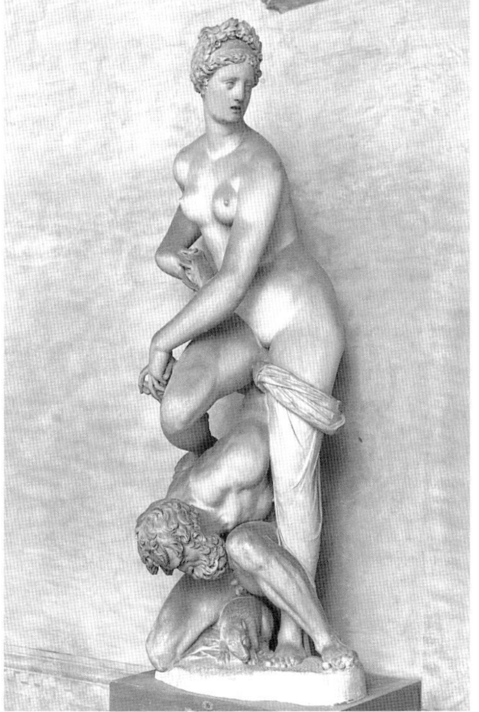

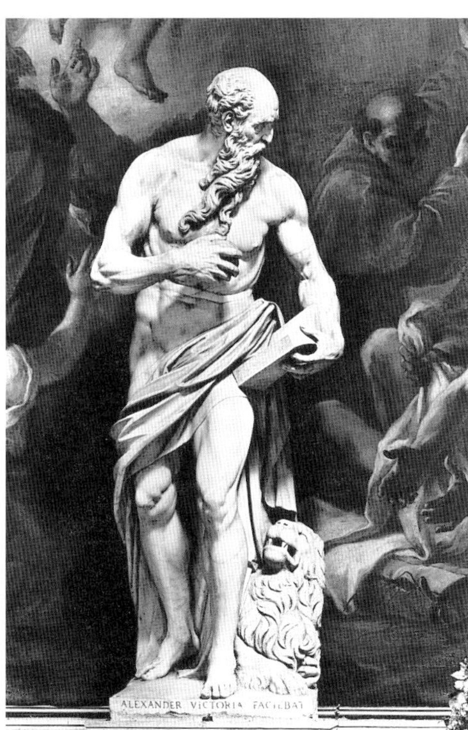

LEFT: fig. 16. Giambologna, *Florence Triumphant over Pisa,* marble, height 260 cm. Museo Nazionale del Bargello, Florence [Fratelli Alinari, 1995]

RIGHT: fig. 17. Alessandro Vittoria, *Saint Jerome,* marble, height 192 cm. Santa Maria Gloriosa dei Frari, Venice [Fratelli Alinari, 1995]

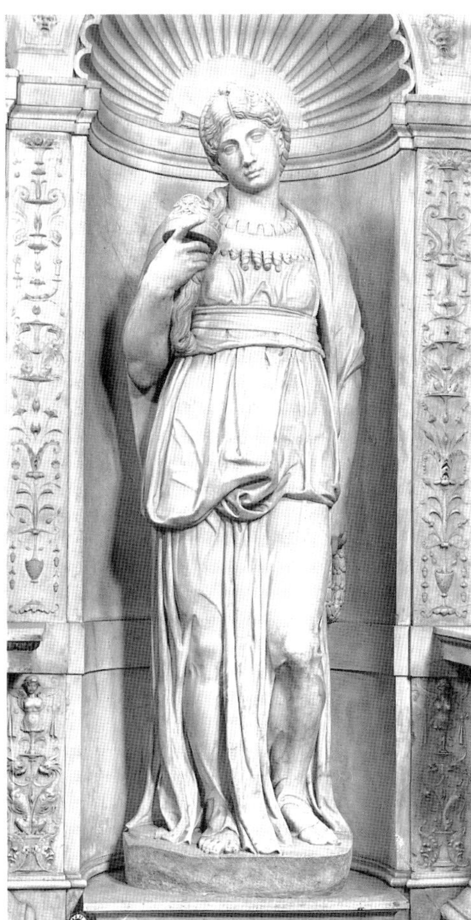

fig. 18. Michelangelo, *Leah*, marble, height 197 cm. San Pietro in Vincoli, Rome [Fratelli Alinari, 1995]

sculpture for much of the rest of the century is largely a response to the aged master's efforts to suppress sensuality and sensuousness in his figures to allow full expression to the spirit. This response, which often failed to appreciate the motivating force of Michelangelo's reductionist style in the *Rachel* and the *Leah* (fig. 18), may also have been encouraged because they presented fewer technical difficulties than Michelangelo's other sculpture. But when a fully fledged reaction against this would-be metaphysical style occurred in the new century, aspects of Michelangelo's own sculpture provided a bridgehead for it. The most inventive Roman seventeenth-century sculptor, Gianlorenzo Bernini, still more dominant in his century than Michelangelo was in the sixteenth, was strongly inspired in much of his early work by Michelangelo's example. Bernini's *Saint Sebastian* (Thyssen Collection, Madrid) is in part modeled on Michelangelo's multifigured *Pietà* (Museo dell'Opera del Duomo, Florence); his *Neptune* (Victoria and Albert Museum, London) is indebted to the *Samson* model; and Bernini alone appreciated fully the pictorial wealth of the Saint Peter's *Pietà*, which he studied for his *Saint Lawrence*, (Palazzo Pitti, Florence, Contini-Bonacossi Collection). This *Pietà*'s treatment of light and shade remained a constant inspiration for his own later work.

Painting

Whereas Michelangelo's influence on sculpture has not been much criticized, it has frequently been said that his painting exercised a destructive effect on the whole of later-sixteenth-century painting, except that practiced in Venice. Michelangelo has been held responsible for a style called mannerism, in which artists produced exaggerated, muscled display figures in uncomprehending imitation of Michelangelo's worst excesses, compounding this by neglecting in their own work the example of Michelangelo's study of life. This view has an element of truth, but its sweeping condemnation is largely a product of nineteenth-century realism and the simultaneous elevation of Pre-Raphaelite and Nazarene models. It equates minor artists, who may mindlessly have imitated Michelangelo's forms, with major ones who understood Michelangelo's aims and aspirations, and developed aspects of his work with sensitivity and intelligence. It is a view that cannot survive twentieth-century efforts to define more precisely later-sixteenth-century artistic personalities. However, for most tasks performed by most artists, Michelangelo's work provided little help: thus it presented few compositional ideas for altarpieces, a staple of most painters' activities. And some of Michelangelo's most memorable images had little progeny: the figures in the *Creation of Adam* on the Sistine ceiling, for example, could hardly be quoted directly; they were too singular and powerful. Raphael's use of elements of Adam's pose in a reclining muse in his *Parnassus* (Stanza della Segnatura, Vatican), could only be surreptitious, and it was, for the most part, the central idea of the divine infusion of life that later artists found productive.

It was in his less forceful, and perhaps less central, works that Michelangelo's influence was more specific: the family groups he devised for the ancestors of Christ, for example, fed easily into compositions of the Holy Family, and were much copied. In general Michelangelo's painting encouraged art of the highest ambition and seriousness, and a stylistic idealism that conscientiously avoided the trivial and attempted to imbue all forms with significance. Such idealism could produce sterile displays of virtuosity, but these are the exception and an unprejudiced consideration of later-sixteenth-century Michelangelesque painting will reveal a still undervalued wealth of beauty and meaning.

The effect of Michelangelo's sculpture on painters was also considerable. By midcentury, plaster and wax reductions of Michelangelo's sculpture circulated widely. In many, perhaps most, cases, obviously so in Venice, painters were instructed by these rather than originals. A drawing in the Ashmolean Museum documents a replica of Michelangelo's *Evening*, showing it supported on a mobile wooden frame much too flimsy to have carried marble (fig. 19). Wax or plaster reductions were more useful for painters than the originals in that they could be studied from any angle. El Greco's only known copy after a statue by Michelangelo shows the *Day* from above, a viewpoint impossible in the chapel and feasible only from a reduction (fig. 20). But reductions encouraged a coarsening of Michelangelo's forms because they blurred the surfaces, textures, and local subtleties of the originals. A similar general point can be made about drawn copies of

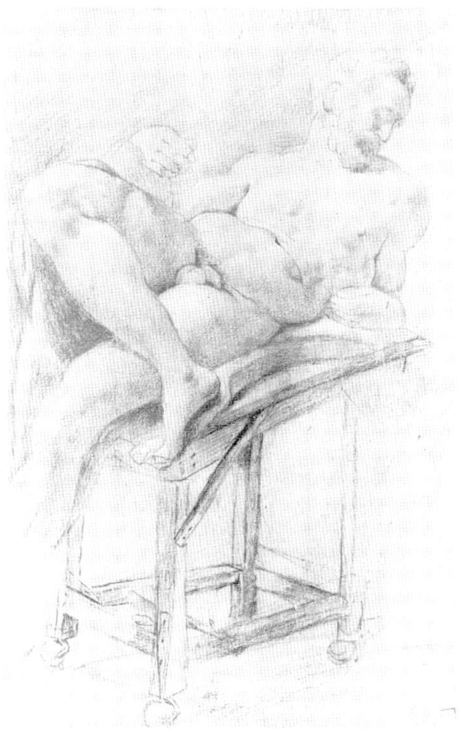

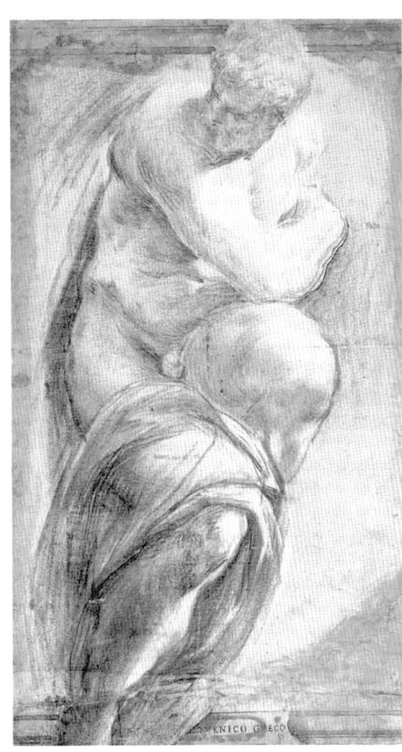

LEFT: fig. 19. Carracci Circle (?) after a Reduction after Michelangelo, *Evening*, red and black chalk, 38.6 x 24.8 cm. Ashmolean Museum, Oxford

RIGHT: fig. 20. El Greco after Michelangelo, *Day*, black chalk with white heightening on blue paper, 59.8 x 34.5 cm. Staatliche Graphische Sammlung, Munich

Michelangelo's Sistine Chapel frescoes: a high proportion was made after earlier drawings or, in the later sixteenth century, after engravings, for the frescoes were difficult of access and neck-breaking to study in situ (fig. 21). Lack of familiarity with the originals could lead to parodic interpretation of their forms, which in part accounts for the view that Michelangelo's influence was negative. Yet copying at second hand could bring advantages for painters of sufficient individuality. Thus the obsessive repetition by Tintoretto and his shop of the *Samson* and figures from the Medici chapel, made from reductions, freed Tintoretto from any obligation to respect Michelangelo's modeling and allowed him to take a proprietary attitude to his forms. Tintoretto proclaimed his allegiance to the *disegno* of Michelangelo and was one of the few artists to match the scale of his projects, but it was to Michelangelo's sculpture that he most looked for inspiration. Figural borrowings or compositional inspiration from his paintings are rare: the most obvious exception is the *Miracle of the Slave* of 1548, which reveals Tintoretto's rapid and confident response to Michelangelo's *Conversion of Saint Paul*, perhaps all the more effective in that Tintoretto never saw the original.

It is probably true that none of his younger contemporaries and few later-sixteenth-century Italian painters remained entirely untouched by or indifferent to Michelangelo's painting, although some ignored his work completely or for parts of their careers. But what painters selected from his work differed widely. Writing in 1584, the Milanese artist and theorist Giovanni Paolo Lomazzo defined three periods in Michelangelo's painting: that of the Sistine ceiling, that of the *Last Judgment*, and that of the Pauline Chapel; this division also applies loosely to the sculpture. In Lomazzo's view these were in descending order of merit. Quite independently, Cellini considered the *Cascina* cartoon, which he saw before it was dismembered, Michelangelo's best work. Thus, knowledge of Michelangelo's early painting persisted alongside experience of his later work and the former was often preferred. But, in broad terms, the response of artists to the different phases of Michelangelo's painting was closely linked with their age, and no painter after Raphael seems to have attempted to shadow Michelangelo in any consistent way. Thus Michelangelo had distinct ranges and generations of followers and these do, approximately, correspond to Lomazzo's divisions.

In its first phase, Michelangelo's influence was mainly exercised by the *Doni Tondo*, the aborted *Battle of Cascina*, and the Sistine ceiling. In Florence the *Tondo* was copied by Michelangelo's friend Francesco Granacci on several occasions, and Raphael, more subtly, inserted figures

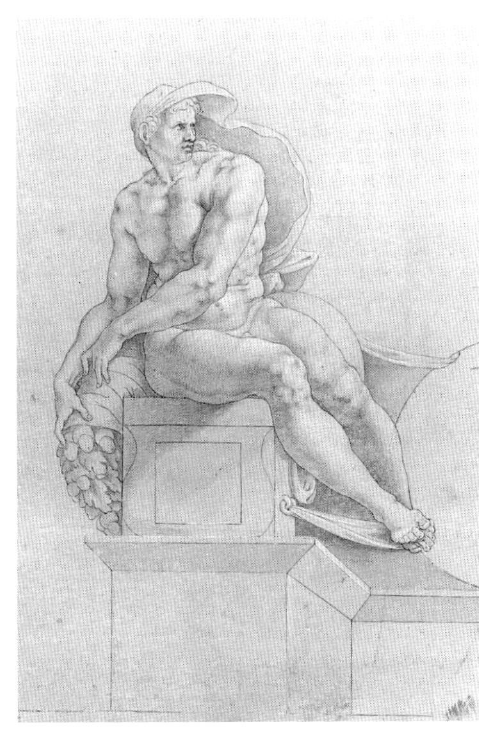

fig. 21. Unidentified Artist after Adamo Scultori after Michelangelo, *The Ignudo to the Left above the Persian Sibyl*, pen and ink and wash, lightly squared in black chalk, 25 x 17.1 cm. The Royal Collection, Windsor Castle

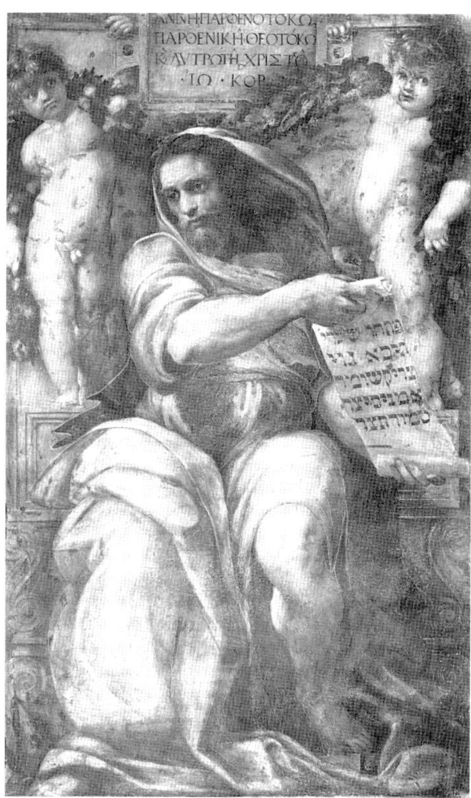

fig. 22. Raphael, *Isaiah*, fresco, 250 x 155 cm. San Agostino, Rome [Fratelli Alinari, 1995]

borrowed from it in other contexts. Michelangelo's unfinished *Entombment* (National Gallery, London) had no effect in Rome, which is surprising, for it seems to have been painted for the Roman church of San Agostino and no documentary evidence places it in Florence. But, it was taken as a compositional model both by Andrea del Sarto in his *Disputà* (Palazzo Pitti, Florence) and by Rosso Fiorentino in his *Marriage of the Virgin* (San Lorenzo, Florence). Andrea, only a few years younger than Michelangelo, was much impressed in his later work by the coloring of the Sistine, but his references to Michelangelo's figure types and poses were circumspect.

While in Florence, Raphael copied everything by Michelangelo that he could: he was the contemporary who best understood Michelangelo's work. In Rome, beginning the Vatican Stanze shortly after Michelangelo began the Sistine, Raphael, according to Vasari, gained access to the chapel and kept a close watch on Michelangelo's work. Awareness of the ceiling and, in all probability, models for the Julius Tomb increasingly infused his work of the early Roman years until, in 1511–1512, he painted heavily Michelangelesque frescoes of *Sibyls* in Santa Maria della Pace and the Prophet *Isaiah* in San Agostino (fig. 22), as well as designing an altarpiece of the *Resurrection* (see cat. 36) deeply indebted to the *Cascina*. But shortly thereafter, Raphael turned from Michelangelo's forms. He was unaffected by Michelangelo's color and did not take up the challenge of superhuman figuration posed by the *Haman*. Nor were his best followers seduced. Giulio Romano, while occasionally lifting motifs from Michelangelo, generally avoided his work. Perino del Vaga borrowed more overtly, but his bias was fundamentally decorative and he tended to interpret Michelangelo's forms with an elegance that drained them of emotion: in this he was highly influential. Polidoro da Caravaggio, who specialized in large-scale façade frescoes, approached more closely the bulk and vigor of Michelangelo's forms, but seems to have been little interested in poses or compositions. However, Raphael's associate Guillaume de Marcillat did utilize some of Michelangelo's Sistine figures and designs for Sebastiano del Piombo in his own vault frescoes in Arezzo Cathedral in the early 1520s, but his ambition so far outstripped his ability as to make his scheme the first of those unintentional parodies of the grand style that fulfill critics' gloomiest apprehension of Michelangelo's influence.

During the period of competition between Raphael and Sebastiano del Piombo, Michelangelo made designs for his *Pietà* in Viterbo, his *Raising of Lazarus* in the National Gallery, and his *Flagellation* in the Borgherini chapel in San Pietro in Montorio (fig. 77); but other compositions by Sebastiano from this time and later were also based on Michelangelo's drawings. Michelangelo simplified figures and, perhaps, compositions to satisfy Sebastiano's innately geometrical sense of form and densely executed surfaces. The resultant images were uniformly grand, rich, and severe. Although their immediate repercussions were few, they exercised enormous influence later in the century: the paintings of Counter-Reformation artists like Girolamo Muziano (see cat. 49) and Giuseppe Valeriano, and the early work of Cesari d'Arpino cannot be understood without them. It was through Sebastiano (see cat. 34) that Michelangelo exercised his greatest influence on altarpiece design.

In Sebastiano's native region, Venice and the Veneto, Titian and Pordenone were the painters most affected by Michelangelo. Titian knew some of Michelangelo's works as early as 1511 and used his knowledge in varied ways and with great intelligence, but it remained indirect until his Roman sojourn of 1545–1546. In the following half decade Titian painted some of his grandest and most powerful pictures: the ceiling canvases of Santo Spirito in Isola and the Scuola di San Giovanni Evangelista and the four damned giants, *Tityus, Sisyphus, Tantalus,* and *Ixion,* for Mary of Hungary, all of which reveal a profound debt to Michelangelo. Pordenone probably visited Rome more than once. Both were aware of at least some drawings by Michelangelo (see cat. 51). Whereas Titian remained primarily concerned with overall equilibrium in his paintings and incorporated borrowings from Michelangelo with discretion, Pordenone pursued the most extreme aspects of his work, his paintings displaying massive discharges of energy. Pordenone died in 1539, before the *Last Judgment* was unveiled, but he would surely have been its keenest pillager; Titian, by contrast, paid little attention to the *Last Judgment* (compare fig. 97), although he cited two of the most violent figures from the Sistine, the *Father Separating Light from Darkness* and the *Haman* (fig. 83). He retained in his approach to Michelangelo a critical detachment akin to that of Raphael. In Parma, Correggio took certain motifs from Michelangelo—his *Jupiter and Io*

(Musée du Louvre, Paris), for example, is inspired by Michelangelo's Sistine *Fall*—but his approach was detached and selective.

Among artists born before 1500, it was probably only Pontormo, whose early work showed little engagement with Michelangelo, who followed him further than his first phase. Although some aspects of Pontormo's figure painting of the early 1520s respond to Michelangelo, it was primarily the master's color that interested him, as can be seen in the *Deposition* and *Annunciation* in the Capponi chapel in Santa Felicità of the late 1520s. Around 1530, he developed close personal links with Michelangelo, executing two paintings from his designs: the *Venus and Cupid* in the Accademia, Florence, (reproduced here in a version by Vasari in the Royal Collection, fig. 23) and the *Noli me Tangere* (versions in a private collection and Casa Buonarroti, Florence). This contact changed the direction of Pontormo's art. His later work, especially the frescoes in the choir of San Lorenzo—worked on for a decade prior to his death in 1556 but destroyed in the eighteenth century—demonstrated a brilliant and radically original response to the *Last Judgment*, which he reinterpreted in a manner inspired by the linear expressionism of the aged Sandro Botticelli.

The unveiling of the *Last Judgment* most deeply affected artists then in their early maturity. Vasari claimed to have made a special trip to Rome to witness the unveiling but his work shows few signs of its influence. Francesco Salviati, on the other hand, responded with a considerable inflation of forms and a bolder manipulation of space. Agnolo Bronzino—who had hitherto largely shunned attempts at Michelangelesque figure style, although marginally responsive to other aspects of his work—was suddenly overwhelmed by the *Last Judgment* after a trip to Rome in 1548 (see cat. 61). He later came to produce paintings that are virtual pastiches of Michelangelesque form but from which Michelangelo's devastating energy is drained (fig. 24). Bronzino's favorite pupil, Alessandro Allori, was still more immediately impressed and, on his return to Florence after 1550, painted in the Montauto chapel in Santissima Annunziata an abbreviated version of the *Last Judgment*. Allori's drawings for this scheme and some of his anatomical studies indicate that he was also aware of Michelangelo's drawings.

The *Last Judgment* was copied in innumerable drawings, and engravings of all or parts of it were printed within a short time of its unveiling. The family of the Farnese pope Paul III, who had commissioned it, also commissioned a large painted copy on panel from the young Marcello Venusti (Museo Nazionale di Capodimonte, Naples). Although the *Last Judgment* alerted artists

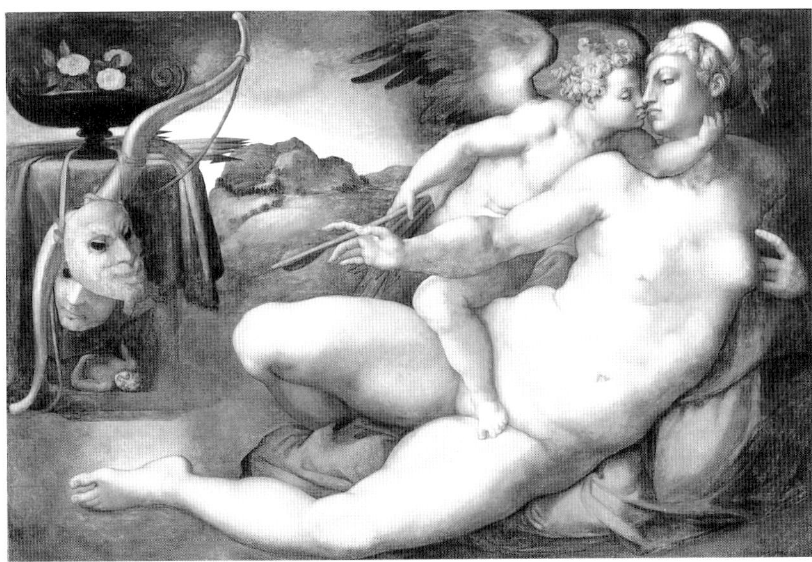

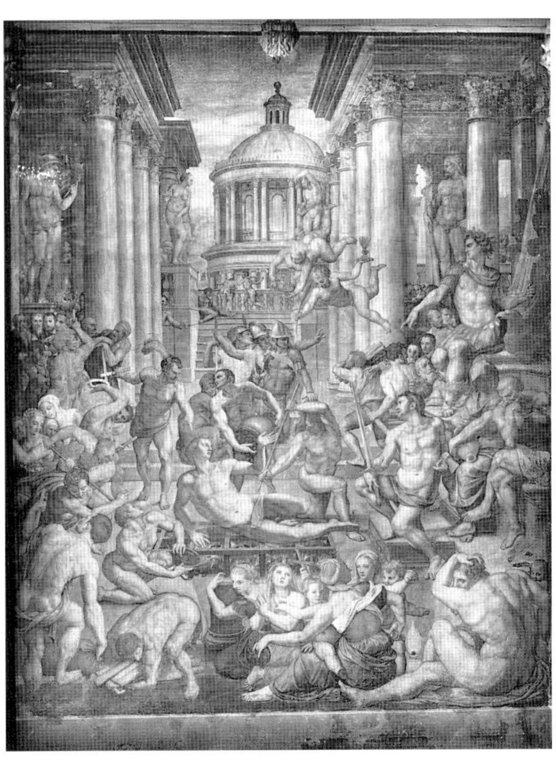

LEFT: fig. 23. Giorgio Vasari after Jacopo Pontormo to Michelangelo's Design, *Venus and Cupid*, oil on panel, 128.6 x 193 cm. The Royal Collection, Hampton Court

RIGHT: fig. 24. Bronzino, *The Martyrdom of Saint Lawrence*, fresco. San Lorenzo, Florence [Fratelli Alinari, 1995]

to the potential of physical power, its positive effects were comparatively slight. It did, however, encourage a certain compositional gigantism: Tintoretto's *Paradiso* in the Doge's Palace, for example, is hardly explicable without its example. But few other artists could cope with it. Thus, while many copies were made by Giovan Ambrogio Figino, these are rarely reflected in his paintings. It was not until Peter Paul Rubens that an artist emerged of sufficiently potent temperament to make use of it productively. Even so ambitious a painter as Salviati consulted it, as it were, in parentheses, and the artist who was closest to Michelangelo in his late years, Daniele da Volterra—who covered some of Michelangelo's more criticized nudities—was sparing in his references to it. Its figures, with their inexorable energy and hard musculature, could not easily be disciplined to act in different roles and it was probably the later-sixteenth-century Romanizing artists of northern Europe, Hendrik Goltzius and Cornelis van Haarlem among others, who acknowledged it with fewest inhibitions.

In some ways more influential, although less widely copied, were Michelangelo's Pauline Chapel frescoes, which, since they decorated a relatively private chapel, were even less accessible than those in the Sistine. As narrative paintings, they were of more immediate relevance to most artists than the timeless display of the *Last Judgment*, but their avoidance of physical beauty and their spatial incongruities might have been expected to alienate. However, a number of artists responded to them very strongly. Among them, Taddeo Zuccaro borrowed both figures and compositions in the years shortly after 1550, exploiting the inflated forms, rope-ridged draperies, and slow or unbalanced movements of Michelangelo's figures in highly imaginative ways (fig. 25; see also cat. 67). Salviati too was much affected, since the softer forms of the Pauline Chapel corresponded more closely than those of the *Last Judgment* to his own figure style (see cat. 64). Muziano, Pellegrino Tibaldi (cats. 65, 66), Giovanni Francesco Bezzi, called Il Nosadella, Bartolomeo Passarotti, and Lelio Orsi were all, to a greater or lesser extent, inspired by the Pauline frescoes and the trend they initiated continued, primarily in Rome and Bologna, until late in the century. Tibaldi, in particular, also turned back to Michelangelo's work on the Sistine ceiling for inspiration (fig. 26). But these artists also looked closely and competitively at each others' work, setting up a pattern of reciprocal influence that, while it operated within Michelangelesque modes, did not necessarily derive directly from them.

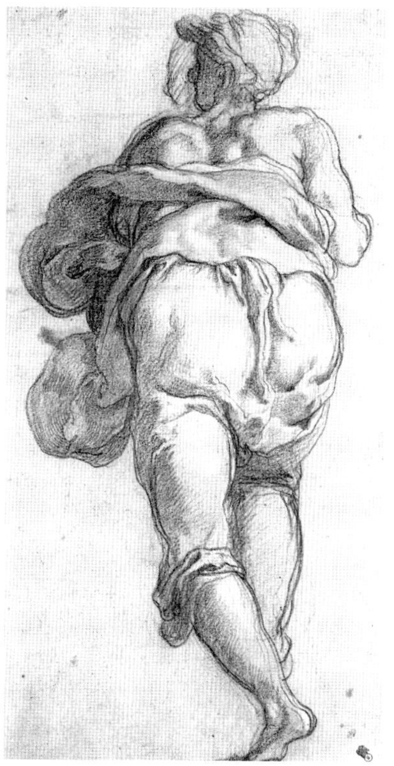

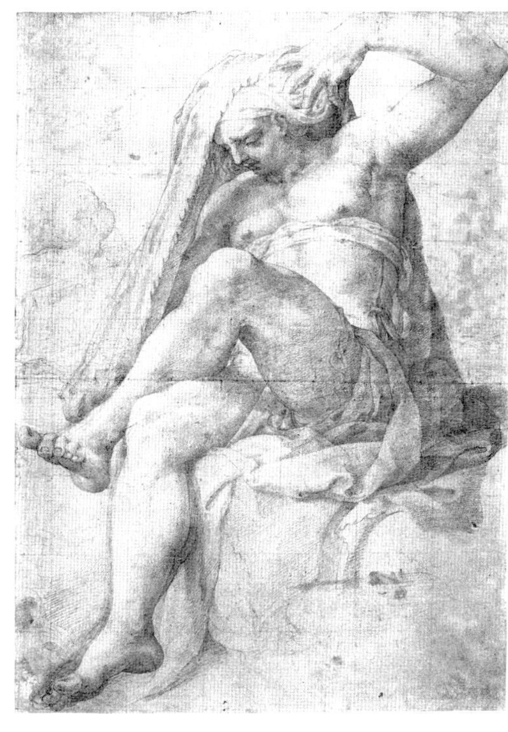

LEFT: fig. 25. Taddeo Zuccaro, *Running Figure*, red chalk and white heightening, 34.4 x 18.8 cm. National Gallery of Art, Washington, Ailsa Mellon Bruce Fund

RIGHT: fig. 26. Pellegrino Tibaldi, *A Seated Sibyl*, red chalk, squared, 47.6 x 34 cm. The Pierpont Morgan Library, New York

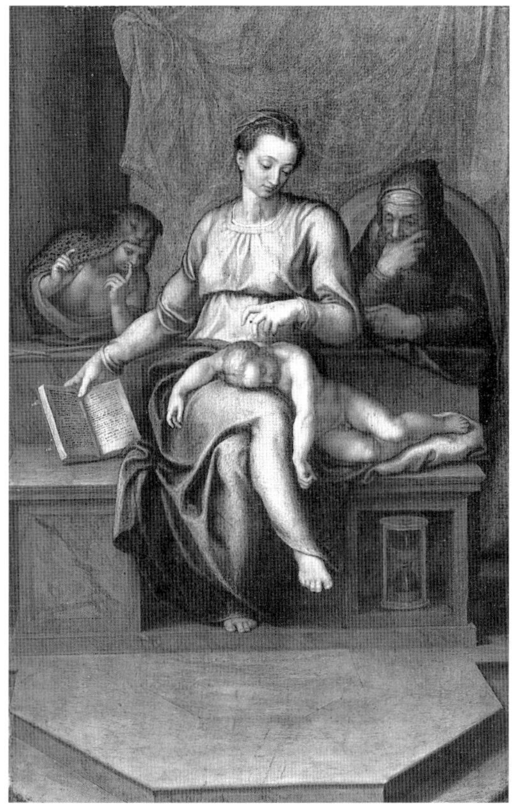

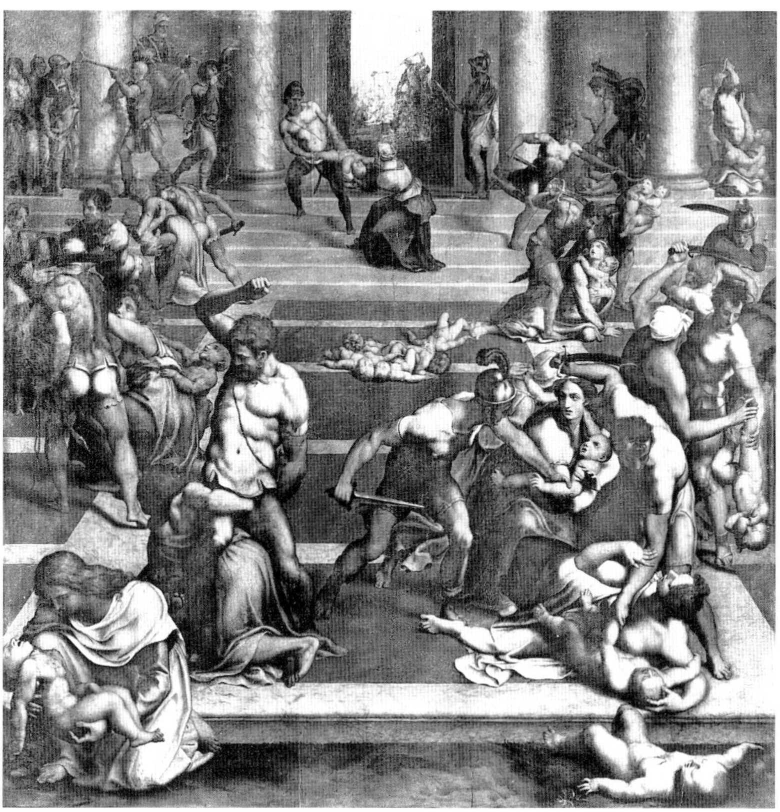

LEFT: fig. 27. Marcello Venusti after Michelangelo, *Madonna del Silenzio*, oil on panel, 43.1 x 28.5 cm. The Trustees of the National Gallery, London

RIGHT: fig. 28. Daniele da Volterra, *The Massacre of the Innocents*, oil on panel, 147 x 144 cm. Galleria degli Uffizi, Florence [Fratelli Alinari, 1995]

Although Michelangelo executed no paintings after the completion of the Pauline Chapel, he nevertheless put both new and revived pictorial ideas into circulation. He made drawings for paintings to be executed by Marcello Venusti and also allowed him to make painted versions of some of his earlier presentation drawings of religious subjects. Marcello's execution, which sweetened the severity of the old master's neo-trecentesque religious style, nevertheless fixed attention on and actively disseminated the master's ideas (fig. 27). Marcello's paintings were influential and much copied. Michelangelo also made drawings for some paintings and sculpture by Daniele da Volterra, whose career he fostered and who was probably his closest friend among Roman artists in his last years. But Daniele was not committed only to Michelangelo's late style: he cited the *Samson* group, devised many years before, in his *Massacre of the Innocents* of 1557 (fig. 28) and, in his late *Baptism* in the Ricci chapel in San Pietro in Montorio, borrowed a figure from the *Cascina*. Nor was he much influenced by Michelangelo in his compositions, except in those small-scale paintings based on Michelangelo's drawings, in which his role paralleled that of Venusti.

Drawing

In addition to influence exercised through his publicly accessible painting and sculpture, Michelangelo also exercised influence, both of style and subject matter, through his drawings. Even El Greco, who expressed dislike of Michelangelo's painting while frequently borrowing forms and ideas from it, admired his powers as a draftsman. El Greco spoke from direct knowledge, for, as a friend of Giulio Clovio and while lodging in the Palazzo Farnese in the early 1570s, he had access to originals by Michelangelo as well as to Clovio's copies. He found inspiration in both.

Knowledge of Michelangelo's drawings came through several avenues. Certain works such as the cartoon for the *Battle of Cascina* (compare fig. 78) were, for a while, on public display. Michelangelo also gave away some works on paper: a cartoon fragment for the Sistine ceiling, now lost, went to his friend Bindo Altoviti, and many drawings and sculptural models were given to Antonio Mini when he migrated to France in 1531. Some became known to Francesco Primaticcio, who quoted figures from them in his own work; it is probable that Mini's cache comprised a high proportion of surviving drawings by Michelangelo datable before 1530. Occasional collaborators

LEFT: fig. 29. Andrea del Sarto, *Study for Saint John the Baptist*, red chalk, 38.5 x 19.5 cm. National Gallery of Victoria, Melbourne, Felton Bequest 1936

RIGHT: fig. 30. Michelangelo, *Study of a Figure for the Battle of Cascina*, pen and ink over black chalk, 24.8 x 9.5 cm. Musée du Louvre, Paris, Département des Arts Graphiques [Photo RMN]

BELOW: fig. 31. Rosso Fiorentino, *Figure Study*, red chalk, 36.5 x 21.5 cm. British Museum, London, Department of Prints and Drawings

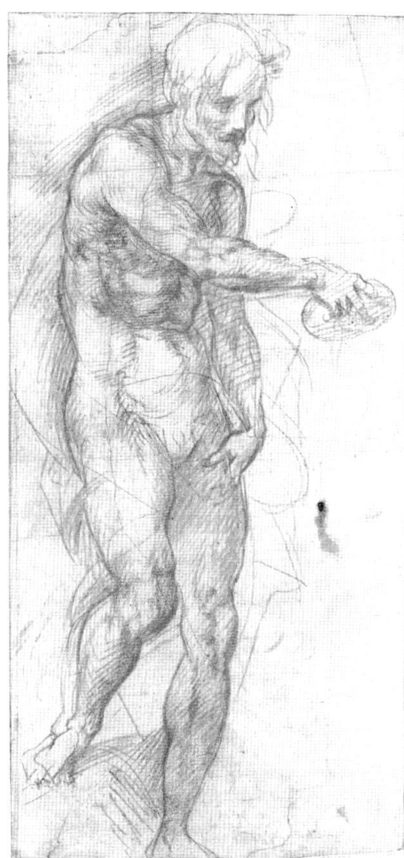

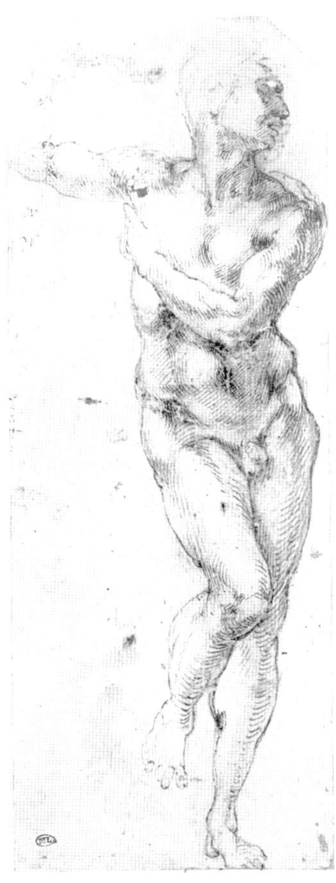

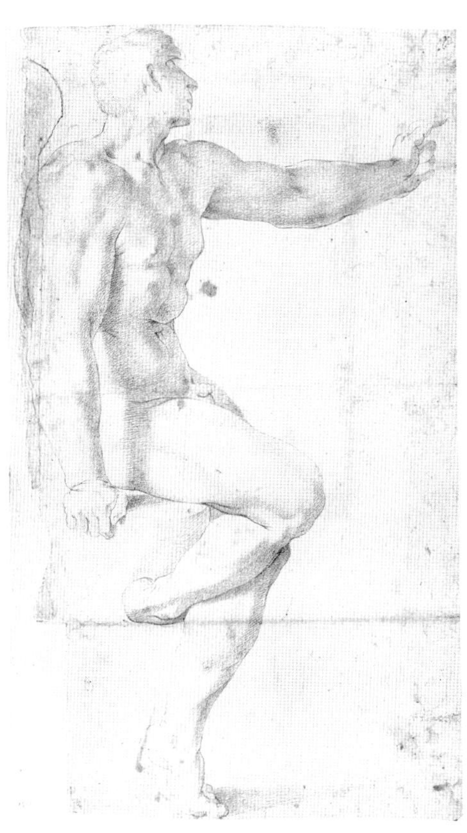

of Michelangelo had access to his drawings and undoubtedly made copies of them, but only a few by Raffaello da Montelupo have been identified. Michelangelo also made drawings or cartoons expressly for other artists: certainly in the cases of Sebastiano del Piombo, Giuliano Bugiardini, Jacopo del Pontormo, Daniele da Volterra, Marcello Venusti, his pupil Ascanio Condivi, and probably also Francesco Granacci. Sebastiano's black chalk drawings, although readily distinguishable from Michelangelo's, are strongly affected by them (see cat. 53); and the later drawings of Pontormo, probably the most brilliant draftsman of all the artists associated with Michelangelo, owe a heavy debt to his drawings of the early 1530s.

In other instances knowledge of Michelangelo's drawings seems clear from the visual evidence. This is especially true of artists who were, either for long or short periods, on friendly terms with Michelangelo. Thus aspects of Andrea del Sarto's red-chalk style, in particular his lively hatching, are difficult to explain without knowledge of Michelangelo's more open pen drawings. An example might be Andrea's study for Saint John the Baptist (fig. 29, National Gallery of Victoria, Melbourne) in the *Baptism of the People* of 1515 in the Chiostro dello Scalzo, which surely shows direct knowledge of Michelangelo's drawing for the *Battle of Cascina* (fig. 30, Musée du Louvre, Paris 712 recto / C. 42 recto) both in pose and in the pen-inspired application of chalk. Most types of drawings by Andrea's one-time pupil Rosso cannot be accounted for without knowledge of Michelangelo's drawings. Rosso's multimedia *modello* style depends directly from *modelli* by Michelangelo and some of his figure (fig. 31) and compositional studies in red chalk would seem to show study of Michelangelo's soft and hard red chalk styles, as found on both sides of his sheet in Christ Church (figs. 8, 9). Links are also clear with two artists who became enemies of Michelangelo. Bandinelli's pen style can hardly have been developed without awareness of Michelangelo's pen drawings (see cat. 31), and it is likely that Raphael too, during his Florentine period, gained access to Michelangelo's portfolios—a replica of a lost Raphael sketch after one of Michelangelo's drawings (fig. 32, Albertina, Vienna Sc. R. 152 recto / C. 22 recto) is in the Metropolitan Museum of Art (fig. 33). And Raphael cannot have been alone, since other artists also

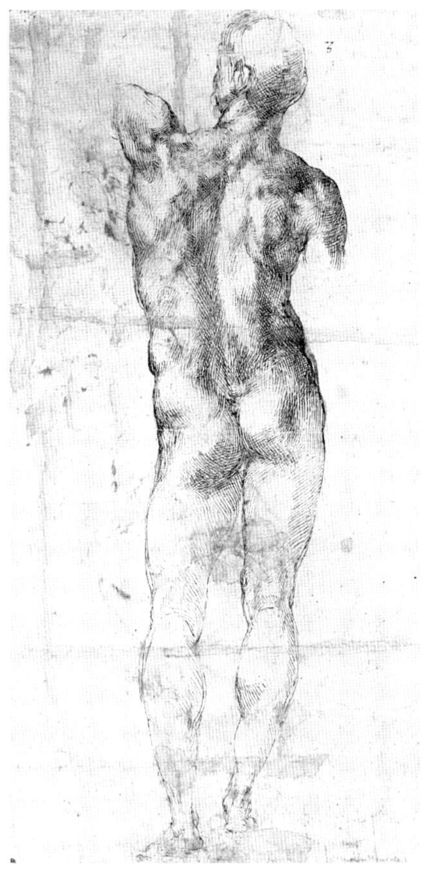

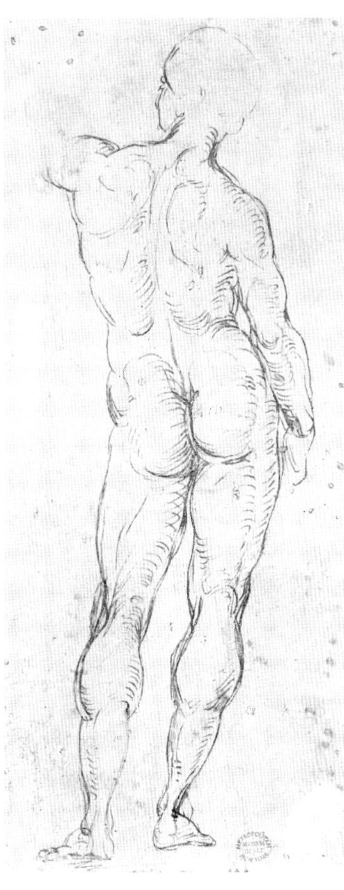

LEFT: fig. 32. Michelangelo, *Male Figure Seen from the Rear*, pen and ink over black chalk, 39 x 19.5 cm. Graphische Sammlung Albertina, Vienna

RIGHT: fig. 33. Unidentified Artist after Raphael after Michelangelo, *Figure Study*, pen and ink, 27.9 x 11.3 cm. The Metropolitan Museum of Art, New York

BELOW: fig. 34. Francesco Salviati after Michelangelo, *Figure Seen from Rear*, black chalk, 25.7 x 18.6 cm. Musée des Beaux-Arts, Lille

demonstrate knowledge of Michelangelo's drawings. Copies of lost or surviving drawings by Michelangelo were made by Biagio Pupini (see cat. 30), Battista Franco, Francesco Salviati, and Alessandro Allori (fig. 82) as well as Giulio Clovio (see cats. 15, 34). It is difficult to judge how many and how widely drawings by Michelangelo circulated. That will have to await more detailed investigation, but it seems certain that some were well known from early on: the drawing copied by Raphael, for example, was also known, directly or indirectly, to Salviati (fig. 34).

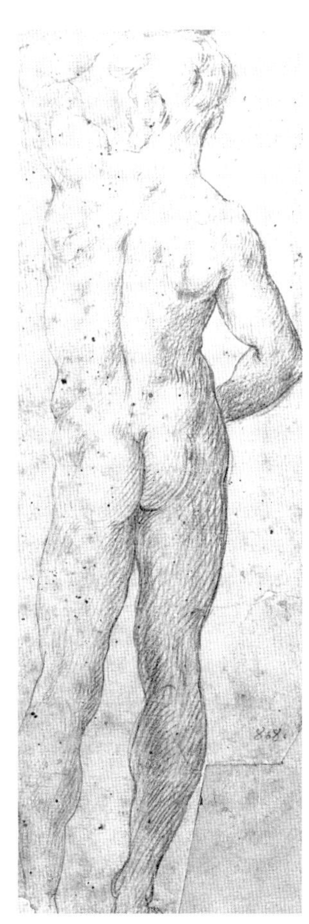

After the mid-1510s Michelangelo began regularly to make presentation drawings as gifts for friends. In the 1520s and 1530s his subjects were mostly secular; later, mostly sacred. Although in his very last years Michelangelo's infirmities precluded the high finish that he probably maintained as late as the early 1550s, it is likely that the practice continued almost to the end of his life. Paradoxically, such drawings, minutely laborious in execution, but miraculously retaining a liveliness in the touch that eluded their copyists, made as gifts for a small number of intimates and carefully guarded as precious objects, soon became well known. Although a few remained concealed by their owners, most seem to have been available for privileged artists to copy from quite soon after their creation. Many exist in multiple copies, which, in turn, spawned others. One of the foremost copyists was the miniaturist Giulio Clovio, whose patronage by Alessandro Farnese and other members of the powerful papal family and whose friendship with Michelangelo would have facilitated access to those who possessed his drawings. But Clovio was not alone and it is probable that too many copies are currently given to him. Alessandro Allori (see cat. 4) and, probably, Bronzino (see cat. 13) made copies, and it is likely that Marcello Venusti did too, although none by him are yet securely identified.

The originals were much sought after by rich or powerful collectors who could not have induced Michelangelo to make presentation drawings for themselves; Aretino long made vain efforts to persuade Michelangelo to send him drawings. Cosimo I obtained nothing from Michelangelo directly: he eventually compelled Tommaso de' Cavalieri to give him Michelangelo's *Cleopatra* and, at their owner's death, obtained the three drawings the artist had given to

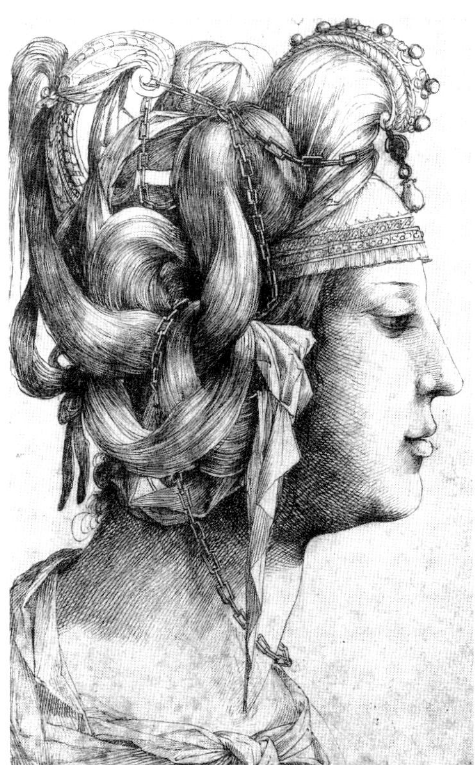

fig. 35. Jacopo Ligozzi, *Ideal Head*, pen and ink over black chalk, 30.6 x 19.9 cm. Private collection

Gherardo Perini. Alessandro Farnese seems to have acquired several presentation drawings at unknown dates before his coup of 1587 when he obtained most of those given to Cavalieri. The preciousness of their execution was obviously seductive and it must also have excited collectors that a master of gargantuan projects could turn his hand to the lilliputian. Furthermore, some of the presentation drawings had the charm of the culturally esoteric, representing recondite allegories that, if not Michelangelo's own inventions, come from literary sources that have evaded identification. Such treatments, establishing the artist as an intellectual, represent a further rise in his status, rivaling the poet as the autonomous creator of both subject and style. Although Michelangelo did not invent this type of image, any more than he invented the presentation drawing, his exploitation of such allegories gave the mode an impetus that carried it through to Netherlandish imagery of the next century. Such rarefied subjects and erudite references had some effect on court art and decoration; one might think of Rosso's frescoes in the Gallery of Francis I at Fontainebleau or Bronzino's *Allegory*, also painted for France, in the National Gallery, London. However, the allegories were not widely imitated, their influence being, so to speak, encapsulated. Among Italian artists, few attempted the combination of elaborate allegory with exquisite execution. Pirro Ligorio, later to become an architectural rival of Michelangelo's, is a rare exception.

The influence of the presentation drawings was widespread and varied. The ideal heads were models for many artists who produced their own variants on the types explored by Michelangelo. They are frequently, of course, to be found in the Florentine school, in paintings by Francesco Ubertini, called Il Bacchiacca, by Bronzino and his followers, and very notably in works by the minor but popular painter Michele di Ridolfo, who seems to have made a speciality in producing highly wrought paintings of heads—and sometimes full figures equipped with such heads—that depended closely from Michelangelo's inventions. Further variants on such types were produced in drawings and prints by artists such as Passarotti, and Jacopo Ligozzi and Goltzius until shortly after 1600 (fig. 35). The effect of the presentation drawings of classical subjects was very great: apart from the large number of direct copies that they inspired, few later treatments of *Phaeton* (see cat. 9) or *Ganymede* (see cat. 15), *Tityus* or *Prometheus* (see cat. 12) could escape their example. Like Titian's mythologies they are among the sixteenth century's most potent legacies to later Western visualization of classical themes.

Still more powerfully impressive were the religious drawings. Not all Michelangelo's graphic treatments of the *Resurrection* were known, but one (British Museum, London, Department of Prints and Drawings w. 52 / c. 258), copied and adapted by both Clovio and Venusti, molded the type for a generation. Michelangelo's *Crucifixion* for Vittoria Colonna (British Museum, London, Department of Prints and Drawings w. 67 / c. 411)—copied in innumerable paintings and engraved both with and without the Virgin and Saint John that Michelangelo later added to the design—exerted a fundamental influence on treatments of the subject from El Greco to Guido Reni. The *Pietà with Angels* (Isabella Stewart Gardner Museum, Boston c. 426) was replicated ad infinitum in all media, and the austerity and willed limitation of these late compositions had considerable impact upon Roman later-sixteenth-century painting. It continued into the late work of Annibale Carracci and the artists affected by that, notably Domenichino and, to a limited extent, Nicolas Poussin. Thus subsidiary parts of Michelangelo's oeúvre retained a germinating power even during a period when his major works were falling from favor.

The Reaction

Reaction against Michelangelo's art came first in his native town. After the death of his great advocate, Vasari, in 1574, Michelangelo's influence waned and little direct stimulus from any phase of his work is found in that of the younger painters, even when they continued to study Michelangelo's figures in drawings, as exercises. Santi di Tito, for example, after an initial Michelangelism in Roman work executed around 1560, seems consciously to have turned against his example, looking to Andrea del Sarto and Raphael for compositional inspiration and to early Bronzino for surfaces. Ludovico Cigoli and Domenico Cresti, called Il Passignano, derived inspiration from the Urbinate painter Federico Barocci, whose work they encountered in Rome, and looked back also to one of his sources of inspiration, Correggio. By 1600, virtually no Michelangelesque painting was being produced in Florence.

In Bologna reaction came a little later. Michelangelo had had a considerable influence there, but Bolognese response was of a dry and rather over-emphatic kind. The delicate substantiality of Michelangelo's modeling was alien to artists like Passarotti and Orazio Samacchini, and they complicated the relative simplicity of his compositions. Around 1580, with the advent of the Carracci, a change occurred. Their leanings were anti-Roman and pro-Venetian and Parmese painting, and they were devoted to life study. In the mid-1590s Annibale Carracci moved to Rome. There, ignoring the painting of late Michelangelesque artists like Jacopo Zucchi, he was able to study Michelangelo's work directly. His attitude modified and "first-phase" forms derived from the Sistine began to appear in his art, initially with an ironic inflection; toward the end of his short life he came to appreciate the more severe aspect of Michelangelo's work. Caravaggio too, although an exponent of naturalism, responded deeply to a range of Michelangelo's forms and in his *Crucifixion of Saint Peter* (Cesi chapel, Santa Maria del Popolo, Rome) produced perhaps the most powerful of all responses to Michelangelo's fresco, whose emotion he felt more intensely than any other painter. But only a single great artist after this date revealed a fundamental inspiration from Michelangelo: this is Rubens, the only seventeenth-century painter who equaled Michelangelo in power and ambition, and who was still more omnivorous. Rubens approached the first two phases of Michelangelo's art with unstoppable energy and was the only artist of his period to make truly creative use of the *Last Judgment.*

Occasional echoes of Michelangelo are found until the middle of the seventeenth century—notably in the work of Guido Reni and Domenichino. Subsequently, while critical admiration was not entirely submerged by hostility, imitation virtually disappeared, and few traces of Michelangelo's stylistic influence can be found until the resurgence of interest in his work, among northern European rather than Italian artists, in the last third of the eighteenth century. It was then that artists who had spent time in Rome—James Barry, Henry Fuseli, and Jakob Carstens in particular—came to undertake renewed study of Michelangelo and his most potent followers. A measure of this change of attitude can be found in Sir Joshua Reynolds. In twenty years of lecturing at the Royal Academy of Arts prize givings, Reynolds, while praising Michelangelo's work, had laid emphasis on the dangers it presented to students and had stressed to his listeners the virtues of restraint and moderation in art. In 1790, his powers fading, knowing death was near, Reynolds devoted his fifteenth and final discourse to one of the most eloquent and deeply felt of all appreciations of Michelangelo's art, based, primarily, on the grandest figures of the Sistine. Michelangelo's style, "may, poetically speaking, be called the language of the gods" and was to be compared with the work of Homer. And, more programmatically than any predecessor, Reynolds recommended Michelangelo as a model: the student should copy his work unceasingly, should cast figures copied from Michelangelo in new roles, should undertake entire compositions made up of figures borrowed from the master, and should invent any additional figures or details in Michelangelo's style. Such a program might seem sterile, condemned to produce pastiches. But, since Reynolds cited as an example the employment of Michelangelo's figures by Titian, he was clearly not proposing slavish imitation, but imitation as inspiration, a means of elevating an artist's consciousness to the grandeur of Michelangelo's conceptions, which could then imbue styles of painting apparently alien to his. Reynolds closed his discourse with an expression of "admiration for that truly divine man . . . I should desire that the last words which I pronounce in this Academy, and from this place, might be the name of—MICHAEL ANGELO." Ironically, Reynolds' apothegm did not mark the beginning of a new phase of Michelangelism in European art: indeed, it came near its end, and Michelangelo was not to be a widespread influence in the nineteenth and twentieth centuries except, sadly, among some of the dreariest exponents of totalitarian art. But when the greatest painters and sculptors of the human figure have wished to strike the major chords, it is to Michelangelo that they have consciously or unconsciously turned: the most ambitious works of Théodore Gericault, Eugène Delacroix, Jean-François Millet, Auguste Rodin, Pablo Picasso, and even Henri Matisse could not have been achieved without his example.

Ideal Heads

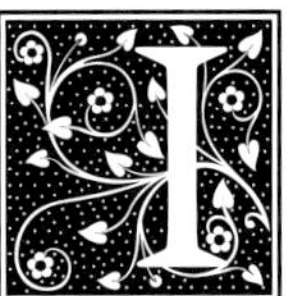

deal heads correspond to what Vasari called *teste divine* (divine heads). Vasari undoubtedly intended a play on the word divine, between the characters represented in Michelangelo's drawings of heads—who are often godlike, although not specifically identifiable with pagan divinities—and the unearthly perfection of their execution, as drawn by the divine Michelangelo. More prosaically, the ideal head can be described as the portrait image, usually elaborately worked, of an imaginary or legendary person, employed by the artist as a vehicle for the representation of moral or spiritual qualities, or physiognomic types. In different forms the ideal head was, for some two decades, an important and highly influential means of expression for Michelangelo. Although he did not invent the genre, he exploited it more fully and with greater imagination than any of his forerunners, and it was predominantly his example that affected later artists. Michelangelo's ideal heads fall into polar groups: the beautiful and the grotesque. Michelangelo is generally associated with the former, which indeed forms the bulk of his output in this genre. Although he did not exploit the grotesque with the same assiduity as Leonardo, and rarely for its own sake, in a number of drawings he made highly inventive use of distorted or tormented facial types.

Many of Michelangelo's heads are seen in profile, the most usual formula for portraits, whose history stretches back to the coinage of antiquity. It was the form in which the portrait medal was revived in the late trecento and then rendered definitive by Pisanello. The profile remained the preferred type of portrait through much of the quattrocento in Italy and not just for its ease of representation. Portraiture was a privileged arena for the development of the overtly beautiful, which took place largely within secular art. Pisanello again, as the most brilliant, and latest, exponent of the International Gothic style, introduced extraordinarily elaborate and refined coiffures into some of his paintings, and it is likely that he contributed to the cult of the court beauty. In Florence too, the profile allowed artists with predominantly linear styles, such as Alesso Baldovinetti, the brothers Pollaiuolo, and, in particular, Botticelli and Piero di Cosimo, to develop portraits into idealized patterns, combining the imaginary with the real and imbuing their subjects with unexpected associations. Some of their work prefigures the "fancy portrait," the personage *en rôle*. For example Botticelli's various versions of the portrait of *Smeralda Bandini* fuse portraiture and ideal type, and Piero di Cosimo's *Simonetta Vespucci* (Musée Condé, Chantilly) can be seen either as casting a modern woman as an historic personage, Cleopatra, or visualizing the Egyptian queen as a modern courtesan.

Fifteenth-century artists also began to show an interest in the contrast of beauty and ugliness, giving them a moral dimension. The investigation and deployment of physiognomical ugliness was practiced most in northern European painting and manuscript illumination, often in a religious context: the suffering Christ, for example, contrasted with his tormentors. But in Italy it was the workshop of Verrocchio that was the crucible of later developments. Verrocchio and his great pupil, Leonardo da Vinci, were alert both to Italian and Flemish themes as well as enraptured by the surface qualities of Flemish painting, of which first-rate examples were available in Italy. Both Verrocchio and Leonardo were enraptured by physiognomical types as well as the revelation of the movements of the mind through facial expression, a preoccupation that reached its apogee in the *Last Supper*. It was also in Verrocchio's workshop that drawing reached extraordinary heights of subtlety and sophistication in the 1470s, when elaborate and beautiful studies of male and female heads were made by Verrocchio and Leonardo. Unlike their Florentine contemporaries, they apparently visualized drawings as independent works of art. A fashion for drawn portraits in North Italy, especially in the circle of Mantegna, may also have inspired them: Verrocchio had visited the Veneto as early as 1468.

It was in the work of Verrocchio and Leonardo—and in that of the sculptor studied by both, Desiderio da Settignano—that a complementary form was exploited: the warrior profile. A number of reliefs of different forms and types were produced by the Verrocchio workshop, although none are certainly autograph. The extension of this into what may be the earliest surviving presentation drawing is exemplified by a large silver-point *Head of a Warrior* in the British Museum (fig. 36), which is one of the young Leonardo's most astonishing achievements. Too elaborate to be a model for another work of art, too much a demonstration of virtuosity not to be a subject of wonder in its own right, it must have been made for sale or presentation. Here too, it may be that Mantegnesque ideas were significant, since a parallel, though less sophisticated, form is found in North Italy in the work of Marco Zoppo, who made numerous drawings and engravings of elaborately helmeted heads of warriors and coiffed females. It is difficult to know how these should be understood. Are they intended to represent historical or mythological figures, like at least some of Verrocchio's reliefs, or are they simply a pattern-book series—more obsessed with the forms of parade helmets than the inner life of his subjects—as their quantity would suggest? However, some emerge as personalities, and since Zoppo tried not to repeat himself, their physical types are varied: perhaps these images show forms planned with decorative intent gradually assuming a life of their own. It is notable, however, that there seems to be little attempt to make ideal heads of religious figures: the early development of the ideal and the grotesque head in Italy seems to have been largely secular.

Late quattrocento drawings and engravings of this type were probably made as collectors' items. But this fashion seems to have lost momentum around 1500, except among Leonardo's Milanese followers, who, in any case, were more preoccupied with painted than drawn images. Michelangelo made much use of idealized and expressive heads, and of elaborate headdresses, in the prophets and sibyls, and the ancestors of Christ on the Sistine vault. But in Florence, the generation that came to maturity around 1500 had largely ignored the ideal head as a separate artistic category until Michelangelo revitalized it circa 1520. Perhaps news of Leonardo's death in 1519 prompted Michelangelo to try himself once more against the work of his old rival, who had made a series of beautiful pen studies for the head of his Leda when he was in Florence circa 1505 as well as dense and precise physiognomic studies in chalk for the *Battle of Anghiari* (fig. 46).

Michelangelo seems to have been the first artist to make a series of large and very elaborately worked drawings of imaginary heads, and although fascinated by elaborate hairstyles and, in his few bellicose male figures, also with helmets, it was the mood and spirit of his subjects that most concerned him. Although frozen and formalized, his heads possess a new intensity of expression. They have inner lives, usually disturbed ones. Female heads predominate and they generally wear hairstyles of fantastic complication that Freudian analysis would treat as fetishistic. Forms that seem peripheral to the main areas of Michelangelesque

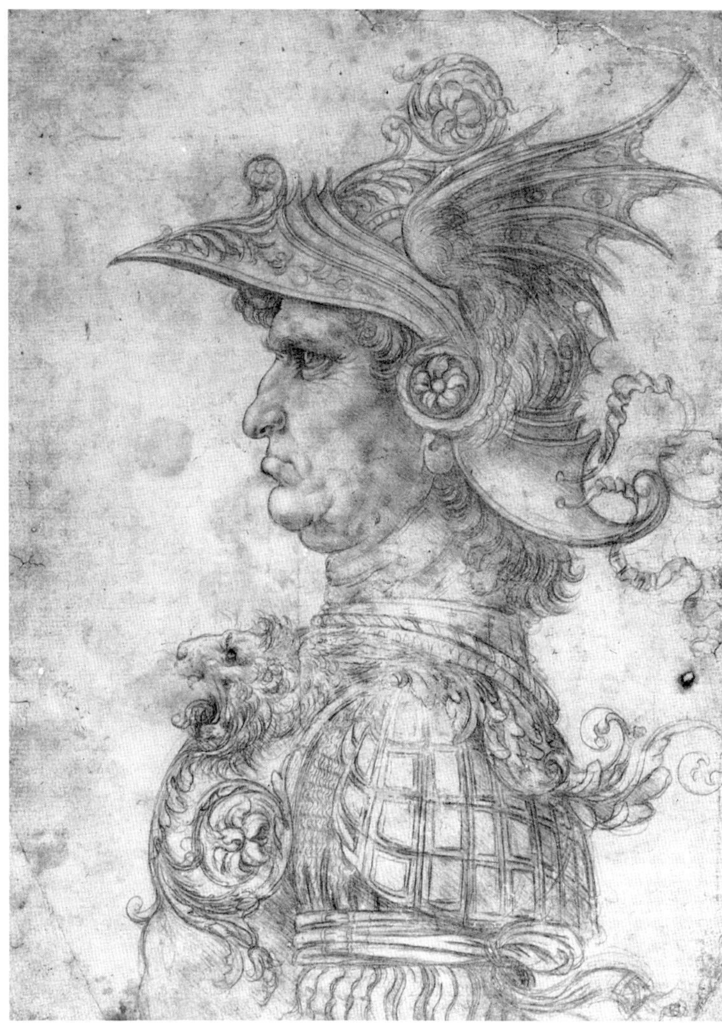

fig. 36. Leonardo da Vinci, *Head of a Warrior*, metalpoint on prepared paper, 28.5 x 20.7 cm. British Museum, London, Department of Prints and Drawings

expression and to have begun life merely as decoration became of obsessive interest to the artist, and as Michelangelo worked, revelatory of the psyche both of his characters—who are usually impassive in proportion to the elaboration of their helmets and coiffures—and their creator. But Michelangelo's heads undoubtedly possessed a further dimension.

The identification, historical implications, literary context, and allegorical dimension of Michelangelo's ideal heads, as well as of those by artists who imitated him, remain largely mysterious, but it is reasonable to suppose that the heads were born from the same poetic instincts that created the imagery of the presentation drawings. Thus the *Count of Canossa* (fig. 44) is not simply the image of a warrior but the evocation of an historical personage whom Michelangelo regarded as an ancestor. *Cleopatra* (Casa Buonarroti, Florence 2F / C. 327), drawn for Tommaso de' Cavalieri and transferred as a forced gift to Cosimo I in 1561, is clearly identifiable, and was named by Cavalieri in a letter to the duke of that year. A third (cat. 4) may well represent the ancient queen *Zenobia* and it seems likely that other heads were intended for specific figures, but, in the absence of hard evidence, their identities remain speculative. Similarly, many of the idealized female heads produced in the School of Fontainebleau would not be recognizable as the more lurid Roman empresses were it not for the fact that they sport name tags.

The significance of Michelangelo's ideal heads, both the beauties and the grotesques, was widely felt, if uncommented. Several of them were engraved, although not to the same extent as the secular and religious presentation drawings. But they engendered numerous graphic copies, sometimes drawings of great accomplishment whose differences from Michelangelo's originals are minimal and whose status has been the subject of dispute. Copies were themselves copied and it is often difficult to decide whether a copy was made after an original or after an intermediate copy: only by minute comparison would it be possible to draw up a family tree of derivations. Copying aside, Michelangelo's examples were rapidly exploited by Rosso (see cat. 8) and by Bacchiacca, who made much use of them in paintings of the 1520s. Both types were eagerly taken up by artists of the following generation, such as Salviati and, to a lesser extent, Vasari and Bronzino. Passarotti was strongly affected by them and made numerous highly finished pen drawings, undoubtedly for sale. His *Head of Minerva* in the Royal Collection (RL 6038 / Popham and Wilde 662) is probably one such. The fashion was given a renewed European dimension with the virtuoso drawings and prints of Goltzius. It was also pursued, in pen drawings of astonishing preciosity, by the Veronese painter Jacopo Ligozzi (fig. 35), who, spending most of his career in Florence, attempted to renew contact more directly with the most crisply executed examples of the Michelangelesque tradition.

Around 1600, however, fashion for heads of this type falters and although etchings after the *Canossa* and the so-called *Vittoria Colonna* were made as late as 1613 by Antonio Tempesta, such interest is rare. Later echoes are, of course, to be found, but these are faint and it is not until the late eighteenth century that there was a revival of interest in heads of both types.

Michelangelo Buonarroti

1a
Head of the Virgin (RECTO)

1b
Head of a Young Woman (VERSO)

c. 1540
black chalk
21.2 x 14.2 (8 3/8 x 5 9/16), upper corners cut; no watermark
inscribed in pen by William Gibson on the verso: *MAngolo.1.4.*
RL 12764

EXHIBITIONS

London 1930, no. 513; Edinburgh 1947, no. 142; London 1950–1951, no. 261; London 1953, no. 59; London 1962, no. 65; London 1972–1973, no. 40; London 1975, no. 130; London 1986, no. 23

LITERATURE

Berenson 1903 and 1938, no. 1608; Thode 1913, no. 533; Popham and Wilde 1949, no. 434; Goldscheider 1951, no. 84; Dussler 1959, no. 715; De Tolnay 1960, no. 154; Goldscheider 1966, no. 90; Hartt 1971, no. 364 (recto); De Tolnay 1975–1980, 2: no. 325; Annesley and Hirst 1981, 608–614; Perrig 1991, 77–78, 139–140

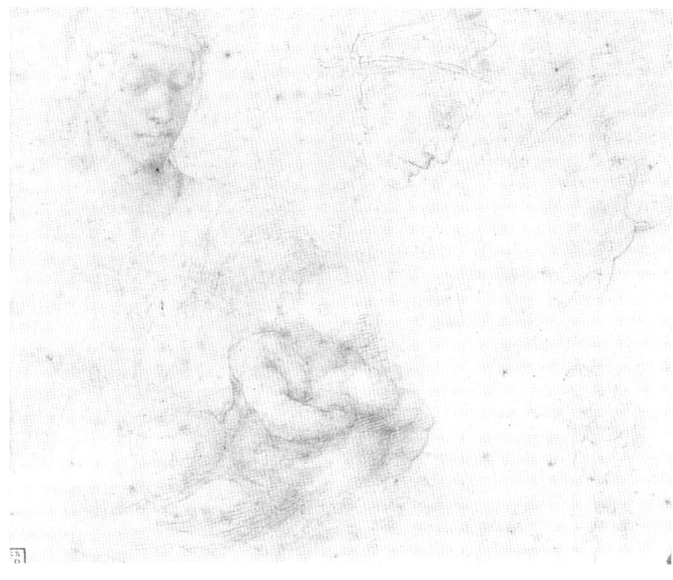

fig. 37. Unidentified Artist after Michelangelo, *The Virgin and Child*, black chalk, 21 x 25.5 cm. Private collection

Highly wrought, the recto head serves as a compelling image of refinement and grace, in which the abstract purity of jawline and extended almond eyes is modulated by the texture of the lips and the slight irregularity of the nose. The detachment and self-sufficiency of the image, in which a geometrical concept is coaxed delicately into human and spiritual life, make it entirely satisfying as an independent work of art. But it was not drawn as such: it was, in fact, created as a developed study for the face of the Virgin in a half-length composition of the Virgin and child, a composition known, as Thode first noted, from a drawing on a sheet formerly in Lord Clark's collection (fig. 37). This sheet, according to the persuasive analysis of Annesley and Hirst, is not autograph, as Wilde finally came to think, but contains copies of drawings from more than one sheet by Michelangelo. The original of the lost Virgin and child study was perhaps intended for another artist, who would execute it as a painting.

Although Michelangelo occasionally drew half-length Madonna and child groups, as in a pair of pen sketches in the British Museum (W. 31 recto / C. 240) and a deservedly famous and beautiful cartoon in Casa Buonarroti (71F / C. 239), they are rare in his work. Michelangelo's preferred format for this subject was the full-length. However a feature that the ex-Clark design shares with Michelangelo's full-length Virgin and child groups is that they too look back to forms developed in Florence during the first decade of the sixteenth century. It is an aspect of Michelangelo's art that remained more or less arrested, in part, perhaps, because treatment of the subject in the first decade seemed to have exhausted further possibilities: it is notable that the half-length Virgin and child is rarely an area of formal innovation in later cinquecento painting.

Michelangelo was always attentive to facial type in his portrayals of the Virgin. He aimed at a regular, youthful, but severe beauty. In the present drawing accidents of nature have been expunged and the rigor and concentration of the technique imbue the Virgin's face with an otherworldly perfection combined with a precision of realization similar to that of Michelangelo's only certain surviving portrait drawing, the *Andrea Quaratesi* in the British Museum (W. 59 / C. 329). Like that, the present drawing displays a solidity of surface equal to the portrait painting of Bronzino. It demonstrates an extraordinary dexterity of touch: had the chalk been applied with fractionally greater pressure in any part, overall tonal unity would have been lost, or could have been recovered only by difficult erasures. Such drawings display a subtlety of modeling previously attained only by Leonardo.

The authenticity of the verso drawing has often been doubted. Even Wilde was at first tempted to give it to Tommaso de' Cavalieri, although he later restored it to Michelangelo. It is highly improbable that Cavalieri would have drawn on a sheet given to him by Michelangelo, and there is no evidence that Michelangelo continued to give him drawings as late as the date of this sheet, circa 1540. It is most reasonable to see it as an autograph sketch for the recto. The type is surprisingly reminiscent of Verrocchio (fig. 38), some of whose elaborate head studies were certainly known to Vasari and probably also to Michelangelo. Indeed, the unusually close link in form is significant, for it again points to the Verrocchio-Leonardo current as one of Michelangelo's principal sources of inspiration for such heads.

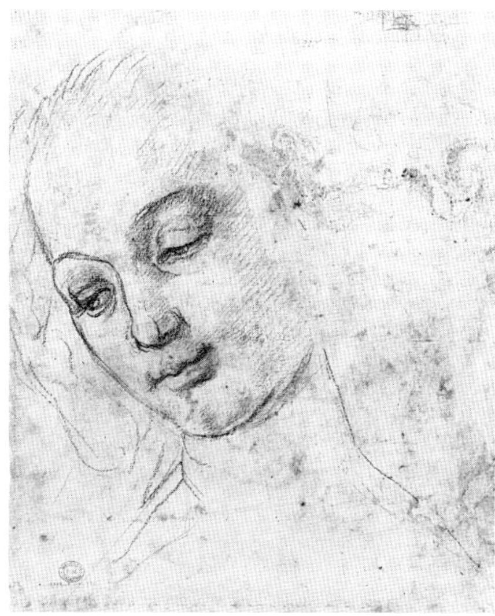

fig. 38. Verrocchio, *Head of a Woman*, black chalk, 32.5 x 27.3 cm. British Museum, London, Department of Prints and Drawings

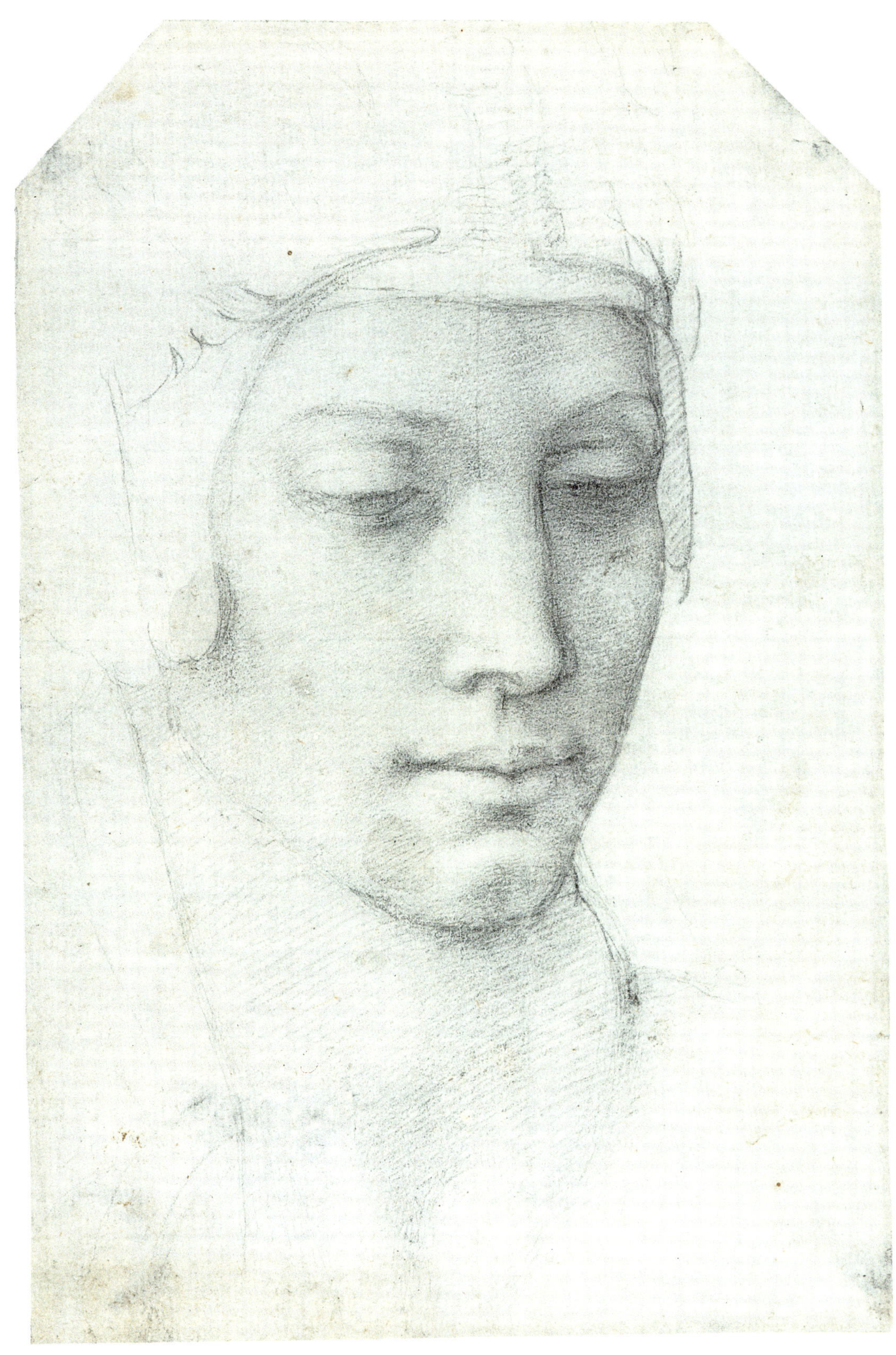

1a

1b

Unidentified (Florentine?) Artist after Michelangelo Buonarroti

2
Imaginary Female Head

c. 1540
black chalk
33.2 x 23.5 (13 1/16 x 9 1/4); no watermark
inscribed in pen by William Gibson on a label affixed to the recto: *Michol. Angollo Buonaroti. 2.4.*
RL 0432

EXHIBITIONS
None

LITERATURE
Frey 1909–1911, see no. 289; Thode 1913, see no. 344; Popham and Wilde 1949, no. 455; Wilde 1953a, see no. 42; Wallace 1995, 127

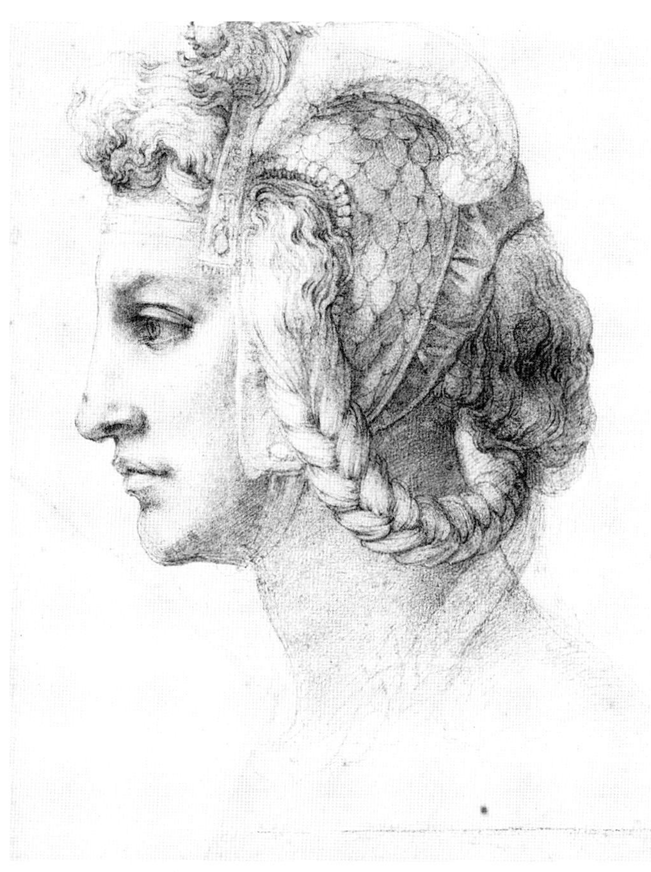

fig. 39. Michelangelo, *Head of a Woman*, black chalk, 28.7 x 23.5 cm. British Museum, London, Department of Prints and Drawings

Although Wilde believed this drawing to be a "relatively late copy" of an ideal head drawn by Michelangelo probably in the early 1520s, and now in the British Museum (fig. 39, W. 42 recto / C. 316 recto), the compiler is inclined to think it of around 1540. A later copy would probably have accentuated the plasticity of the original, rather than reducing it, as here. Sharp and a little dry in handling, it was certainly made directly from the original, whose slightest lines, like those under the chin, it attempts to preserve. William Gibson priced it at £2, double the price of cat. 1, and undoubtedly believed it autograph.

Michelangelo's drawing would have been made as a gift. The young Florentine nobleman, Gherardo Perini, who was given three other sheets of ideal heads by Michelangelo in the early 1520s, would be an obvious candidate as the recipient, but the British Museum drawing cannot be traced to his possession. However, despite its provenance from the Casa Buonarroti, whence it was acquired by Jean-Baptiste-Joseph Wicar, it seems unlikely that such a drawing would have remained in Michelangelo's Florentine workshop to be inherited by his nephew Leonardo. It was probably acquired later, perhaps by Leonardo's son, Michelangelo Buonarroti the Younger, who made strenuous efforts to build up the family's collection of his ancestor's drawings in the early seventeenth century.

The rather brittle modeling of the original and its sharp profile are characteristic of Michelangelo's ideal heads of the 1520s and can be seen in drawings such as another of those owned by Perini, the *Three Heads* now in the Uffizi (599E / C. 308). These drawings tend to be crisp and severe in characterization, less densely worked and more lightly burdened with mood and meaning than later heads. The profile copied in the present drawing, or one of similar type, was among the models for Rosso's drawing of an ideal head in the Fogg Art Museum, Harvard University, Cambridge, Massachusetts (Inv. 1979-67). The influence of drawings of this type may also be seen in the crystalline and clear-cut forms of Andrea del Sarto.

The subject's identity is uncertain. Her cherub headdress, more fully preserved in this copy than in the trimmed original, might suggest a saint or the Virgin. The head was etched in 1613 by Antonio Tempesta as a portrait of Michelangelo's close friend, Vittoria Colonna, marchioness of Pescara. But Michelangelo met Vittoria only in the 1530s and her features bore no resemblance to those of the present drawing. The fact that the image was etched as a pair with another of Michelangelo's ideal heads, that of the *Count of Canossa*, which Tempesta identified correctly, may suggest that Michelangelo himself envisaged the pairing and that the head is indeed of an aristocrat: perhaps the legendary count's equally legendary countess.

Although the present drawing is of high quality and clearly by a very competent artist, no attributions have been suggested. It may be by the same hand as the British Museum copy of the *Count of Canossa* (fig. 44, W. 87).

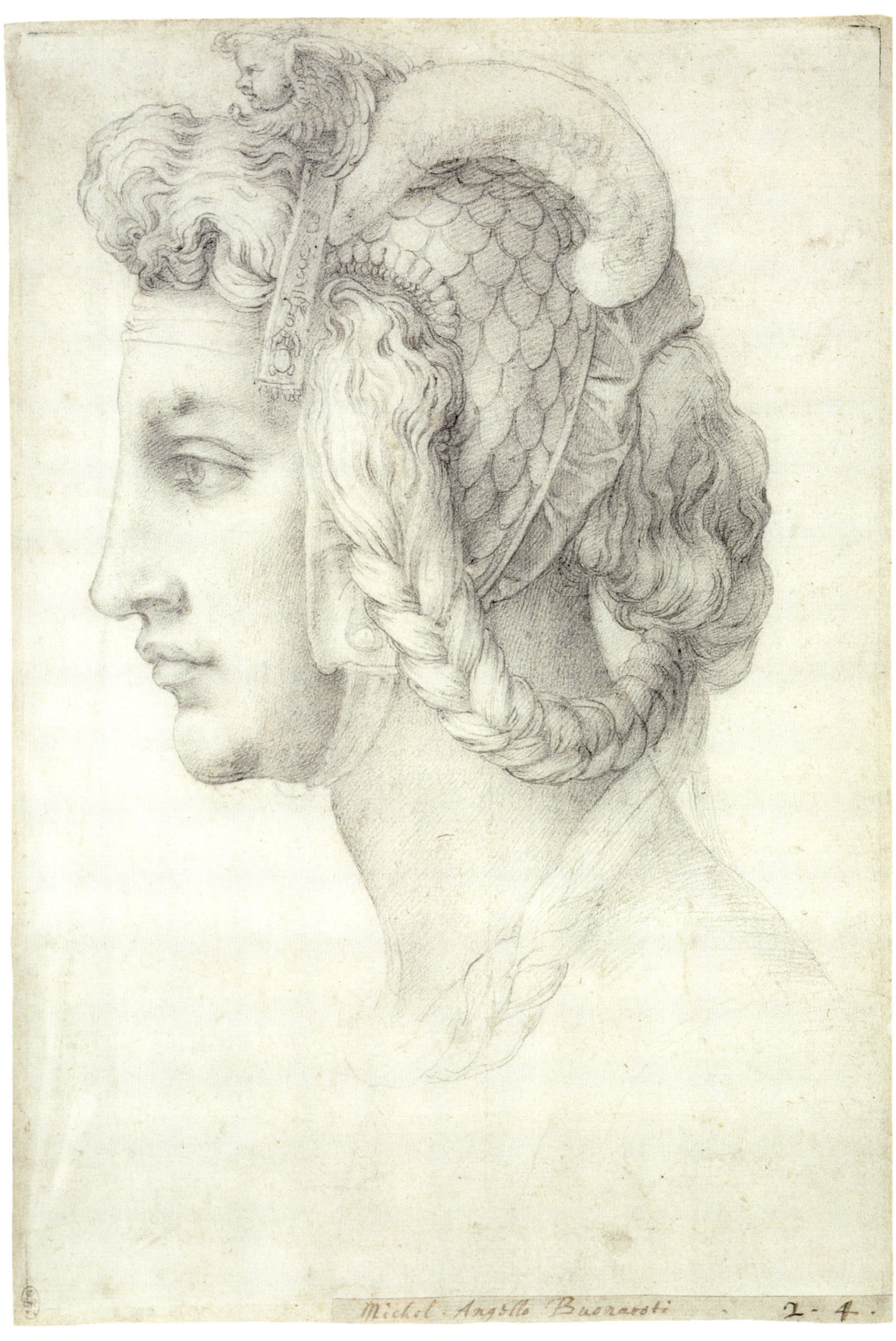
Michel · Angello Buonaroti · 2 · 4 ·

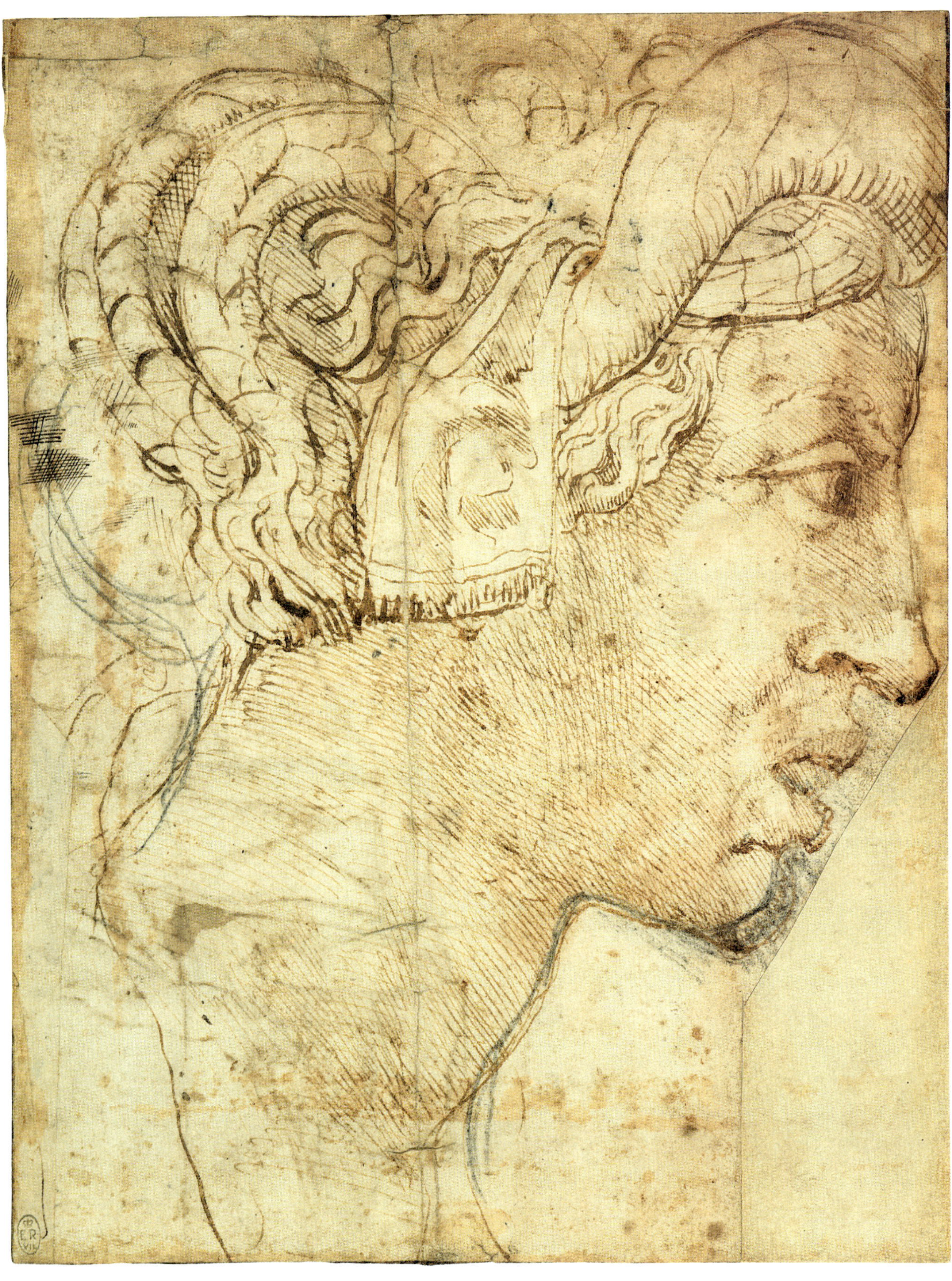

Raffaello da Montelupo

3
Imaginary Female Head

c. 1533
pen and ink, in part corrected with black chalk
26.8 x 20.6 (10 9/16 x 8 1/8), the lower right corner cut and made up; no watermark
inscribed in pen on the verso, upper left: *micael angnillo* and two illegible words; lower center more elaborately: *Micael angnilo bonarota.*
RL 0417

EXHIBITIONS
None

LITERATURE
Popham and Wilde 1949, no. 786

Raffaello's father, Baccio da Montelupo, had completed Michelangelo's now-lost bronze *David* in 1509, and this link may have encouraged Michelangelo to employ Raffaello in the last phase of work on the New Sacristy, between 1532 and 1534. In September 1534 Michelangelo moved finally to Rome and abandoned his Florentine projects. For the tomb of the Magnifici, which remained unfinished, Raffaello executed the *Saint Damian* who sits at the *Madonna's* right. His work was sufficiently satisfactory for Michelangelo to ask Raffaello to assist him again in the last stages of work on the tomb of Julius II. In this project, however, he acquitted himself poorly, and by 1550 Michelangelo could counsel against employing him in the Del Monte chapel in San Pietro in Montorio, a project that went to Ammanati.

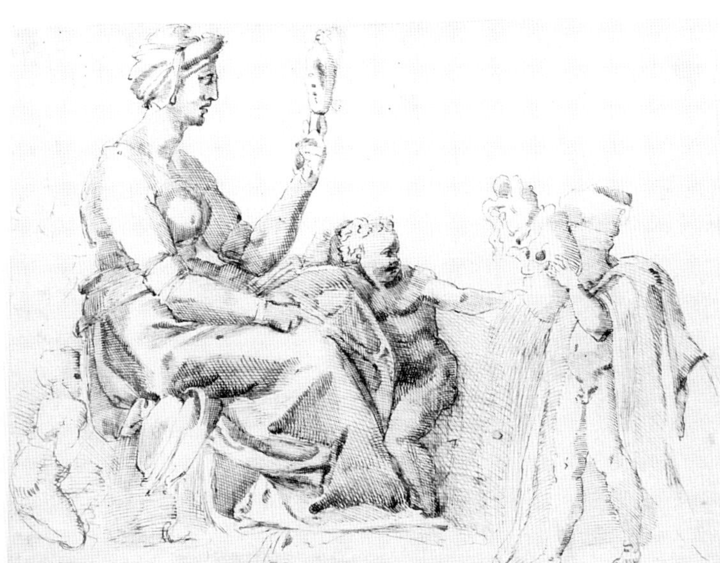

fig. 40. Raffaello da Montelupo after Michelangelo, *Allegory of Prudence*, pen and ink, 26.1 x 35.9 cm. British Museum, London, Department of Prints and Drawings

During his time with Michelangelo, mostly in 1533, Raffaello had access to some of the master's drawings and made copies of them: the versions of Michelangelo's lost composition of *Prudence* in Chantilly (Inv. [36] 30) and the British Museum (fig. 40, w. 89 recto) are probably both by Raffaello (see also cat. 10). The present drawing, on the recto of the sheet, may reflect a lost drawing by Michelangelo rather than be a pastiche entirely due to Raffaello. The particular elaboration of the coiffure and the sausagelike forms into which the hair is bound correspond closely with Michelangelo's experiments with ideal heads in the 1520s, and the slightly open mouth is also found in drawings by him. There is a similarity with a lost ideal head by Michelangelo recorded in a copy formerly in the Mond Collection (Borenius and Wittkower 153). Raffaello's drawings have not been the subject of sustained study, but in his brief autobiography he says that he always drew left-handed, although able to work ambidextrously, and those drawings generally accepted as his display left-handed hatching. They are all in pen, and Raffaello's drawing in other media remains to be identified. Black chalk employed to correct pen, as here, is rare in High Renaissance drawing. It sometimes occurs in Michelangelo's work, and Raffaello may have adopted the practice from him.

While no ideal heads in pen by Michelangelo are known, there is every reason to suppose that he made them, and it may be that a pen drawing by Michelangelo was Raffaello's inspiration in the present head. In the Louvre is Michelangelo's amusingly grotesque *Head of a Satyr* (Inv. 684 recto / c. 95 recto), drawn in vigorous pen over a weak chalk copy by his pupil, Antonio Mini, of the same lost *Ideal Head* of a woman copied in the ex-Mond drawing. The pen work of the *Satyr* reaches a very high level of finish, and while in all probability begun as a witty critique of his pupil's drawing, it may, as Michelangelo worked on it, have developed a life of its own and metamorphosed into what is virtually a presentation drawing.

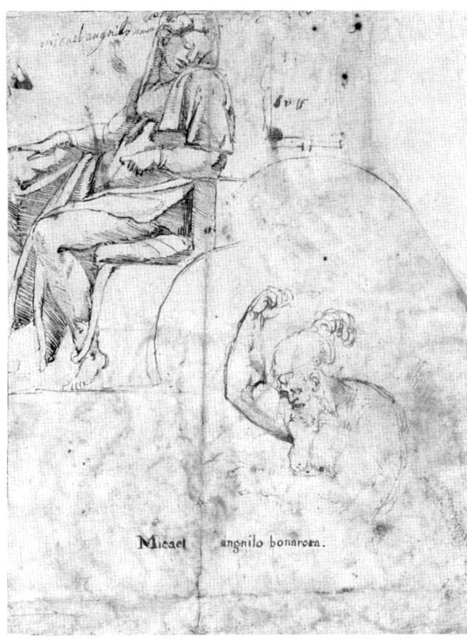

fig. 41. Raffaello da Montelupo, *Copy of Michelangelo's Abias and an Unrelated Figure Study*, pen and ink, 26.8 x 20.6 cm. (verso of cat. 3)

On the verso of the present sheet are two small sketches (fig. 41). The upper, which has been indented, is a copy of *Abias*, one of the ancestors of Christ frescoed by Michelangelo on the Sistine ceiling; the figure would presumably have been seen by Raffaello when he worked in Rome in the 1520s, but he may have been reminded of it by material in Michelangelo's studio. Otherwise it would have to be presumed that he copied the figure when in Rome, carried the sheet with him to Florence, and then re-used it—or vice versa, if the recto is dated first. The lower sketch is of a bearded man wearing a plumed helmet. It seems unlikely that he represents a figure at a forge of Vulcan; rather, he may be a soldier in some historical or religious composition. Similar types are found on a sheet in the British Museum (1946-6-13-373). No connection can be established with any composition by Michelangelo.

Attributed to Alessandro Allori after Michelangelo Buonarroti

4
Zenobia

c. 1560
black chalk
30.5 x 23.7 (12 x 9 5/16); watermark: crown and star, close to Briquet 4833
RL 0419

EXHIBITIONS
None

LITERATURE
Thode 1908, 344; Popham and Wilde 1949, no. 454; Giononi-Visani and Gamulin 1980, 103; Wallace 1995, 127

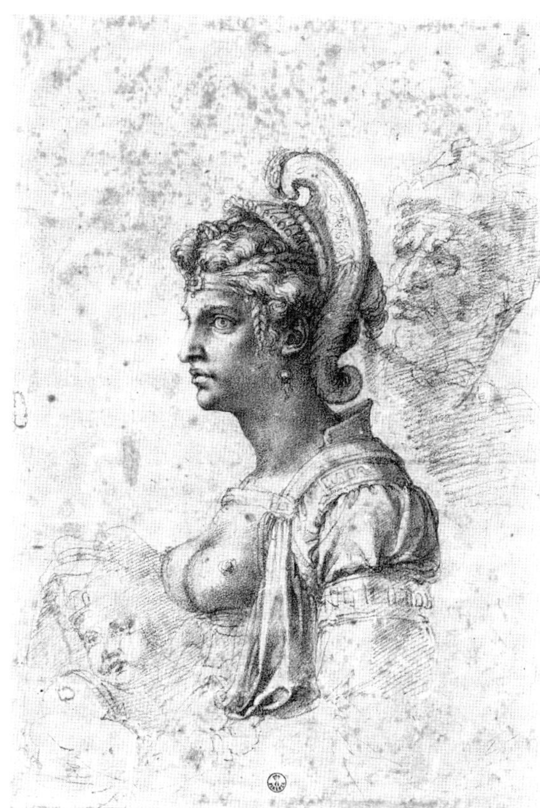

fig. 42. Michelangelo, *Zenobia*, black chalk, 35.7 x 25.1 cm. Gabinetto Disegni e Stampe degli Uffizi, Florence

This drawing is a copy of Michelangelo's famous ideal head in the Uffizi (fig. 42, 592E recto / C. 307 recto) traditionally known as *Zenobia*. The original was one of the three sheets presented by Michelangelo to his young friend Gherardo Perini in the early 1520s (see also cat. 8). It is unclear how and when the subject acquired its name, but it may be correct. Zenobia was a third-century heroine, a fearless and successful warrior queen of Palmyra, who, finally defeated by the Emperor Aurelian, was allowed to live out her life in exile in Rome. Zenobia, celebrated in Boccaccio's *De Claris Muliebris*, was not commonly represented in Renaissance art, but Boccaccio describes her in terms that would have appealed to Michelangelo: physically powerful, of masculine energy, chaste, and refusing intercourse with her husband except for procreation. Conjugal chastity was a theme that, as Sir Ernst Gombrich (1986) has proposed, Michelangelo implied in his late *Epifania* cartoon (British Museum, London W. 75 / C. 389), and it may also be represented here. Zenobia was Syrian, and the features of this woman could well suggest an Eastern origin. If this identification is correct, she would presumably be ignoring her husband to concentrate on her child.

Other identifications suggested for the composition have been *Venus, Cupid, and Vulcan* or *Combat of Mars and Venus*. The former is improbable, since the helmet worn by the man is inappropriate for Vulcan and the child bears none of the attributes of Cupid. That Michelangelo drew a *Combat of Mars and Venus* is likely, since a treatment of the subject ascribed to him, copied by Giulio Clovio, was recorded in Clovio's inventory. However, while aversion and disdain might be suggested by the present drawing, it is difficult to see it as a combat. Such a description better fits a puzzling drawing in the Louvre (Inv. 2767), clearly by Clovio, which treats a battle between groups of gods, but they are divided according to reason and passion, with Mars and Venus fighting on the same side. This multifigured drawing might be that recorded in Clovio's inventory, but that is not entirely trustworthy (see cat. 16). Whether it copies a composition by Michelangelo is questionable, for the figural inventions seem unlike his.

Whatever the identity of the actors in this drama, the theme seems to be of desire and rejection. A comparable scene is represented in another presentation drawing of a male and female head (Uffizi, Florence 603E / C. 2:97), probably made a little before the *Zenobia*. This is often dismissed but the compiler believes it to be autograph. Here too the arrangement implies a narrative rather than an allegory, and a similar tenseness of mood is seen. In the *Zenobia*, the woman's hair has become helmet-like, and matches, even overpowers in plastic force, the bellicose portrayal of the man.

The composition is unusual in a Florentine context and suggests Michelangelo's awareness of the half-length narratives pioneered by Venetian painters, most notably by Titian and Giorgione, some of whose work Michelangelo might well have seen by the time this drawing was made. Since this Venetian mode was largely inspired by experiments by Leonardo and Mantegna, it would have been readily acceptable by Michelangelo.

The present copy was formerly attributed to Clovio. If this were correct, it would presumably have been executed during his period in Florence in 1551–1553, a date consistent with the most similar watermark found in Briquet, datable to 1549. However, the compiler finds it difficult to see in it Clovio's tricks of hand and would prefer to give it to Alessandro Allori, a view endorsed by Martin Clayton. Direct comparison with Allori's *Studies of a Left Foot* at Windsor (RL 0216 / Popham and Wilde 1096 as anonymous, but given to Allori by Pouncey [oral attribution recorded in Popham and Wilde 1949, 401] and Lecchini Giovannoni [1991, 309–310]) strongly supports this attribution; the treatment of the shaded areas is identical.

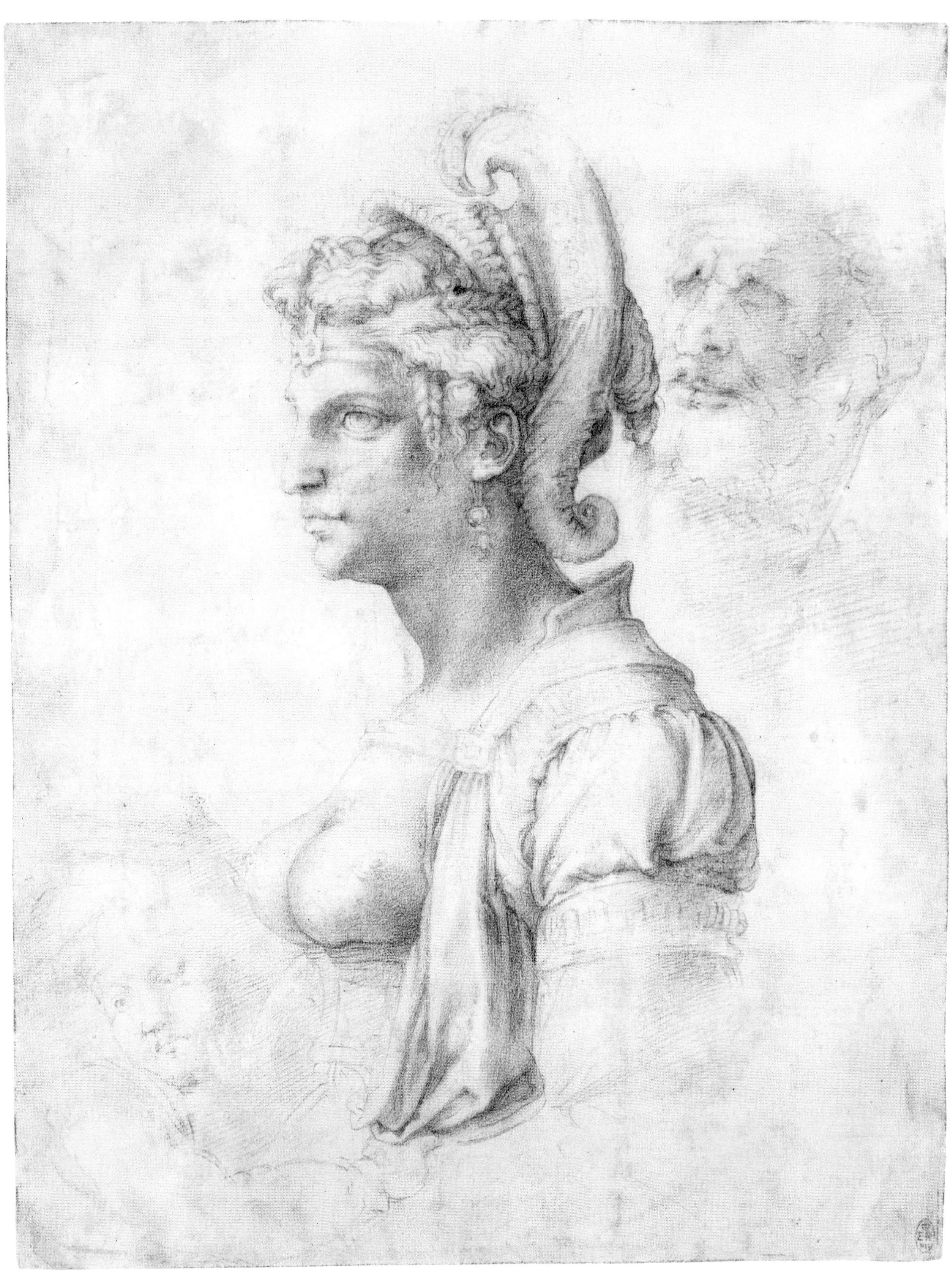

Giulio Clovio

5
Head of Minerva

c. 1540
gray chalk, extensively damaged and made up along the right margin and Minerva's chin
28 x 19.7 (11 x 7 3/4); laid down
RL 0453

EXHIBITIONS
None

LITERATURE
Popham and Wilde 1949, no. 243; Giononi-Visani and Gamulin 1980, 102

This drawing was classed as from the school of Michelangelo before Popham attributed it to Giulio Clovio. As Popham noted, the head recurs in very similar form, although much smaller, in a marginal illumination in *The Commentaries upon Saint Paul* commissioned from Clovio by Cardinal Marino Grimani and now in Sir John Soane's Museum (fig. 43). The manuscript is datable to the mid-1530s. Although little hard evidence supports the contention, it seems likely that Clovio, a gifted executant but without great inventive powers in figure drawing, repeated his own compositions as readily as his copies after Michelangelo. Thus several miniatures by Clovio also exist in drawn versions that seem to have been made as independent works, and this is probably the case here.

Minerva, the goddess of wisdom, born from the head of Jupiter, is the ideal subject for an ideal head. But, although of considerable beauty and executed at Clovio's highest level of refinement, it is notable that, despite its formal debt to Michelangelo's profiles, it lacks their allusiveness and psychological complexity. It is probable that, in producing such an image, Clovio was also inspired by antique cameos and it was a simulated cameo that he painted in the margin of the *Commentaries*. Antique cameos present the image rather than the inner being, which in Michelangelo's hands even the personification of reason would have acquired. However, the fallen putto on Minerva's helmet, which is not found in the miniature, is very Michelangelesque and may well depend from an invention by him. Medusa's head on Minerva's breast plate has a complex ancestry that includes Leonardo and Raphael as well as Michelangelo's own *Damned Soul* (see cat. 8).

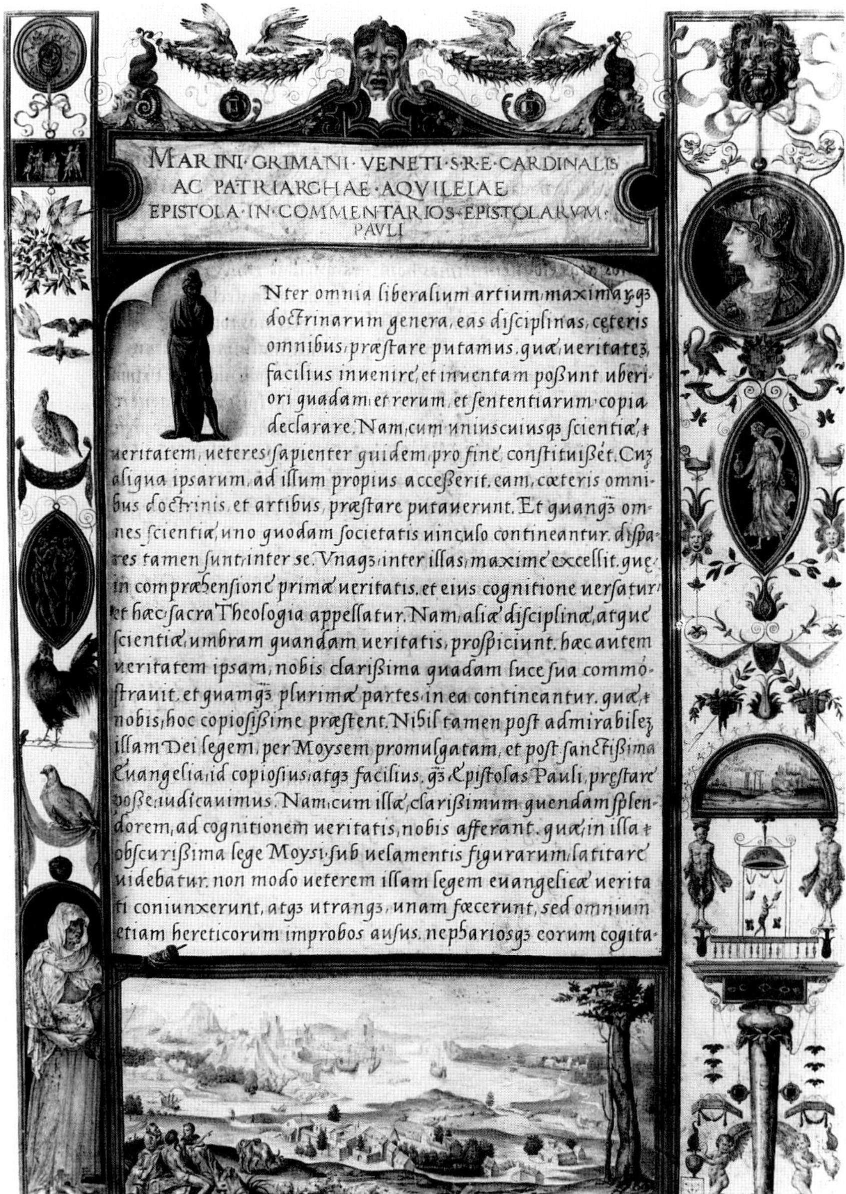

fig. 43. Giulio Clovio, *The Commentaries upon Saint Paul*, miniature, page 1, 42.9 x 30.5 cm. By courtesy of the Trustees of Sir John Soane's Museum, London

The overall appearance of Clovio's head is remarkably neoclassical. Minerva was a subject much loved by artists at the turn of the eighteenth and nineteenth centuries, and the drawing might at a casual glance be mistaken for a work by Anne-Louis Girodet de Trioson. It is thus not surprising that it was copied in an etching by the eldest daughter of George III, Charlotte Augusta Matilda, princess royal, in 1785.

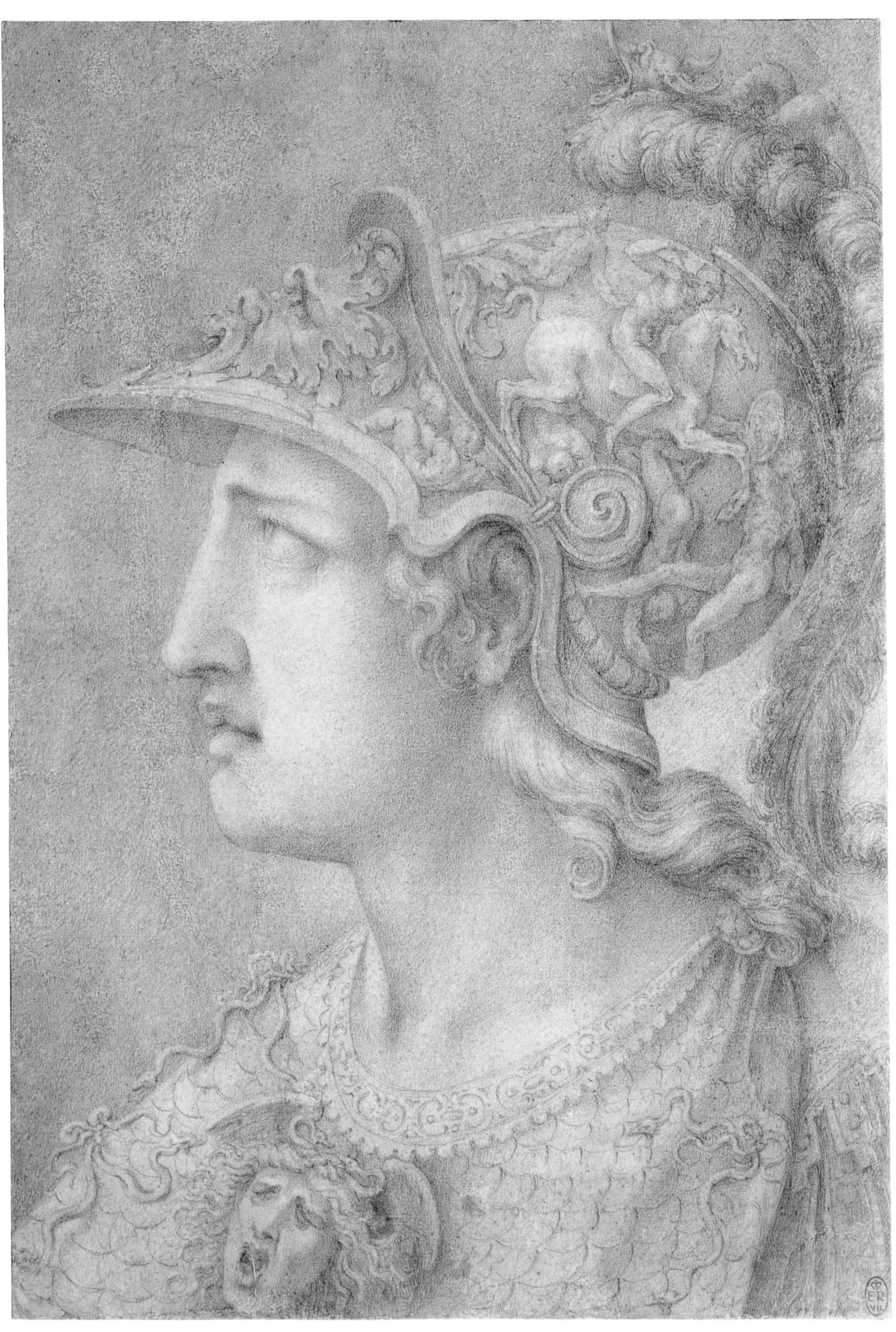

Francesco Salviati

6
Head of a Warrior

c. 1545
red chalk
26.3 x 20 (10 3/8 x 7 7/8); no watermark
inscribed in pen on the verso by William Gibson:
M. Angolo. 5.2.
RL 0463

EXHIBITIONS
None

LITERATURE
Popham and Wilde 1949, no. 68 (as attributed to Bacchiacca)

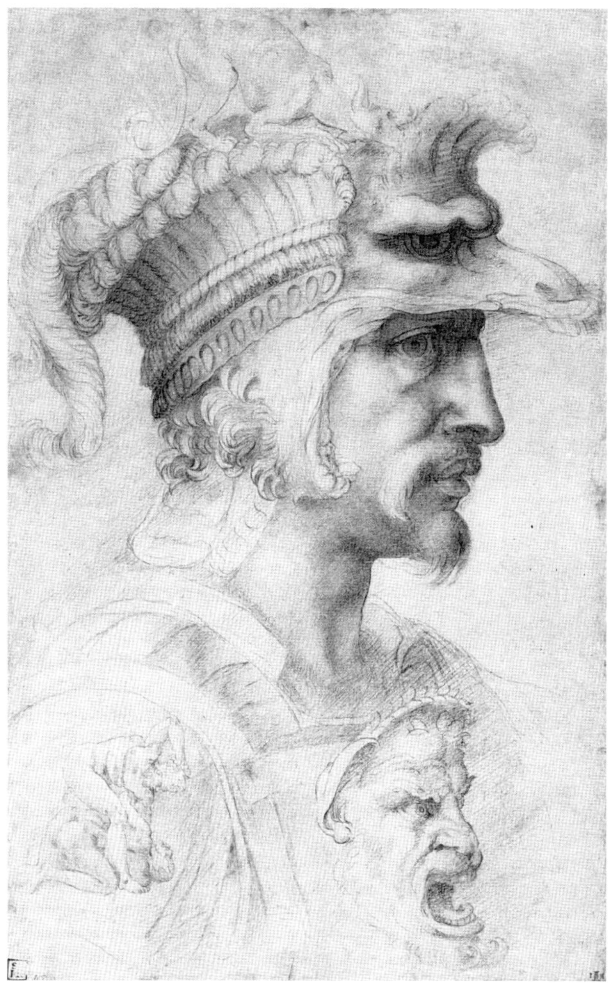

fig. 44. Unidentified Artist after Michelangelo, *Count of Canossa*, black chalk, 41 x 26.3 cm. British Museum, London, Department of Prints and Drawings

Heads of warriors in elaborate helmets were pioneered by Verrocchio and Leonardo in Florence, and Zoppo and others in North Italy also produced many examples. Michelangelo had experimented with such heads in pen drawings of circa 1505 (see Louvre Inv. 737 / c. 34). These are generally associated with the *Battle of Cascina* project but were probably made instead for a composition of the *Martyrdom of the Ten Thousand*, which he seems to have devised around the same time. The present drawing is more immediately reminiscent of Michelangelo's famous *Count of Canossa*, made in Florence circa 1520. The original is now lost, but a fine copy is in the British Museum (fig. 44, w. 87) and others also survive.

In 1520 Michelangelo was in correspondence with the then Count of Canossa, Alessandro, to whom he believed himself related and who responded to him as a kinsman. It may be that Michelangelo made the drawing for the count, as an evocation of their common ancestor. Michelangelo's Canossa was certainly known by 1538 to Battista Franco, who included a motif taken from it, the struggling figures on the epaulet, in his *Battle of Montemurlo* (Palazzo Pitti, Florence) probably painted that year.

Despite similarities of type and scale, the present draftsman made no effort to imitate Michelangelo's drawing style, and other currents are present in the handling, which is both confident and distinctive. The attribution to Francesco Ubertini, called Il Bacchiacca (1494–1557), proposed by Pouncey, who dated it in the 1540s, cannot be sustained by comparison with drawings certainly by him. While this minor and eclectic artist exploited ideas and forms derived from Michelangelo, among many others, nothing in his work of any period approaches either the characterizational acuity of this drawing or its power of relief. By 1540 Bacchiacca was nearing the end of his career and nothing in his known work of this period suggests he would have been capable of the self-renewal his authorship of this drawing would imply.

The long parallel hatching lines that surround the bust and lay in an indeterminate setting derive ultimately from Leonardo but more immediately from Andrea del Sarto and Pontormo; the employment of stumping in the head of the putto on the helmet, which produces a smooth, slightly slick surface, and the sharp herringbone hatching on the neck are technical traits found in the work of both artists. But they seem to occur combined only in the drawings of an artist heavily influenced by both: Francesco Salviati. The particular type, thin and somewhat angular, with a long neck and stringy features, against which wire-like hair is strongly emphasized, is very much in Salviati's mode in the period of his work in the Sala d'Udienza in the Palazzo Vecchio in Florence. The present drawing was probably made at around the same date, in the early to mid-1540s.

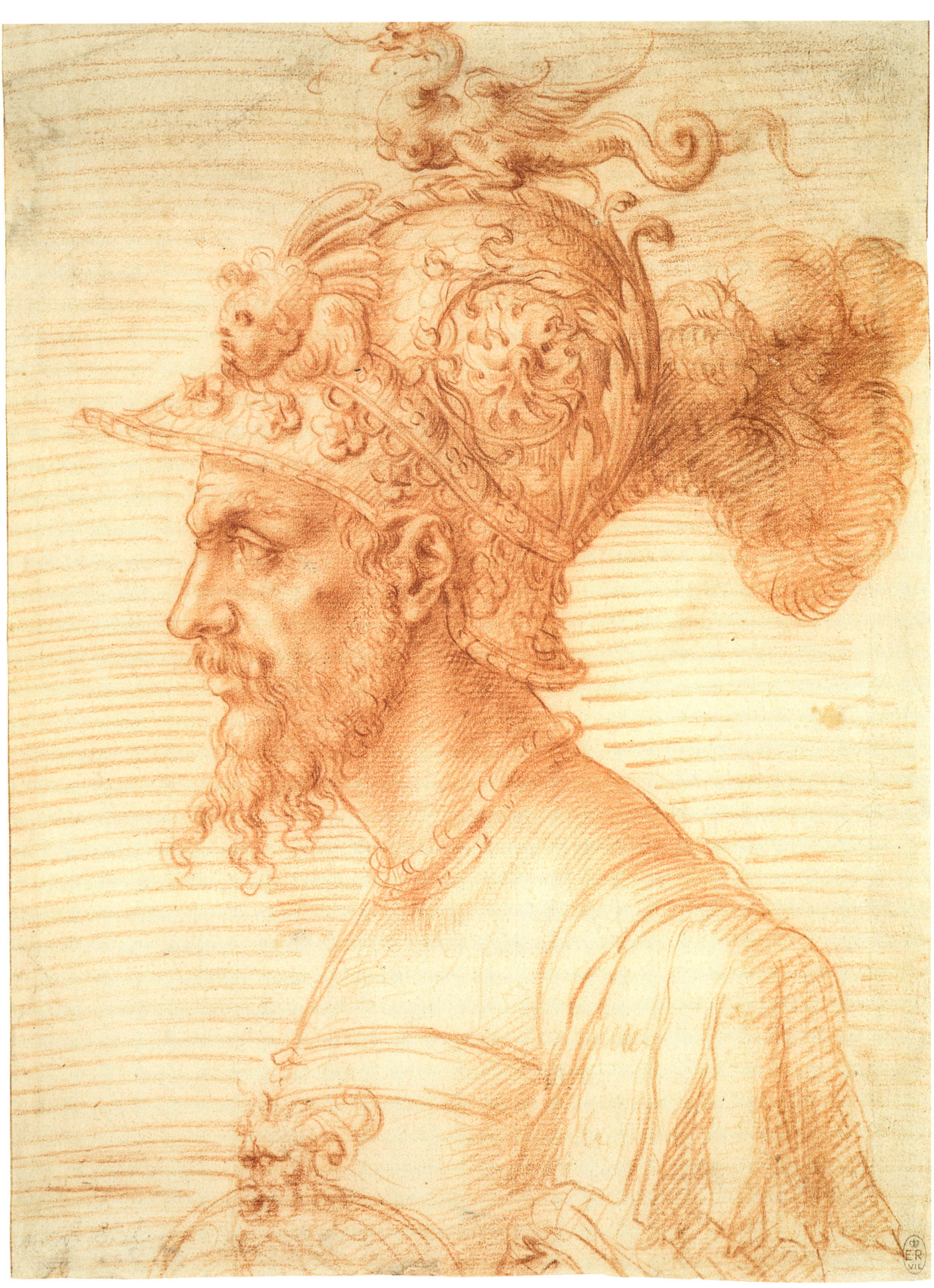

Michelangelo Buonarroti

7
Grotesque Mask

c. 1525
black chalk over and with red chalk
24.8 x 11.9 (9 3/4 x 4 11/16); no watermark
RL 12762

EXHIBITIONS
London 1953, no. 111; London 1972–1973, no. 43; London 1975, no. 64; Sydney-Brisbane-Melbourne 1988, no. 16

LITERATURE
Berenson 1903 and 1938, no. 1610; Frey 1909–1911, no. 212A, 213B; Thode 1913, no. 535; De Tolnay 1948, no. 93; Popham and Wilde 1949, no. 425; Goldscheider 1951, no. 63; Dussler 1959, no. 237; Berti 1965, 448; Goldscheider 1966, no. 70; Hartt 1971, no. 497; De Tolnay 1975–1980, 2: no. 236bis; Hirst 1988, 74

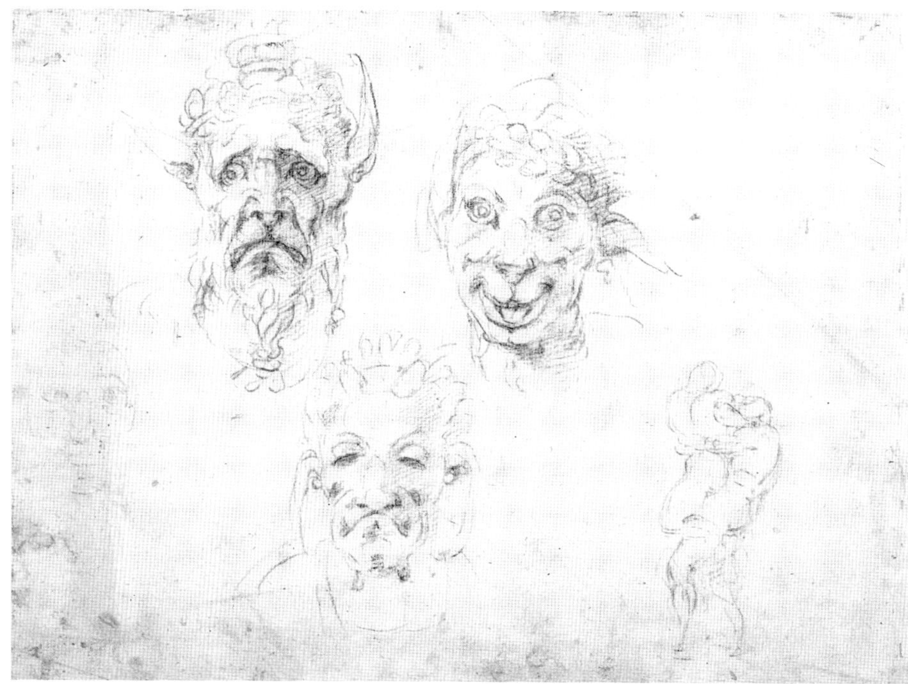

fig. 45. Michelangelo, *Grotesque Heads*, black and red chalk, 25.5 x 35 cm. British Museum, London, Department of Prints and Drawings

This drawing on the recto of the sheet contains, in addition to the main face, another looser, less developed face at lower right. This is now fragmentary but the curving lines surrounding its lower part, which are also found in the more finished study, suggest that Michelangelo drew them as alternatives. The drawings show Michelangelo's interest in distorted, even tormented facial expressions and also, indirectly, in the other form of the grotesque, the fanciful images in antique painting that, found in the grottoes of imperial Rome, greatly excited sixteenth-century artists. Heads of similar type had been included by Michelangelo among the vegetal and animal forms in the decorative carving of the architecture of the tomb of Julius II and, in the form of lion masks, on the exterior of the Chapel of Leo X in the Castel Sant'Angelo. A much later work that shows a persistence of such interests is the keystone of Porta Pia, for which, Wilde suggested, Michelangelo may have remembered this drawing and used it as a model. But, for Michelangelo, decorative form was never merely decorative, and his approach sometimes demonstrates an explicit vitalism: in a drawing now in Casa Buonarroti (10A recto / C. 201 recto), Michelangelo added eyes to an architectural profile to transform it into a human one.

Although the present drawing has been linked with the row of formalized masks on the ducal tombs, these would not have required such animated preparation. Wilde's suggestions of the mask on the cuirass of *Giuliano* underway in the mid-1520s or, just conceivably, the diadem of *Leah* (fig. 18), probably begun in the early 1530s, seem more plausible. But it may be, given the elliptical shapes below both heads, that Michelangelo was planning an actual piece of metalwork, the upper section of the cuirass of a suit of parade armor. However, whether or not Michelangelo had a specific sculptural or architectural purpose in mind, drawings of this type allowed his imagination rather free rein and gave him the opportunity to exercise his visual wit. In this respect, as in many others, the influence of Leonardo remains a constant in his work. It is to be seen, on occasion, at fuller strength, in the direct juxtaposition of the beautiful and ugly within the same frame, as in Michelangelo's idealized *Profile Bust of a Young Man* in Princeton (1947–134), which contains the ugly profile of an older man concealed in its shoulder. Such interests informed the treatment of the *Damned Soul* (see cat. 8), roughly contemporary with the present sheet, the more lighthearted treatment—one of them is grinning!—of grotesque faces in the British Museum (fig. 45, W. 33 recto / C. 222), and the facial types of the devils in the *Last Judgment.*

Here Michelangelo has focused particularly on the hollowed-out pupils of the eyes and the furrowed brow. The use of these elements of emphasis returns to Michelangelo's interest in Verrocchio, who had employed them in his head of *Bartolommeo Colleoni*, seen by Michelangelo during his Venetian sojourn of 1494 and adapted by him in the *Saint Proculus* of 1495 and the *David* of 1501–1504. But the present drawing incorporates a pictorial emphasis in that Michelangelo seems to have used red chalk for color as well as form, reserving it for the flesh areas that are given a fiery hue.

The fragmentary drawing is harder to analyze, but this type of head, of which Michelangelo must have drawn many examples, seems to have affected drawings from Michelangelo's school, such as the treatments of grotesque faces in the Louvre (Inv. 719) and the Musée des Beaux-Arts, Lille (Inv. 95). In both, the forms of the visage seem to extend into quasi-geometrical forms.

The sheet has been severely cut, truncating the verso copy of Michelangelo's drawing of *Samson and Delilah*, now in the Ashmolean Museum (P. 319 / C. 297). Wilde plausibly attributed this copy to Antonio Mini and, if correct, it would probably have been drawn late in Mini's stay with Michelangelo, toward 1530. Michelangelo devised his great *Samson and the Philistines* group in 1529, and the Ashmolean composition may be a by-product of his thoughts about the hero as well as a warning to his pupil about uncircumspect passion, to which Mini was vulnerable.

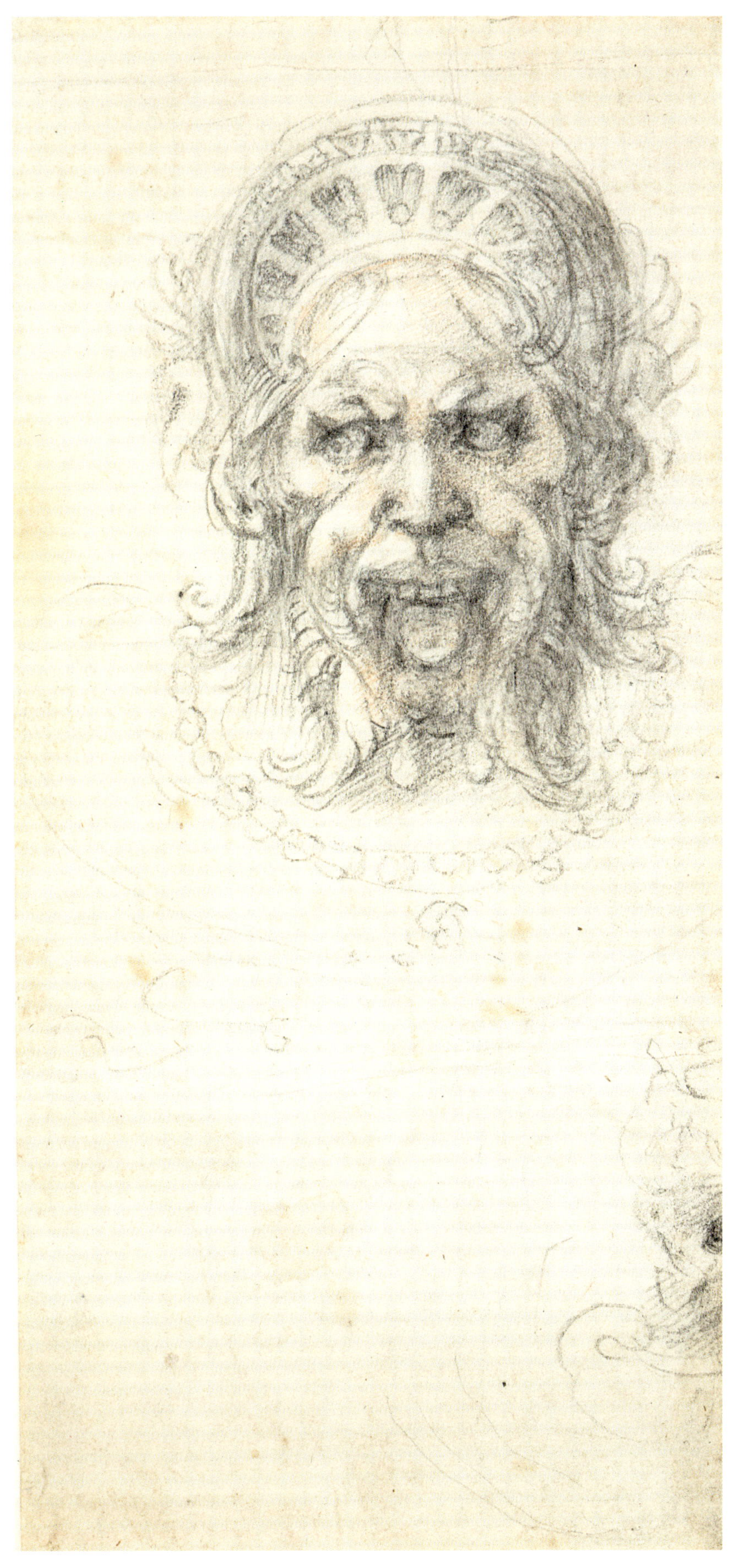

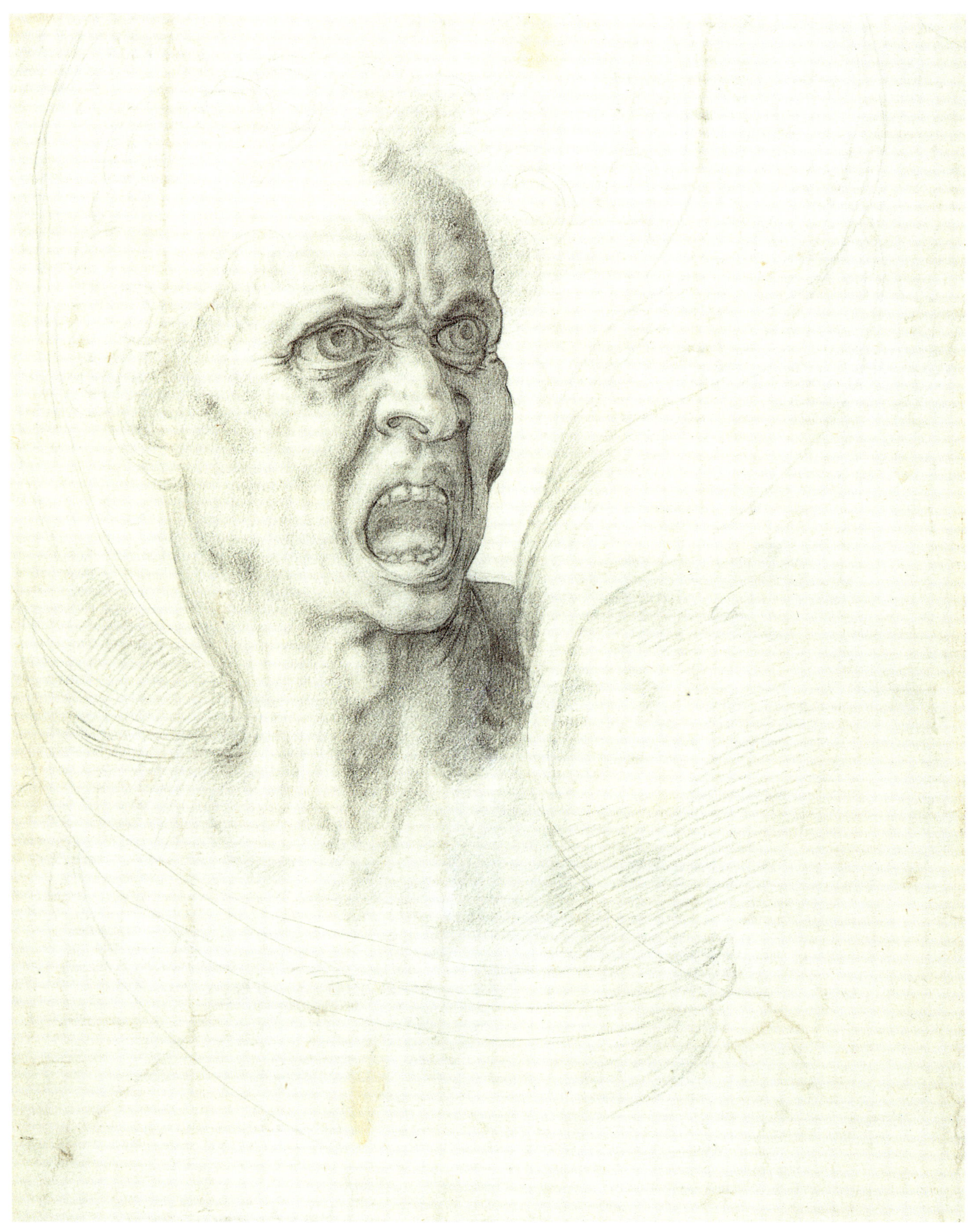

Unidentified Artist after Michelangelo Buonarroti

8
Damned Soul

c. 1560
black chalk
26.2 x 21.3 (10 5/16 x 8 3/8); watermark: arrows with star, not in Briquet
RL 01365

EXHIBITIONS
None

LITERATURE
Berenson 1903 and 1938, no. 1619; Thode 1913, no. 544; Popham and Wilde 1949, no. 453

This is a copy of a drawing, the famous *Damned Soul*, given by Michelangelo to Gherardo Perini in the early 1520s. It was probably not made directly from the original, whose handling it does not imitate, but from an intermediate copy.

The original entered the grand ducal collection in 1565 at Perini's death, together with the two other drawings given to him by Michelangelo; all three are now in the Uffizi. The *Damned Soul* (601E / C. 306) is inscribed, probably, as Wilde suggested, by Perini himself, with Perini's own name and MICHELAN / BONAROTI / FACIEB / AT. It was engraved at an uncertain date, but probably very early—although not necessarily directly from the original—by Antonio Salamanca. By the mid-1520s it was known to Rosso Fiorentino, who adapted it in his own *Fury* engraved by Jacopo Caraglio, as Gilbert (1992) has demonstrated. Rosso was surely friendly with Perini for he also knew the *Three Female Heads* (Uffizi 499E / C. 308), as did Bacchiacca, who quoted heads from the sheet in his *Moses Striking the Rock* (National Gallery of Scotland, Edinburgh), of around 1525. It is unclear how available Michelangelo's drawings were to artists once they had entered the collection of the Medici, but Perini himself seems to have been generous in allowing access to them.

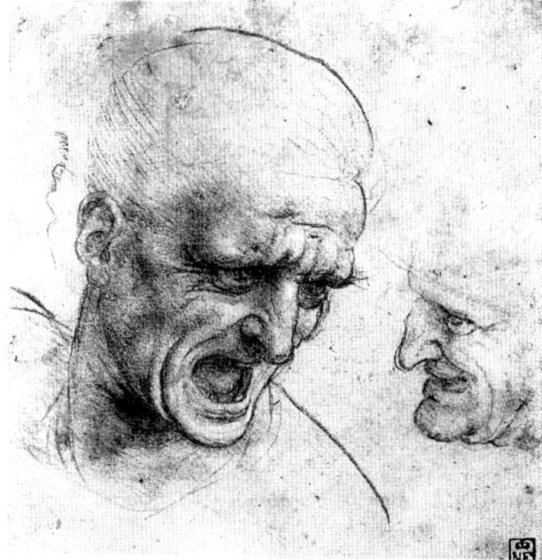

fig. 46. Leonardo, *Head of a Warrior for the Battle of Anghiari*, red and black chalk, 19.2 x 18.8 cm. Szépmüvészeti Múzeum, Budapest

The *Damned Soul* may owe something to Dante, with its emphasis not merely on the external pains of damnation, but on the soul's inner torment, a development from simple exteriorized representation to psychological analysis. As Wilde noted, Michelangelo reused the head in the *Last Judgment*, which may imply that it was intended to represent a specific character. The *Damned Soul* was quoted by Cellini in his relief of *Perseus Rescuing Andromeda* on the base of his *Perseus*; Vasari refers to a gem engraved after it by Giovanni Bernardi da Castel Bolognese; and a painting, based on the drawing, currently on loan to Casa Buonarroti, has been attributed by Pilliod (private communication, 1993) to Pier Francesco Foschi (a further copy of the *Damned Soul*, in pen, in the Albertina, Birke and Kertesz 62, may be after the painting). It was also the ultimate model for the young Bernini's self-portrait as the *Damned Soul*. The invention, however, is far from original. More obviously than any other presentation drawing by Michelangelo, it is based on a famous example by Leonardo: his head of a Milanese cavalryman in the *Battle of Anghiari*. The *Damned Soul* corresponds less closely to Leonardo's final helmeted figure than to his highly finished preparatory drawing, now in Budapest (fig. 46), which Michelangelo may have known. Leonardo's head had earlier appealed to Raphael, who had used it for the Medusa embossed on the shield held by the simulated statue of Minerva in the *School of Athens*.

The present sheet was dated by Wilde after 1589. He inferred this from the fact that on the verso (fig. 47) is a copy of Michelangelo's fragmentary *River God* model as it was set up that year—incorrectly in relation to Michelangelo's original conception—in the Accademia in Florence. However, this argument is not firm, for the *River God* was much replicated in clay and bronze reductions that might have been set up in any number of ways and that were

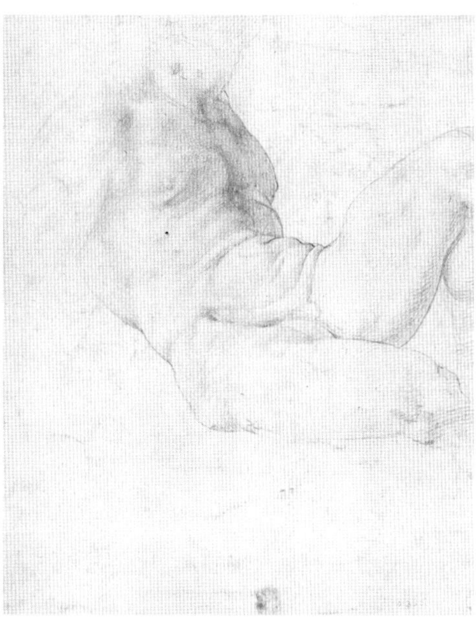

fig. 47. After Michelangelo, *Reclining River God*, black chalk, 26.2 x 21.3 cm. (verso of cat. 8)

themselves copied. Some of these replicas were made before the life-size model entered the Accademia and the verso drawing could have been made after one of them. The argument is also insecure since we do not know how Michelangelo's figure was displayed before 1589: it might well have been resting on its back, as in the verso drawing. On balance, the style of both recto and verso suggests a rather earlier date, around the middle of the century. Another, much livelier, copy in red chalk of the same fragment from the same angle, with conjectural additions, is in the British Museum (W. 104): its style is somewhat reminiscent of Salviati's.

The recto copy is refined in execution and, while it makes no attempt at facsimile reproduction, achieves a real vivacity. The outlining of the far side of the face is a little lumpy but the drawing's liveliness makes it possible to understand why Berenson believed it to be the original. The recto is indubitably more successful than the verso, but they might have been drawn a few years apart by the same draftsman rather than by different ones. Allori would be a possible attribution for the recto, but less likely for the verso. However, since the verso seems to show a trace of Bronzino's style, it may be by another of his pupils.

Presentation Drawings: Mythologies and Allegories

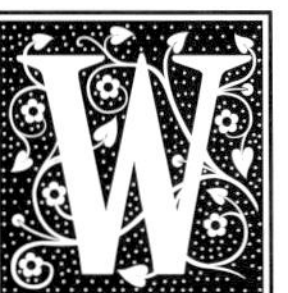hile not the originator of the genre of highly finished drawings of narratives or allegories made as self-sufficient works and intended as gifts for friends, Michelangelo exploited it more fully than any of his predecessors and contemporaries. His presentation drawings were demonstrations both of virtu and of affection, and vehicles for experimenting with personal or recondite subjects. There was and remains an inherent surprise in the master of works on a gigantic scale disciplining his genius to the confines of a sheet of paper, and in the painter who could cover square meters of fresco in a day producing drawings of watchmakerly precision. These factors have ensured for his drawings a fame that even their extraordinary quality might not have gained. Michelangelo made presentation drawings both of secular and religious subjects, but after the mid-1530s all of such drawings are of Christian themes.

Between drawings made as gifts for friends—never, apparently, for patrons—and drawings made as *modelli* for compositions that others might execute, the distinction is slight, and the two categories overlap. Thus Michelangelo's lost *modello* made for Sebastiano's fresco of the *Flagellation* in 1516 (see cat. 34) was highly finished and a striking small picture in its own right. Similarly, toward the end of his career, the *cartonetti* that Michelangelo made for Marcello Venusti's small paintings of the *Annunciation* and the *Agony in the Garden* were themselves displayed like paintings when they entered the collection of the Medici (now Uffizi, Florence 229F / C. 393, 230F / C. 409). Venusti also executed painted versions, generally the same size as the originals, of presentation drawings made by Michelangelo with no thought of reproduction (for example, fig. 27). The level of execution is the same for both categories, and such an overlap may suggest that the presentation drawing originated as an offshoot from the *modello*. Drawn models for engraving could often be very elaborate, as, for example, were those by Mantegna. But Mantegna's designs were made in line and wash, whereas pure pen or chalk were more suitable for translation into engraved line. Raphael's single surviving finished drawing for an engraving, his *Massacre of the Innocents* of circa 1510 (Museum of Fine Arts, Budapest Inv. 2195), is in pen, but later engraver's models made by his studio are mostly in red chalk.

The practice of making highly finished narrative or allegorical drawings as ends in themselves seems to have been invented by Leonardo. Vasari records an elaborate drawing made by Leonardo, for his friend Antonio Segni, of a scene from the *Aeneid*, the *Quos Ego*, which represents Neptune calming the waves. This is lost but a study for it is at Windsor (RL 12570), a collection that also houses one of Leonardo's elaborate allegorical drawings, showing a wolf in a boat and an eagle on a globe (RL 12496). It was for Segni, incidentally, that Botticelli painted his *Calumny*, now in the Uffizi, and it may be that Botticelli too made presentation drawings: an unfinished *Abundance* in the British Museum (Popham and Pouncey 24) could well have been intended as a gift. Significantly, both subjects are classical or classicizing and Michelangelo's rivalry with Leonardo and his interest in Botticelli's work may have prompted him to pursue the same path.

Michelangelo probably made some drawings as gifts for friends and colleagues from very early in his career. A very highly finished pen drawing of a *Standing Philosopher* in the British Museum (W. 1 recto / C. 6 recto) could serve as an independent image, although this example was evidently not given away since it bears a later sketch on its verso. But survivals, contemporary testimony both documentary and visual, and the account of Vasari suggest that Michelangelo began to make presentation drawings in red or black chalk extensively only in the 1520s, initially of heads. Highly elaborate treatments of classical or allegorical subjects seem to have begun later, in the early

1530s. These were probably developed principally for Tommaso de' Cavalieri, although a number of Michelangelo's presentation drawings cannot be traced to Cavalieri's possession and one, the *Archers* (cat. 16), is generally thought to antedate Michelangelo's meeting with the young Roman nobleman. The subjects of some of Michelangelo's presentation drawings are elaborate inventions that are difficult to interpret and for which no textual source has been found. As gifts, they undoubtedly comment, directly or obliquely, upon the relation between the artist and the recipient, although in a number of cases the recipient is unknown. Much has been made of homoerotic content in the drawings given to Tommaso, but this is not true of all of them and even the most pagan and sensual are somber in mood. Michelangelo's view of life was not cheerful, and the uninhibited expression of pleasure, erotic or otherwise, is rare in his art.

While much can be inferred from their correspondence, from Vasari, and from the content of Michelangelo's gifts, the nature of the friendship between Michelangelo and Tommaso de' Cavalieri is uncertain; so, surprisingly, is Tommaso's date of birth. There can be little doubt that Michelangelo's primary—although not necessarily exclusive—erotic orientation was toward his own sex. It was hinted by Aretino, in a letter to Michelangelo of November 1545, and is often taken for granted that his relation with Tommaso was actively homosexual. However, this seems unlikely, for, as Gerda Panofsky-Soergel (1984) has argued, Tommaso was probably no more than twelve or thirteen when Michelangelo met him, and, indeed, his earliest letters to Michelangelo have a childish quality both in their expression and their unformed handwriting. Michelangelo was then in his late fifties, he would never have children, and it is likely that his love of Tommaso was as much paternal as sexual, and the drawings made for him less visual love poems or confessions—although they are also that—than carefully cogitated moral allegories. Certainly nothing was covert about his gifts.

Among the drawings that Michelangelo gave to Cavalieri were the *Ganymede* (see cat. 15); the *Cleopatra* in Casa Buonarroti (2F / C. 327), which Cavalieri was compelled in 1561 to donate to Cosimo I; and three drawings now at Windsor: the *Phaeton* (cat. 9a), the *Tityus* (cat. 12a), and the *Bacchanal of Infants* (Popham and Wilde 431 / C. 338). All these are mentioned by Vasari, who notes that Michelangelo also drew a now lost portrait of Tommaso "in un cartone, grande di naturale" (life-size in a cartoon) (Vasari-Barocchi 1962, 1:118), which, according to a later writer, showed him "vestito all'antica, e in mano tiene un ritratto o medaglia" (dressed in the antique manner and holding in his hand a portrait or medal) (Vasari-Barocchi 1962, 4:1905), perhaps a portrait of Michelangelo himself. There may have been further gifts: several surviving allegorical and narrative compositions—such as the *Dream of Human Life* (Courtauld Institute, London, Prince's Gate Collection / C. 333), the *Archers* (cat. 16), the *Hercules* (cat. 18)—cannot be linked with any recipient, and it remains an open question whether these too might have been given to Tommaso. The fact that the two last are at Windsor would support such a provenance. It is also possible that some, although certainly not all, of Michelangelo's beautiful series of *Resurrection* drawings (compare cat. 39) of the early 1530s were given to Cavalieri.

Most of Michelangelo's presentation drawings were engraved and were reproduced in other media, such as rock crystal (fig. 49). Many drawn copies were also made, including a number by Giulio Clovio, some possibly in multiples; several copies of Michelangelo's *Ganymede*, in addition to cat. 15, have reasonably been attributed to Clovio. Alessandro Allori seems also to have made copies and Marcello Venusti probably did so too, although the attribution of drawings to him remains very uncertain.

Following Michelangelo's example, a few other artists—Salviati and Pirro Ligorio, for instance—made what seem to be presentation drawings in chalk of narrative or allegorical subjects, but these lack the density of meaning and intensity of emotion that characterize the drawings of the master. They did not attain public status, and the genre did not become widespread. Elaborate pen drawings are more commonly found, sometimes even executed on vellum, thus blurring the boundary with miniatures. Such pen drawings as these, however, circle back to printmaking, which may have provided one of the initial stimuli for the development of presentation drawings. Such highly developed pen drawings seem to have been more widely produced in northern Europe than in Italy, and often within the milieux of engravers. It is significant that some of the most elaborate and beautiful drawings of this type, the *federkunststücke,* were made by Goltzius, who began his career as an engraver and whose most refined pen work explicitly challenges the clarity of the engraver's line.

Michelangelo Buonarroti

9a
The Fall of Phaeton (RECTO)
1533
black chalk

Antonio Mini (?) and Michelangelo Buonarroti

9b
Bust of a Woman (VERSO)
c. 1531
red chalk

41.3 x 23.4 (16 1/4 x 9 3/16); no watermark
RL 12766

EXHIBITIONS
London 1950–1951, no. 269; London 1953, no. 91; London 1962, no. 70; London 1972–1973, no. 41; London 1975, no. 126; Washington-Paris 1988–1989, no. 42; Montreal 1992, no. 111

LITERATURE
Berenson 1903 and 1938, no. 1617; Frey 1909–1911, no. 58 (recto); Thode 1913, no. 542; De Tolnay 1948, no. 119 (recto); Popham and Wilde 1949, no. 430; Goldscheider 1951, no. 96; Dussler 1959, no. 238; De Tolnay 1960, 167 (verso); Berti 1965, 454–455, no. 156; Goldscheider 1966, no. 93; Hartt 1971, nos. 358 (recto), 369 (verso); De Tolnay 1975–1980, 2: no. 343; Hirst 1988, 111–115; Donati 1989, 84–86; Perrig 1991, 45–46 (recto), 123 (verso)

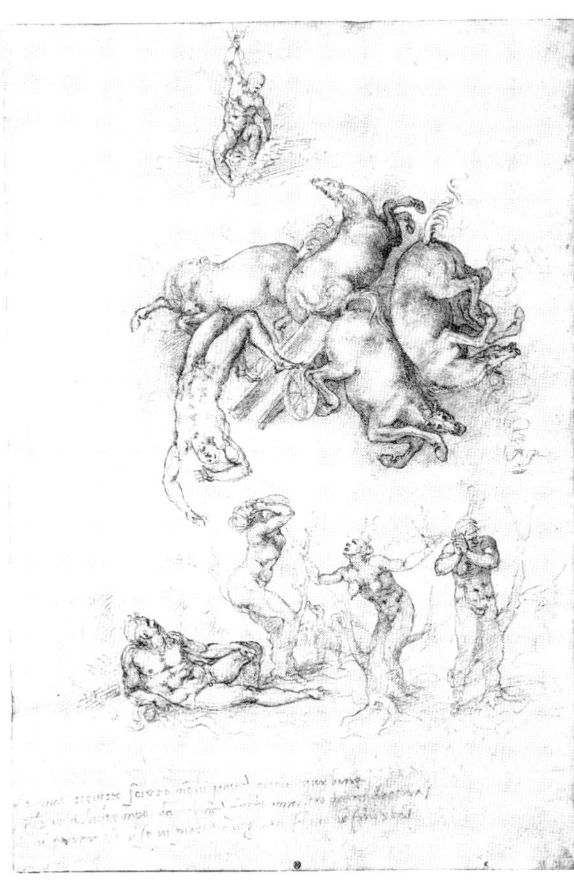

fig. 48. Michelangelo, *The Fall of Phaeton*, black chalk, 31.3 x 21.7 cm. British Museum, London, Department of Prints and Drawings

Phaeton, whose story is told most accessibly in Ovid's *Metamorphoses*, was the son of Apollo. Exploiting his father's offer to grant any wish, Phaeton demanded to drive the chariot of the sun. Disaster followed. Phaeton lost control of the chariot and to save the earth from incineration, Jupiter destroyed him. The youth's sisters, the Heliades, while mourning him, were transformed into trees and his relation Cycnus, into a swan. Phaeton's fall is an obvious image of hubris but it need not refer to Michelangelo's own sense of unworthiness in relation to his beloved Cavalieri. Phaeton is a youth, not middle-aged. He is the victim not of desire but of vanity, and he causes disaster not only for himself but for his family. Such a fable is more appropriate as a warning to a young man than a covert confession by an aging one.

Three autograph versions of the *Fall of Phaeton* survive, all in black chalk. The earliest, now in the British Museum (fig. 48, w. 55 / c. 340), was drawn in Rome, probably in June 1533. This bears a message from Michelangelo to Cavalieri, offering either to draw another version the next evening if Cavalieri does not like it, or to finish it if he does. The sequel is uncertain, but it may be that Michelangelo next drew the version in the Galleria dell'Accademia, Venice (Inv. 177 recto / c. 342 recto), which also bears a message, now only partly legible. This retains the three-tier arrangement, but shows Phaeton and his chariot falling more precipitately. Michelangelo perhaps offered Cavalieri a choice between the two versions. Wilde and Hirst have argued that the Venice drawing is a later variant, of circa 1535, and the fact that its verso carries a sketch for a figure in the *Last Judgment* would support such a dating. Michelangelo may simply have re-used the sheet after Cavalieri returned it; however, for Michelangelo to have repeated both subject and message, after a two-year interval, following the "definitive" Windsor drawing would be a strange duplication. A fragment of a compositional sketch for still another version, in red chalk, is at Haarlem (A. 31 / c. 341).

The Windsor *Phaeton* is the most refined of the three, but it shows many signs of reworking and contains numerous, carefully erased *pentimenti*. The Heliade at the far right, for example, at first had both arms raised and, more important, the main airborne group was tried lower down, with Phaeton's arms silhou-

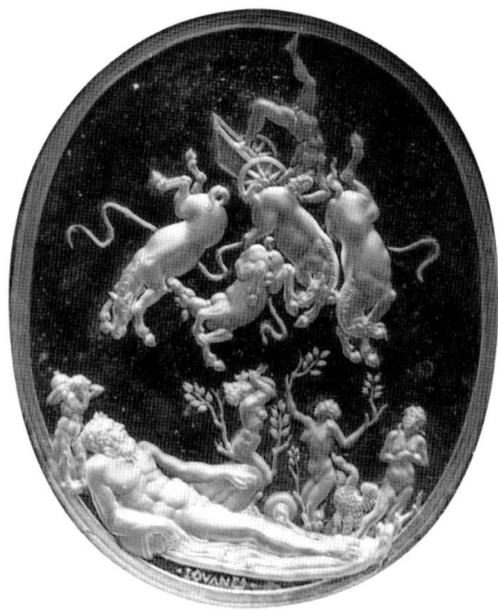

fig. 49. Giovanni Bernardi da Castel Bolognese after Michelangelo, *The Fall of Phaeton*, engraved crystal, 7.3 x 6.2 cm. The Walters Art Gallery, Baltimore

etted against the sky. Of all Michelangelo's presentation drawings, this is perhaps the one that displays most fully a controlled variety of touch.

The Windsor *Phaeton* was drawn not in Rome but in Florence, where the composition was copied in a loose pen drawing (cat. 10) by Raffaello da Montelupo. Michelangelo's drawing was sent, probably in late August 1533, to Cavalieri, whose letter of acknowledgment is dated 6 September. Its arrival in Rome was a public event: Tommaso told Michelangelo that he was visited by the pope, Cardinal Ippolito de' Medici, and "ognuno" (everyone). The cardinal studied all Cavalieri's Michelangelos and asked to have the *Tityus* and *Ganymede* reproduced in crystals by Giovanni Bernardi da Castel Bolognese. Cavalieri presumably lent the cardinal only one drawing at a time. Vasari adds that Bernardi also engraved the *Phaeton* for the cardinal; the three crystals were probably completed before Ippolito's death in 1536. Since Giovanni's small crystal (7.3 x 6.2 cm) of the *Fall of Phaeton* in the Walters Art Gallery, Baltimore (fig. 49), combines elements from both the Windsor and the British Museum drawings, Tommaso Cavalieri probably retained the latter (first recorded in the Moselli collection in Verona in 1760), and made it available to Giovanni. Given the thirst for knowledge of Michelangelo's drawings, this drawing too was copied: a very early replica, probably a tracing, whose mount bears a cross very similar to the mark of Francisco de Hollanda, is in the Louvre (Inv. 829). But the Venice version seems to have remained entirely unknown: no copies of it have been found and its provenance is obscure.

Giovanni Bernardi carved a second set of crystals, differing slightly from Ippolito's in both design and scale (approximately 9 x 6 cm), after Michelangelo's three drawings. This set, now known only from metal plaquettes, was probably ordered from him circa 1540 by Pier Luigi Farnese, who commissioned further complementary crystals from designs by Perino del Vaga. All these crystals were to be set in a casket whose design was entrusted to Francesco Salviati (Robertson 1992; reproductions of both series of crystals in Donati 1989).

Even so carefully worked a drawing as the *Phaeton* was not made on a fresh sheet of paper, for the verso drawing was undoubtedly made first. Michelangelo's authorship of this female figure is often denied and it is difficult to believe that the awkward bust and arms are his. The drawing probably repeats a pattern of

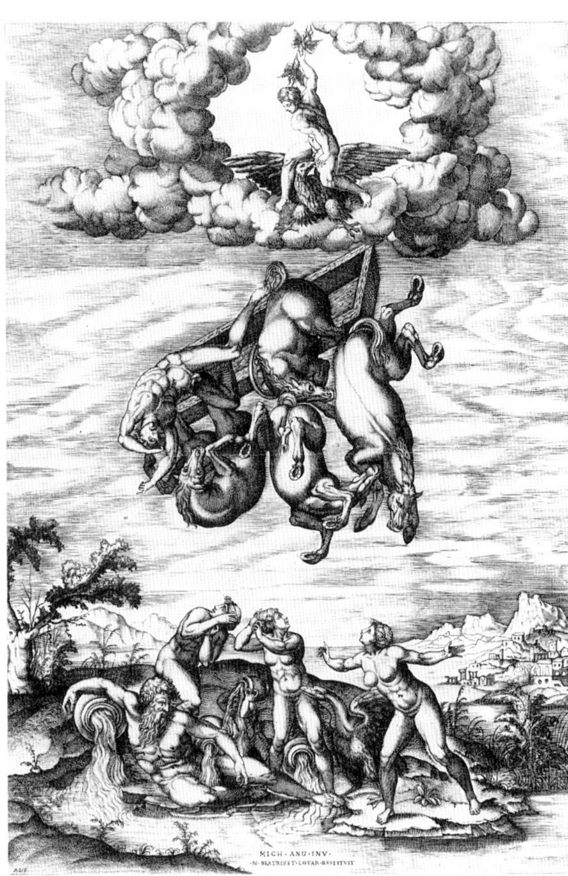

fig. 50. Nicolas Beatrizet after Michelangelo, *The Fall of Phaeton*, engraving, 41.7 x 29.2 cm. The Royal Collection, Windsor Castle

work found elsewhere in the 1520s, in which one of Michelangelo's pupils made a drawing, perhaps a copy of one by Michelangelo, that the master then worked over. Here it seems likely that the outline is by Antonio Mini, as Berenson suggested, but that the dense hatching on the face is Michelangelo's. Wilde suggested that the bust reflected an idea for the statue of *Leah*, included in the final version of the Julius Tomb, referred to as far advanced in a petition of Michelangelo's of July 1542. It may have been planned a decade earlier, when Michelangelo considered preparing models for the figures on the tomb. In that case, the present drawing would suggest that by late 1531, when Antonio Mini left Florence for France, Michelangelo had already decided to discard the niched groups of *Victories* and perhaps also the *Slaves*.

The Windsor *Phaeton* was engraved by Nicolas Beatrizet at an uncertain date but probably in the 1540s (fig. 50).

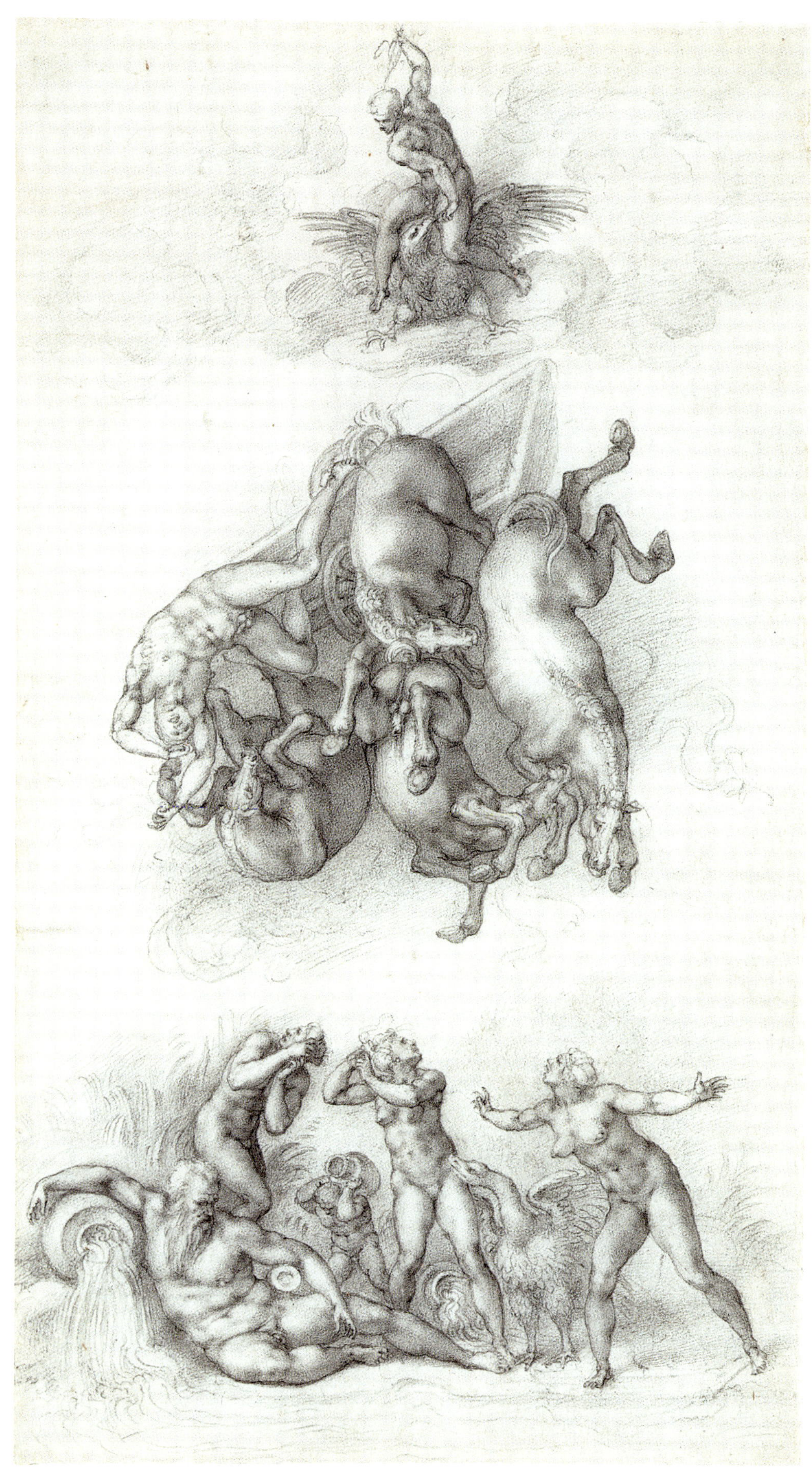

9a

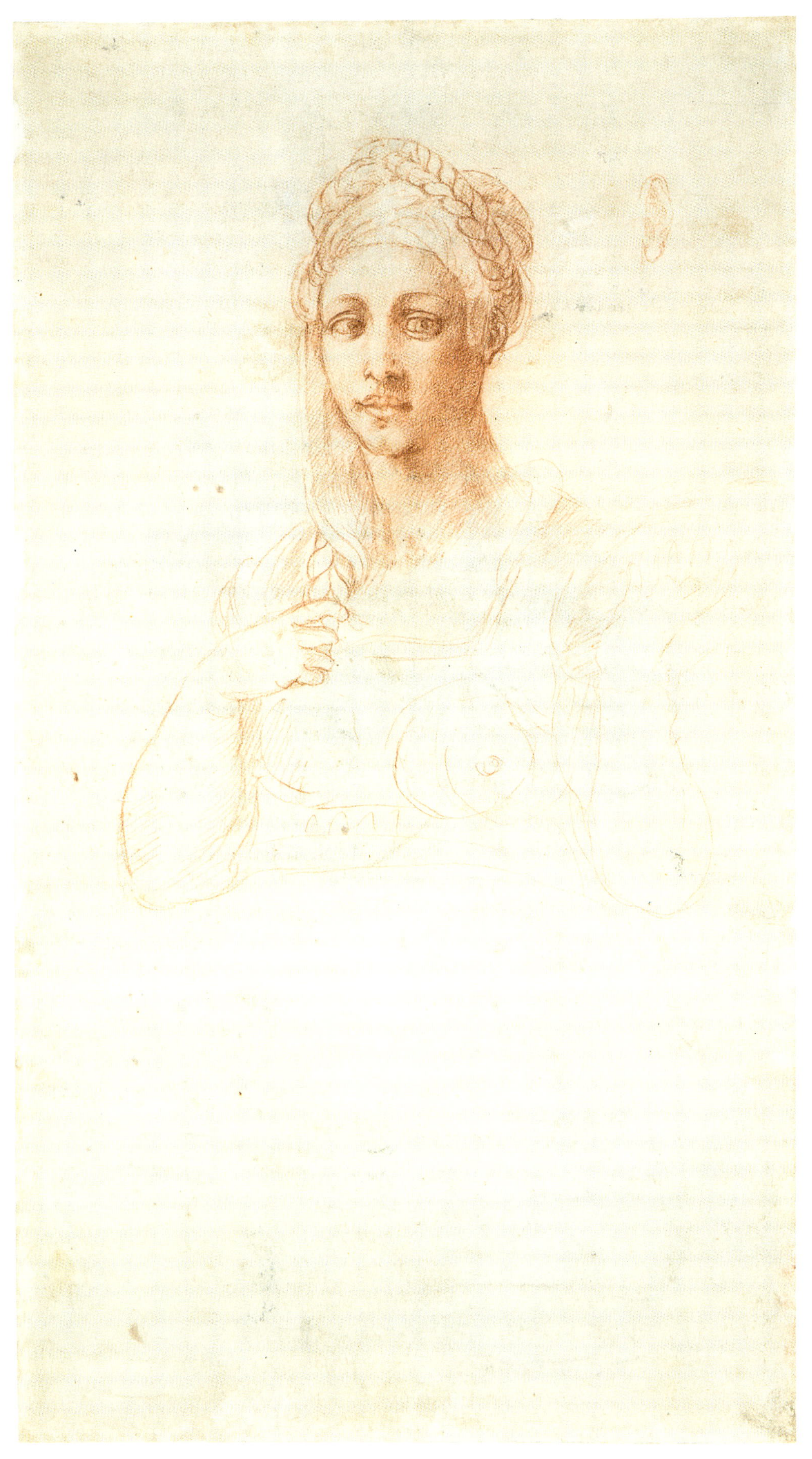

9b

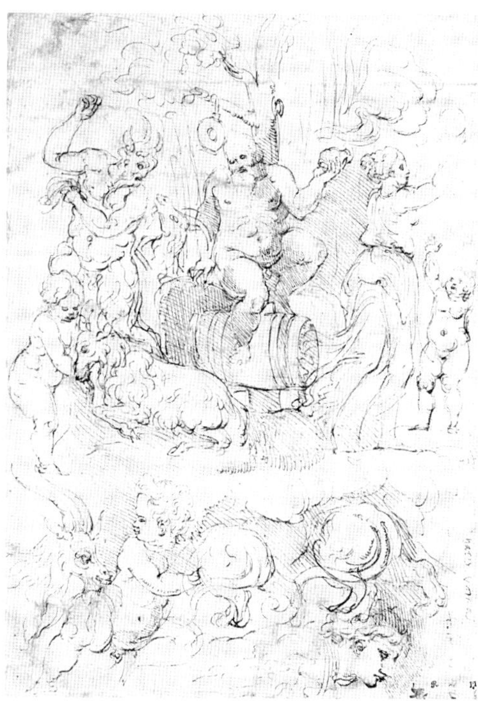

fig. 51. Raffaello da Montelupo, *Bacchic Scene and Other Sketches*, pen and ink, 34 x 23.8 cm. (recto of cat. 10)

Raffaello da Montelupo after Michelangelo Buonarroti

10
The Fall of Phaeton, and an Architectural Sketch

1533
pen and ink
34 x 23.8 (13 3/8 x 9 3/8); watermark: anchor in circle with star, not in Briquet
inscribed on the recto, lower right, probably in the hand of the artist: *pacis Ultima Copia/fecit raffaello*
RL 0505 verso

EXHIBITIONS
None

LITERATURE
Popham and Wilde 1949, no. 787 (verso)

Although rapidly and loosely drawn, this *Fall of Phaeton*, on the verso of the sheet, is unmistakably based on the composition of the version in Windsor (cat. 9a) rather than those in London or Venice. It was presumably made when Raffaello da Montelupo was collaborating with Michelangelo in mid-1533. He probably saw Michelangelo at work on the original but the variant positions of the arms of the Heliades are more likely his own experiments than records of Michelangelo's ideas. His copy, which makes no effort to record the detail of the original but which does capture something of its energy, is a vivid example of Raffaello's pen style at its loosest and most rhythmical. Such flowing pen work is rare among his drawings, but it reveals a draftsman of greater vitality than most of his surviving work would suggest. Battista Franco, who worked with Raffaello for a period in the mid-1530s, modeled aspects of his pen style on drawings such as this. Shortly after he made the present sketch, Raffaello made a larger and more prosaic copy, also in pen, of probably the latest of the gifts that Michelangelo sent to Cavalieri from Florence, the *Bacchanal of Children* (Popham and Wilde 431 / C. 338). This copy is now in the Ashmolean Museum, Oxford (P. 410).

The Phaeton copy was made after the three-bay architectural form had been drawn on the sheet, for Raffaello had to change the layout of the Phaeton to fit his sketch into the available space. This architectural scheme, probably an altar rather than a wall-tomb, is not directly related to any known Michelangelo drawing, but the arrangement clearly reflects some of Michelangelo's architectural ideas, as illustrated in various projects for altars and, perhaps, freestanding tombs. The relation of the reclining figures and the volutes on either side of crowning pediment suggest that Raffaello was familiar with early designs for the tombs in the New Sacristy, and the diamondlike form in the center of the broken pediment—itself based on the sarcophagus lids of the ducal tombs—may indicate a Medici project.

That Raffaello made free use of Michelangelo's ideas with some confidence is shown also by the upper drawing on the recto (fig. 51). This Bacchic scene is in part inspired by Michelangelo's drawings of children at play, such as that on the verso of the drawing recently acquired by the Getty Museum, and in part by Michelangelo's design for a relief of the *Nymphs in the Garden of the Hesperides*, an early design for the Magnifici tomb that is known in developed form only in copies (for example, Uffizi 607E). The scene may also be indebted to Michelangelo's project for a painting—probably the *Bacchanal of the Andrians*—for the *camerino d'alabastri* of Alfonso d'Este, a project for which a figure study has been identified (Louvre Inv. 697 / C. 69). In Raffaello's composition, however, Michelangelo's forms are much coarsened. A faint echo of the recto drawing can also be found in the allegorical relief on the tomb of Jacopo Sannazaro in Santa Maria del Parto in Naples, which was worked on by Montorsoli, Silvio Cosini, and Ammanati: the first two had assisted Michelangelo and the third knew his work well (see cat. 11).

That Raffaello was ready to parody Michelangelo's forms and ideas appears from a drawing in the Rijksmuseum (1981–23), a composition of a *Sleeping Venus*—whose figure, based on Michelangelo's *Dawn*, is surrounded by a group of exceptionally delinquent putti. This is mischievously based on Michelangelo's *Dream of Human Life.*

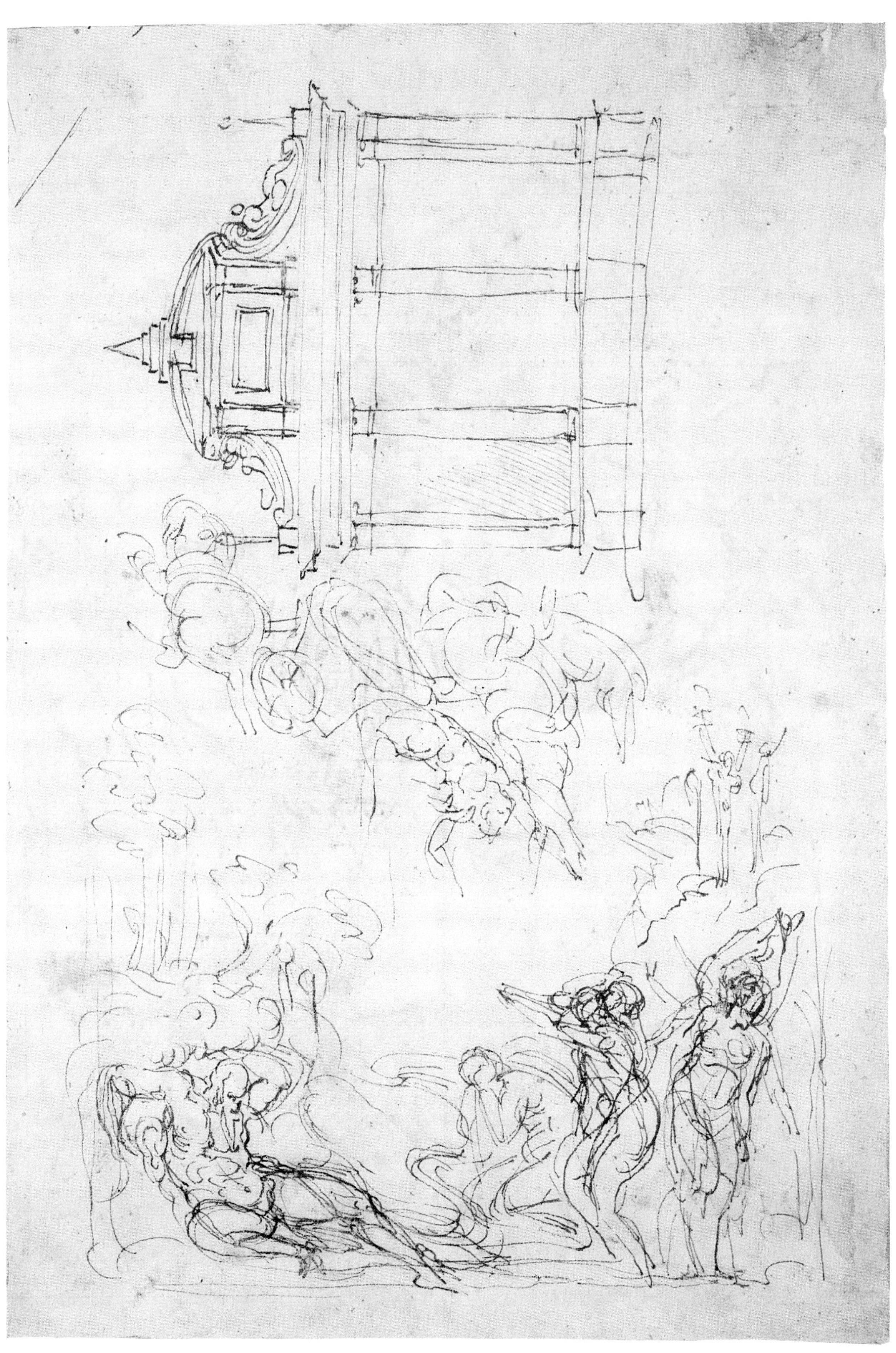

Unidentified Florentine Artist (Bartolommeo Ammanati?)

11
River God

c. 1550 (?)
black chalk
22.4 x 22.5 (8 13/16 x 8 7/8); no watermark
RL 0444

EXHIBITIONS
Florence 1980, no. 25

LITERATURE
Popham and Wilde 1949, no. 1090

This figure is similar in pose, build, and facial type to the reclining River Po in the lower left of the *Fall of Phaeton*, a figure itself developed in part from the river gods that Michelangelo intended to place in pairs at floor level either side of the ducal tombs in the New Sacristy (fig. 52, Inv. 838 / C. 186). The drawing's technique also reflects knowledge of those chalk drawings that Michelangelo made to prepare his most muscled allegorical figures for the New Sacristy and was to develop further in his semi-*écorché* drawings for the *Last Judgment*. It should be compared with cat. 55 verso.

The author of this splendid study has eluded secure identification. The powerful three-dimensionality of modeling suggests a sculptor—although this impression was not shared by Popham—and the face is reminiscent of the types favored of Jacopo Sansovino, with lavish moustaches and flowing beards that combine to submerge their mouths. But the body appears more compact and rhythmical than those in Jacopo's sculpture, and the drawing's style bears little resemblance to the very few drawings that have been given to him.

More attractive is an attribution (suggested in Florence 1980) to a sculptor by whom no figure drawings in chalk are securely identified and arguably no figure drawings at all: Bartolommeo Ammanati. Although he later diverged from close imitation of Michelangelo's forms, Ammanati was, as a young man, obsessed with Michelangelo's work, to the extent of breaking into Michelangelo's Via Mozza studio and stealing some of his drawings. Michelangelo recovered them, but not before Ammanati studied them. Much of his sculpture of the 1530s and early 1540s is modeled on Michelangelo's designs. Ammanati worked in Venice in the early 1540s under Jacopo Sansovino, carving spandrel figures of river gods for the Marciana Library, figures in which Michelangelesque inspiration is clear and whose facial types are close to those of the present drawing and of Sansovino. An attribution of the present drawing to the young Ammanati would thus conveniently explain those qualities in it that are reminiscent both of Michelangelo and Sansovino. Nevertheless, caution is required. The musculature and posing of the figure in the drawing are so much more vital and mobile than those of Ammanati's sculpted nudes, whose torsos are never as powerful and whose articulation tends to stiffness, that a bridge from one to the other is difficult to construct. The confidently vigorous application of chalk suggests a practiced and fluent draftsman, and the manner in which the right arm and the right side of the chest are shaded, in soft strokes that have been carefully stumped to create a form that is dense and rotund but simultaneously soft-textured, is reminiscent of the later manner of Salviati, whose drawings the present draftsman might have known.

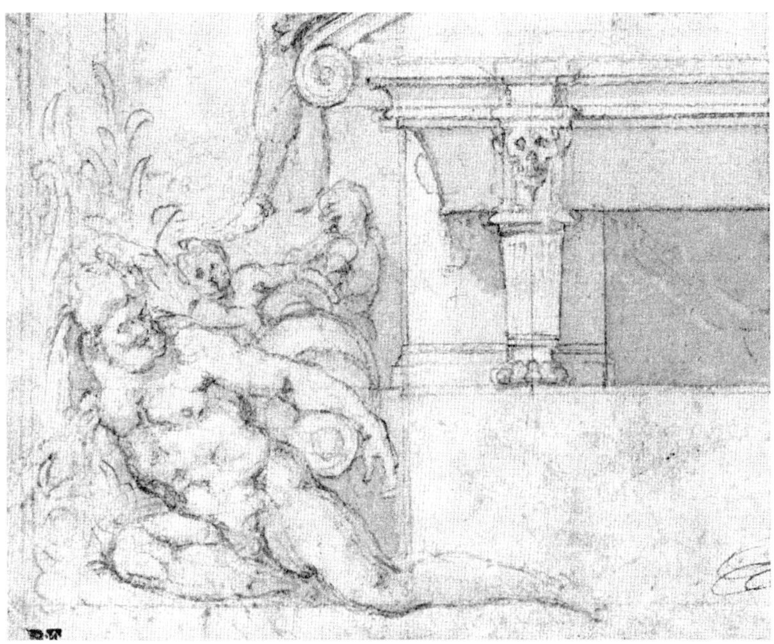

fig. 52. Michelangelo, *River God*, detail from the *modello* for the Tomb of Duke Giuliano, black chalk and wash over stylus indentation, 32.1 x 20.5 cm. Musée du Louvre, Paris, Département des Arts Graphiques [Photo RMN]

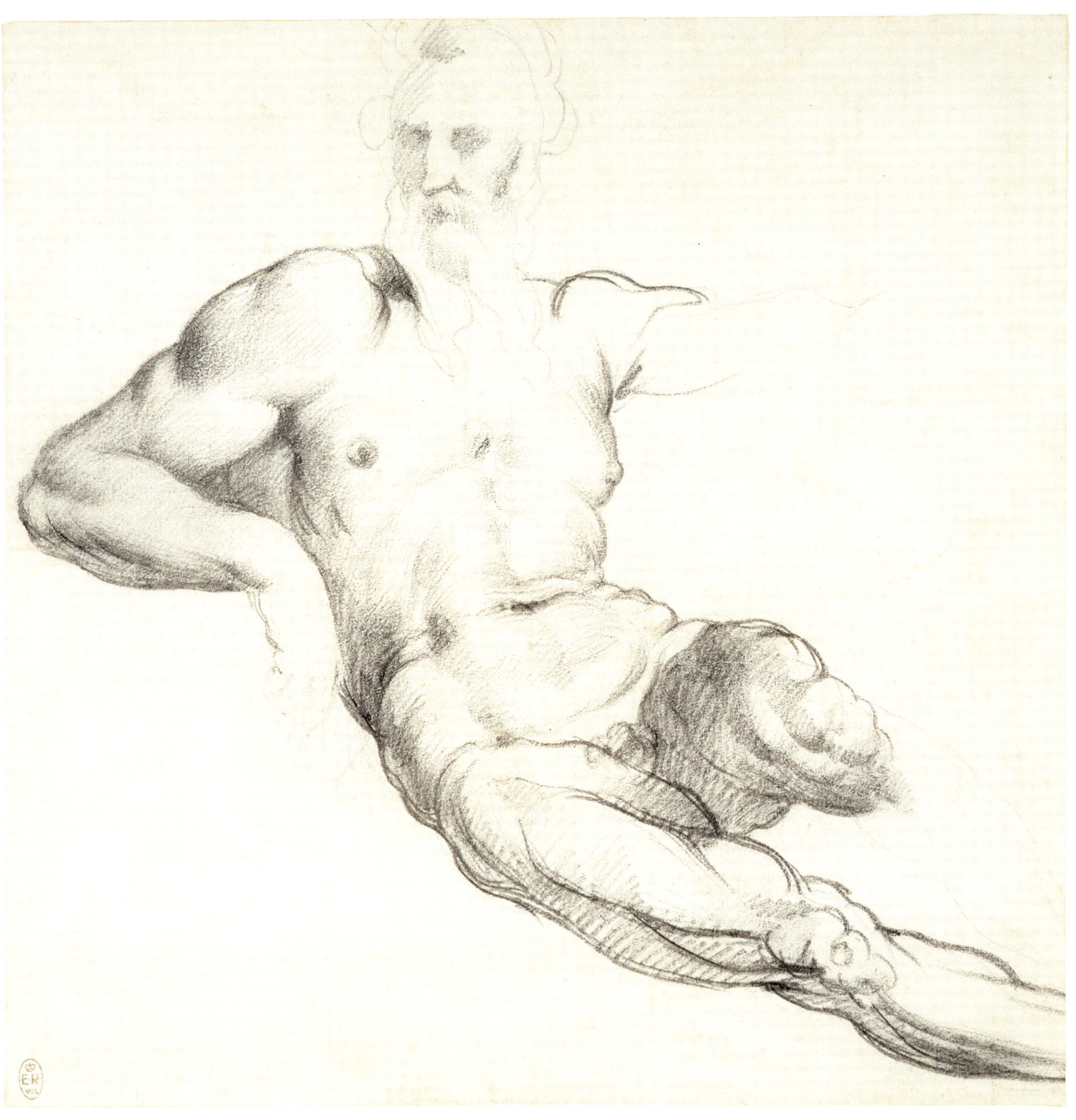

Michelangelo Buonarroti

12a
Tityus (RECTO)

12b
The Risen Christ (VERSO)

1532
black chalk
19 x 33 (7 1/2 x 13); no watermark
RL 12771

EXHIBITIONS
London 1930, no. 515; Edinburgh 1947, no. 145; London 1950–1951, no. 266; London 1953, no. 92; London 1962, no. 68; Florence 1964, no. 134; London 1972–1973, no. 44; London 1975, no. 123; London 1986, no. 24; Washington-Paris 1988–1989, no. 43; Montreal 1992, no. 108

LITERATURE
Berenson 1903 and 1938, no. 1615; Frey 1909–1911, no. 6; Thode 1913, no. 540; De Tolnay 1948, no. 115; Popham and Wilde 1949, no. 429; Goldscheider 1951, no. 74; Dussler 1959, no. 241; Berti 1965, 455, no. 157; Goldscheider 1966, no. 75; Hartt 1971, no. 353; De Tolnay 1975–1980, 2: no. 345; Hirst 1988, 112–113; Donati 1989, 78–80; Perrig 1991, 44 (recto), 76–77 (verso)

This sheet, combining an exceptional refinement of surface with a remarkable variety of touch, represents Tityus, one of the giants of antique mythology, who was punished by the children of Leto for attempting to rape her. Chained to a rock, he was condemned to an appropriate torment: his liver, regarded as the seat of lust, grew back each night to be devoured again by a vulture the next day. Below him a crab seems to be climbing toward him, presumably to add its minor torment. To the right, the screaming face within the tree is of another sinner tormented in Hades and this, although not mentioned in connection with Tityus in the *Metamorphoses*, may have been suggested by tree-bound beings elsewhere in Ovid's text.

Michelangelo's interest in pictorial treatments of the *Metamorphoses* may have been fired by the mythologies by Titian and others that he saw in Ferrara during his visit to Alfonso d'Este in 1529. In the early 1530s Michelangelo painted the *Leda* for Alfonso d'Este, designed the *Venus and Cupid* for his friend Bartolommeo Bettini to be painted by Pontormo, sculpted a statuette of *Apollo* for Baccio Valori, and made his most elaborate presentation drawings. The *Tityus* was drawn in Rome late in 1532 and was given directly to Tommaso, probably at the same time as the *Ganymede*. The theme, the punishment of lust, has often been interpreted as a confession of Michelangelo's own sinful love for the young man, but its application is more general: it is a moral lesson, that heterosexual passion should be controlled, and as such Tityus was represented, in the knowledge of Michelangelo's design, by Titian in a painting for Mary of Hungary, of 1549.

The theme is related to that of Prometheus and it may be that this connection was in Michelangelo's mind. It is, indeed, mainly the

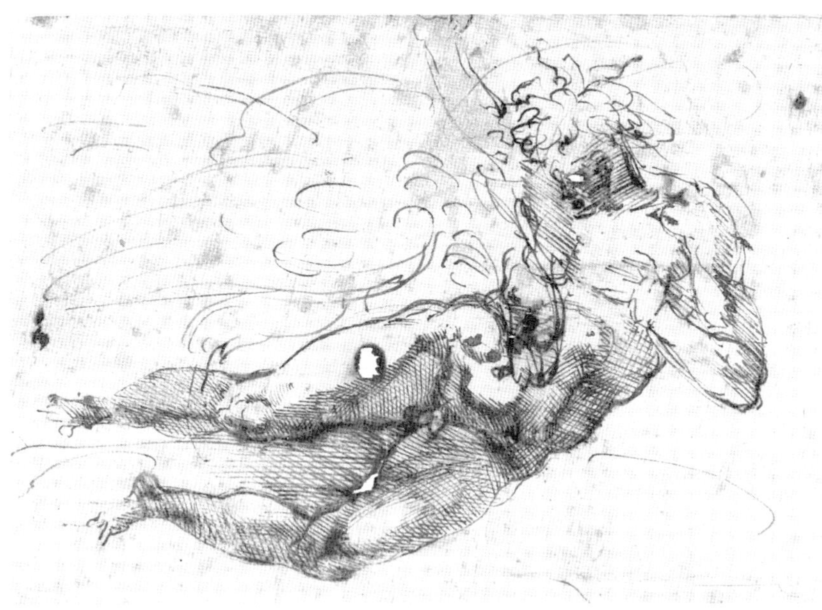

fig. 53. Raffaello da Montelupo, *Tityus or Prometheus*, pen and ink, 16.6 x 24 cm. Musée des Beaux-Arts, Lille

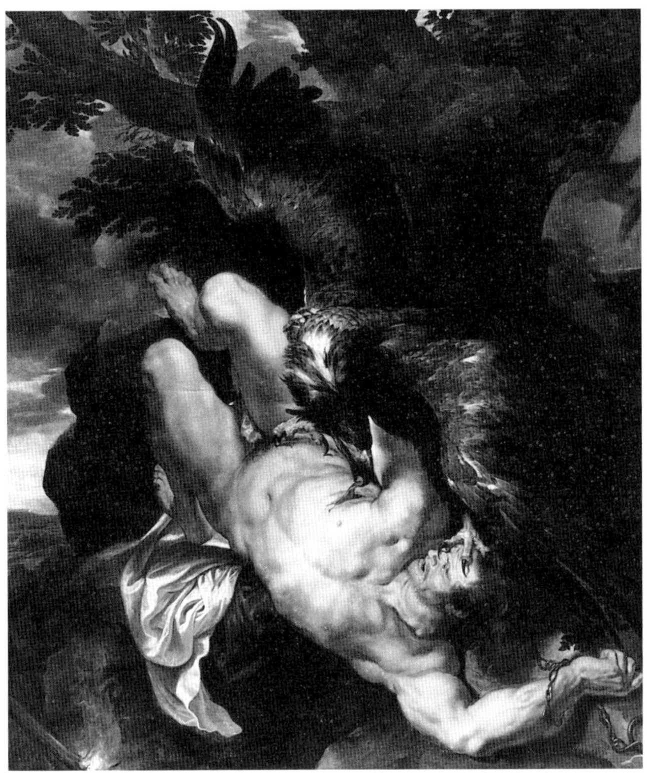

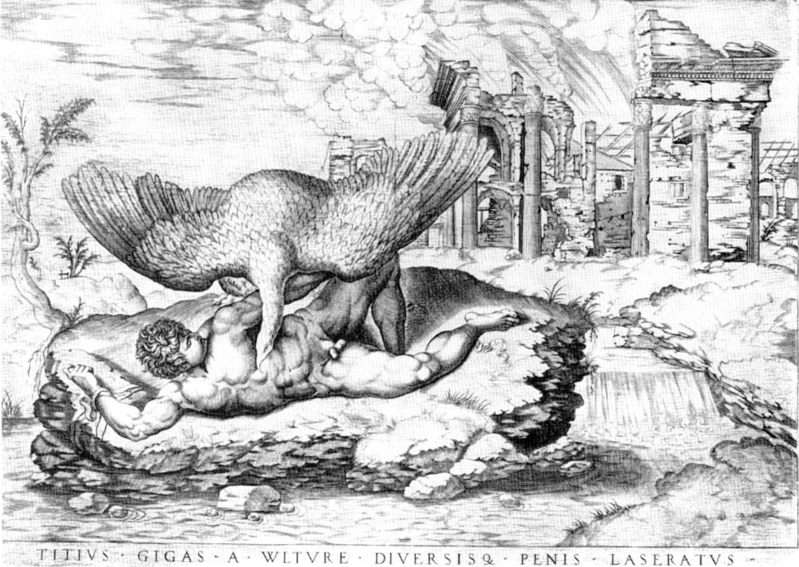

ABOVE: fig. 55. Nicolas Beatrizet (?) after Michelangelo, *Tityus*, engraving, 28.1 x 37.4 cm. The Royal Collection, Windsor Castle

LEFT: fig. 54. Peter Paul Rubens, *Prometheus*, oil on panel, 240 x 189 cm. Philadelphia Museum of Art, The W. P. Wilstach Collection

screaming head of the soul imprisoned in the tree, a Bellinian or Titianesque detail, which identifies the setting as Hades rather than the Caucasus, where the giant Prometheus is tortured by an eagle (which Michelangelo's bird resembles more than a vulture) in a like manner for his theft of fire from the gods. The heroic and in no way degraded appearance of Michelangelo's figure, whose gloriously modeled body shows no wounds and whose facial type suggests heroism rather than degeneracy, may have been intended to evoke Tityus' noble counterpart. The figure may have been interpreted in this sense by Raffaello da Montelupo, in a drawing in the Musée des Beaux-Arts, Lille (fig. 53, Pluchart 90). It was certainly interpreted in this sense by Rubens, when he came to paint his *Prometheus* (fig. 54). He also used it for his *Death of Hippolytus* (Fitzwilliam Museum, Cambridge). Rubens would certainly have known the *Tityus* through Nicolas Beatrizet's engraving, probably made during the 1540s (fig. 55), but he may also have seen one of the drawn copies of the original. Copies of the *Tityus*, with modifications, were made by Giovanni Bernardi, once again in two different sizes.

The strong, blockishly formed sketch on the verso of the sheet is partly traced from the recto: Tityus is rotated 90 degrees to create a Christ emerging from the tomb. This verso figure is remarkable and unparalleled. Michelangelo's presentation drawings often contain slight or awkward sketches on their versos (compare cat. 9), but he rarely re-used sheets on which he had already made finished drawings. That he did so here suggests he was suddenly seized by inspiration. In several examples among his drawings, Michelangelo made verso tracings after recto figures had been completed (for example, Louvre Inv. 688 / C. 20 and Inv. 712 / C. 42), but the present sheet is the only occasion when Michelangelo made a tracing—slightly modified, with a changed position of the legs—of a completed presentation drawing. And there is no example of tracing used to cast the same figure in two radically different roles; indeed, the thematic contrast between them is as extreme as could be imagined. On the recto, a sinner is tormented in a hell that may not be Christian, but that is its equivalent; on the other side the selfsame figure, differently oriented, becomes Christ emerging from the tomb after hell's harrowing. It would be tempting to suggest that Michelangelo deployed this contrast consciously—visual and verbal puns were by no means unknown to him—but had that been his intention he would surely have produced a more fully finished image. While this double image displays Michelangelo's extraordinary grasp of the diverse potentialities of a single figure, it is surely also an indication of his unconscious fears and hopes. The message of the two sides of this drawing taken together is akin to that of Michelangelo's *Dream of Human Life*.

A further truncated sketch on the right, a variant of the *Resurrected Christ*, shows Michelangelo's imagination stretching in a different direction, back toward his *God the Father Separating Light from Darkness* on the Sistine vault. This sketch was probably the germ of one of the most expressive and passionate of Michelangelo's Resurrection drawings, the *Risen Christ* (cat. 39).

A copy of the *Tityus* sold at the Hotel Drouot, Paris, 25 February 1924, no. 44, from the Robinson and Marignane collections, was described in the sale catalogue as having an "academie d'homme au verso," and it may therefore have contained copies of both sides of the original.

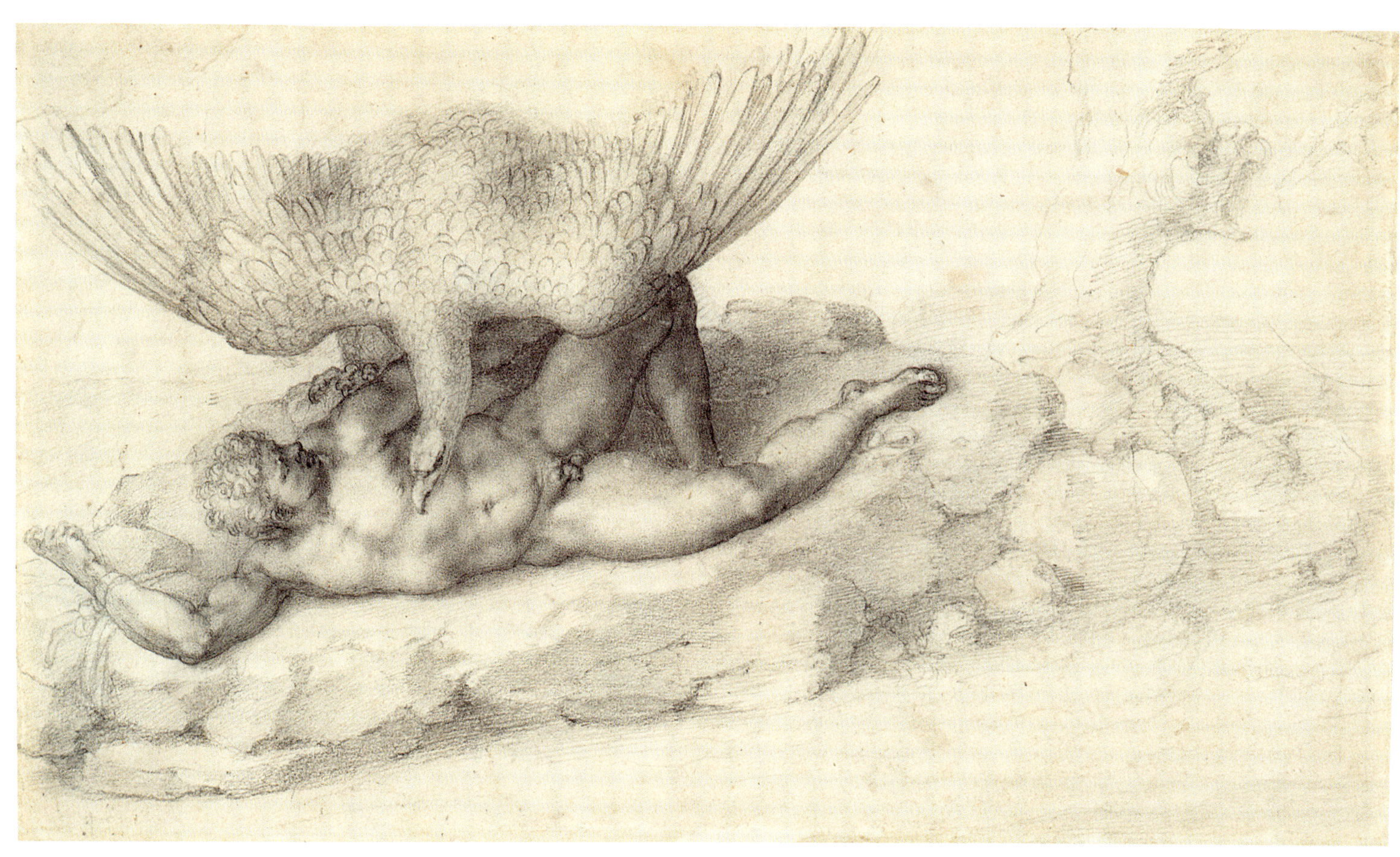

12a

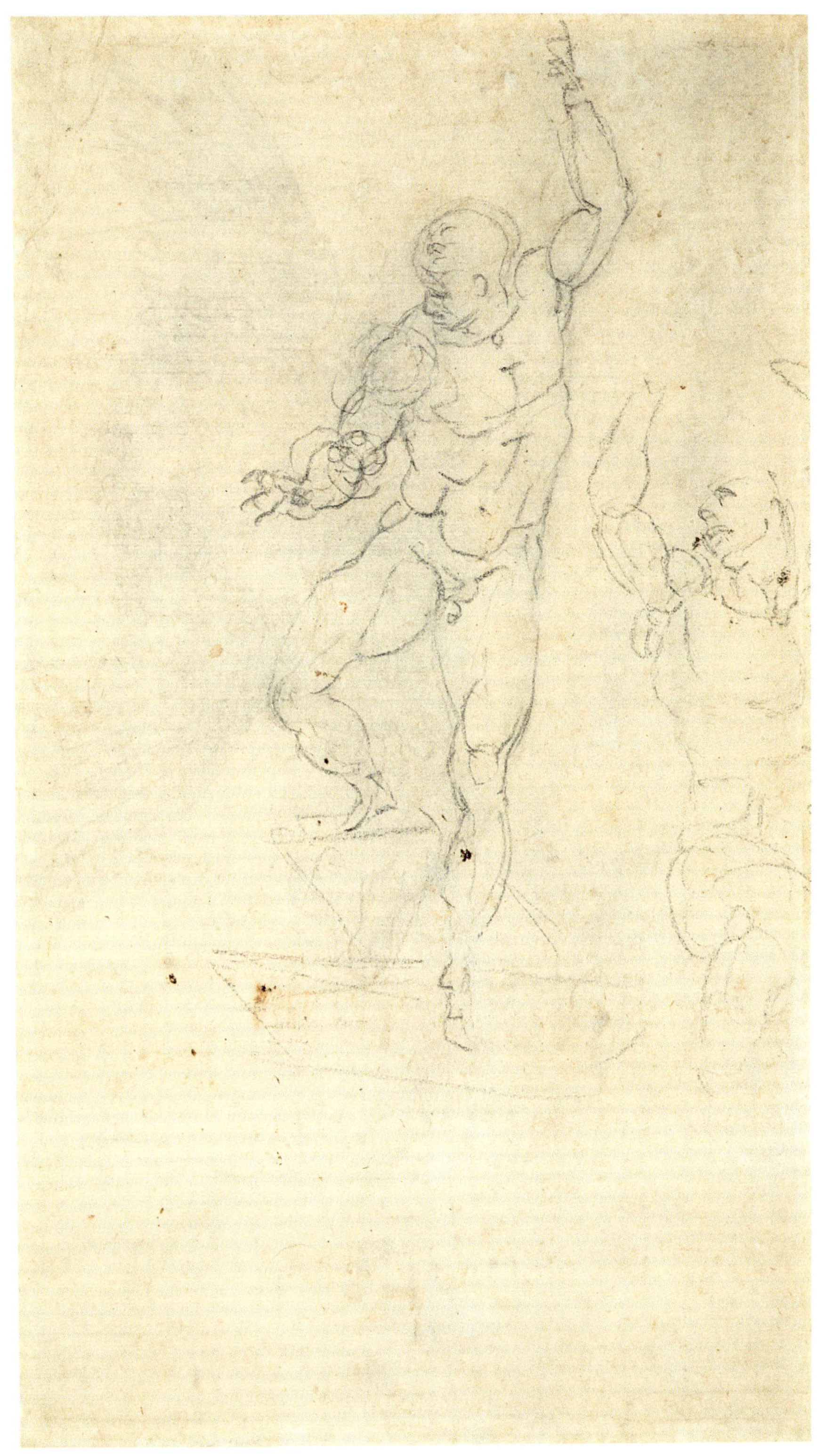

12b

Agnolo Bronzino (?) after Michelangelo Buonarroti

13
Tityus

c. 1550 (?)
black chalk
21.2 x 32.2 (8 3/8 x 12 11/16); watermark: fleur-de-lys in circle with star, not in Briquet
inscribed upper left in pen: *sei/cinque;* and at lower right in pen in a different hand: *Del*
RL 0471

EXHIBITIONS
None

LITERATURE
Popham and Wilde 1949, no. 458

This is an accurate and sensitive copy of Michelangelo's *Tityus* (cat. 12a). Its closeness of touch to the original suggests that it was made directly from Michelangelo's drawing, rather than from an intermediate copy, probably while it was still in Cavalieri's possession. Unlike most drawings of this type, it has not been attributed to Giulio Clovio and, indeed, no name has been put forward. But a suggestion made to the compiler by Elizabeth Pilliod deserves to be taken very seriously. This is for the drawing's attribution to Agnolo Bronzino.

Bronzino did not pass extended periods in Rome, but he visited the city in 1548 and probably made other short trips. He might well have had access to Tommaso de' Cavalieri's house and his collection. The technique of the present drawing bears some similarities to that of drawings by Bronzino, for example, Uffizi 6704F, made in preparation for the *Crossing of the Red Sea* in the Chapel of Eleanora of Toledo, in 1540 or 1541, although it is less like his *Nude Man* (cat. 61). But, given the extreme paucity of drawings firmly established as by Bronzino, any attribution is difficult to sustain without a direct connection with a painted work. The interpretation of *Tityus*' facial type is also reminiscent of Alessandro Allori—which would maintain the drawing in Bronzino's circle—but it is more even-toned and less vigorous than other drawings attributed to Allori.

Another copy of the *Tityus* in the Uffizi (248F, black chalk over traces of red chalk, 22.2 x 33.9 cm), given to Bronzino in the nineteenth century but subsequently transferred to Allori, is very similar in handling to the present copy. However, while Tityus' body and the bird are more richly defined in the Uffizi drawing, the surroundings are more sketchily treated. The differences and similarities between the present copy and that in the Uffizi might be explained by two closely allied artists—Bronzino and Allori—making independent copies of Michelangelo's drawing, with the master's version more hesitant, if more precise, than that of his pupil. But, were it necessary to emphasize further the fragility of such hypotheses, it should be noted that Uffizi 248F has recently been given by Giovanetti (1991, no. 18) to Francesco Morandini, called Il Poppi.

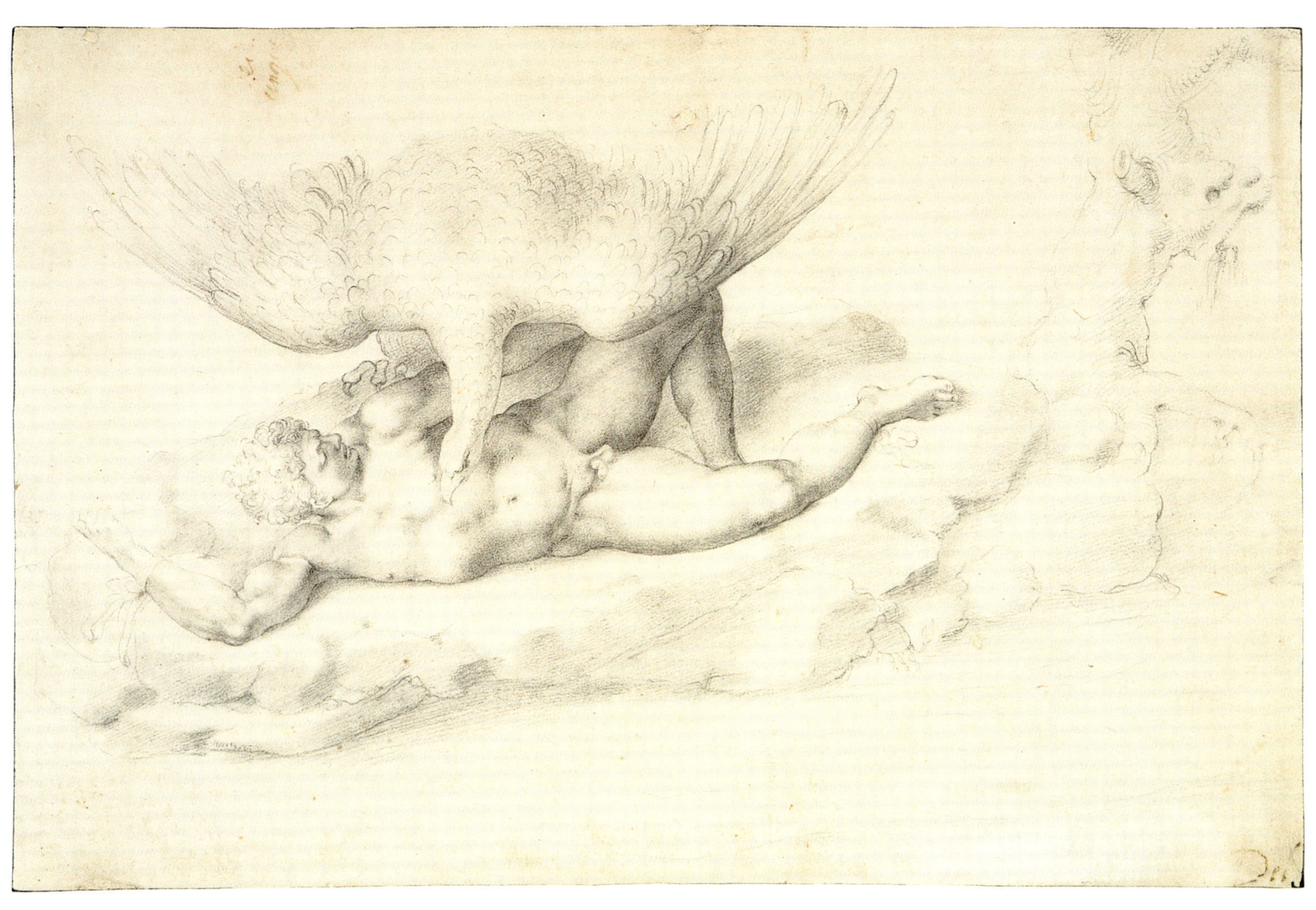

Unidentified Artist after Michelangelo Buonarroti

14
Tityus

c. 1550
black chalk
20.3 x 29 (8 x 11 7/16), upper corners cut; watermark: anchor in circle surmounted by a star, not in Briquet
inscribed in pen on verso: *Michel;* and in the hand of William Gibson: *Julio Clovio d MAngolo Buonarottj/3.3.*
RL 0472

EXHIBITIONS
None

LITERATURE
Popham and Wilde 1949, no. 459; Giononi-Visani and Gamulin 1980, 105; London 1986, 45; Perrig 1991, 26–27, 44

The inscription on the verso of the present sheet was accepted by Wilde as by a sixteenth-century hand and he also accepted its statement that the drawing was by Giulio Clovio, as did Giononi-Visani and Gamulin. However, Martin Clayton's suggestion to the compiler that the inscription is, in fact, English, of the seventeenth century, and by William Gibson was confirmed when the drawing was lifted in preparation for the present exhibition to reveal Gibson's pricing code, previously concealed by the mount. Clayton also remarked that the diagonal trimming of the upper corners is frequently found in drawings that have passed through English seventeenth-century collections.

That the inscription is later than Wilde thought need not cast doubt upon the information it conveys. But, as the *Resurrection* (cat. 38) shows, even verso inscriptions datable within or just after Clovio's own lifetime are not necessarily to be trusted, and, on visual grounds, the compiler finds the attribution of the present drawing to Clovio very difficult to accept. The present abbreviated copy is neither a particularly accurate nor a sensitive version of the original, unlike Clovio's replica of Michelangelo's *Ganymede* (cat. 15) or his copy of the *modello* for Sebastiano's *Flagellation* (cat. 34), although in both those cases Michelangelo's originals are lost. Nor does the application of the chalk seem to possess Clovio's characteristics. The fine if rather tentative contour generally to be found in Clovio's drawings is not seen here, the internal hatching is quite brisk and coarse, emphatic in a manner alien to Clovio's more delicate and fastidious procedures, and the details of physical form, the characteristic outlining of the extremities of fingers and toes, for example, which in Clovio always seem slightly timid, are here executed with confidence but without expression.

The style of this drawing suggests to the compiler a Florentine draftsman of the generation that came to maturity around 1550. The breadth of handling of the chalk is reminiscent of the rather open and simplified manner of an artist like Tommaso Manzuoli, although this drawing displays neither his confidence nor his tricks of hand. It is probably by one of his contemporaries rather than one of Clovio's. A version of the *Tityus* sold at Christie's on 3 April 1986, lot 6 (black chalk, outlines indented, 19 x 27.3 cm, with the fragmentary watermark Briquet 561 and from Lanier's collection), seems to be a still coarser derivative of the present drawing or its model.

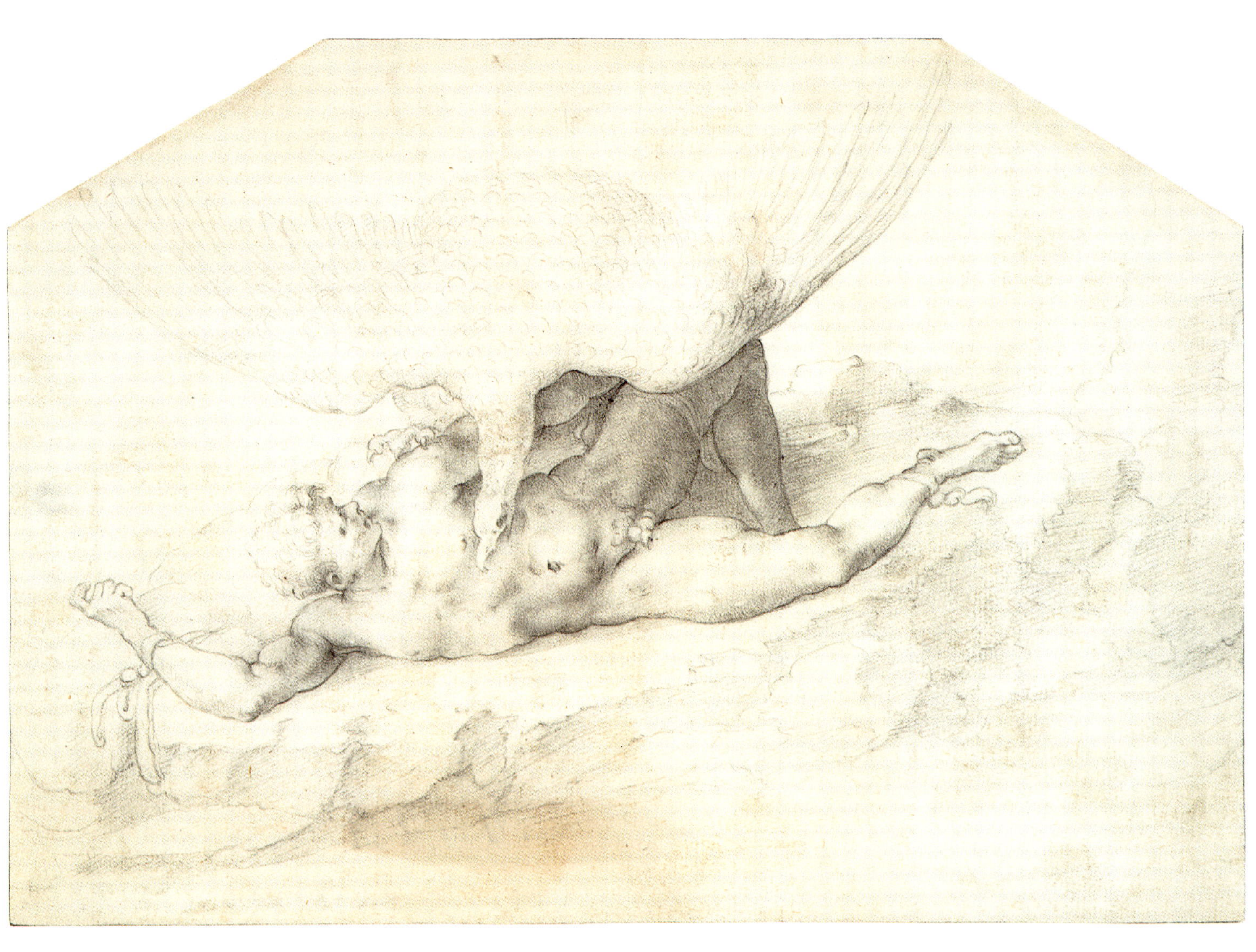

Giulio Clovio after Michelangelo Buonarroti

15
Ganymede

c. 1540 (?)
black chalk
19.2 x 26 (7 9/16 x 10 1/4); no watermark
inscribed in black chalk on verso: *Ex divino Raffael Urbinas.*
RL 13036

EXHIBITIONS
London 1972–1973, no. 48; London 1975, no. 124; Lisbon 1983; Montreal 1992, no. 109

LITERATURE
Berenson 1903 and 1938, no. 1614; Frey 1909–1911, no. 18; Thode 1913, no. 539; De Tolnay 1948, no. 116; Popham and Wilde 1949, no. 457; Giononi-Visani and Gamulin 1980, 105–106; Donati 1989, 82–83; Perrig 1991, 43–44

This drawing is fully acceptable as by Clovio: it displays his slightly tentative handling of contour, his distinctive formulation of extremities, his habit of building up forms by thin hatching lines, rather regularly applied, which are then worked over. It is, in all probability, a partial copy of a presentation drawing in vertical format made late in 1532 by Michelangelo for Tommaso de' Cavalieri. Indeed, it may have been cut down, for the hatching extends to the edges of the sheet.

The problem of Michelangelo's *Ganymede* composition is complicated and can only be summarized here. Versions exist in two formats. One is vertical in orientation, with Ganymede and the eagle in the sky and, below, a landscape with the boy's crook, bundle, and startled dog. The other consists solely of Ganymede and the eagle, and is horizontal. The best example of the horizontal format is the present drawing. This type seems to have been more widely copied than the vertical version. There are no significant differences between the "vertical" and the "horizontal" in their common feature, the group of the boy and the eagle. This identity therefore raises the questions of whether Michelangelo himself produced the same design in both a vertical and a horizontal format, and whether an autograph version in either format survives. The compiler's answer to the first would be no; to the second, perhaps.

The reason for the first denial lies precisely in the fact that in both formats the boy and eagle are identical. There exists no secure example of Michelangelo making a line-for-line copy of one of his own drawings, and such a course of action seems temperamentally improbable for him. When repeating a subject, Michelangelo invariably visualized it differently, as the *Phaeton* drawings demonstrate. (It might be noted that another, much looser red-chalk drawing of *Ganymede* by Michelangelo of circa 1530, in the Uffizi [611E / C. 298], is radically different in composition.) It would follow that the horizontal *Ganymede* represents a reduction of Michelangelo's vertical *Ganymede* by another artist. Of course, in theory, Michelangelo could himself have cut down a drawing made in vertical format, of which copies would have been made before he did so, but this seems highly unlikely. It may be that the horizontal version, which forms a neat, self-contained image, was created to translate into crystals and plaques, but not by the master. A crystal by Giovanni Bernardi does not survive, but it is recorded in numerous bronze plaquettes.

In 1975 Hirst published a *Ganymede* in vertical format in the Fogg Art Museum, Cambridge, Massachusetts (fig. 56, 1955–75 / C. 344), as an original by Michelangelo. This view is accepted by Perrig and—in an oral

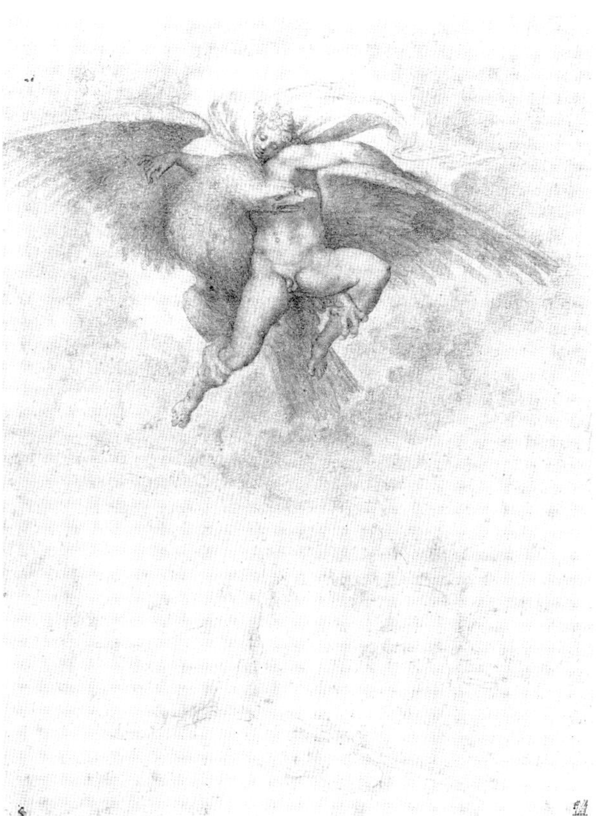

fig. 56. Michelangelo or after, *Ganymede*, black chalk, 36.1 x 27.5 cm. President and Fellows of Harvard College, Harvard University Art Museums, Fogg Art Museum, Cambridge, Massachusetts

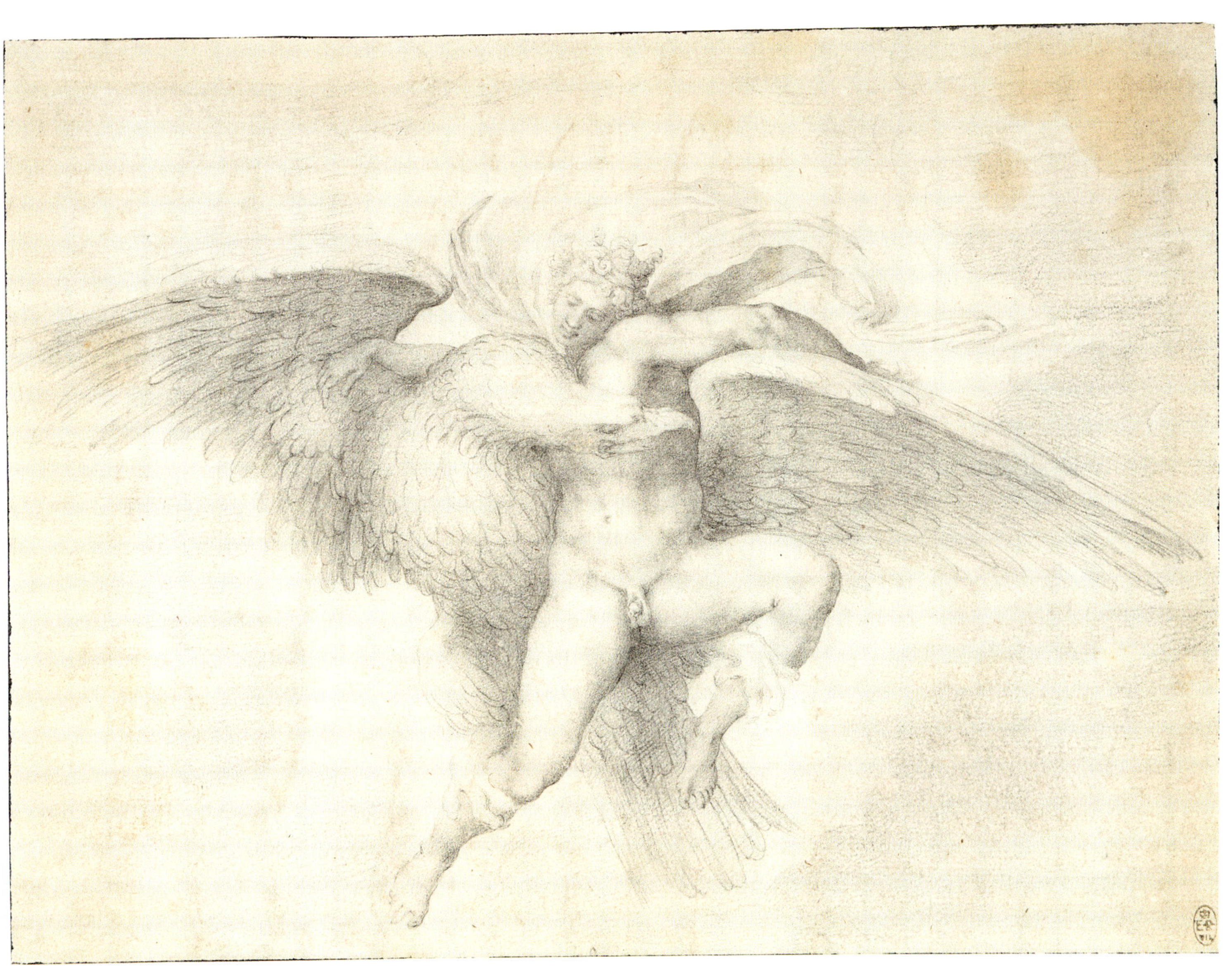

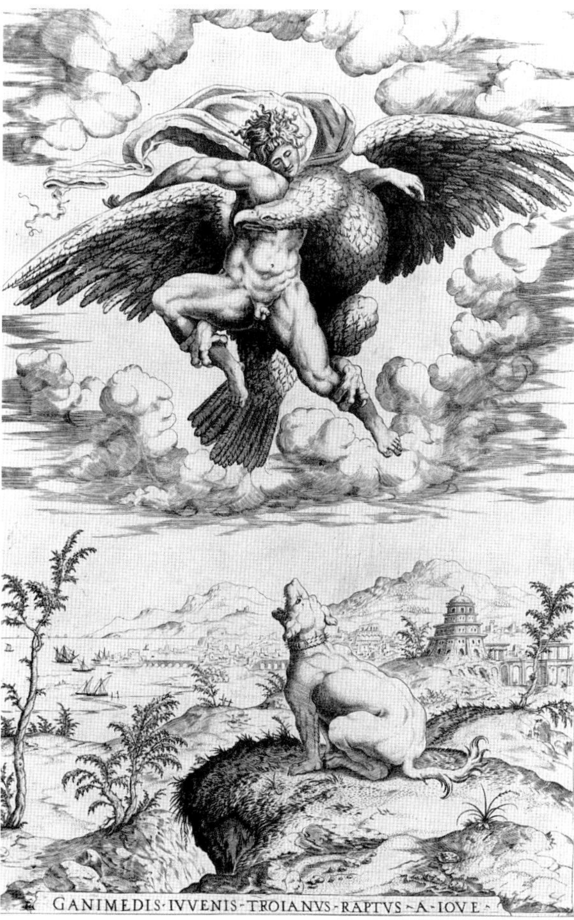

fig. 57. Nicolas Beatrizet (?) after Michelangelo, *Ganymede*, engraving, 42.5 x 28.2 cm. The Royal Collection, Windsor Castle

communication to William Robinson—by Sylvia Ferino Pagden, but opposed by De Tolnay and Frommel (1979). The compiler, who has not seen the Fogg drawing unglazed, remains uncertain. The upper group has been severely damaged by extensive stylus incising, presumably to transfer it to another sheet, and it would be surprising if a genuine Michelangelo drawing, let alone one belonging to Cavalieri, had been so treated. Notable in the Fogg drawing is that the whole earthly scene is very lightly indicated. Such an extreme discrepancy between parts occurs in no other finished presentation drawing by Michelangelo (the Venice *Phaeton* was clearly left incomplete). Consequently, it might be argued that the Fogg drawing was copied from Michelangelo's lost original before the master had completed its lower section: he certainly sent drawings in progress to friends for their comments and might have done so with the *Ganymede*. But against this hypothesis is the fact that comparable discrepancies of finish occur between the upper and lower sections in the "verticals" in the Louvre (Inv. 826) and at Chatsworth (Jaffé 1994a, no. 45), which suggests that this was a feature of the original. The Louvre and Chatsworth drawings, however, do not agree completely either with each other or with the Fogg drawing. The status of the last must for the present remain unresolved: a report on it by Leslie M. Schick, generously made available to the compiler by William Robinson, confirms that no watermark is to be found on its paper. However, if not a damaged original, the Fogg sheet is the best surviving copy of the vertical image, and the main group is also superior in the refinement of its execution to that of any of the horizontal, abbreviated images.

The theme of *Ganymede* is inherently homoerotic, but it was frequently transformed. Sebastiano suggested to Michelangelo in a letter of 17 July 1533 that a Ganymede with a halo might be painted in the lantern of the New Sacristy and called a Saint John. This was no more than a risqué joke. But in 1538 Battista Franco did adopt Michelangelo's *Ganymede* as an image of the divine elevation of Cosimo de' Medici at the *Battle of Montemurlo* (Palazzo Pitti, Florence) and he would hardly have done so had the image carried an exclusively homosexual meaning. Xenophon had interpreted the Ganymede story allegorically as a divine elevation and this seems to be the message of Michelangelo's design. The *Ganymede* is thus linked positively with Michelangelo's contemporary *Resurrection* drawings and negatively with his *Fall of Phaeton*, which was surely a conscious pendant; the dimensions of the two would have been close. It has often been proposed that the *Ganymede* was, rather, a pendant to the *Tityus* and it is true that the two drawings seem to have been executed at the same time. But, the horizontality of the *Tityus* would have made the visual pairing much less effective. It is possible, however, that a subsidiary reason for the creation of the horizontal image was to establish such a pairing retrospectively.

A *Ganymede* in vertical format, with a lower section whose details do not correspond precisely with any of the other known versions, was issued in an unsigned engraving that, as first observed by Price Amerson (1975), is dated 1542 on the tongue of Ganymede's dog (fig. 57). Unlike the engravings after the *Phaeton* and the *Tityus*, it is in reverse, but the technique strongly suggests that it too is by Beatrizet.

Michelangelo Buonarroti

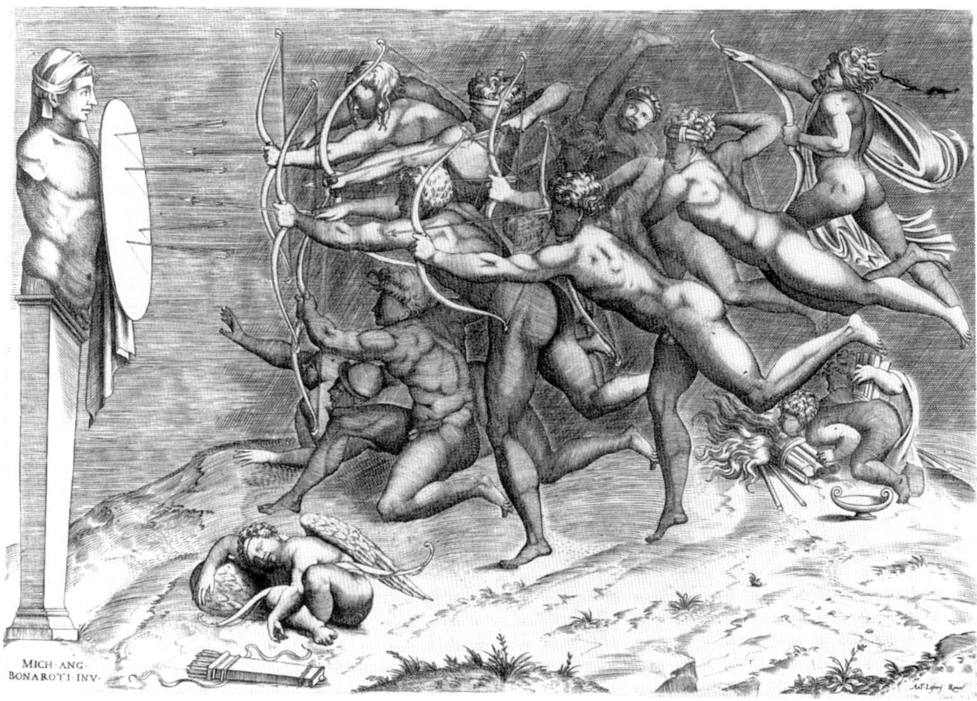

fig. 58. Unidentified Engraver after Nicolas Beatrizet (?) after Michelangelo, *The Archers*, engraving, 23.5 x 34.9 cm. The Royal Collection, Windsor Castle

16
The Archers

c. 1530
red chalk
21.9 x 32.3 (8 5/8 x 12 11/16); watermark: crossbow in circle, close to but not identical with Roberts Crossbow D / Briquet 762
inscribed in ink on verso in two different hands: *andrea quaratesi venne . quj a di/12 . di . ap[r]ile . 1530 edebbe . α. 10 p[er] man[d]/are . asuo . padre . apisa* and *D. Giulio Clovio copia di/Michiel Angel.*
RL 12778

EXHIBITIONS

London 1930, no. 504; Edinburgh 1947, no. 140; London 1950–1951, no. 260; London 1953, no. 90; Amsterdam 1955, no. 217; London 1962, no. 72; London 1972–1973, no. 42; London 1975, no. 127; London 1986, no. 22; Montreal 1992, no. 103

LITERATURE

Berenson 1903 and 1938, no. 1613; Frey 1909–1911, no. 298; Thode 1913, no. 538; Popp 1925–1926, 75; De Tolnay 1948, no. 121; Popham and Wilde 1949, no. 424; Goldscheider 1951, no. 73; Dussler 1959, no. 721; Berti 1965, 456, no. 159; Goldscheider 1966, no. 74; Hartt 1971, no. 362; De Tolnay 1975–1980, 2: no. 336; Wilde 1978, 154; Hirst 1988, 11–113; Perrig 1991, 33–34, 42–43

The verso inscription giving the present drawing to Giulio Clovio is not a signature nor is there any evidence that its writer was, as Popp suggested, a pupil of Clovio's. But whether, as Wilde suggested, it was made a few days before Clovio's death, when an inventory of his collection was taken, or later in the sixteenth century, the inscription demands serious consideration, especially so as "il saggittario di Michelagniolo fatto da D. Giulio" is listed in the inventory. Another inscription in the same hand is found on the *Resurrection* (cat. 38), giving that drawing also to Clovio.

However, quite apart from the evidence provided by the present sheet and cat. 38, there are indications that the inventory of Giulio Clovio is not fully accurate. Cardinal Alessandro Farnese was warned by Bishop Alessandro Rufino in 1577 that the *Farnese Hours* should be removed from Clovio because the aged artist might damage the book, and it seems likely that he suffered from senile dementia in his last years. It may be that the writer of the inscription was a later Farnese employee who, based on his knowledge of the inventory, simply mistook Michelangelo's original for a copy of the *Archers* by Clovio that has since disappeared.

With the exception of Popp and Perrig, no modern critics have credited the ascription of the present drawing to Clovio. Quite apart from the characteristics of the handling, which are entirely compatible with the drawings made by Michelangelo for Tommaso de' Cavalieri in the early 1530s, the other inscription, probably by an assistant of Michelangelo, refers, as Wilde elucidated, to a continuing series of payments made in 1530 by Michelangelo and his brothers, who sent money from besieged Florence to their aged father in Pisa, through the Quaratesi bank. To attribute the drawing to Clovio, one would have to assume that an otherwise blank sheet of paper dated 1530, bearing a private memorandum from Michelangelo's Florentine studio, was some years later passed on to Clovio in Rome—or handed over to him during his Florentine sojourn in the early 1550s—so that he could make a copy of the lost original of a presentation drawing that, coincidentally, was made around 1530.

The recipient of the *Archers* is unknown. It is unlikely that it was executed for Cavalieri even though, like other drawings he owned, it too was engraved, probably by Beatrizet, and this engraving was itself replicated (fig. 58). Apart from the *Cleopatra*, which he was compelled to donate to Cosimo I, Cavalieri seems to have retained all his gifts from Michelangelo until the end of his life. The *Archers* was prob-

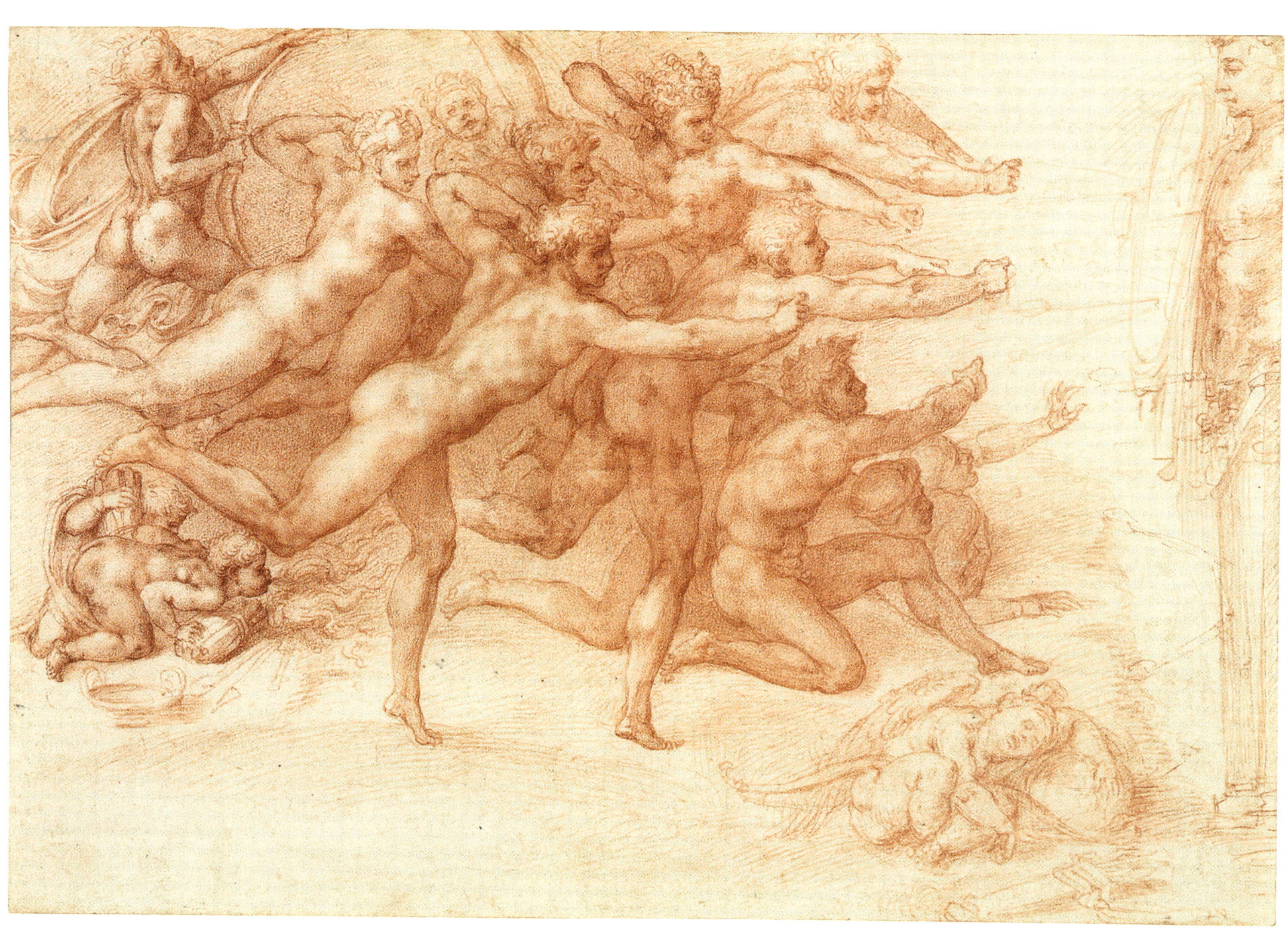

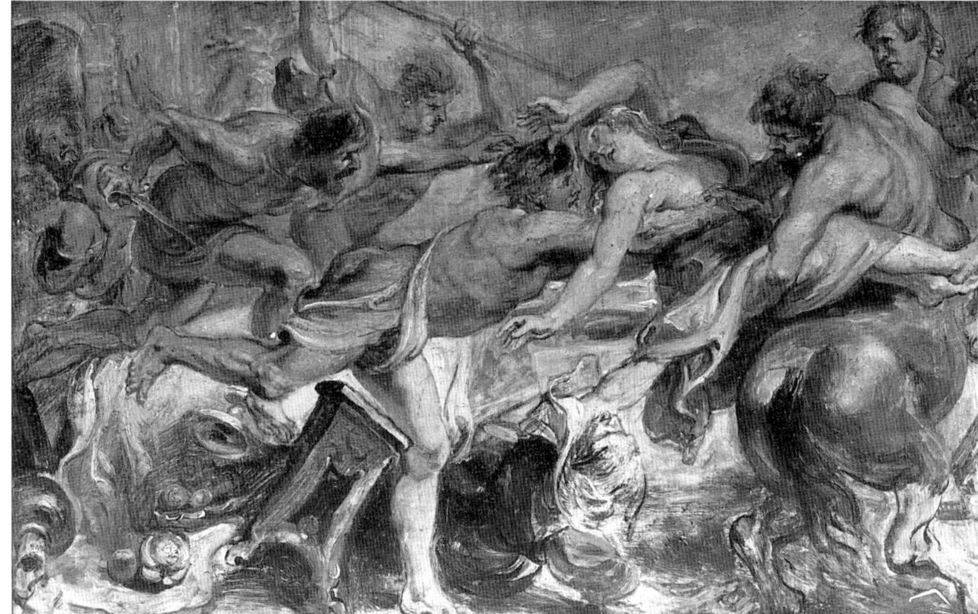

fig. 59. Peter Paul Rubens, *The Rape of Hippodamia*, oil on panel, 25.9 x 40.3 cm. Musées Royaux des Beaux-Arts de Belgique, Brussels

ably in Farnese possession by 1572: this is indicated by a book published that year, Girolamo Ruscelli's *Le imprese illustri con espositioni, et discorsi*, which employs the herm and shield from Michelangelo's drawing to illustrate the impresa of Cardinal Alessandro. The other obvious candidate for the *Archers'* recipient, Andrea Quaratesi, whose name is on the verso, seems to have kept secret Michelangelo's drawn portrait of him, and it would be surprising, had he owned the *Archers*, if he had allowed it to be engraved or ceded it to the Farnese.

The subject is loosely inspired by an antique stucco relief once in the Golden House of Nero, which is known in a copy drawing by Michelangelo's friend, Francisco de Hollanda. But the figures in the relief are standing, not airborne, and the arrangement is not close visually to Michelangelo's drawing: it can have provided no more than a starting point. Interpretation of the drawing is problematic. That none of the archers carry bows may not be a point of meaning but simply a way of disencumbering the composition: it is interesting that in a fresco based on the drawing, probably painted in the mid-1540s and once associated mistakenly with Raphael (Galleria Borghese, Rome), this lack is supplied. The basic message seems to be of aspiration and qualified success: only four of the arrows fired by the archers attain the target, the shield suspended loosely on the herm that has to be hit squarely for the shaft to fix, and not one comes near its center. The archers' erratic aim may be due to lack of guidance from Cupid, who lies curled in slumber at lower right, while they are simultaneously impelled and confused by the fire and smoke blown forward by his mischievous little apprentices at the left. Alternatively, the archers might be a materialization of the dream of the sleeping Cupid, a vision of how badly things proceed without his guidance. The view that the sleeping Cupid represents divine love, while the other two are representatives of earthly passion, seems less likely, given the comic qualities in their posing.

The drawing is not so highly finished as the *Phaeton* (cat. 9a) or the *Bacchanal of Children* (RL 12777 / Popham and Wilde 431). This need not be because it is earlier but may be a device to increase the effect of lightness and elegance. Michelangelo shows an unexpected interest in weightless figures. The central archer, poised on one leg like an ice skater, may have inspired Giambologna's *Mercury*, and it was borrowed again in the 1630s by Rubens, in his *Rape of Hippodamia*, for the Torre de la Parada and now in the Museo del Prado, Madrid. His lively sketch for it is in Brussels (fig. 59). It is significant of their difference of temperament that the effort of Michelangelo's young man is unrewarded, whereas Rubens' figure succeeds in his rescue.

A drawing in the Louvre (Inv. 707 / C. 71) is often claimed as a study for the leftmost figure in the *Archers*, but it seems, rather, to be of circa 1505, perhaps for the *Battle of Cascina*.

Bernardino Cesari after Michelangelo Buonarroti

17
The Archers

c. 1600 (?)
red chalk
25.7 x 37.2 (10 1/8 x 14 5/8); no watermark
inscribed on verso in pen in two different hands, left of center: *M B.C Apn.*; and below: *Copiato da Bernardino Cesari.*
RL 0442

EXHIBITIONS
None

LITERATURE
Thode 1913, see 366; Frey 1909–1911, see no. 298; Popham and Wilde 1949, no. 456; Perrig 1991, 33–34, 42–43

Bernardino Cesari, identified as the author of this copy by the inscription on the verso, was the younger brother and assistant of Giuseppe Cesari, called Il Cavaliere d'Arpino (1568–1640). In 1589 the Cavaliere d'Arpino organized the catafalque for Cardinal Alessandro Farnese, which suggests that the painter had close connections with the Farnese family. Cardinal Alessandro Farnese had inherited Giulio Clovio's collection of drawings in 1578 and had also acquired those owned by Tommaso de' Cavalieri after Tommaso's death in 1587: presumably both Giuseppe and Bernardino were permitted access to Michelangelo's drawings in the Farnese palace. However, it seems unlikely that the present drawing is the work of the seventeen year old, and more likely that Bernardino's activity as a copyist of Michelangelo's drawings took place after Cardinal Alessandro's death, perhaps around 1600. Presumably the brothers continued to enjoy access to the collections in Palazzo Farnese.

As Wilde noted, Giovanni Baglione, writing in 1642, remarked that Bernardino had copied some of the drawings Michelangelo had given to Cavalieri; therefore it seems that they had achieved some renown. Baglione added that Bernardino's copies were indistinguishable from the originals, a claim of a type frequently made for other copyists of Michelangelo drawings such as Dionisio Calvaert and Toussaint Dubreuil, and sometimes taken by modern critics as significant evidence when they wish to eliminate authentic drawings by Michelangelo. However, when examined closely, anecdotes of this kind invariably prove to be either hearsay or boasting or both, and no indication is ever provided of the knowledge or sophistication of the collectors who are supposed to have been fooled. It is very likely that a collector who had studied no original drawings, or very few, by Michelangelo—the position, before the invention of photography, of virtually everyone without access either to the Casa Buonarroti or the Farnese collection—might have taken competent copies for originals, but it is difficult to believe that anyone knowing presentation drawings by Michelangelo in the original would have included this copy among them.

The present drawing is probably among the latest copies to be made after presentation drawings by Michelangelo, for interest in them does not seem to have persisted much after the first decade of the seventeenth century.

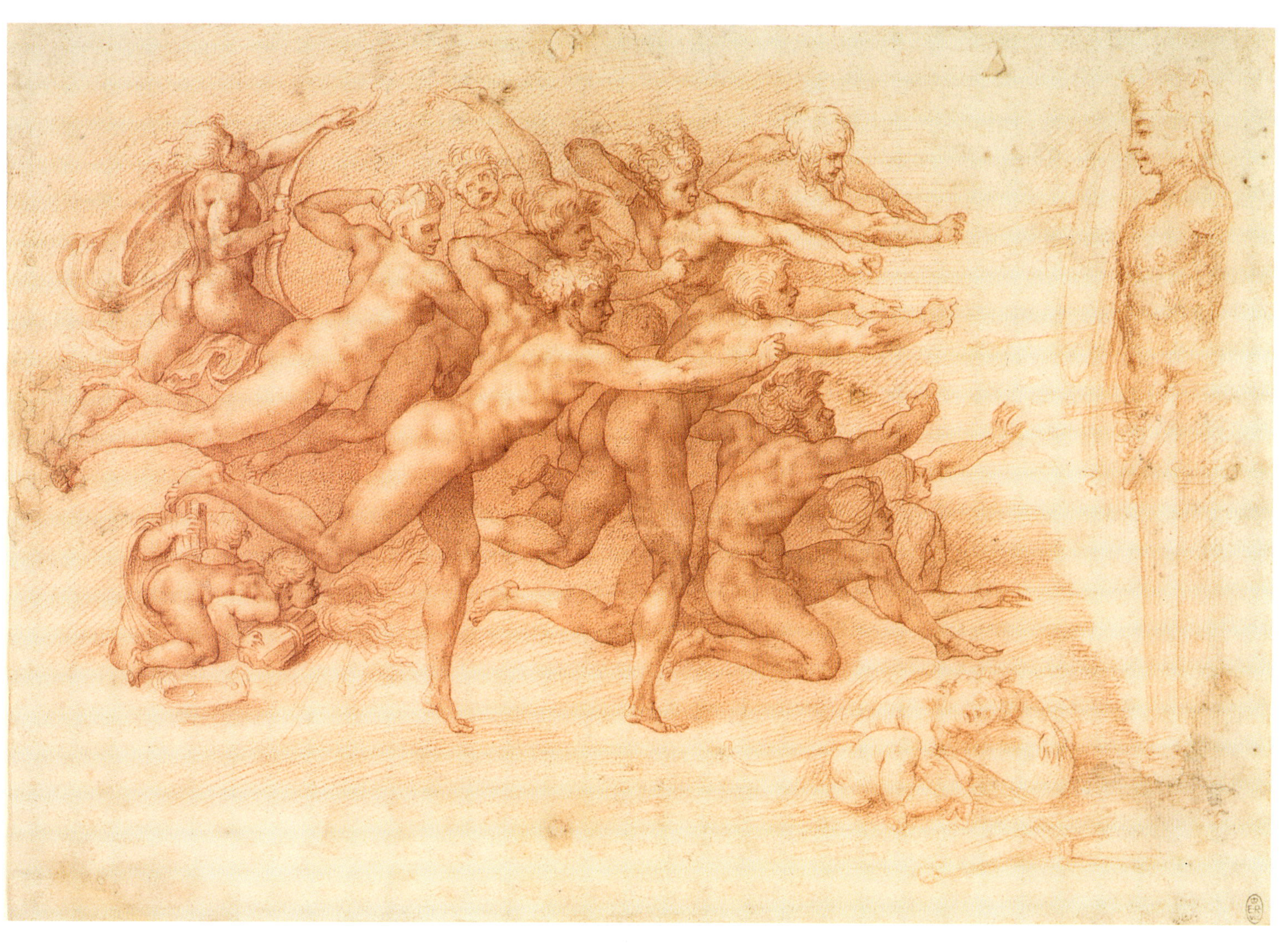

Michelangelo Buonarroti

18
The Three Labors of Hercules

c. 1530
red chalk
27.2 x 42.2 (10 11/16 x 16 5/8); watermark: anchor in circle with star, Roberts Anchor G
inscribed by Michelangelo above the left-hand group: *questo e ilseco[n]do leone ch[e] ercole / am[m]azzo*
RL 12770

EXHIBITIONS

London 1930, no. 510; Edinburgh 1947, no. 144; London 1950–1951, no. 262; London 1953, no. 73; London 1962, no. 69; London 1975, no. 120; Washington-Paris 1988–1989, no. 42

LITERATURE

Berenson 1903 and 1938, no. 1611; Frey 1909–1911, no. 7; Thode 1913, no. 536; De Tolnay 1948, 185; Popham and Wilde 1949, no. 423; Goldscheider 1951, no. 68; Dussler 1959, no. 363a; Berti 1965, 456; Goldscheider 1966, no. 73; De Tolnay 1968a, 206–210; Hartt 1971, no. 360; De Tolnay 1975–1980, 2: no. 335; Hirst 1988, 110–111

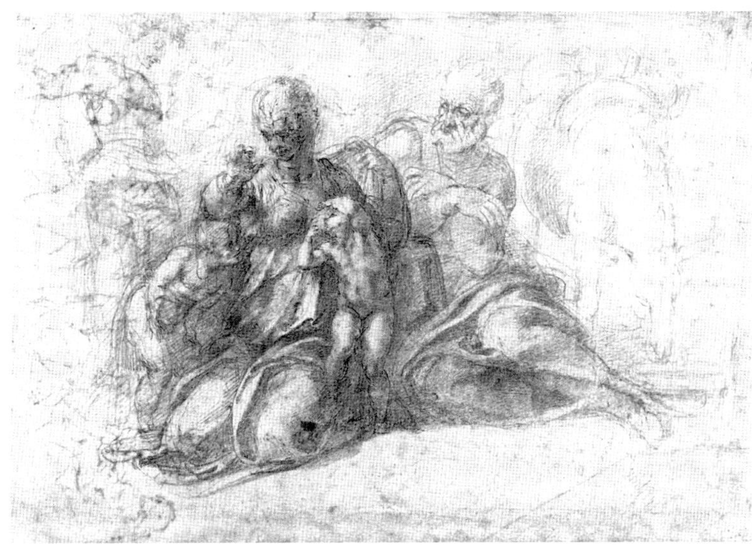

fig. 60. Michelangelo, *The Rest on the Flight into Egypt*, black and red chalk with pen and ink over stylus indentation, 27.9 x 39.1 cm. Collection of the J. Paul Getty Museum, Malibu, California

The episodes shown are, from left to right, the Killing of the Nemean Lion, Hercules Wrestling with Antaeus, and Hercules and the Hydra. Three different types of drawing are on the sheet: the left-hand group is brought to a very high level of finish, with great emphasis on the surface of Hercules' body; the second is in softer focus, corresponding to the group's deeper position in space; the third is broader in treatment, concentrating on form rather than texture. The groups also display, as Wilde noted, "three typical views of the human figure, frontal, profile, and three-quarters profile." These two trios are accompanied by a third: in the first labor Hercules is a young beardless man; in the second he appears somewhat older; in the third he is as traditionally represented, mature and with a heavy beard. The scheme embodies three ages, and it may be permissible to see in this a strand of autobiography: from the easy victories of Michelangelo's youth, through the combats with opponents like Bramante and Raphael in his middle years, to the oppressive struggle with commissions that, around 1530, threatened to strangle him.

Wilde's detailed discussion of the drawing and its sources, both antique and quattrocento, need not be repeated here, but a few additional points may be made. First, the three episodes chosen were, as noted by Hirst, the subjects of three canvases painted by the brothers Pollaiuolo in 1464 for the Medici palace. These are lost, but small replicas of two of them survive in the Uffizi. Thus the drawing must in part reprise Michelangelo's earliest artistic experiences in the Medici palace. It was probably as a beardless young man that Michelangelo had represented Hercules in his own early statue, now lost; it had been sent to France in 1530, which perhaps contributed to reviving his interest in the hero at this time. A further retrospective link is with a pen drawing of *Hercules and the Nemean Lion* in the Louvre (Inv. 687 / c. 12), which, although not by Michelangelo himself (the compiler believes it to be by his associate Piero d'Argenta, plausibly identified by Hirst [1994–1995] as the so-called Master of the Manchester Madonna), closely reflects his style. Finally, Hercules would have been much in Michelangelo's mind in the 1520s and 1530s because the commission for a group of *Hercules and Antaeus* originally awarded him in 1508 had been revived by Clement VII in 1524 but transferred by the pope to Bandinelli, much to Michelangelo's chagrin. Michelangelo regained the block during the republic of 1528 after Bandinelli had worked on it; forced to redesign his group, Michelangelo produced his famous, extraordinary model of *Samson and the Two Philistines.* Bandinelli in turn regained the block after the fall of Florence, and carved his *Hercules and Cacus.* The present drawing may be connected with Michelangelo's thoughts about this problem.

The inscription suggests that the drawing was made for someone not fully familiar with Hercules' labors. It is reminiscent of those on two of the *Phaeton* sketches that Michelangelo made for Cavalieri. Perhaps this too was intended for Michelangelo's young friend, as another moral lesson, stressing the hero's achievements and his courageous struggles.

In the right-hand group the body of the Hydra is seen from behind in sharp foreshortening, and in this respect it links closely with the ass in the drawing of the *Rest on the Flight into Egypt* (fig. 60), which is shown in steep foreshortening from the front. Both the sheets are on a large scale, and the drawings were probably done around the same time.

It is probable that the present drawing was made in Florence. Wilde refers to a pen copy, now lost, which was etched by Metz in 1789 as by Bandinelli, and a Florentine pen drawing of the left-hand group—which also bore an incorrect attribution to Bandinelli—is in the Accademia, Venice (Inv. 187). It is unlikely that Michelangelo and Bandinelli were on speaking terms by 1530, but by no means impossible that Bandinelli could have known of Michelangelo's drawing through some intermediate copy. His pupil, Vincenzo de' Rossi, included a figure derived from the present drawing in a design for a fountain, sold at Christie's, 9 December 1982, lot 23.

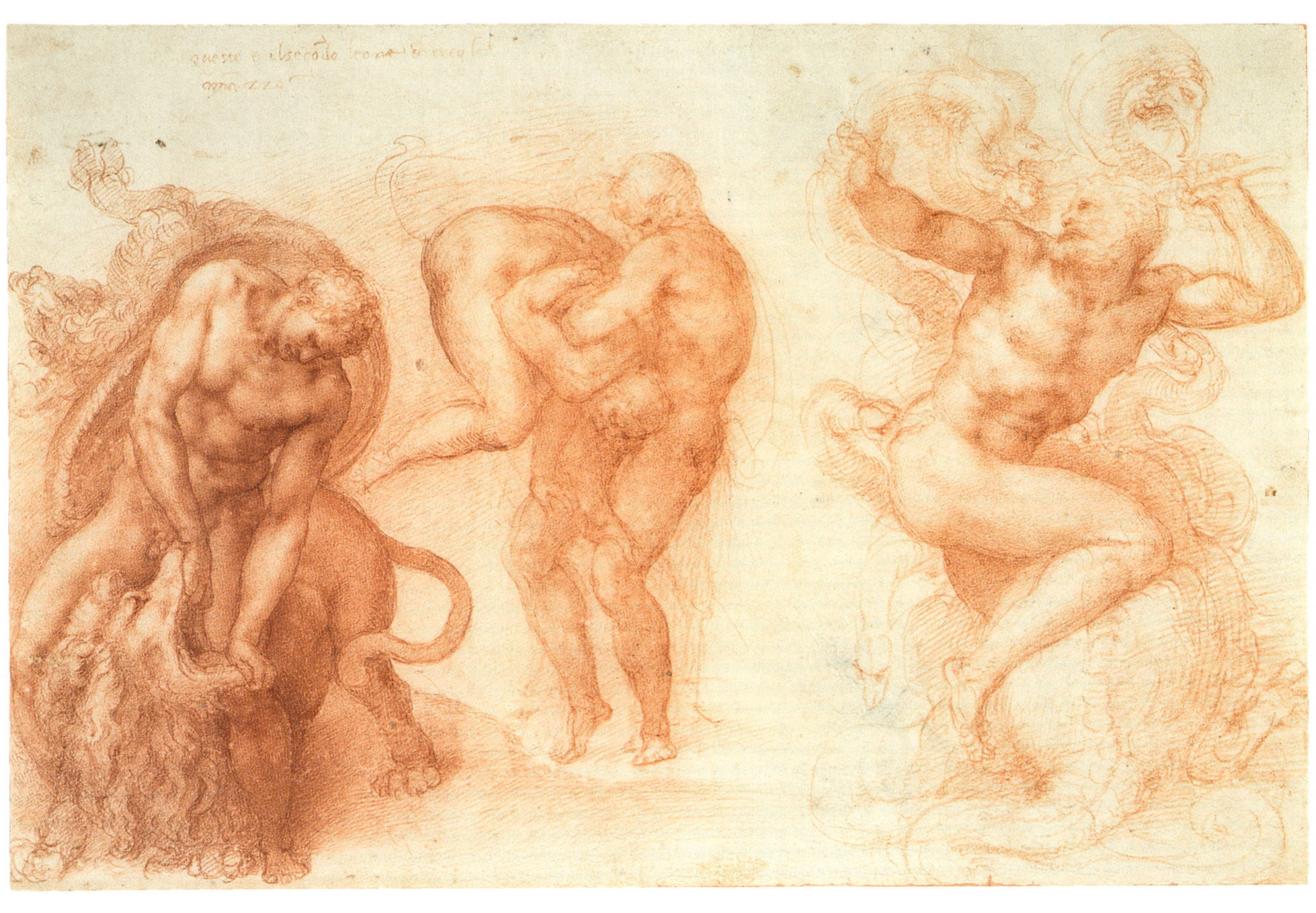

Presentation and Finished Drawings: The Sacred

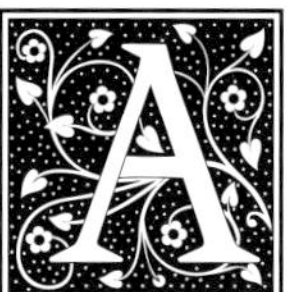

Although not particularly thought of as a designer of Madonna compositions, Michelangelo in fact produced a number of graphic treatments of the subject. Some may have been made for others since Michelangelo seems to have made designs for artist friends from his earliest years. Vasari and Condivi relate that during his first Roman sojourn Michelangelo made a cartoon of the *Stigmatization of Saint Francis* to be executed in fresco in San Pietro in Montorio. It is likely that a still-earlier drawing by Michelangelo inspired his friend Francesco Granacci's *Holy Family*, now in the National Gallery of Ireland, Dublin. It is well known that Michelangelo provided drawings and *modelli* for several major paintings by his friend Sebastiano del Piombo—one for the *Flagellation* in San Pietro in Montorio survives in Giulio Clovio's copy (cat. 34). But Michelangelo also made drawings for lesser paintings by his friend, including a sketch now in the Museum Boymans-van Beuningen, Rotterdam (I. 198 / C. 85), for Sebastiano's *Virgin and Child* of 1525, now in Olomouc in the Czech Republic. Michelangelo's cartoon for a half-length *Madonna* in the Casa Buonarroti (71F / C. 239) may have been made for his long-standing friend Giuliano Bugiardini, to whom Berenson thought of attributing it: although no painting to this design by Bugiardini survives, the facial type of the Virgin is echoed in some of his Madonnas of the 1520s. A finished drawing in the British Museum of a *Virgin, Child, and Saint John* (fig. 61, W. 58 / C. 245) was copied by other artists both in drawing and in painting, and examples of such derivations could be multiplied.

Apart from drawings intended to assist other artists, it is likely that some of Michelangelo's surviving treatments of the *Virgin and Child* were made as presentation drawings, although none have securely been identified as such. The theme of mother and child was one to which Michelangelo continually returned. It was of fundamental importance to him and emerged from the deepest levels of his personality. He had lost his mother when he was six, and his treatments of mother and child themes invariably suggest loss, while simultaneously embodying a yearning for attachment. Together with Raphael—who also lost his mother as a child, but whose less melancholic treatments of the theme suggest that he was not affected in the same way—Michelangelo was the most profound designer of the theme in his period. It is perhaps significant that the drawing, which has good claim to be the latest Michelangelo made, is of a standing *Virgin and Child* elemental in the nudity of the figures and the simplicity of pose (British Museum W. 83 / C. 391). In this drawing Michelangelo recalled a formulation that he had considered employing in 1505, during his work on the tomb of Julius II: the funereal association is appropriate and was surely intentional.

Michelangelo apparently began to make presentation drawings of the Crucifixion only around 1540, when he sent to his friend Vittoria Colonna a drawing of *Christ on the Cross Between Two Mourning Angels*. Christ is still alive: the moment chosen is that of his cry, "Father, Father, why hast thou forsaken me?" (Mark 15:34). This drawing, which Vittoria Colonna realized should be examined through a magnifying glass, is now in the British Museum (W. 67 / C. 411). Another, whose recipient is unknown but which was probably made around the same time, is in the Prince's Gate Collection of the Courtauld Institute (Inv. 423 / C. 410).

As far as is known, Michelangelo did not again produce drawings of the Crucifixion until toward the end of his life. In a series of which six "finished" versions survive, Michelangelo experimented with different interpretations of the scene, and different moments in Christ's Passion. Although it may have been a sculptural project that initially prompted Michelangelo to create this series (see cat. 23), there can be little doubt that they became au-

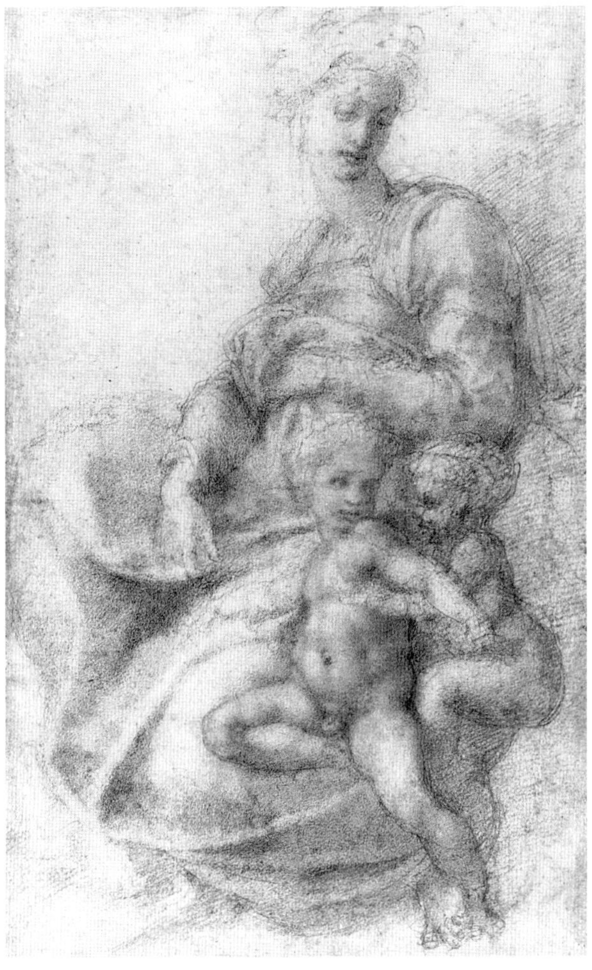

fig. 61. Michelangelo, *The Virgin, Child, and Saint John*, black chalk, 31.4 x 20 cm. British Museum, London, Department of Prints and Drawings

tonomous images. They have the character of private works, and it is likely that they performed for the aged Michelangelo the function of spiritual exercises, images designed to focus his attention on Christ's agony and meditation on death and the dissolution of the body. None of these drawings now remain in Casa Buonarroti, although those that have a Casa Buonarroti provenance were probably obtained by Michelangelo's nephew Leonardo after his death. However, the fact that two of the series are at Windsor, and that another, in the Louvre (Inv. 700 / c. 414), has a Jabach provenance, would also suggest that Michelangelo gave some of the *Crucifixion* drawings away before his death. A further point that corroborates this is that in a drawing of the *Wedding Feast at Cana* by Dionisio Calvaert—which exists in at least three autograph replicas made in the 1590s (the earliest, dated 1591, is in the British Museum 1895.9.15.1014)—the figure of the Virgin is derived directly from the *Crucifixion* drawing by Michelangelo in the Louvre, which proves that that sheet, at least, had some circulation.

Several drawings in this series employ a mixture of media, which is uncommon in Michelangelo's figure drawings and does not occur in his earlier presentation drawings, in which Michelangelo prided himself on his rigor and austerity of technique. In these drawings, which display the same characteristics as those for the Porta Pia, the artist works and reworks the same image, attempting to bring it into focus by the application of wash and white heightening. But now the different layers have become less distinct and the final effect is of indefiniteness and mystery. In such intensely pictorial images Michelangelo approaches the late style of the artist generally regarded as his antithesis, Titian. Both the supreme sculptor and the supreme painter, in the obsessive reworkings that characterize their last images, converge in their portrayal of the evaporation of the physical.

Michelangelo Buonarroti

19
The Virgin, Child, and Saint John

c. 1532
black chalk
31.7 x 21 (12 1/2 x 8 1/4); no watermark
RL 12773

EXHIBITIONS
London 1950–1951, no. 267; London 1953, no. 75; London 1962, no. 74; London 1972–1973, no. 39; London 1975, no. 117; Washington 1987, no. 22

LITERATURE
Berenson 1903 and 1938, no. 2504; Frey 1909–1911, see no. 34; Thode 1913, no. 549; Dussler 1942, 179–181; Palluchini 1944, 82, 180; Popham and Wilde 1949, no. 426; Dussler 1959, no. 719; De Tolnay 1968b, 343–345; De Tolnay 1975–1980, 2: no. 247

Dated by Wilde around 1532, this masterly exercise in modeling in different depths of shadow nevertheless displays a composition that could have been designed twenty years earlier. A *retardataire* quality is common to many, although not all, drawings of the Holy Family and the Virgin and child made around this period; in some cases, there may be a political reason for this. For example, a drawing in the Louvre of circa 1530 (Inv. 692 verso / C. 246 verso) reprises the arrangement of a central group in Fra Bartolommeo's great unfinished altarpiece of 1512, painted for the Sala del Cinquecento in the Palazzo della Signoria, the parliament of Florence's republican government. It may be significant that the earlier republic was recalled at a moment when the current one was beleaguered. It is otherwise difficult to explain why Michelangelo should have designed a variant of a composition by Fra Bartolommeo.

In the present drawing, on the recto of this sheet, reference to the past is more private: the Baptist is shown with his legs crossed, an arrangement that Michelangelo probably employed in his lost *Hercules* of circa 1494; the emphasis on the tufts of the Baptist's goatskin robe is reminiscent of another early work, the *Manchester Madonna*; and the Virgin's drapery recalls that of the *Delphic Sibyl* on the Sistine ceiling. These features and the completeness of the image might suggest that the drawing was made for another artist, perhaps an old friend like Granacci who would have appreciated Michelangelo's loyalty to his earlier work, but no painting following it is known. However, paintings are recorded, by unidentified artists who seem to be Florentines working in the 1530s, after two comparable drawings by Michelangelo. The present group is compact and could have served for sculpture. However, in a first idea, which would have modified its solidity of effect, Michelangelo sketched the head of the Virgin a little higher and turned upward. The angle of the infant Baptist's head has also been changed so that he looks forward rather than up toward Christ. This reinforces the apparent detachment of the figures, all of whom face forward, without overt emotional links. But their psychological separation is counteracted by a series of unifying formal devices, as unconnected words can be linked by meter and rhythm. The outer vertical fold of John's goatskin falls directly into the ridge of the Virgin's drapery; the inner one parallels his front leg and that of the Virgin; the smooth tightening of drapery over the Virgin's left shoulder parallels the angle of the child's body and his raised leg; and the lower part of the composition is tightened by the curving ridge of the Virgin's drapery. The mood is also modified by the lithe movement of child, which is not unlike that of the child in Raphael's *Aldobrandini Madonna*; by the unusual feature of the Virgin's arm placed under his left thigh; and, most obviously, by the affectionate motif of the cheeks touching, while the faces remain averted.

An unremarked feature is the form behind Saint John's cross. It would be customary to find Joseph in some such position and what Michelangelo intended here is unclear.

The verso, a copy in red chalk after an antique bas-relief, is not by Michelangelo and was presumably drawn by a pupil or associate who has so far remained unidentified.

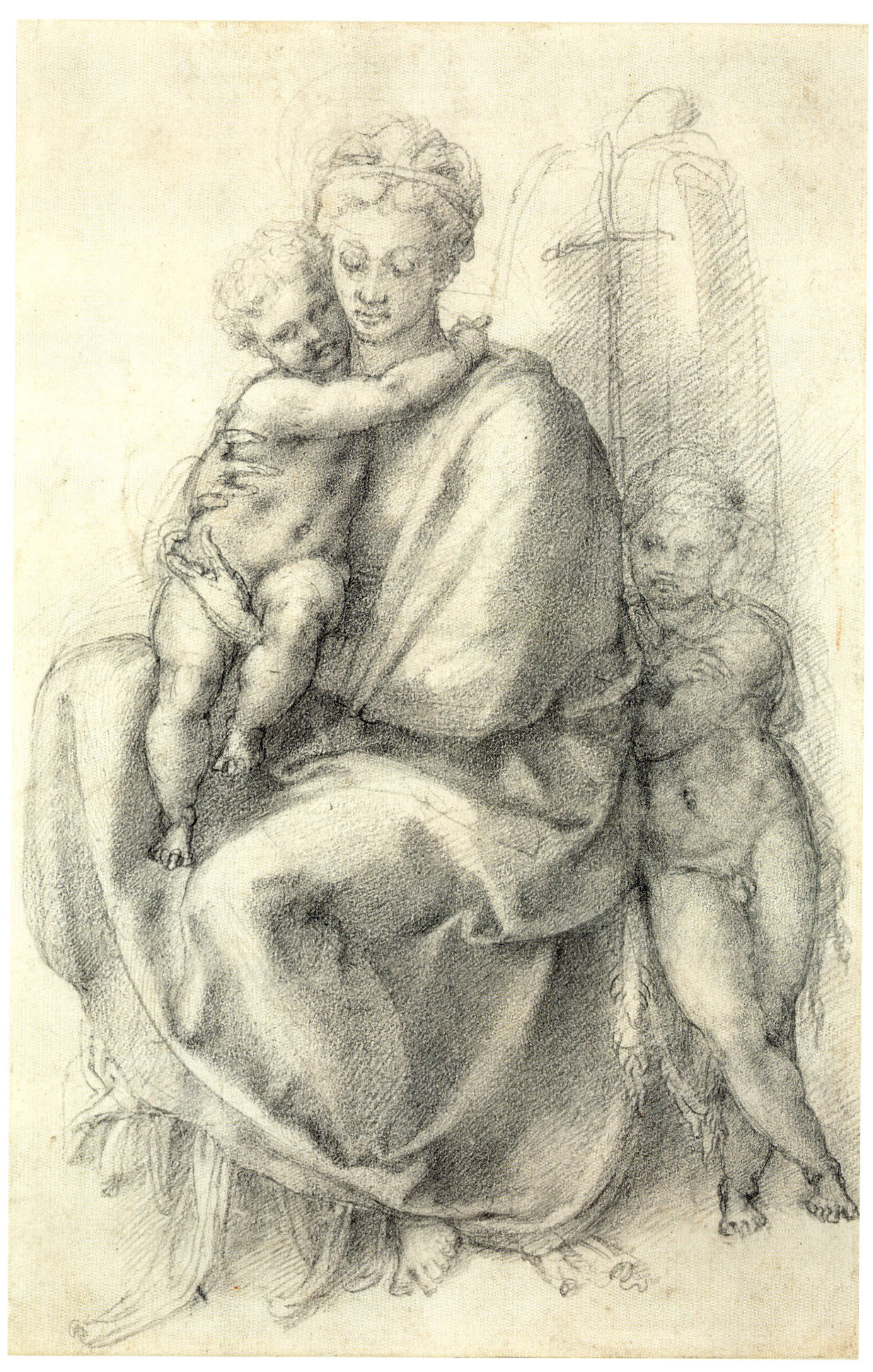

Sebastiano del Piombo

20
A Donor Presented to the Christ Child

c. 1530
black chalk, heightened with white
26.7 x 21.9 (10 1/2 x 8 5/8); no watermark
inscribed on verso: *di Fra Bast.o dl piombo*
RL 4813

EXHIBITIONS
London, Royal Academy 1950, no. 283; London, Queen's Gallery 1972–1973, no. 96; Sydney-Brisbane-Melbourne 1988, no. 19

LITERATURE
Berenson 1938, no. 2505A; Dussler 1942, no. 177; Popham and Wilde 1949, no. 923; Hirst 1981, 138

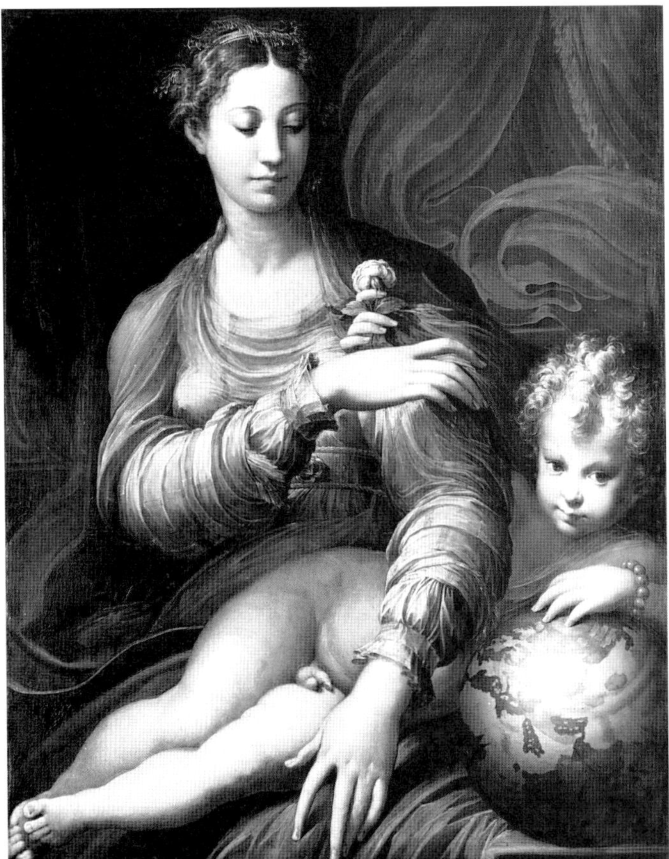

fig. 62. Francesco Parmigianino, *Madonna della Rosa*, oil on panel, 109 x 88.5 cm. Staatliche Kunstsammlungen, Dresden

The drawing on the recto of this sheet cannot be connected with any painting by Sebastiano del Piombo either surviving or known from written sources, and no further drawings for the composition have been identified. The bearded figure kneeling before the Christ child might, as Berenson suggested, be Pope Clement VII, in which case the drawing would be datable after the Sack of Rome in 1527, when Clement, like Julius II before him, grew a penitential beard. The most likely date is 1530, when Sebastiano traveled to Bologna in the pope's entourage, to meet and effect a reconciliation with the emperor, Charles V. Clement, if it is he, is shown presented by Joseph to the Christ child, who holds a celestial orb. This motif is immediately reminiscent of a panel that Francesco Parmigianino painted in Bologna in 1530 or 1531, and that Clement owned, the *Madonna della Rosa* now in Dresden (fig. 62), in which the Christ child, carried in the Virgin's lap, rests his arm upon the orb. Parmigianino's painting presents directly to the spectator a vision comparable to the one that Clement experiences in this drawing.

The energy and power of the forms are very Michelangelesque, as are the complex pose of the Christ child, the expression and gesture of Saint Joseph, and the movement of the Virgin, which echoes the figure that Michelangelo designed (Museum Boymans-van Beuningen, Rotterdam Inv. I. 198 / c. 85) for Sebastiano's *Madonna del Velo* of 1525, now in Olomouc in the Czech Republic. The relation of child and orb is also loosely reminiscent of one of Michelangelo's most famous presentation drawings, his *Dream of Human Life*, of circa 1532, but there is probably no direct connection. However, in his figure drawing—which tends toward a geometrical simplification of physical form, producing somewhat blocklike shapes—Sebastiano simultaneously remains true to his own proclivities and anticipates a direction that Michelangelo's art was to take only in the 1540s. Despite his pleas for Michelangelo's assistance, Sebastiano was never slavishly in thrall to his friend's ideas. Nor is it likely that the present composition is indebted to Michelangelo: Sebastiano had employed a similar arrangement in the late 1510s in the *Borgherini Holy Family* (National Gallery, London) and the motif of a bust-length donor presented, usually by his or her patron saint, to the child was frequent in Venetian painting.

In the lower left-hand corner of the sheet Sebastiano tried a different pose for the child and placed Saint Joseph behind him, supporting him. Thus Sebastiano created a closer link between the donor and the child, and reduced Joseph's commanding presence. He also described in more detail the rocky shelf on which the child is seated and the lower shelf on which the globe is placed. Overall, the iconography is unusual. That the child is not supported by the Virgin; that the pope is introduced to the child by Saint Joseph rather than, as would be expected, by Saint Peter; that the Virgin's role is peripheral and not clearly defined will probably be explained only if the circumstances of the presumed papal commission are defined more closely. Sebastiano tried the Christ child again on the verso.

Another drawing by Sebastiano, in the Metropolitan Museum of Art, New York (1975.89), shows a mystic dialogue between the Christ child holding the orb and the infant Baptist holding a lamb. It seems to be an independent image, however, and related to this sheet only in the motif of the orb.

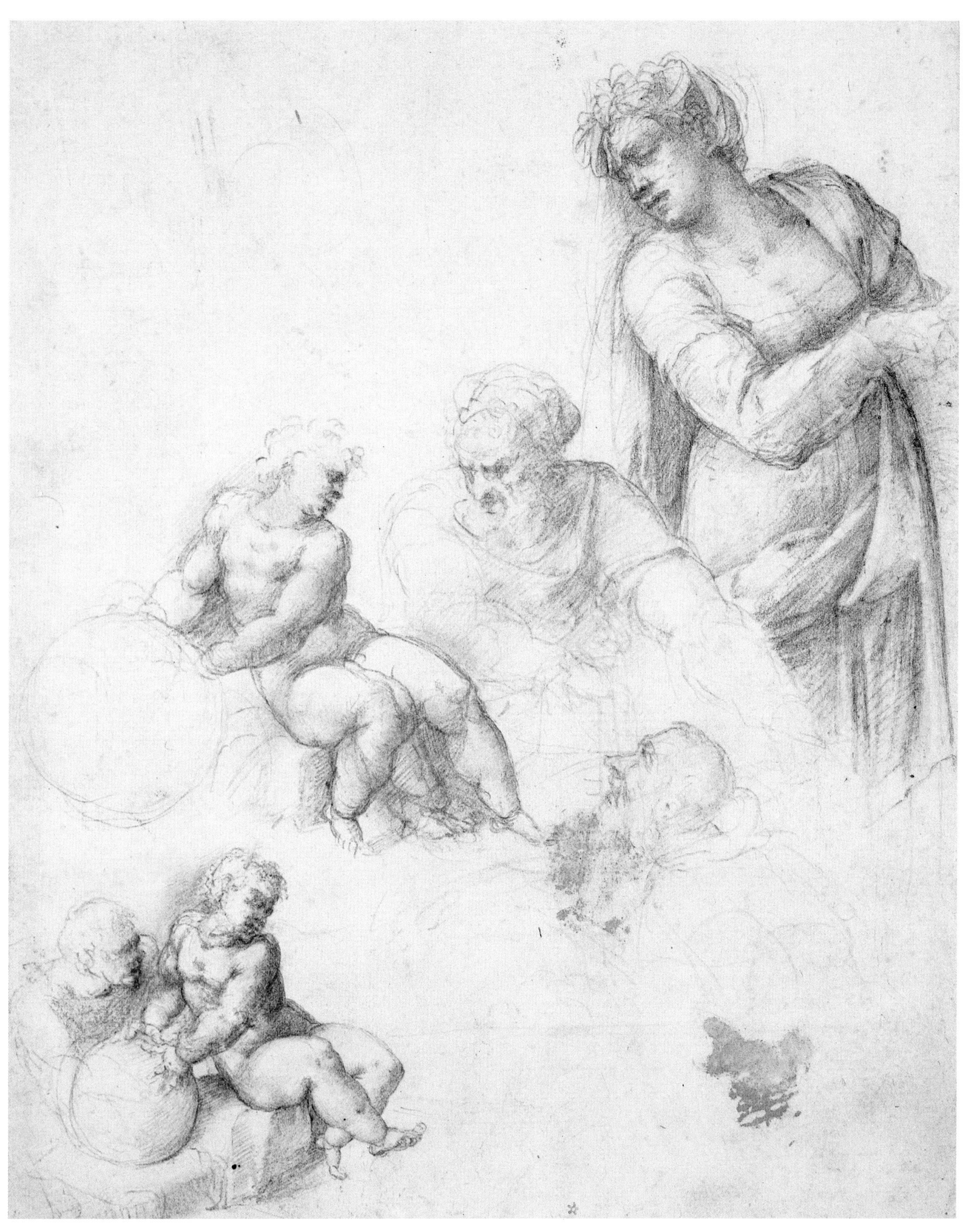

Michelangelo Buonarroti

21
The Virgin and Child

c. 1545
black chalk, over red chalk underdrawing that was largely covered when the group was silhouetted in gold paint, and remains partly obscured following its removal
22.5 x 19.4 (8 7/8 x 7 5/8), a strip 15 mm wide at the right cut from the sheet and then reattached; watermark: Roberts Char A
RL 12772

EXHIBITIONS
London 1950–1951, no. 273; London 1953, no. 96; London 1962, no. 71; London 1972–1973, no. 50; London 1975, no. 143

LITERATURE
Berenson 1903 and 1938, no. 2505; Frey 1909–1911, no. 34/35B; Thode 1913, no. 550; Popham and Wilde 1949, no. 435; Dussler 1959, no. 242; De Tolnay, 1960, no. 237; De Tolnay 1968b, 9; Hartt 1971, no. 439; De Tolnay 1975–1980, 3: no. 390

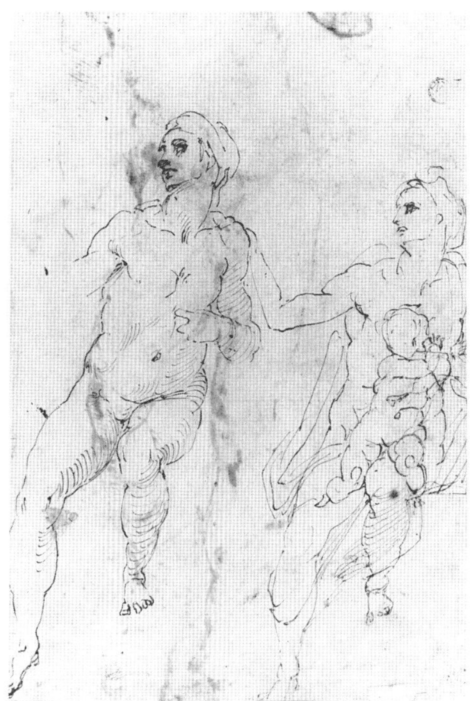

fig. 63. Michelangelo, *The Virgin and Child*, pen and ink, 25.3 x 17.5 cm. Musée du Louvre, Paris, Département des Arts Graphiques [Photo RMN]

Repetition of forms and arrangements, embodying themes central to Michelangelo, can be found through much of his oeuvre, and the arrangement of figures in the present drawing is a notable example of such thematic continuity. First adumbrated in a thumbnail sketch on a sheet in the Uffizi (233F recto / C. 37 recto), developed in larger drawings of circa 1504 in Paris (fig. 63, Inv. 689 verso / C. 23 verso) and Vienna (Sc. R. 152 verso / C. 22 verso), the motif of the Christ child seated astride his mother's lap, facing forward but simultaneously turned round to her breast, was re-used in the Medici chapel *Madonna* in the 1520s and in a drawing in the British Museum in the 1530s (fig. 64, W. 65 / C. 248). It finds its latest known variant here, in this drawing on the recto of the sheet, with the child turning to kiss the Virgin rather than seeking her breast. The arrangement is a poignant formulation of the motifs of attachment and loss: it plays on the facts of the child's inevitable maturation and departure from his mother, his assumption of independence, and his role as Savior. It is the motif of the child's first step, the beginning of the path that will lead to Calvary, registered in the pull of his weight on the Madonna's drapery, which provides the dramatic focus of the Bruges *Madonna*. It was while Michelangelo was contemplating that statue that he produced his first version of the central motif of the present drawing. The motif is rich, for the child is also Everyman, who turns away from his fate toward the Virgin who represents the church that provides universal nourishment and love. And the child represents Everyman in another sense: departure from the mother inevitably foreshadows death, and it is this universal truth that Michelangelo exploits in his sequence of drawings.

As Wilde pointed out, an engraving of a painting after this composition was published in Richard Duppa's *Life of Michelangelo* in 1807. This painting, then in the collection of Richard Cosway, is now lost, but was plausibly attributed to Marcello Venusti. It is not impossible that Michelangelo actually made the drawing for Venusti, but it seems more likely that he made use of an existing design. It is revelatory of its pictorial effect that the drawing itself was also transformed into, in effect, a painting in grisaille. The dark area surrounding the Madonna is the remains of preparation for gold paint that at one time silhouetted the group and that was later removed as a deforming addition. It was certainly an addition but it is likely that the gold was added early to realize the group's potential as a devotional image. The drawing's level of finish and the isolated intensity of its form make it a self-sufficient image of considerable power. But unlike most drawings by Michelangelo that are finished to *modello* or presentation level, it was made on a page on the verso of which Michelangelo had already written a poem. This writing, visible from the recto, does not interfere with the image, but it does affect the field around it. It was probably in part to conceal this writing that the gold was applied, perhaps with Michelangelo's cognizance. The result would have been to elevate the drawing into a displayable image.

The gold might have been applied for yet another reason. Even before severe criticisms of the nudities in the *Last Judgment* modified the direction of Michelangelo's art, he had begun to change direction. His aim was to create a pietistic art that, while it conceded nothing to facility, would communicate a severe, unrelenting, but reassuring spirituality. To achieve this Michelangelo turned to the past, to the art of the dugento and the trecento, and that of the north, which had fascinated him in first youth. This archaism became increasingly insistent as Michelangelo approached the end of his life, and it probably constituted a conscious—and in part self-proclaimed—pro-

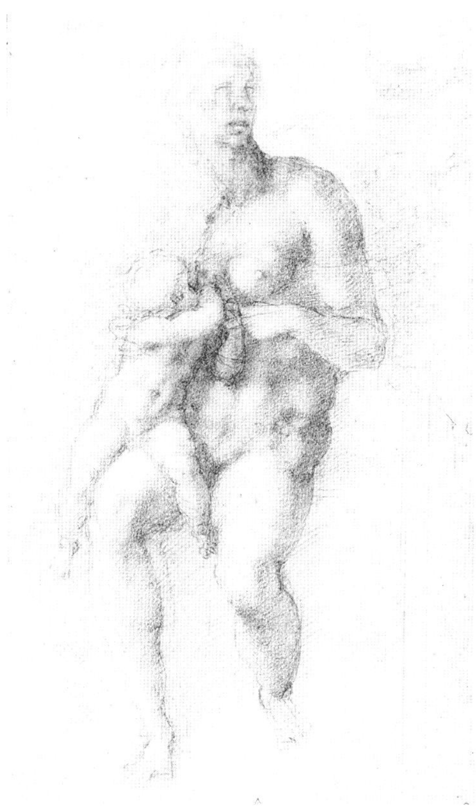

fig. 64. Michelangelo, *The Virgin and Child*, black chalk, 31.7 x 19.1 cm. British Museum, London, Department of Prints and Drawings

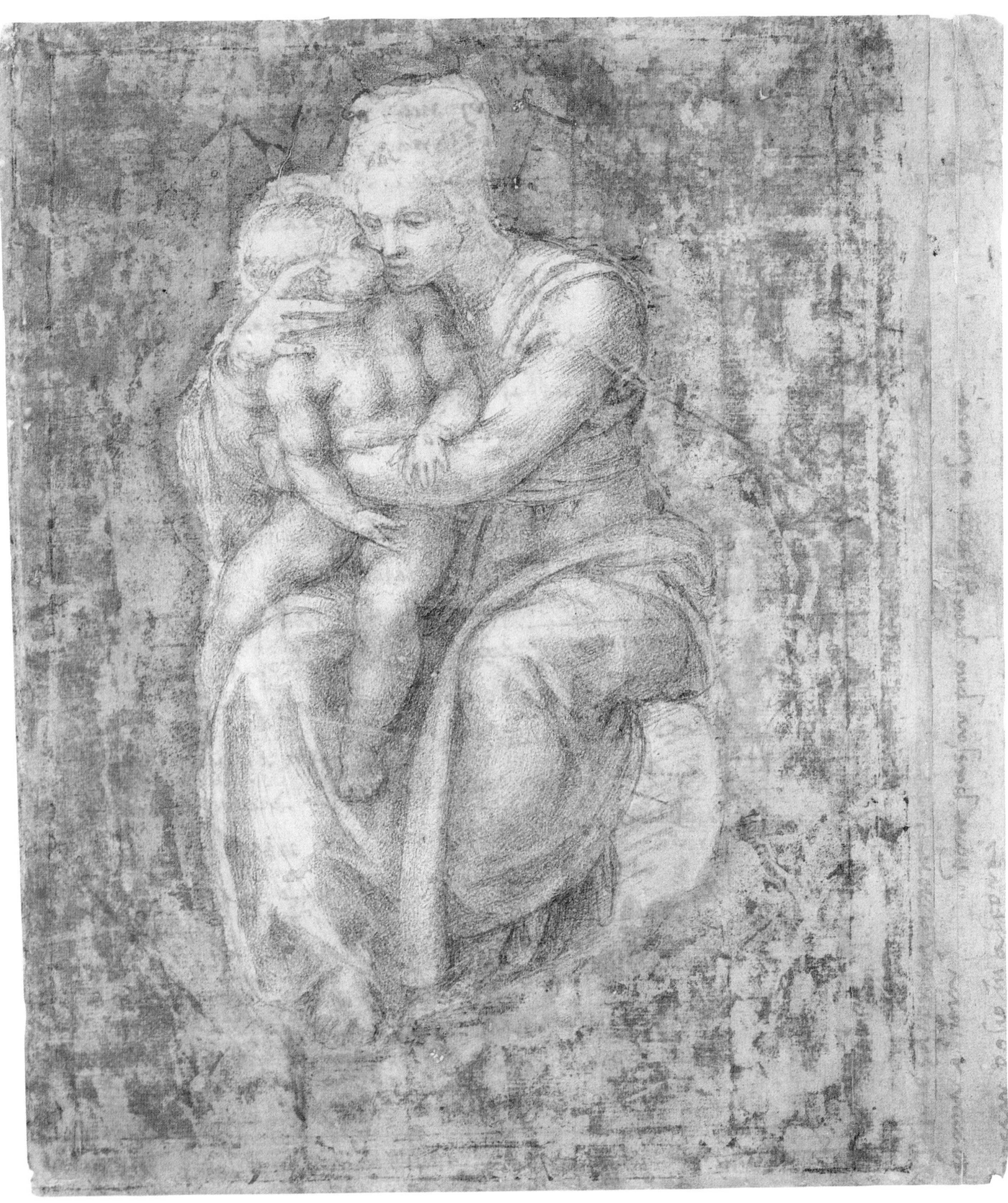

gram. The addition of gold paint to this image of the *Virgin and Child* would have bestowed upon it the air of a modernized trecento painting, a grisaille on gold ground, and the severity and compactness of the form, although not directly Giottesque, would nevertheless have echoed his art. Michelangelo criticized pietism and simplifications, but his pietism and his simplifications were not like those of others.

Drawings such as this, in which figures are brought to a high level of finish while settings are either ignored or merely indicated, are typical of those made by Michelangelo for Marcello Venusti, of which the earliest documented examples are of around 1550, a few years after this drawing was made. This approach was adopted by a number of other artists both within and without Michelangelo's immediate circle. Stony-textured, minutely finished, contextless figures were drawn by Daniele da Volterra, Siciolante da Sermoneta, Bronzino, and others who remain to be identified: this "impersonal" mode presents considerable problems for connoisseurship.

Giulio Clovio

22
The Virgin and Child with Saints John the Evangelist, Anne (?), Joseph, and a Female Saint

c. 1537
gray chalk, the Virgin's halo added in gold paint
28.1 x 21 (11 1/16 x 8 1/4); no watermark
RL 0462

EXHIBITIONS
None

LITERATURE
Popham and Wilde 1949, no. 242; Giononi-Visani and Gamulin 1980, 103–104

The present drawing shows an interesting combination of modes. The main figure group is clearly adapted from a composition by Michelangelo such as that seen in the *Virgin and Child* (cat. 21), although it is unlikely to have been inspired directly by that drawing. The motif of the child seated facing forward, while turning round to the Virgin's breast was (as noted in cat. 21) a persistent theme in Michelangelo's work and one that seems not to have been pursued by any other artist in this form. This Michelangelesque group, however, has been placed within a domestic setting of a type that Michelangelo seems never to have employed for a Virgin and child, although he did indicate a domestic interior in his designs for two Annunciations made for Marcello Venusti around 1550. Here, the group has been placed within a setting that might have been designed by Giulio Romano, who, in a series of paintings executed both before and after Raphael's death, made highly imaginative and expressive use of different types of interior. Obvious examples of this are the small *Hertz Madonna*, in the Galleria Nazionale d'Arte Antica in Rome, and the *Madonna della Gatta* in the Museo Nazionale di Capodimonte, Naples. Perhaps closest of all to the setting of the present drawing is that of an engraving by Marcantonio (fig. 65) of the Holy Family with Saint Anne in an interior that is generally regarded as after Raphael, but that was more probably designed by the young Giulio Romano.

Giulio Clovio, a protégé of Giulio Romano's in the early 1520s, would have met his mentor again in Mantua around 1530, and he may have seen Michelangelo's Medici *Madonna* on his trip south to Rome. Given its strong links with Giulio Romano's work, it may be that the present sheet dates relatively soon after his return to Rome, around the mid-1530s.

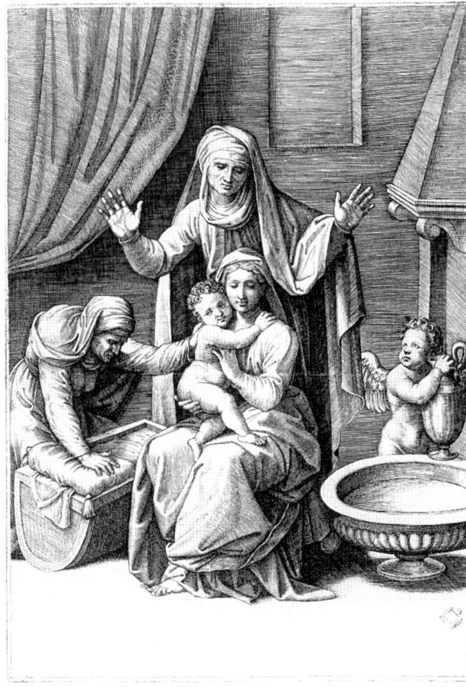

fig. 65. Marcantonio Raimondi after Raphael or Giulio Romano, *The Virgin and Child with Saint Anne and a Holy Woman*, engraving, 24.5 x 17.3 cm. British Museum, London, Department of Prints and Drawings

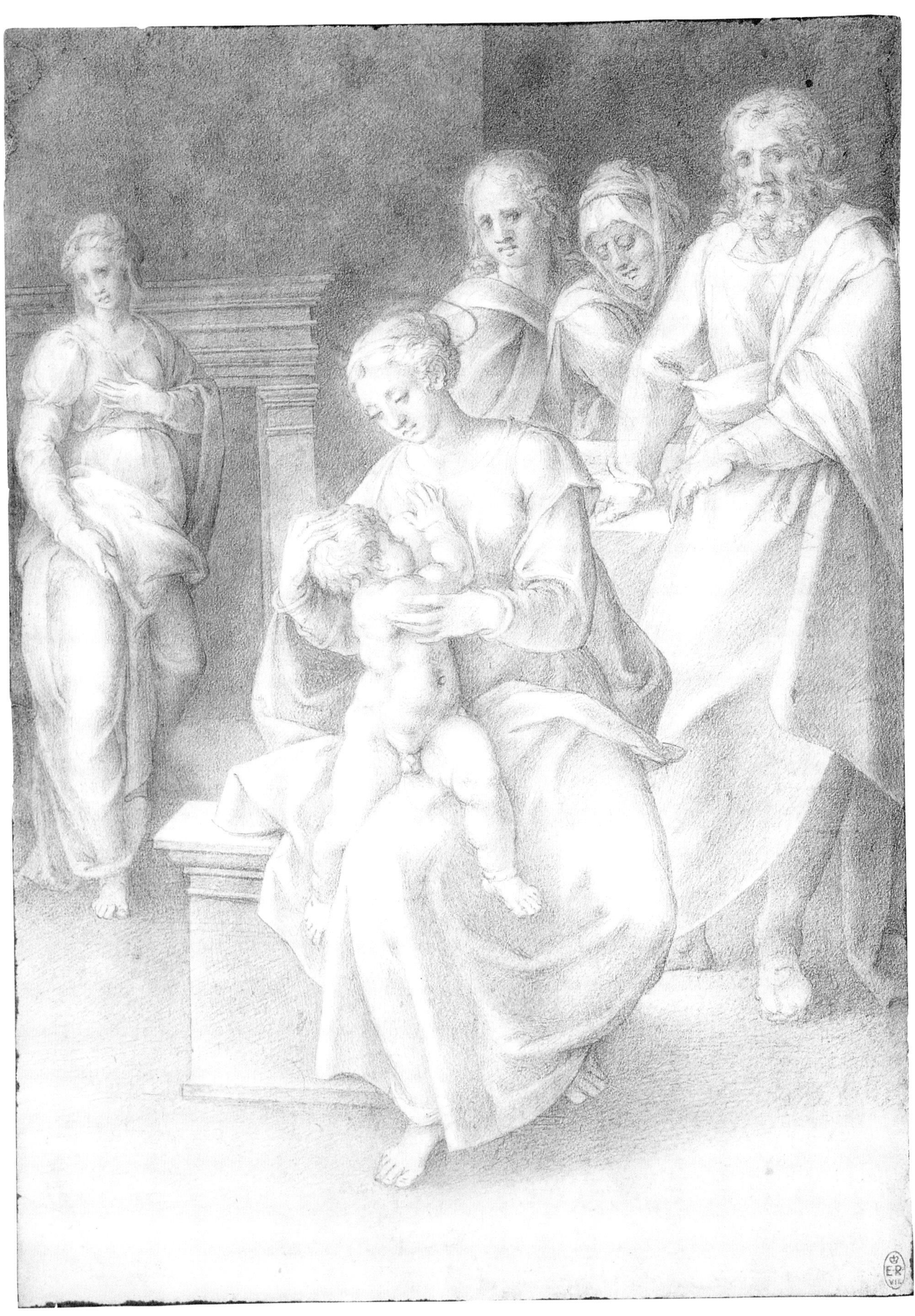

Michelangelo Buonarroti

23
Christ on the Cross with the Virgin, Saint John, and Mary Magdalen

c. 1562
black chalk with traces of white heightening and a touch of red chalk
40.5 x 21.8 (15 15/16 x 8 9/16); watermark: crossed arrows with star, Roberts Arrows B / Briquet 6291
RL 12761

EXHIBITIONS
London 1930, no. 516; London 1950–1951, no. 277; London 1953, no. 101; London 1972–1973, no. 52; London 1975, no. 178; Washington-Paris 1988–1989, no. 59

LITERATURE
Berenson 1903 and 1938, no. 1621; Frey 1909–1911, no. 129; Thode 1913, no. 547; Popham and Wilde 1949, no. 437; Goldscheider 1951, no. 128; Dussler 1959, no. 236; De Tolnay 1960, no. 252, 253; Berti 1965, 481, no. 202; Goldscheider 1966, no. 126; Hartt 1971, no. 425 (recto), 422 (verso); De Tolnay 1965, 97; De Tolnay 1975–1980, 3: no. 416; Hirst 1988, 57–58; Perrig 1991, 94–98

The present drawing, on the recto of the sheet, and *Christ on the Cross* (cat. 24) are two of a series of the Crucifixion by Michelangelo, of which six complete images and several sketches survive. It is universally agreed that they were drawn late in Michelangelo's life, but their datings are uncertain. Most scholars place the series in the mid-1550s but it is the compiler's view that it dates to the last two years of Michelangelo's life and that Michelangelo probably made many more drawings of the subject than now survive. The present sheet provides the most solid evidence of what might have prompted Michelangelo to draw such a series.

Letters of August 1562 from two of his associates in Rome to his nephew Leonardo in Florence reveal that Michelangelo planned to carve a *Crucifix* out of wood and wanted woodworking tools to be sent to him. Thus, as very old artists often return to the interests of their youth, Michelangelo—who had probably not executed wood carvings in the intervening years—reverted to the conception of the *Santo Spirito Crucifix* (fig. 67), which he had carved exactly seventy years earlier in 1492—an extraordinary emotional resurrection. It was probably in preparation for this that Michelangelo whittled the small model, also in Casa Buonarroti, which was reevaluated by De Tolnay in 1965. In 1960 he had been the first to point out that the verso of the present drawing carries a triangular line encompassing the recto figure of Christ, and to suggest that this represented the outline of a block from which the figure was to be carved. De Tolnay thought that the block was to be of marble, but it is much more likely, for practical reasons, that it was to be of wood and that the outline simply indicates the dimensions and shape of another small model, which Michelangelo may or may not have carved.

It seems that the scheme to carve a wooden *Crucifix* proceeded no further. Instead, Michelangelo continued to labor fitfully on the Rondanini *Pietà*, which he had been working on for several years. He was still working on it only a few days before his death on 18 February 1564. But the theme of the Crucifixion haunted him, and Michelangelo's visual ideas pursued the archaizing path that they had followed for some years. When writing about the *Pietà* that Michelangelo had drawn for Vittoria Colonna, probably toward the mid-1540s, Condivi remarked that the Y-shaped cross under which the Virgin was seated was that carried by the Bianchi during the great plague of 1348. This was hardly a fact that Condivi would have known otherwise, and he must have learned of it from Michelangelo. Together with the fact that in the *Pietà* the cross' upright bears a quotation from Dante, it emphasizes that Michelangelo was turning consciously to archaic sources. Once again this marks a return to Michelangelo's youth, for what is generally recognized as his earliest drawing is a copy after Giotto. In the present drawing, the Bianchi cross is used again, and, in the sideway slew of Christ's body on the cross, there is a link—perhaps in this instance coincidental, but surely part of a general intention—with the painfully intense small-scale crucifixes executed in wood and ivory by Giovanni Pisano or a close follower (fig. 66).

The sense of pain is dramatically increased in the present drawing by a very unusual feature: on Christ's visible foot is a patch of red chalk. In an uncharacteristic burst of color, Michelangelo evoked the redemptive flow of blood immediately above the shadowy figure of the Magdalen crouched at the base of the cross.

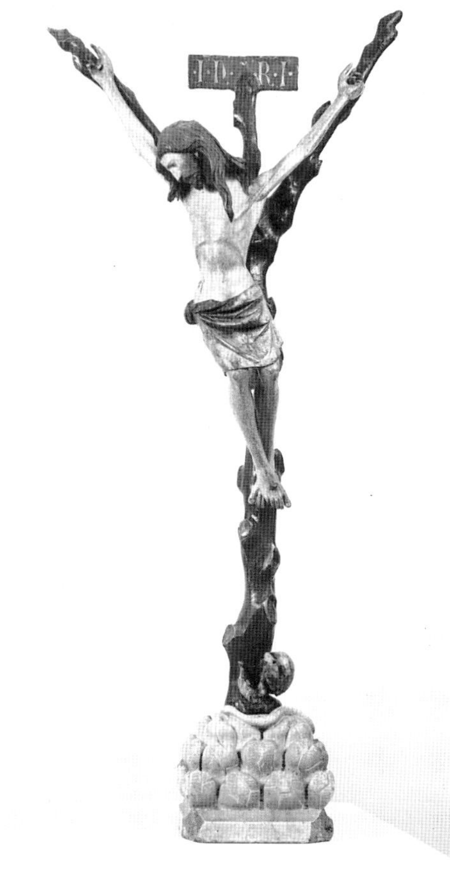

fig. 66. Giovanni Pisano (?), *Crucifix*, wood, height 75 cm. Museo dell'Opera del Duomo, Siena [Soprintendenza B.A.S. Siena su concessione del ministero per i beni culturali e ambientali]

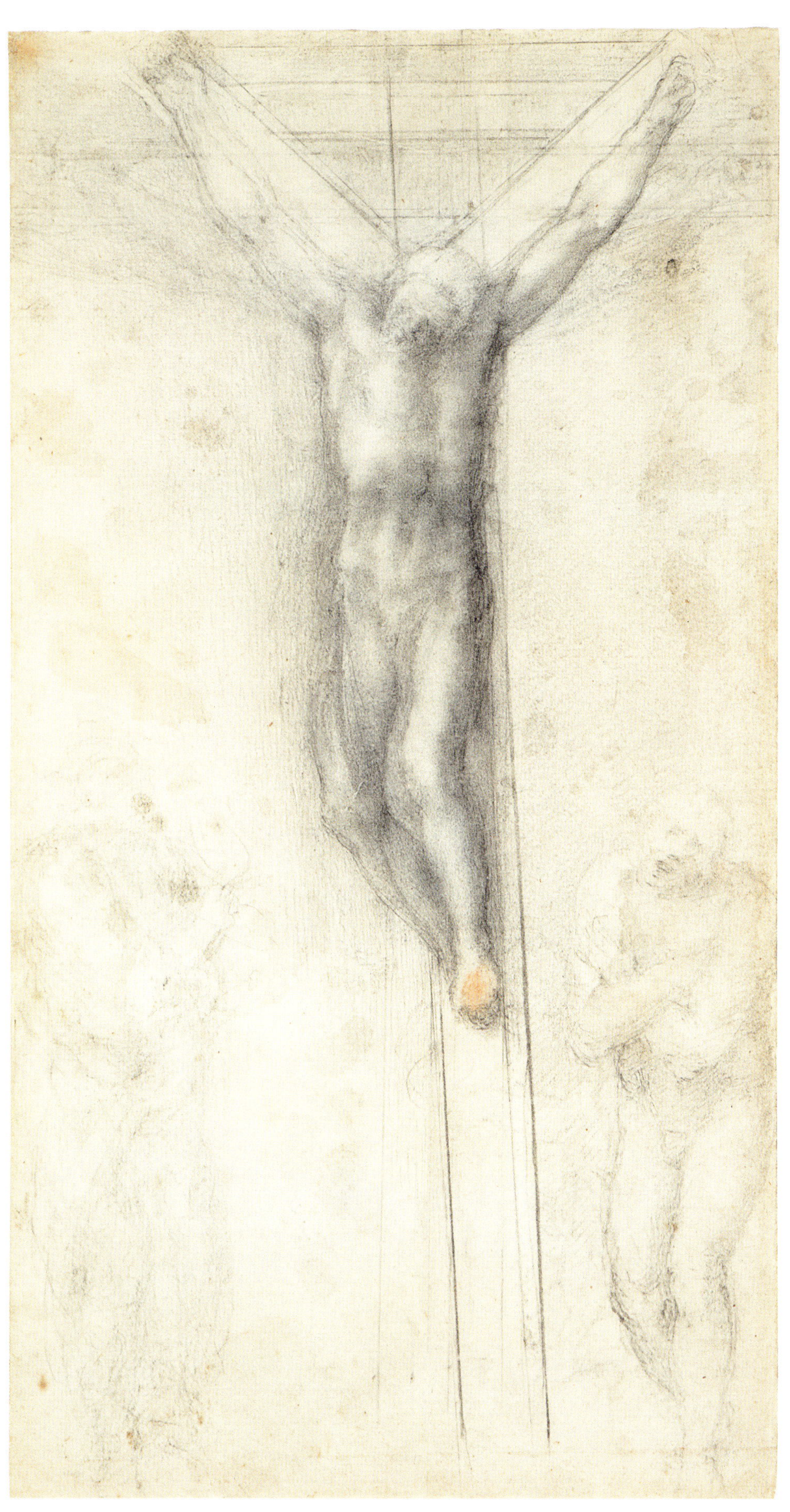

Michelangelo Buonarroti

24
Christ on the Cross between the Virgin and Saint John

c. 1562
black chalk with white heightening
38.2 x 21 (15 1/16 x 8 1/4); no watermark
RL 12775

EXHIBITIONS
Edinburgh 1947, no. 141; London 1950–1951, no. 275; London 1953, no. 99; London 1972–1973, no. 49; London 1975, no. 182; Washington-Paris 1988–1989, no. 58

LITERATURE
Berenson 1903 and 1938, no. 1622; Frey 1909–1911, no. 130; Thode 1913, no. 548; Popham and Wilde 1949, no. 436; Dussler 1959, no. 204; De Tolnay 1960, nos. 250, 254; Berti 1965, 481, no. 199; Hartt 1971, no. 423; De Tolnay 1975–1980, 3: no. 418; Hirst 1988, 58; Perrig 1991, 94–98

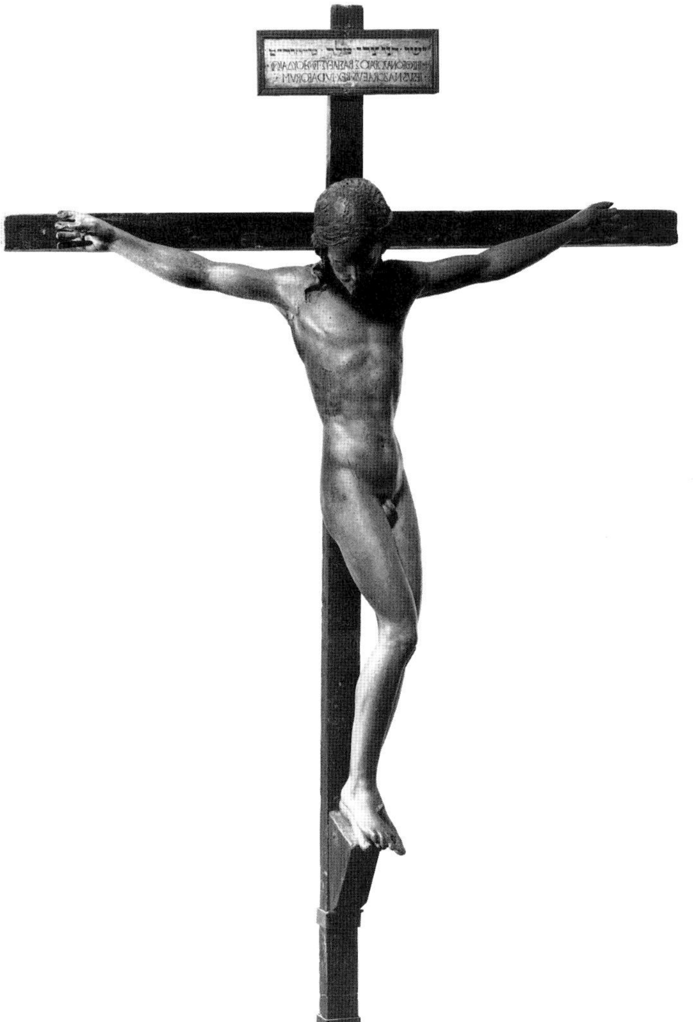

fig. 67. Michelangelo, *The Santo Spirito Crucifix*, pigmented wood, height 135 cm. Casa Buonarroti, Florence

In this drawing Michelangelo showed the head of Christ turned downward both toward the Virgin and toward Saint John in an unresolved *pentimento*. The moment is that in which the dying Christ says to Saint John "Son, this is thy mother" and to the Virgin "Mother, this is thy son" (John 19:26–27). That Christ's head is shown in two positions and that his body is less defined than those of the other figures permits the viewer a freedom of interpretation that, however unintentional, is powerfully evocative.

It was remarked earlier that in his 1562 project to carve a *Crucifix* in wood, Michelangelo was returning to the idea of a work of his earliest youth, the *Crucifix* he had carved for Santo Spirito (fig. 67). A further echo of this early *Crucifix* may be found in the present drawing, in which the movement and slim form of Christ's hips are strongly reminiscent of those of the adolescent Christ that he had carved seventy years before. According to Vasari, Michelangelo had a tenacious memory and never forgot an image that he had produced.

The handling of this drawing and of the others in the series is novel in Michelangelo's work. It must, in part, be a consequence of decreasing muscular control; he stated in a letter to his nephew of 23 December 1563 that he would no longer write letters, but would simply sign them, yet this letter itself is autograph. Here the blurred effect of superimposed media technique was deeply appropriate to the subject. Michelangelo had, even in the Sistine period, occasionally employed wash and white heightening as well as pen and chalk for figure drawings, and he had always done so for *modelli* for architectural-sculptural projects. It had also been a characteristic device of his to employ one medium to correct another. But in his work of the period approaching 1560, which was primarily architectural, he tended to lay forms over forms in a way that risked confusing and blurring them, and then to bring them into focus with wash and liberal applications of white heightening. It is this technique, developed in his architectural practice, which is largely employed in the Crucifixion drawings. The effect is to produce highly pictorial images in which the sharp definition and sharp focus of Michelangelo's earlier work is lost. Coincidentally, in these late Crucifixion drawings, the technique—sketching out an arrangement, drawing over it, reworking it in wash and white heightening—corresponds to the pictorial approach of the aged Titian. Michelangelo seems to have extended this refusal of closure to his last sculpture, the Rondanini *Pietà*. Perhaps the failure to complete, which in earlier life had so tormented him, no longer seemed entirely a negative; the unfinished process of creation had become for him a spiritual journey.

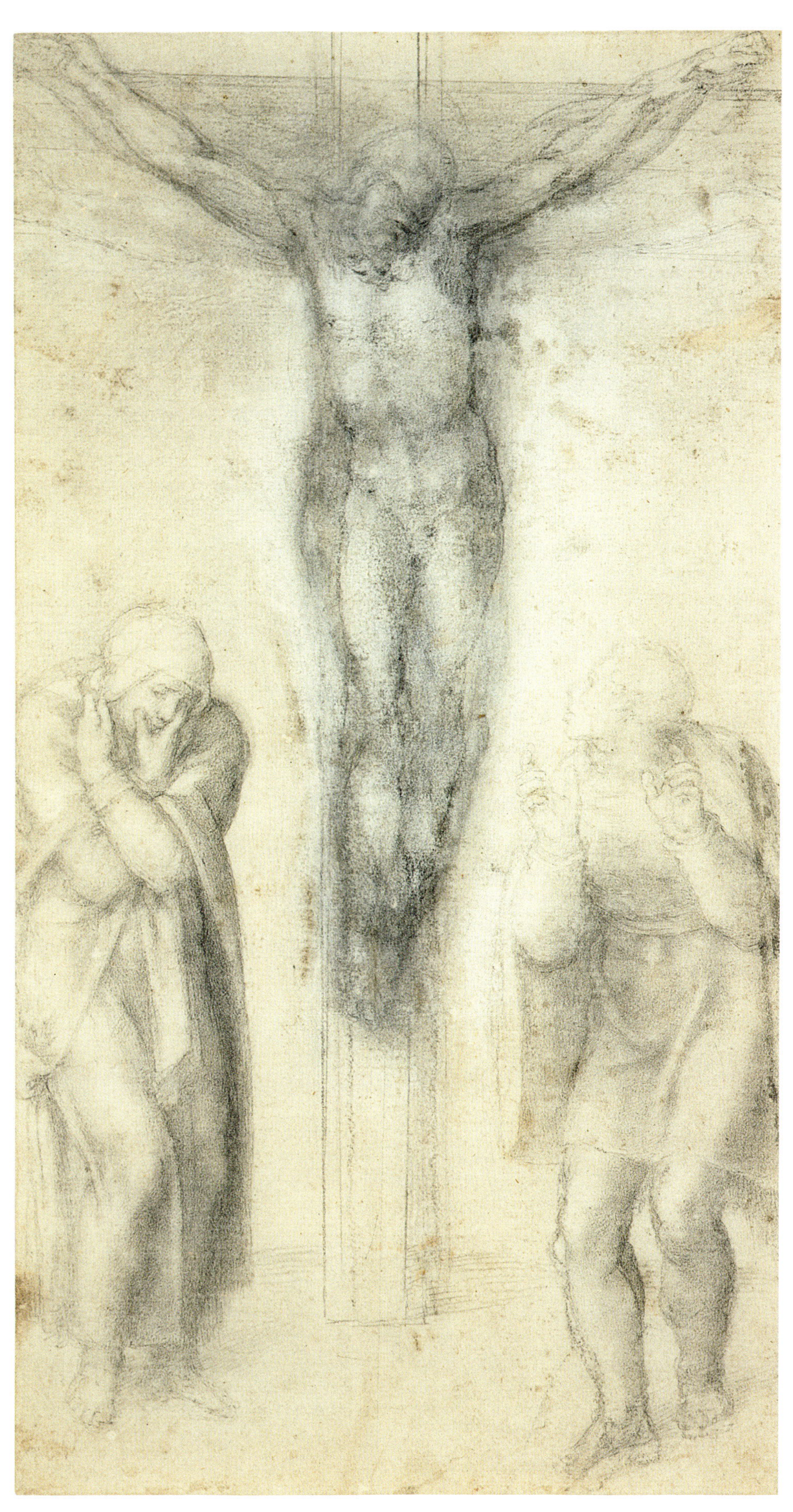

Attributed to Giulio Clovio after Michelangelo Buonarroti

25
Christ on the Cross

c. 1545
black chalk on vellum
24.6 x 12.4 (9 11/16 x 4 7/8)
RL 12774

EXHIBITIONS
None

LITERATURE
Frey 1909–1911, see no. 129; Thode 1913, no. 546; Delacre 1938, 315; Popham and Wilde 1949, no. 460; Dussler 1959, no. 720

Another version of this drawing, identical in every particular but on paper rather than vellum, is in the Louvre (Inv. 739bis); it is probably by the same hand. Both must be facsimiles of a lost drawing by Michelangelo. The type of Christ is similar to that of the Christ in Michelangelo's *Pietà with Two Angels* now in the Isabella Stewart Gardner Museum in Boston (c. 426). That drawing was made for Vittoria Colonna around 1540, which also seems appropriate for the original of the present drawing. The careful, somewhat labored style of this copy—and use of vellum, characteristic of a miniaturist—suggests Giulio Clovio, and this is supported by the tentative handling of the feet and toes, a common feature in Giulio's copies.

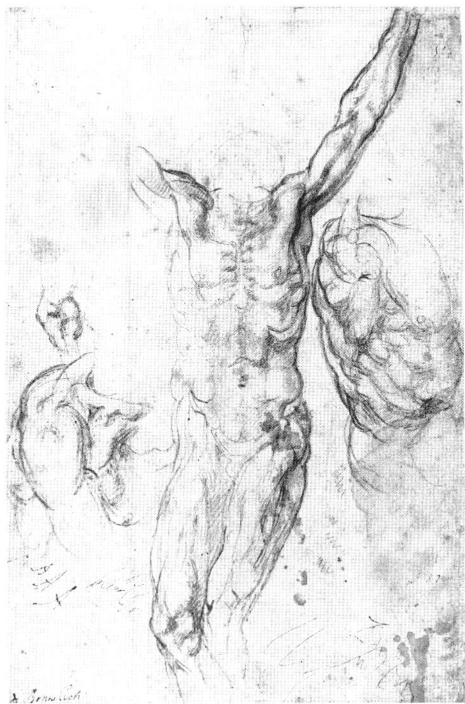

fig. 68. Michelangelo, *Christ on the Cross*, black chalk, 33.1 x 22.9 cm. Teylers Museum, Haarlem

Michelangelo was, in general, attracted to the motif of crossed legs, which frequently recurs in his work, both in upright and reclining figures. It allowed the legs further expressive possibilities and arranged the body in a cone-like form with the ankles as the point, thus drawing the viewer's concentration toward the abdomen, torso, and head. In the present instance he also demonstrated an allegiance to the Gothic motif—more northern European than Italian but rare anywhere—of Christ crucified with his legs crossed at the ankles, an early example of the archaism that was to be so significant a component of his work after 1540. But although the technique of the present drawing suggests that the original it followed was begun, although presumably never finished, as a presentation drawing rather than a sketch for painting or sculpture, its composition connects with a number of other works produced either by Michelangelo or in his orbit, which were probably intended for a sculptural project. Thus the present arrangement is most similar to that of a black chalk drawing in the Teylers Museum, Haarlem (fig. 68, A34 recto / c. 250 recto), clearly of the *Last Judgment* period, which shows, in views both from the front and the side, Christ crucified with his legs, as here, crossed left over right at the ankles. But despite the closeness, Haarlem A34 depicts a more robust Christ, and is more sculptural in emphasis.

It is likely that this was a project that had been underway for some time. A pen drawing in the Louvre (fig. 69, Inv. 10903) in the characteristic left-handed technique of Raffaello da Montelupo also shows the crucified Christ from both the front and the side, but in a pose closer to that of a figure of Christ known in a bronze *Golgotha* group in the Metropolitan Museum and from which separate figures are found elsewhere. The Metropolitan group is generally believed to copy a lost wax model by Michelangelo, and there seems no good reason to doubt this, at least so far as the figures of Christ and the Bad Thief are concerned. Sixteenth-century drawn copies of the model of the latter survive in Haarlem inscribed *il ladrone di Michelangelo* (De Tolnay 1960, no. 332), and in the Fogg Museum (Mongan and Sachs 173), as school of Rosso. However, Raffaello's drawing cannot have been made directly after Michelangelo's model, since the arrangement of the legs differs, and this fact, together with the drawing's style, suggests that it copies a lost pen drawing by Michelangelo himself, made in preparation for the model. It is probable that Haarlem A34 represents a further development of this project, in which the physical attributes of Christ were more fully worked out. The present drawing exemplifies the final utilization of this figure, elongated and dematerialized, in a presentation drawing.

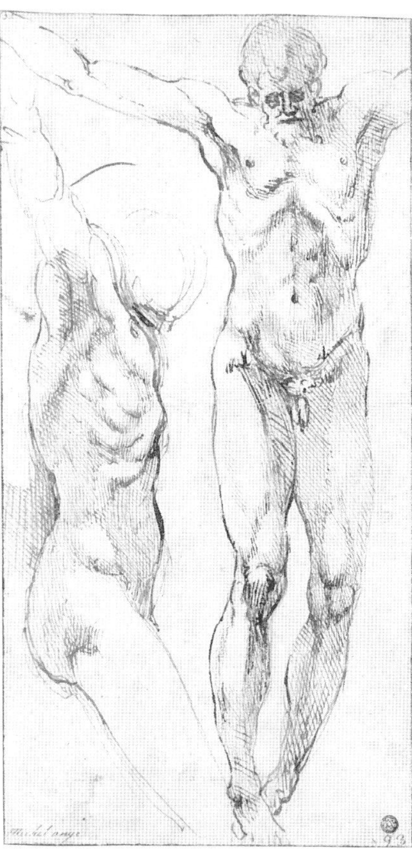

fig. 69. Raffaello da Montelupo after Michelangelo, *Christ Crucified*, pen and ink, 24.4 x 12.3 cm. Musée du Louvre, Paris, Département des Arts Graphiques [Photo RMN]

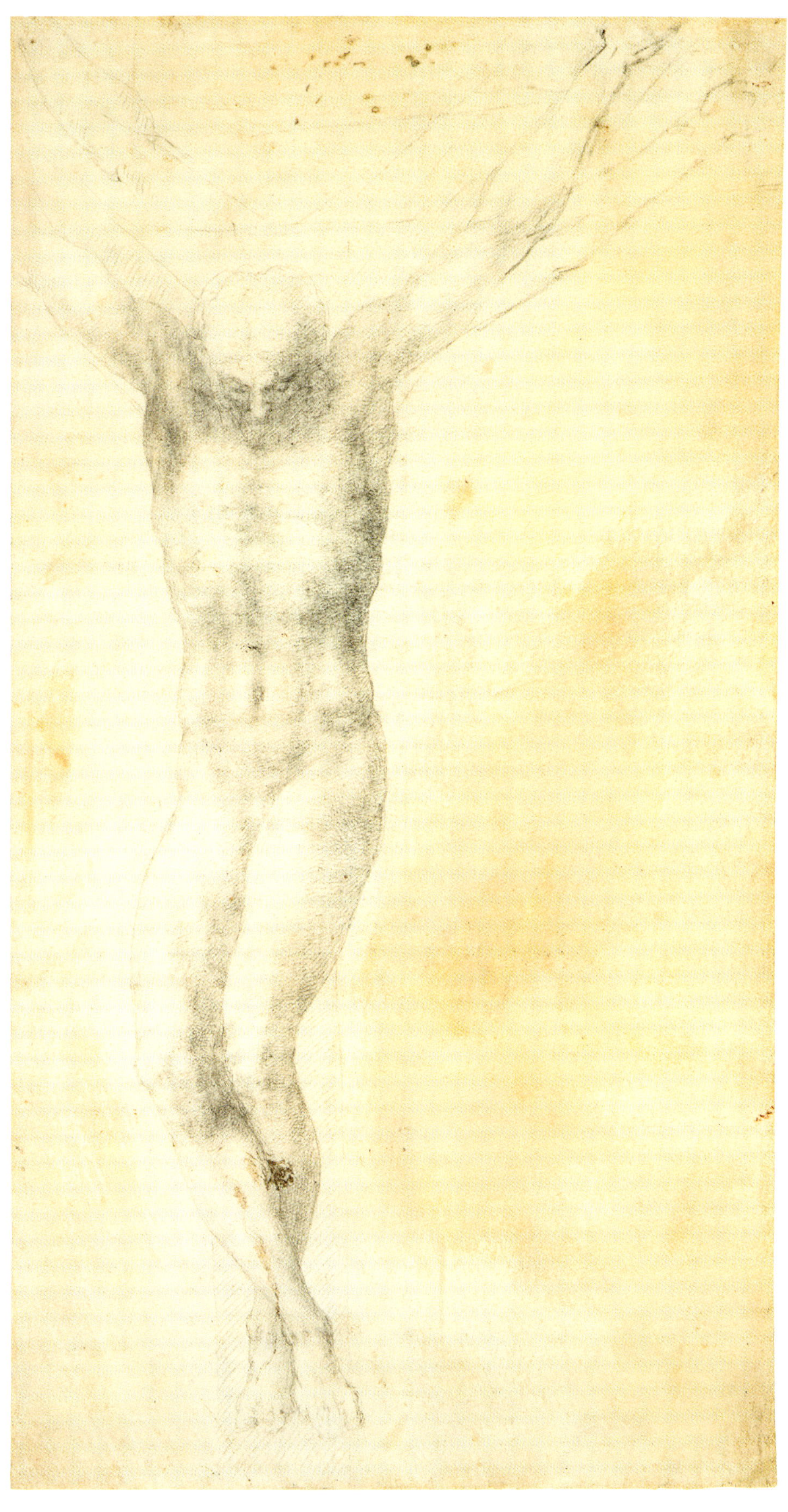

Pen Drawings

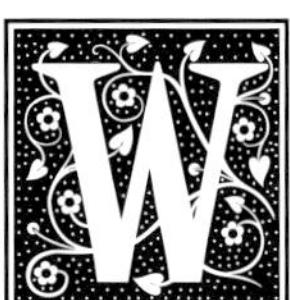

When Michelangelo was growing up, four dominant graphic media were employed in Florence and especially in the workshop of Ghirlandaio. They were charcoal, for loose preparatory sketches of which few survive—although some drawings until recently believed to be in lead-point are in fact in compressed charcoal; metal-point on prepared paper, of which only a couple by Michelangelo are known; multimedia drawings employing pen or chalk, wash and white heightening, which Michelangelo tended to reserve for architectural-sculptural *modelli*; and pen. Pen seems to have been Ghirlandaio's preferred medium, especially for sketches and figure studies. Only a few drawings by Michelangelo survive that can confidently be dated before 1500. All these are in pen. It is not until the period of the preparatory studies for the *Battle of Cascina* that chalk can be found extensively in Michelangelo's work, and while this must be in part due to accident of survival, it is also likely that this is a response to the return to Florence of Leonardo, who seems to have pioneered the use of red and black chalk in Central Italy. Michelangelo's apparent lack of interest in chalk before this time may also in part reflect his dominant preoccupation in the 1490s with sculpture, whose polished surfaces and sharp contours could best be evoked by pen lines.

Ghirlandaio was a master of pen drawing. He employed a vigorous and sharply abbreviated style for figural *concetti*, and closely hatched, carefully worked drawings, both solid and straightforward, for more developed figure studies. But Ghirlandaio was never as interested in volume or plasticity as Michelangelo, and, in consequence, his drawings tend to look slight and weightless when placed beside those of his dynamic pupil. Michelangelo took both of Ghirlandaio's modes much further, and while his drawings frequently reveal graphic tricks derived from his master, he took pen drawing to new heights. Ghirlandaio of course was not the only source. Michelangelo made extraordinarily potent use of pure outline to define form, evoking with exactitude and force the volumes of a body or the contrasting musculatures of a forearm and an upper arm by a system of slight breaks and minute swellings. This method derives from the outline drawing of Antonio Pollaiuolo, but takes it to a level of precision that has not subsequently been equaled. Michelangelo also developed varieties of curved hatching that could bring out the relief modeling of a sculptural form with an open economy in which the solid and wiry are simultaneously evoked. But Michelangelo's best-known, most beautiful, and most brilliant drawings were made in crosshatching, a technique that Ghirlandaio had employed with considerable efficacy, but to which Michelangelo brought new rigor. He employed much tighter meshes of lines than Ghirlandaio, and his registration of varying densities of light and shade to evoke the modeling, say, of a rib cage or leg muscles was of a precision and flexibility that no follower or imitator could match. Michelangelo's method demanded the highest degree of dexterity, for it did not allow error. One or two mistaken pen lines could be covered over, but not more, and any excessive application of ink would cause the form to be lost. Michelangelo's virtuosity in the use of crosshatching was unequaled. There is even a drawing (Hamburger Kunsthalle Inv. 21094 / C. 35), probably made as a demonstration piece, in which he conjured from the page a mouth and chin solely by the use of crosshatching, without any bounding or contour lines. But such a technique was risky and very time consuming, even for an artist who worked as fast and as confidently as Michelangelo. It is dangerous to generalize from what is inevitably an arbitrary survival rate, but it seems that when he began to undertake his first major painting, the *Battle of Cascina*, Michelangelo used chalk and pen in a planned sequence. Soft black chalk was used both for preliminary sketches, to obtain the broad massing that he wanted, and for more richly worked studies of background figures or those that Michelangelo did not intend to place in sharp focus. In some cases, he also used a harder chalk, applied less densely and pictorially, for foreground figures. But it seems that those figures that were to be most prominent or pivotal in his composition were worked up in closely crosshatched pen; the same seems to have been true of drawings made for a roughly contemporary composition of the *Martyrdom of the Ten Thousand*. Although any artist of intelligence employs different media with different objectives in mind, Michelangelo's use of his graphic tools was highly conscious, and it seems that at this stage it was calculated to establish a dialogue between media, in which creative options are continually being reconsidered.

When Michelangelo came to paint the Sistine ceiling, although he seems to have begun by using techniques developed for *Cascina*, he gradually reduced the roles both of pen and black chalk to certain specific tasks: thumbnail preparatory sketches tended to be made in pen; broad layout studies for figures, and one magnificent portrait head, in black chalk. But in the developed figure studies made for the second half of the ceiling, the roles previously performed both by black chalk and pen are taken over by red chalk.

At the end of his work on the ceiling, Michelangelo reverted for a while to his earlier method of pen crosshatching. His study for the *Risen Christ* in Santa Maria sopra Minerva, probably of 1514 (private collection / C. 94), is very close in technique to studies made ten years earlier. But increasingly chalk, usually red in the 1510s but returning to black in the 1520s, came to be used even for studies for sculpture, with pen being reduced to an adjunct role. He employed pen for some anatomies in the second decade, and, in the third, for some quasi-anatomical drawings in which he wished to lay out the underlying musculature of his Medici chapel figures with the most vigorous and jabbing strokes, as though assaulting the paper (for example, Casa Buonarroti 44F / C. 299). He made some drawings in pen as demonstrations of virtuosity, and in these, he tended to create somewhat more caricatural and grotesque types than in the past. His crosshatching becomes less precisely evocative, coarser, and more dramatic. His studies in pen tend to employ line work in a way that calls attention to itself, and that seems more about the expressive virtuosity of the draftsman than the apparent requirements of the subject. But this energetic spasm of the 1520s marked the effective end of Michelangelo's work as a draftsman in pen, and while the instrument was probably never abandoned entirely for drawing, very few pen studies of any consequence survive for the last thirty years of Michelangelo's life.

Although copies demonstrate that Michelangelo's early pen drawings gained some renown, the models they proposed were very difficult ones. Raphael, the most intelligent and ambitious of Michelangelo's contemporaries, attempted some pen drawings in a Michelangelesque vein, but the manner did not come very naturally to him and he did not persist with it. It was the broader and coarser pen studies of the later teens and the twenties that offered the most imitable models. These were employed particularly by Bandinelli in Florence, who produced an enormous number of drawings in crosshatched pen, some of which were certainly made for sale. His technique tended to inflate and simplify physical form and to produce smooth, bland surfaces where Michelangelo concentrated on what might be called nodes of expression. Bandinelli's pen drawings are highly efficient but frequently seem mechanical. Some exist in several versions, and the difference between prime originals and autograph copies and between autograph copies and copies by others is not always obvious. Bandinelli's drawings have little of the textural subtlety that characterizes Michelangelo's earlier pen drawings, and they tend to miss the energy and vitality that imbue his later ones. But Bandinelli's manner was extremely influential and his drawings, and copies of them, were both better known and circulated more widely than those of Michelangelo. It is clear, for example, that Bandinelli's drawings had a greater influence upon Passarotti than those of Michelangelo. It was not until the Carracci and Rubens that crosshatched and outline pen drawing regained something of the constructive energy of Michelangelo. How much of that was due to direct knowledge of the master's work in pen is difficult to elucidate.

Michelangelo Buonarroti

26
Anatomical Studies

c. 1520
pen and ink
28.3 x 19 (11 1/8 x 7 1/2); no watermark
inscribed in pen at the top right of the recto: *no.39* and *36*; on the verso: *di Michel Angelo bona Roti*
RL 0474

EXHIBITIONS
London 1975, no. 83; Washington-Paris 1988–1989, no. 27

LITERATURE
Popham and Wilde 1949, no. 442; Dussler 1959, no. 708; Blunt 1971, 100; De Tolnay 1975–1980, 1: no. 106; Hirst 1988, 14

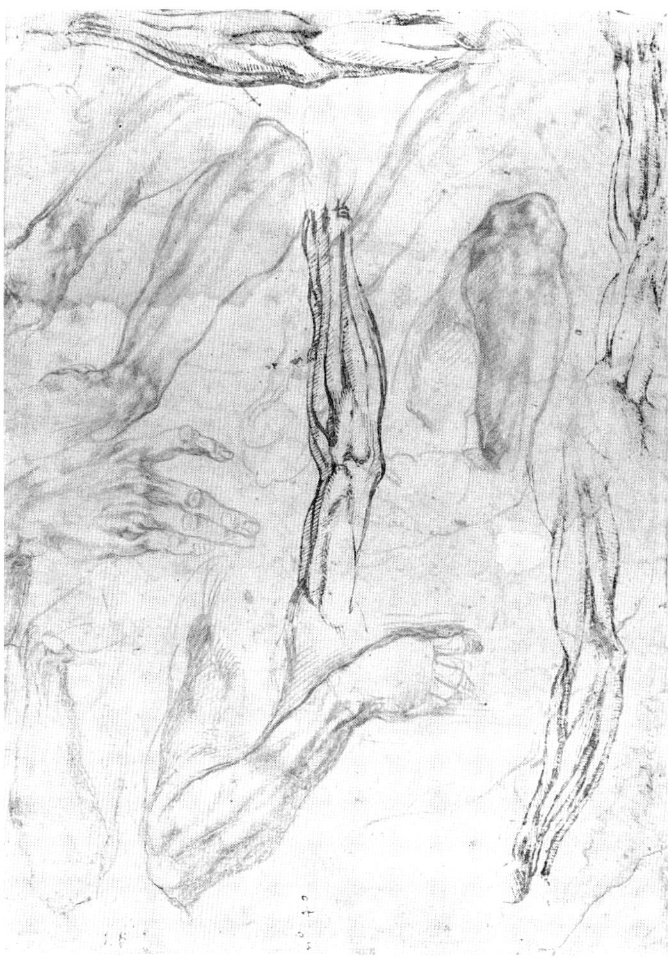

fig. 70. Michelangelo, *Anatomy Study for the Dying Slave*, red chalk and pen and ink, 28.5 x 25.7 cm. Teylers Museum, Haarlem

Two sheets of anatomical studies in pen (cats. 26, 27) were attributed to Michelangelo's studio in Popham and Wilde's catalogue. Reportedly, Popham opposed Wilde, who wished to accept both, and they were reinstated as by Michelangelo only in Blunt's supplement. Both are similar in style to another sheet of anatomical studies in Haarlem (fig. 70, A. 28 recto / C. 108 recto), but that was made in preparation for the statue of the *Dying Slave*, whereas the present drawings, which are a little freer and which probably date to the later 1510s, cannot be linked with a specific project. Anatomical studies of different sorts, examining different levels of the human body, were obviously central to Michelangelo's work. He must have made many of them, although few survive.

The present drawings are included here primarily to demonstrate Michelangelo's pen technique. But in his anatomical drawings Michelangelo's style is more diagrammatic than in his usual pen studies. The present drawings are concerned with structure, not surface, and make no attempt to convey light and shade. Nor do they attempt to evoke form, as Michelangelo so brilliantly could, by stressed outlines and broken contours. They are strictly practical, slightly dry, end-directed drawings, and in them we can see clearly the strength and single-mindedness of the artist's endeavor. They are designed to reveal mechanical functions of the sinews and tendons of the legs. In this they compare interestingly with those anatomical drawings in red chalk in which Michelangelo is more concerned with surface appearance. The pen drawings lay out the substructure of bones and tendons, whereas the red-chalk drawings represent the subcutaneous musculature. It is in the latter that subtleties of emotional expression begin to be defined. In these studies Michelangelo seems to be attempting, probably with sculpture in mind, to stress the broad plates of the musculature and the hard protrusion of the ribs. The effect is as though the torso becomes a cuirass, and the legs and buttocks tensile support.

Like the two anatomical drawings in red chalk (see cats. 41, 42), the present drawing was made from a single model, probably in wax or clay. This is most obvious in the present drawing in the treatment of the back, which is a more analytical, simplified version of that in cat. 42. The side view connects rather less clearly with cat. 41, and one would have expected a greater emphasis on the upward stretching movement, which Michelangelo here seems consciously to have diminished. Although, as remarked elsewhere, no figure precisely identifiable with this model appears in Michelangelo's work, echoes of it are to be found. Thus the way that the back is sketched here is reminiscent of the back of the devil seen from the rear in the lower center of the *Last Judgment*.

The technique of the present drawing compares closely with the analytical study of the abdomen of a seated figure probably made in preparation for one of the dukes in the Medici chapel (Casa Buonarroti 10F / C. 224), but that is probably a few years later.

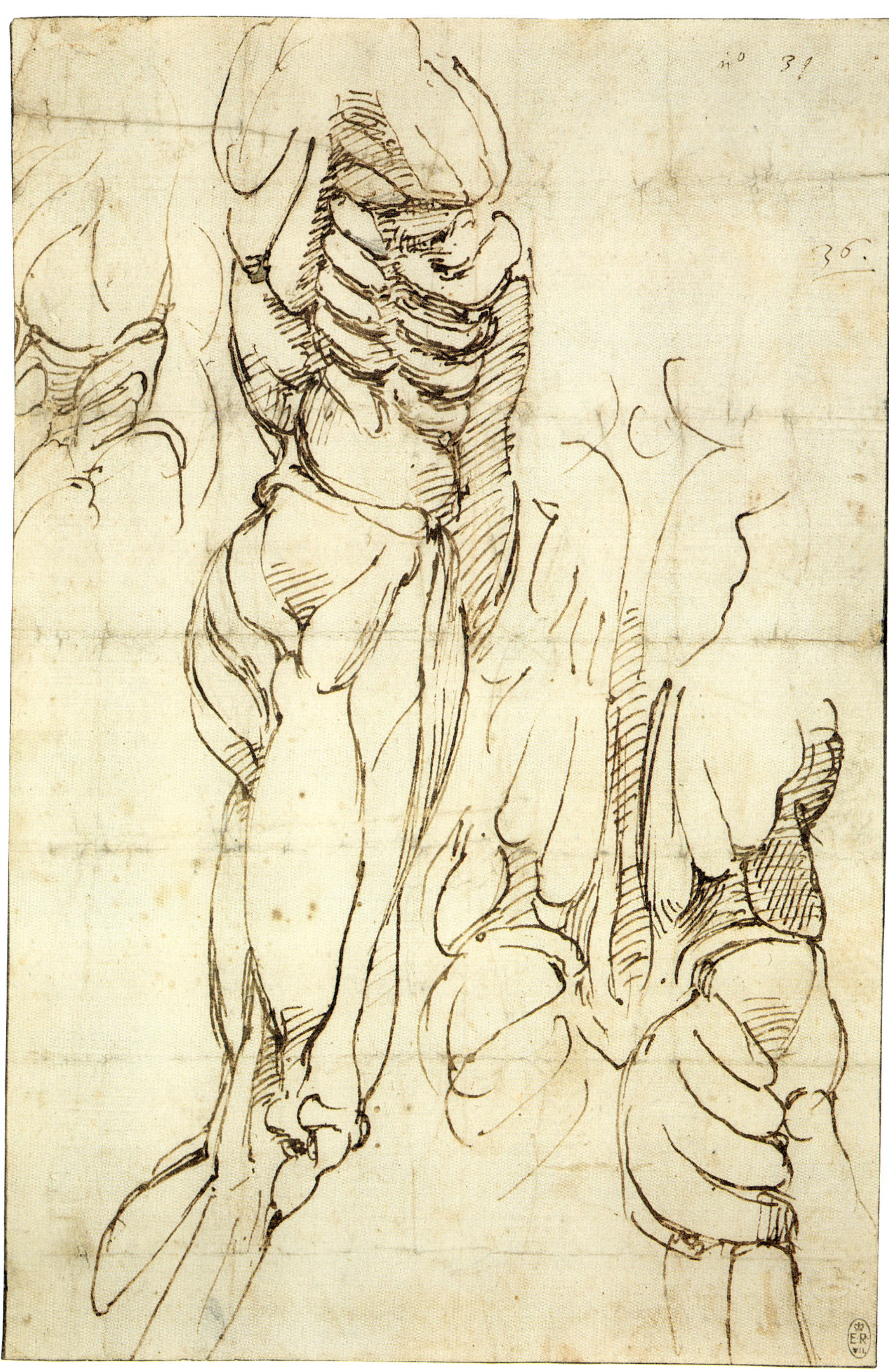

Michelangelo Buonarroti

27
Anatomical Studies

c. 1520
pen and ink
27.8 x 20.3 (10 15/16 x 8); no watermark
inscribed in pen at lower right of verso: *no. 43*; and at lower center of verso: *Michel Aglo Buona Roti*
RL 0475

EXHIBITIONS
London 1975, no. 84

LITERATURE
Popham and Wilde 1949, no. 443; Dussler 1959, no. 709; Blunt 1971, 100; De Tolnay 1975–1980, I: no. 107

The drawing on the recto of this sheet, like cat. 26, shows Michelangelo's pen style applied not to the main areas of the body, but to expressive units, particularly the knee joints and the neck muscles. The knees would be particularly relevant to seated figures, and Michelangelo always endeavored to give his seated figures, whether in painting or sculpture, a sense of imminent or potential movement. As indicated elsewhere (cat. 41), the turned head is taken from the same *écorché* model as the studies in red chalk, but the other drawings would have been after a different model or, possibly, different models. A sheet in the Uffizi (234F) that shows similar forms was probably copied by a pupil or associate of Michelangelo's after a drawing such as this. Further anatomical studies by Michelangelo are also found on the verso of the sheet.

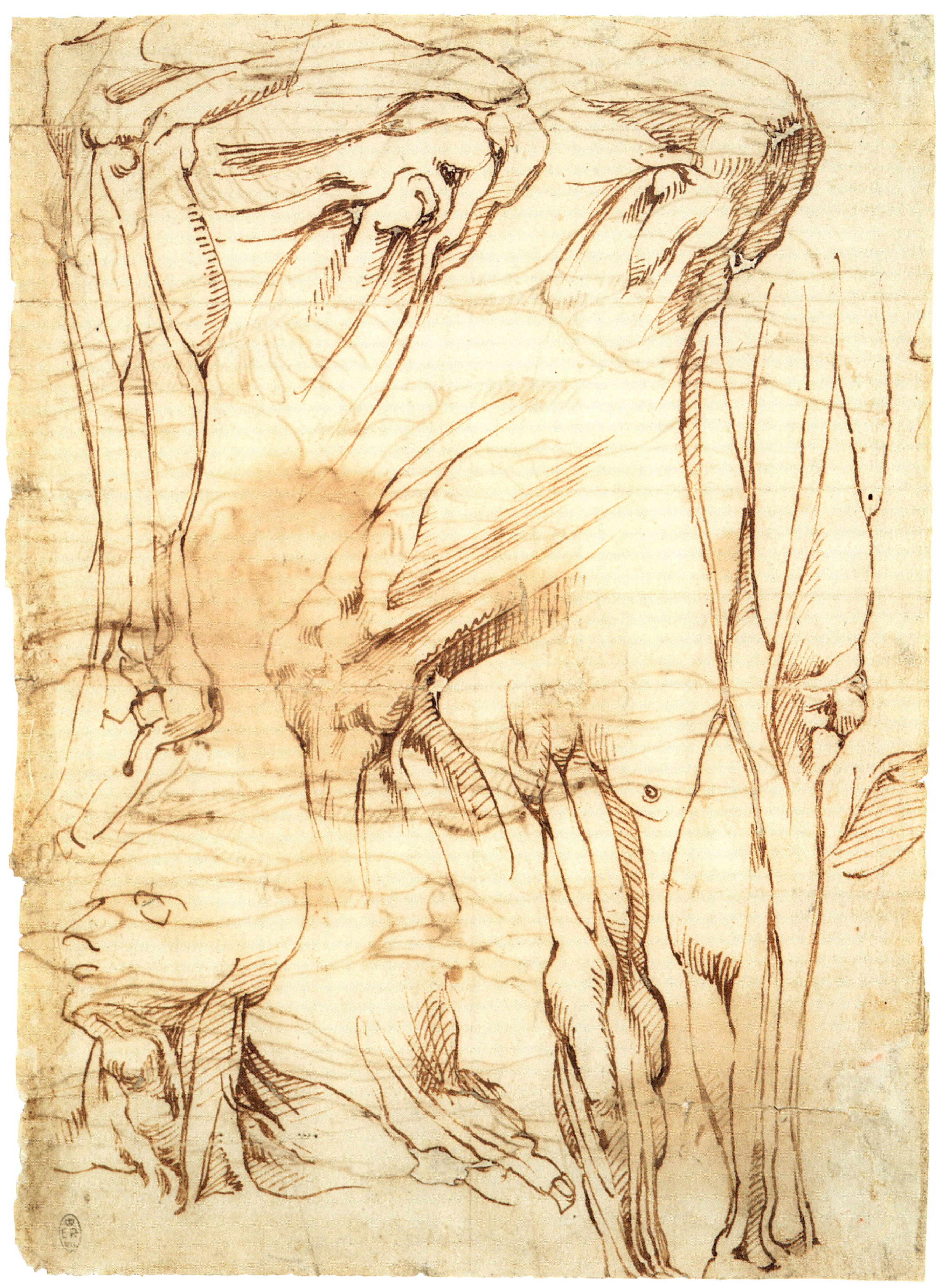

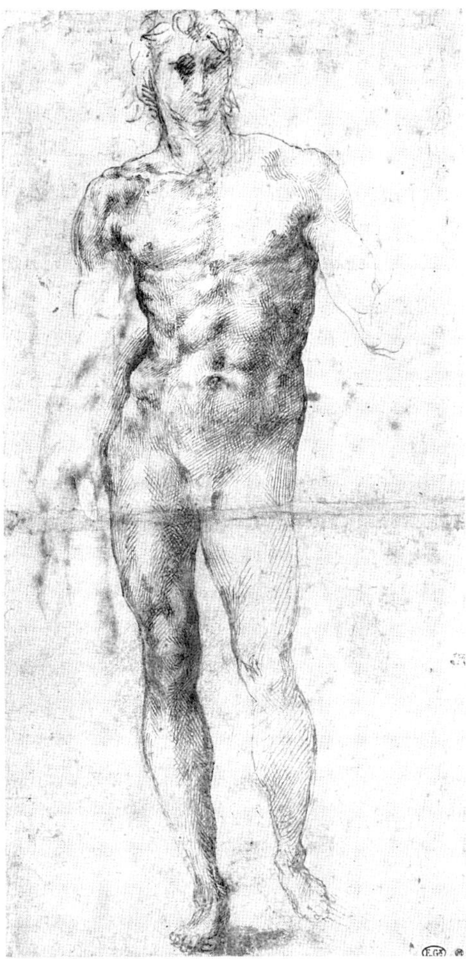

fig. 71. Michelangelo, *Standing Male Nude*, pen and ink, 31.6 x 15.2 cm. Musée du Louvre, Paris, Département des Arts Graphiques [Photo RMN]

Unidentified Artist after Michelangelo Buonarroti

28
Studies of a Male Nude

c. 1520 (?)
pen and ink
33.3 x 26.7 (13 1/8 x 10 1/2); watermark: crossed arrows with star, not in Briquet
RL 0433

EXHIBITIONS
None

LITERATURE
Berenson 1938, no. 1749A; Popham and Wilde 1949, no. 461

The recto of this page probably repeats a lost original by Michelangelo. The main study is related to an exceptionally beautiful original by Michelangelo in the Louvre (fig. 71, RF 1068 recto / C. 21 recto), which is universally dated circa 1505–1506. But although very similar to that figure, this is not a copy of it: there are significant differences in the position of the legs and the rhythm of the torso, and the head is here excluded. The main drawing must be a copy of a lost variant study for the same figure as the Louvre drawing. Since the figure in the Louvre drawing is close in pose to another figure found on a further pen drawing in the Louvre (Inv. 688 recto / C. 20 recto)—the so-called *Mercury-Apollo*, which probably represents, as Thode suggested, *Mercury's Invention of the Lyre*—it is probable that Michelangelo, in both of the Louvre drawings and in the lost original of the present drawing, was experimenting with Mercury's pose. The purpose of the *Mercury* is unknown, but it is marginally more likely that it was sculptural rather than pictorial. Michelangelo was certainly involved, at one level or another, in many more projects than Vasari was aware of or that we know today. But it is worth making a suggestion. The Julius Tomb, which, in its first freestanding version of 1505, was to be placed in the choir of Old Saint Peter's between two banks of choir stalls, was planned to contain large figurative reliefs on either flank. There is no information on what the subjects of these might have been, but, given the context, scenes with a musical content are a strong possibility, in which case Mercury's invention of the lyre would have made an appropriate, although pagan, theme. Whether or not this suggestion is correct further research may determine. But support for the probability that Michelangelo did plan a "musical" composition around this time is provided by another copy of a contemporary lost drawing (Louvre Inv. 18368) of a nude figure playing a tambourine.

The subsidiary figure on the left is a variant of the main figure, with slightly narrower waist and legs placed closer together. It is close to another drawing, on the verso of Louvre 688 / C. 20. The pen drawing of the pelvic girdle is not paralleled among Michelangelo's surviving works, but it is related to the pose of the main figure, and thus it would be an unusual addition for a copyist to have made. Compared with a similar study made by Fra Bartolommeo a few years earlier (Louvre RF 5586), the present study displays a much more convincing picture of the jointing of pelvic girdle, thighbones, and spine. Martin Clayton, observing that the sacrum is oversimplified and the loops of the lower pelvis misunderstood, suggests that the present drawing is a poorly comprehended copy of an accurate original.

Although Wilde rejected it, the sketch of the child at lower left is convincing to the compiler as a copy of a lost drawing by Michelangelo. The pen work suggests a date of 1505–1506 and the pose of the child is reminiscent of that of the Christ child in one of Michelangelo's most famous drawings of this period, the *Virgin, Child, and Saint Anne* (Louvre Inv. 685 recto / C. 26 recto).

Throughout the drawings on the recto of this sheet, the draftsman has employed a finer pen than is found in Michelangelo's drawings, and has interpreted rather than followed his hatching system. The effect is to diminish Michelangelo's vigor and ruggedness, and to accentuate his elegance.

The verso sketch of the bones of a hand is in a style not usually associated with Michelangelo, who very rarely used wash in conjunction with pen outlines, but so few studies of bones by the artist survive that it is difficult either to accept it or reject it as a copy of a lost original. Those on the verso of an early drawing in Munich (Inv. 2191 / C. 4 verso), probably datable some ten years before the original of the present sheet, are loosely comparable in content, but not in style. However, the fact that the Casa Buonarroti owns a rather similar drawing (26F), which is usually rejected but which may be autograph, would support the view that such a drawing was within Michelangelo's range.

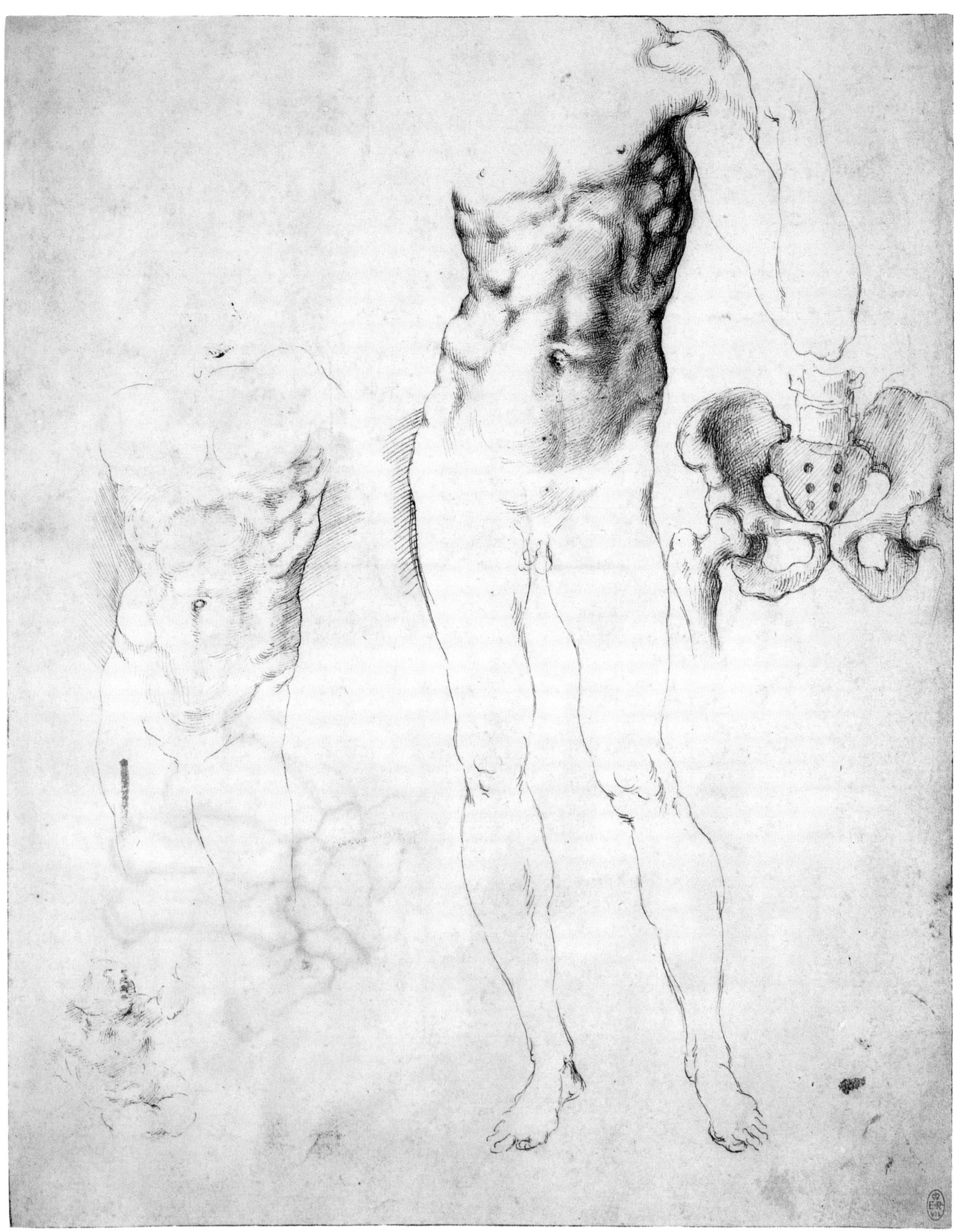

Raphael

29
Hercules and the Hydra

c. 1507
pen and ink over black chalk
39 x 27.2 (15 3/8 x 10 11/16); no watermark
RL 12758

EXHIBITIONS
London 1983, no. 66

LITERATURE
Fischel 1898, no. 504; Fischel 1913–1941, 4: no. 190; Popham and Wilde 1949, no. 791; Joannides 1983, no. 189; Knab et al. 1983, no. 229

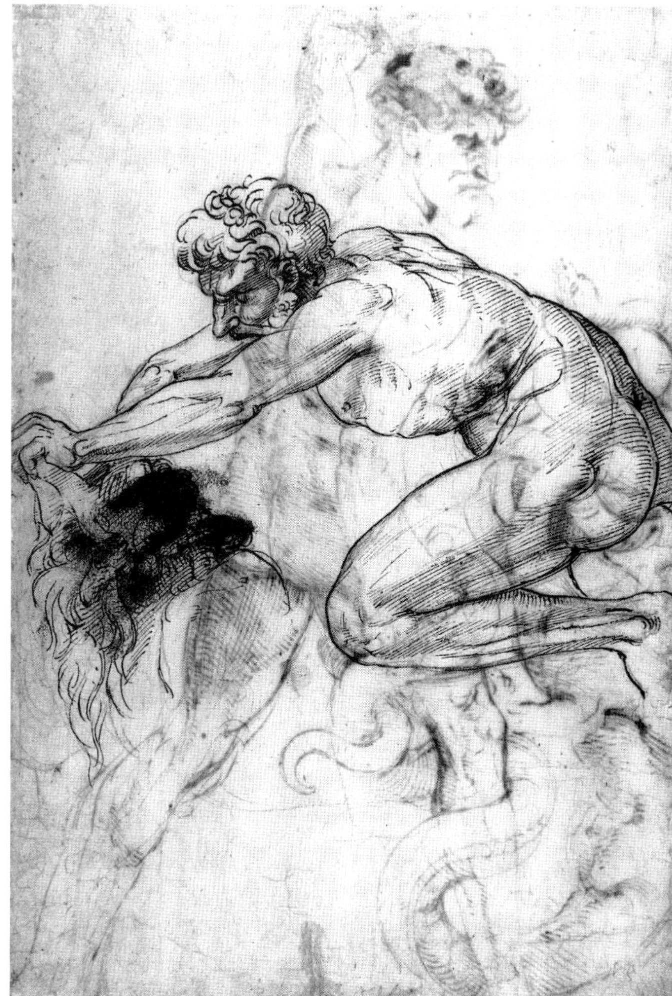

fig. 72. Raphael, *Hercules and the Nemean Lion*, pen and ink over stylus indentation, 37.2 x 39 cm. (verso of cat. 29)

In a letter of 1542 Michelangelo wrote, "what Raphael had of art, he had of me." His bitterness toward Raphael, even twenty years after the younger artist's death, suggests something more profound than jealousy of the man who had been his most dangerous competitor, the one Central Italian contemporary whose intellect, visual inventiveness, and productiveness matched his own and who was infinitely more skilled as a diplomat and courtier. It seems likely, though evidence is lacking, that the two artists were personally close during the short period that they overlapped in Florence and perhaps also during the years 1508–1510 in Rome. Michelangelo was often generous in providing models for younger artists, and Raphael may have had access to Michelangelo's studio, as is suggested by a number of borrowings from the latter's painted and sculpted work. He also knew some of Michelangelo's drawings. The Metropolitan Museum of Art in New York owns a copy of a lost drawing by Raphael (fig. 33) that is clearly based on Michelangelo's drawing in the Albertina (fig. 32, see page 31), although Raphael did not attempt to replicate Michelangelo's handling of the pen.

The present drawing, on the recto of the sheet, is generally dated to circa 1507. It is looser and wilder in its pen work than drawings of comparable technique and scale by Michelangelo himself. Despite the obvious effort to think big, Raphael, at this stage, could not match Michelangelo's inherent control of form, and he attempted to achieve a strength and grandeur matching the subject by a somewhat bombastic exercise of the pen. Raphael's graphic work is inherently rhythmical, precise, clean, and clear, and his efforts to communicate energy through a rougher manner of handling were not, finally, successful. Raphael did not continue with this manner of pen drawing; it remains the product of a particular moment in his work. But it had considerable influence. One drawing of this type by Raphael, in the Albertina (Sc. R. 151), was long attributed to Bandinelli, and it was a Michelangelism seen through this phase of Raphael's interest in Michelangelo that seems to have affected Bandinelli as much as direct knowledge of Michelangelo's works. Aspects of this style too were taken up by Raphael's pupils, notably Gianfrancesco Penni, whose study, also at Windsor (RL 0804 recto / Popham and Wilde 811), for the statue of *Jonah* in the Chigi chapel in Santa Maria del Popolo, looks back to Raphael's late Florentine pen style.

The purpose of the present drawing, which treats the same subject as the right-hand group on the *Three Labors of Hercules* (cat. 18); of its verso (fig. 72); and of three other sheets of studies by Raphael of the *Labors of Hercules* (Ashmolean Museum, Oxford, P. 540 and 463; British Museum, Pouncey and Gere 22), has never been elucidated. However, their sculpturesque nature suggests that they may have been made for a Hercules cycle to be executed in relief in the courtyard of a private palace or, perhaps, to adorn the base of a statue of *Hercules*. Michelangelo was commissioned in 1508 to carve a *Hercules* as a pair to his *David*, and it may be that Raphael's drawings reflect discussion of the project in Florence while Michelangelo was still in Bologna.

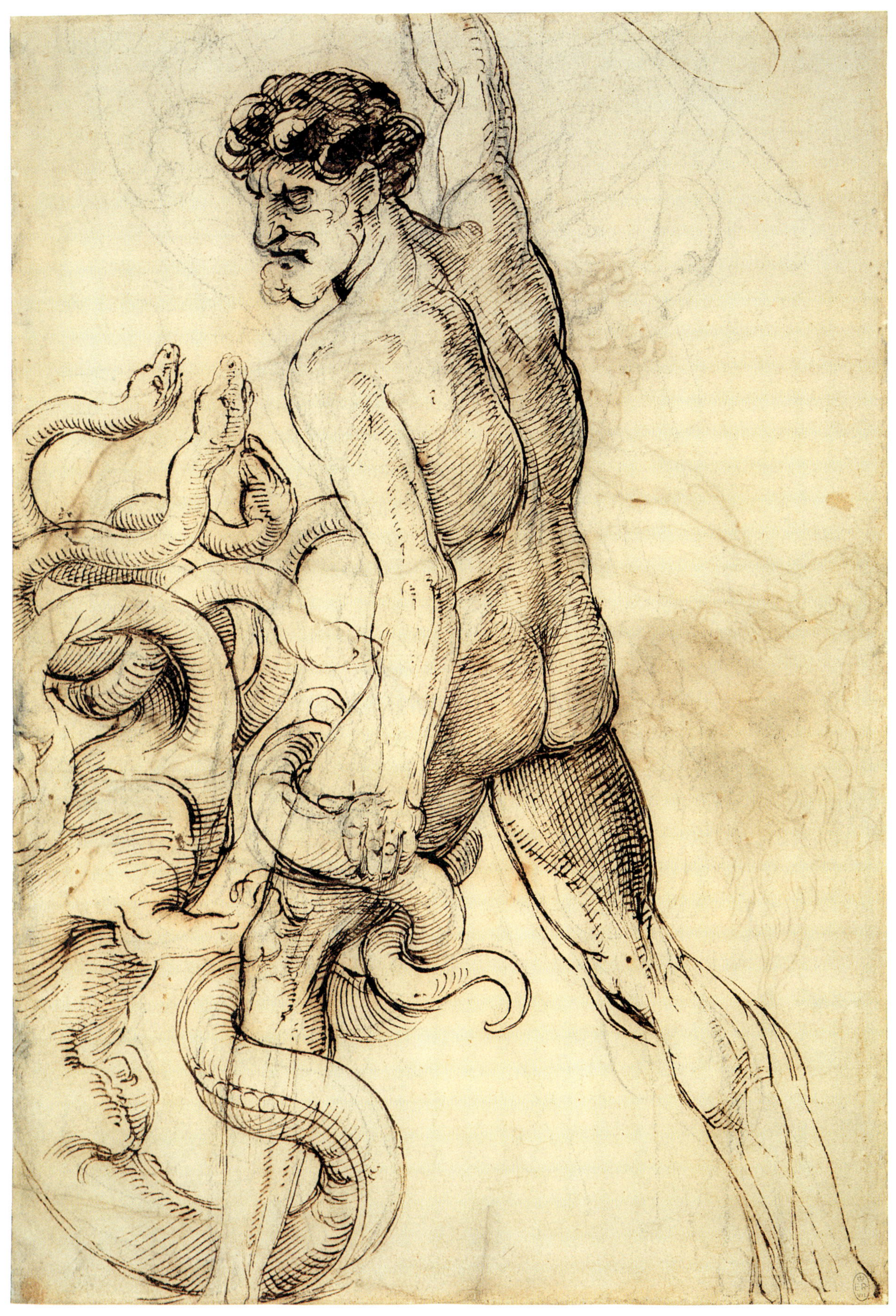

Biagio Pupini after Michelangelo Buonarroti

30
Studies for the Libyan Sibyl and Other Sketches

c. 1530
pen and ink with white heightening rubbed over with yellow pastel on the right-hand side of the page
20.2 x 29 (7 15/16 x 11 7/16); no watermark visible
RL 5435 verso

EXHIBITIONS
None

LITERATURE
Popham and Wilde 1949, no. 785 (verso)

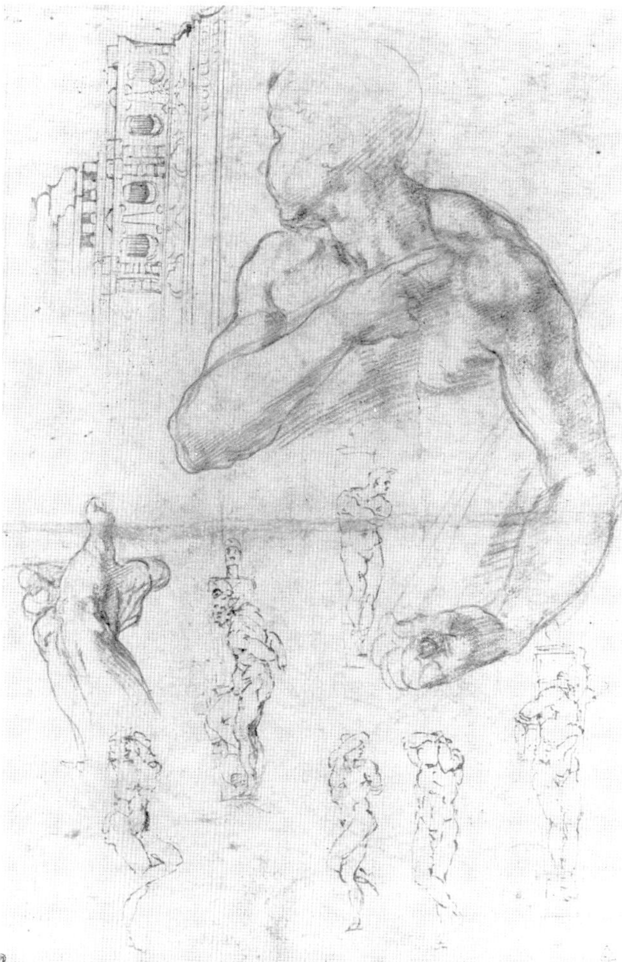

fig. 73. Michelangelo, *Study for the Genius Accompanying the Libyan Sibyl and Sketches for the Julius Tomb*, pen and ink and red chalk, 28.6 x 19.4 cm. Ashmolean Museum, Oxford

It remains unexplained how the relatively minor Bolognese painter and prolific draftsman Biagio Pupini knew some of Michelangelo's drawings. Pupini seems to have passed an early phase in Rome, in undefined association with the workshop of Raphael, with whose drawings he was also acquainted. Although it is difficult to believe he had direct access to Michelangelo's studio, he certainly knew some drawings made by Michelangelo for the Sistine ceiling: a drawing by Pupini that probably copies a lost sketch for the Sistine is in the Louvre (Inv. 748 verso). In the present drawing on the verso of this sheet, the figures are the same size as those they copy, found on a famous page now in the Ashmolean Museum, Oxford (fig. 73, P. 297 recto / C. 157 recto). The putto accompanies the *Libyan Sibyl*, one of the most refined of all the figures on the Sistine ceiling, and the sketched right hand is that of the Sibyl herself. Michelangelo's originals, however, are in red chalk, not pen, and Pupini's copies are therefore of motif, not of medium, with no effort to imitate Michelangelo's technique. It is as if Pupini decided to copy Michelangelo's sketches in the style of Michelangelo's pre-Sistine pen drawings. However, Pupini does not use the pen dynamically, but rather to build up a web of light and shade. His modeling of the forms is not forceful.

The other two drawings on this side of the sheet may also copy drawings in red chalk by Michelangelo, this time lost ones. Despite its comparative awkwardness of pose and proportion, the full-length figure on the left, who seems to be beckoning, is comparable in type and definition of musculature with the most elaborate of Michelangelo's red-chalk *écorchés*, which are generally thought to date to the later 1510s. These were posed in a quasi-narrative manner (see cats. 41, 42)—whether or not Michelangelo intended to employ them in compositions—and the same is true of the present figure. It is probable that the small sketch at the bottom right is also after a sketch by Michelangelo: there is some relation of form and pose with the putto supporting the throne of the prophet *Joel*, but the similarity is insufficient to warrant claiming a connection.

In the absence of any chronological analysis of Pupini's drawings, the date of this drawing is difficult to determine. But the head of the main copy after Michelangelo is treated in a rhythm so reminiscent of Parmigianino's pen style that it is difficult to believe that it was drawn before the young Parmese artist's style began to exercise a serious influence, in the mid-1520s. On the other hand, it is virtually certain that Michelangelo's Ashmolean sheet, whose first recorded appearance is in the Crozat collection, was known to Primaticcio, who copied a figure from it (Joannides 1994a). Therefore, it is likely to have been one of those taken to France by Michelangelo's pupil, Antonio Mini, at the end of 1531. Pupini's copy, therefore, was probably made in the late 1520s.

The drawing on the recto of the sheet, a *Battle of Hercules and Theseus against the Amazons* in the manner of a relief, may be after a lost design by Giulio Romano rather than after an antique.

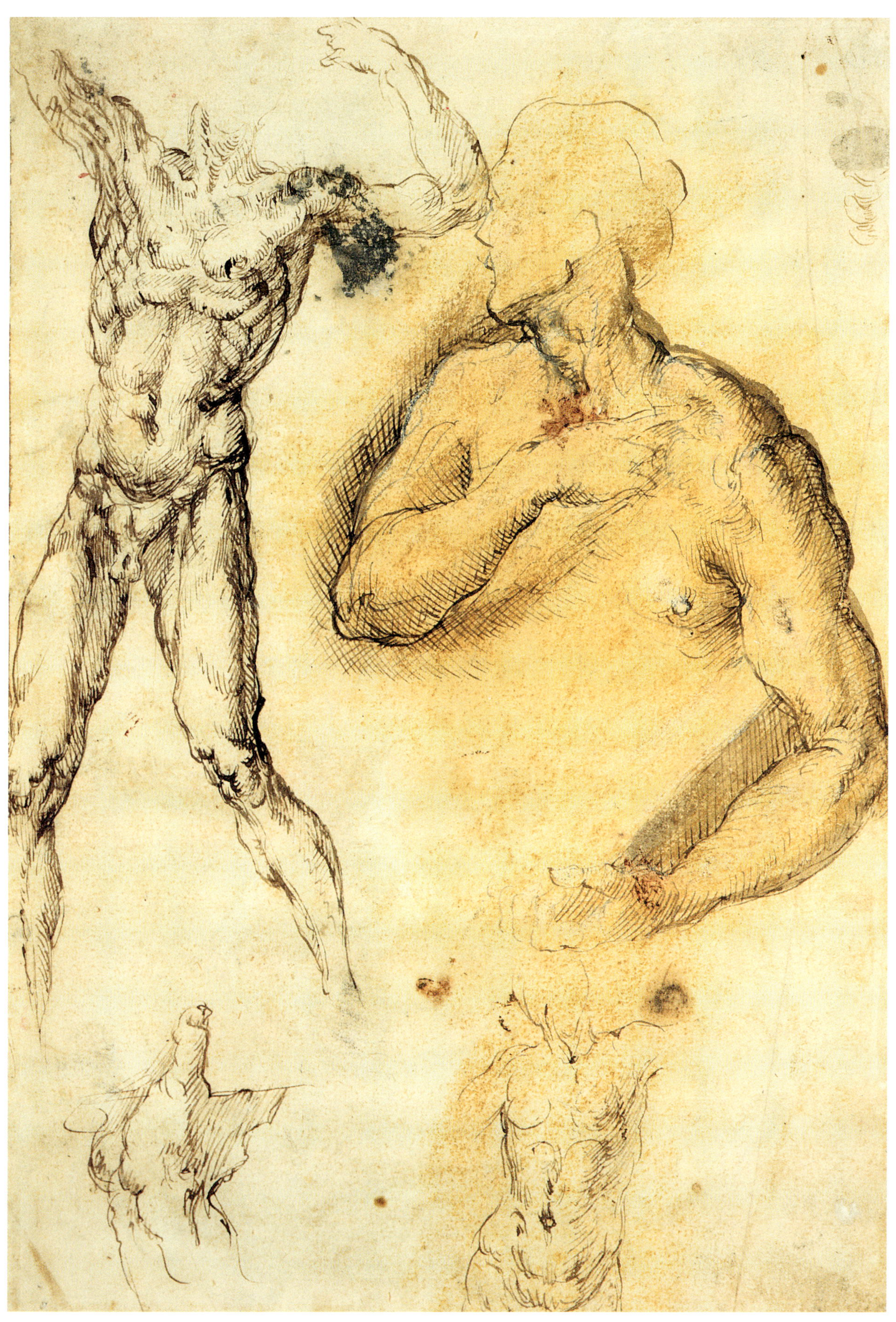

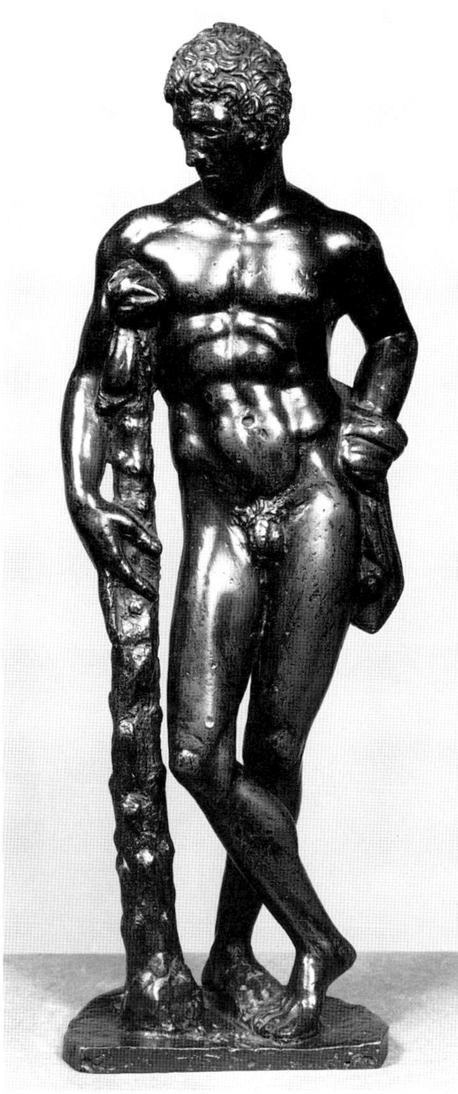

fig. 74. After Michelangelo (?), *Hercules*, bronze, height 33 cm. The Board of Trustees of the Victoria and Albert Museum, London

Baccio Bandinelli

31
Three Male Nudes

c. 1520
pen and ink
27.2 x 20 (10 11/16 x 7 7/8); laid down
RL 0376

EXHIBITIONS
None

LITERATURE
Popham and Wilde 1949, no. 75; Ward 1982, no. 419

The present drawing is characteristic of Bandinelli and a fine example of his work. As here, he generally used a thicker nib than Michelangelo habitually employed and was correspondingly less interested than Michelangelo in local subtleties of modeling. Whereas Michelangelo aimed for the maximum of muscular expressiveness within the containing envelope of the skin, Bandinelli, whose early experience with Leonardo—a strong critic of what he called "anatomical painting"—would have reinforced an innate preference, chose smoother, more idealized form. It is appropriate that one of Bandinelli's most successful statues, the *Orpheus* carved for the Palazzo Medici circa 1519, is closely based on the *Apollo Belvedere.* When Bandinelli attempted a more muscular style, as in his *Hercules and Cacus* in the Piazza della Signoria, a project taken over from Michelangelo, the forms he produced were based on Leonardo's more static anatomical mode rather than on Michelangelo's mobility and asymmetricality of form, and the consequent effect was one of stiffness.

Nevertheless, despite the essential difference in their styles, which cannot have escaped Michelangelo, Bandinelli and Michelangelo were in close contact in the period following 1516. At this time Michelangelo attempted to promote Bandinelli's career by employing him as a collaborator on the massive sculptural program of the façade of San Lorenzo, a favoritism that earned Michelangelo bitter reproaches from Jacopo Sansovino, who believed that he was to be a collaborator and who felt betrayed. Although relations between Michelangelo and Bandinelli had soured by the mid-1520s, there was a period when they were close, and in this context it is understandable that Bandinelli made a highly finished life-size portrait drawing of Michelangelo in pen, and then the painted portrait based upon it, dated 1522, both of which are now in the Louvre. Bandinelli's authorship of the drawing (Inv. 2715 / c. 118), often called a self-portrait of Michelangelo, has frequently been denied, but the attribution of Pouncey (1963) seems manifestly correct and also explains the qualities of the painting, in which the influence of Bandinelli's friend Andrea del Sarto is plain.

In the *memoriale* that he prepared for his children toward the end of his life, Bandinelli remarked that Michelangelo had always praised his drawings, some of which, he boasted, had been sold for considerable sums. The present drawing was dated by Popham circa 1525–1530, a view with which Ward concurred, but it may have been drawn a few years earlier, during the period of Bandinelli's closest association with Michelangelo. The figure on the far left is a variant of the pose found in a famous statuette of *Hercules* (fig. 74), which probably reproduces Michelangelo's lost early statue. Here, in an unusual view, the figure is not isolated, but seen as part of a group and from the side. It seems likely that Bandinelli had learned more than one lesson from Raphael in the fluent integration of forms, and he showed himself to be a remarkably successful inventor of multifigure compositions. His *Martyrdom of Saint Lawrence* and *Massacre of the Innocents*, both engraved by Marcantonio Raimondi, are among the most impressive attempts of their time to create crowd scenes out of highly wrought and expressive individual figures.

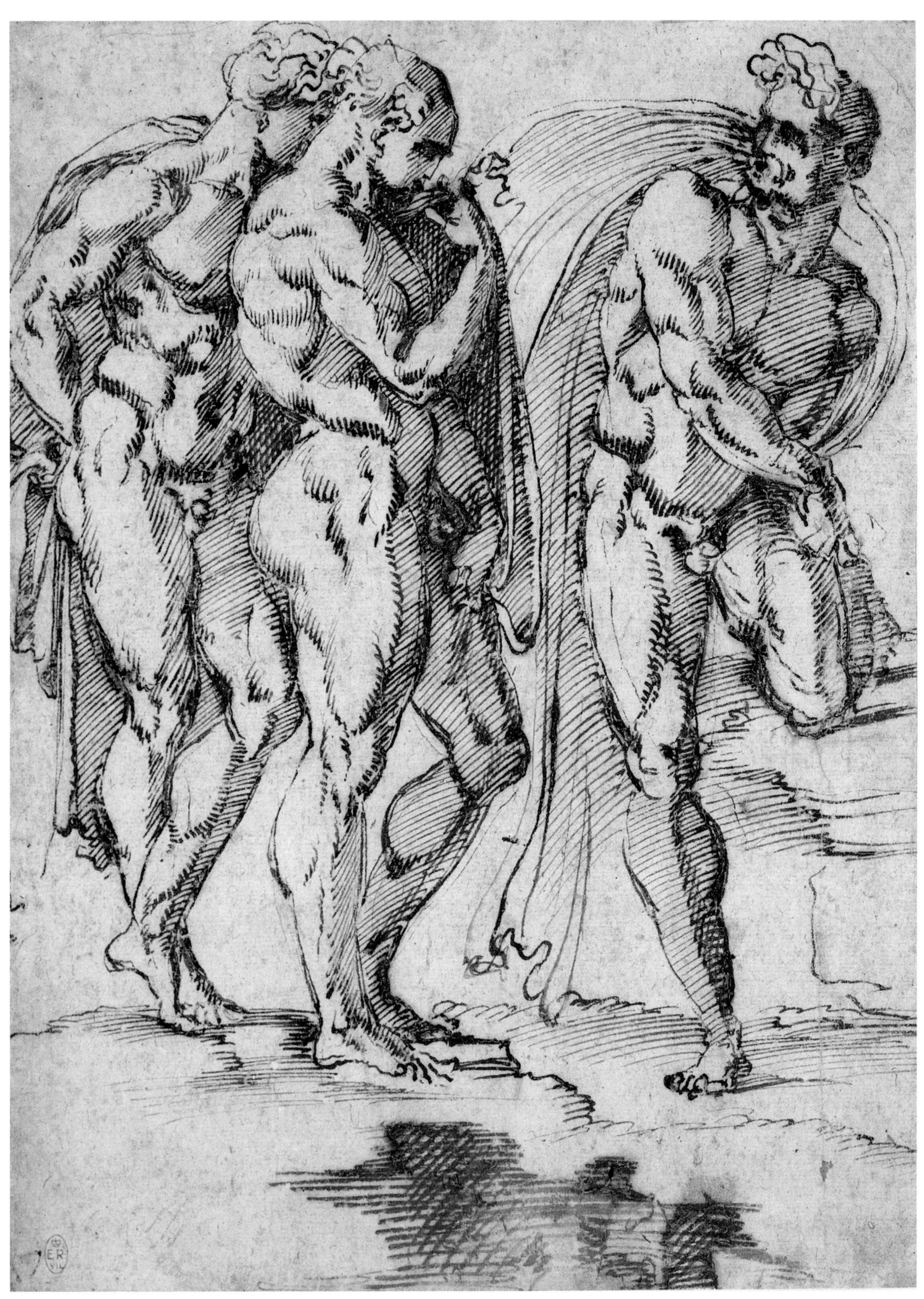

Bartolomeo Passarotti

32
Nude Figures

c. 1560
pen and ink
39.2 x 25.8 (15 7/16 x 10 3/16); no watermark
inscribed on the verso by William Gibson: *Bartolomeo Passorotto 2.3 / 8.1.*
RL 6041

EXHIBITIONS
None

LITERATURE
Popham and Wilde 1949, no. 662; Höper 1987, z. 342

Passarotti's use of a thick pen and an uninflected and broad crosshatching link this drawing more closely with the style of Bandinelli than that of Michelangelo, and demonstrate the significance of Bandinelli in promulgating a Michelangelesque drawing style that varied considerably from that of the master. Passarotti copied Bandinelli's public works as well as those by Michelangelo. Whereas Passarotti seems not to have been intimate with Michelangelo or with those who possessed his drawings, he probably had direct access to drawings by Bandinelli: the two artists' pen drawings have often been confused. Passarotti became a virtuoso in pen, a skill further developed by his work as an engraver, but there is often a stiffness and excessive systematization in his handling. Passarotti seems to have made drawings for sale, and it is probable that, like Bandinelli, he made replicas of his own drawings.

Exaggerated vigor of handling with loose and rumbustious pen work was intended to convey energy, as in Raphael's drawing (cat. 29). But, in the absence of a sophisticated grasp of three-dimensional form, this style of pen drawing can seem vapid and devoid of any engagement with life. Nevertheless, Passarotti's pen style had a productive influence, in particular on the early drawings of Agostino Carracci, for a period his pupil. Whereas Agostino controlled this facile expressivity with renewed study of the living model, Passarotti seems never to have been interested in the textures of the body, although he produced a number of anatomical drawings. There are very few surviving studies in chalk, a medium invariably employed by artists who wished to capture the movement of light on skin and of muscles below it. The overriding impression of Passarotti's painted work is of compositional inventiveness untempered either by narrative subtlety or by physical sensuousness. He aimed for the most part at extreme elongations of form, radically unbalanced compositions, violent and complicated poses and movements. The figure style of drawings like the present—and even something of their handling—looks forward to protoromantic artists like Barry and, especially, Fuseli. Indeed, there is some, certainly coincidental, similarity between the present composition and Fuseli's *Oath on the Ruttli.* In the eighteenth century, before large numbers of genuine Michelangelo drawings came onto the market, sheets by Passarotti were routinely given to Michelangelo, and protoromantic Michelangelism was based less on the master's own work than on that of relatively distant followers like Passarotti. Their simplified and flashy dynamism and drama broadcast a distorted picture of the master's graphic manner.

Höper suggests that the present drawing was made in preparation for the right-hand figure in a compositional drawing by Passarotti, also in the Royal Collection (RL 6039 / Popham and Wilde 659), which depicts the *Flagellation.*

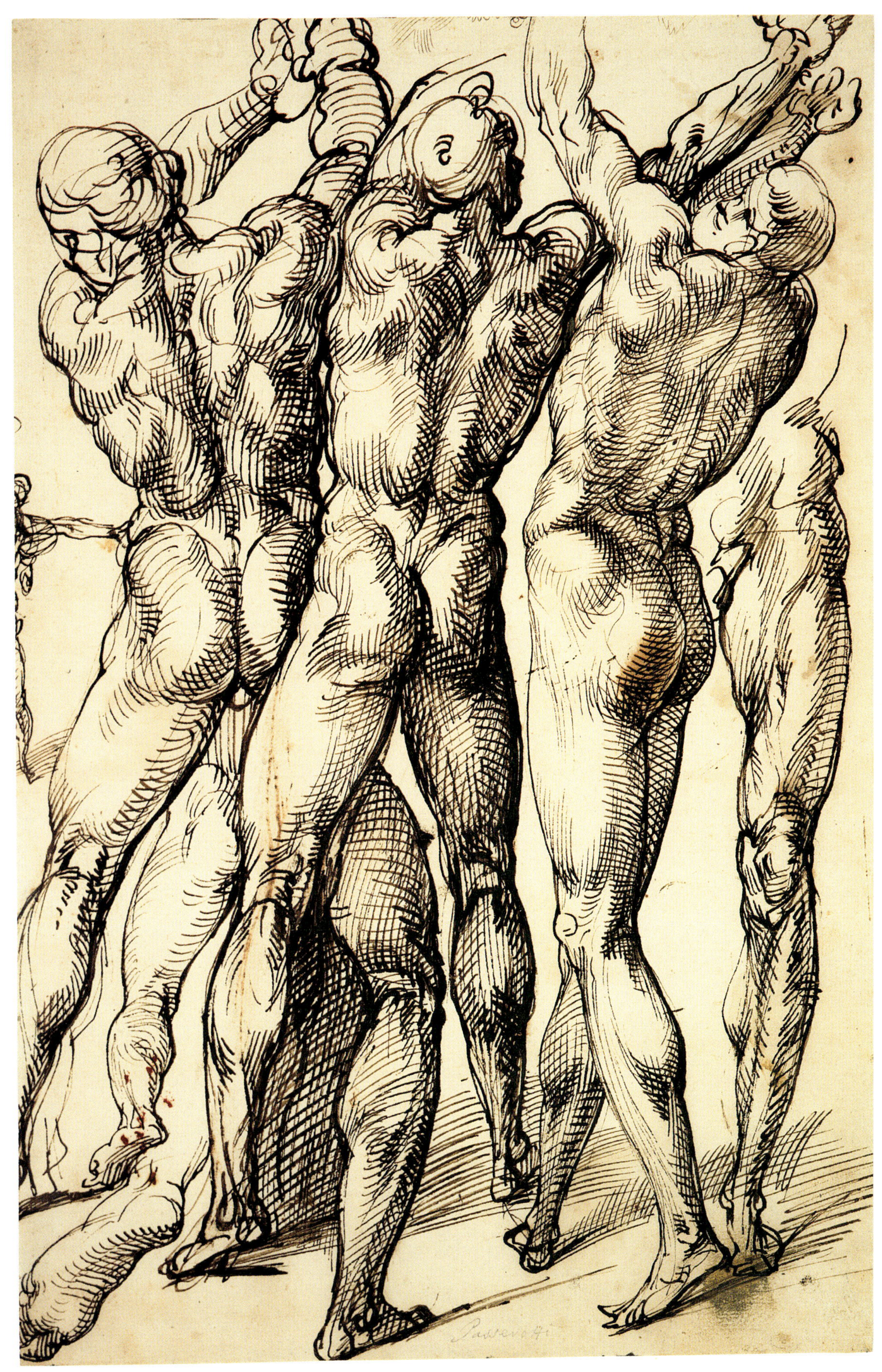

The Expressive Nude in Chalk

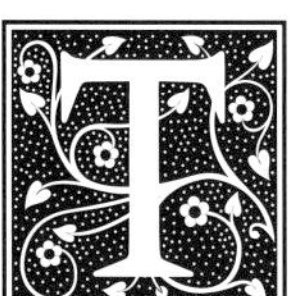

he expressive nude was the central preoccupation of Michelangelo's art. He sought forms to which the beholder would respond with empathy, from knowledge of his or her own body. For although Michelangelo's most profound commitment was to the male body, he was also deeply responsive to the expressive potentialities of the female form. He was particularly alert—with a perception that was certainly innate but that may have been sharpened by knowledge of Botticelli's work—to the physical foci of emotion. Thus in his earliest surviving sculpture, the relief of the *Virgin and Child* in Casa Buonarroti, carved when he was about sixteen years old, emotion is focused in the nude child's head and hand. His head turns against his broad and simplified back in an arrangement suggesting death as much as sleep; his right hand, turned upward and outward in an arrangement deriving from a *Pietà* by Filippo Lippi (Museo Poldi-Pezzoli, Milan), was re-used by Michelangelo sixty years later in his own late *Pietà* (Museo dell'Opera del Duomo, Florence). In the *Bacchus*, carved in Rome in 1496–1497, the god of wine is unbalanced, creating a physical unease in the spectator and an awareness of the god's irrationality and power. In the *Pietà*, carved at the end of the century for the chapel of Santa Petronilla attached to Old Saint Peter's, the right shoulder of Christ, lifted by the Virgin's hand, actualizes his death as a man with unequaled pathos. In order to achieve such focus and precision, Michelangelo must have made innumerable studies of the details of bodies as well as of their overall structure.

As Leon Battista Alberti had advised, Michelangelo made nude studies even of figures intended to be heavily draped. Thus the British Museum houses a superb small pen sketch, made from a nude male model for the Bruges *Madonna* (w. 5 verso / c. 46 verso), even though the drapery of that figure had been a key expressive feature from its conception. But to be able to deploy all the expressive resources of the nude body was Michelangelo's central aim, one which he had achieved at the beginning of his career in his pseudo-antique *Battle of the Centaurs*, of 1491–1492, for which, regrettably, no drawings survive. It was the *Battle of Cascina,* commissioned in 1504, that provided his next opportunity, and this scheme marked a major breakthrough for Michelangelo. It was to be frescoed in the great hall of the republic, the Sala del Cinquecento in Palazzo della Signoria, in conjunction with Leonardo's *Battle of Anghiari.* The two frescoes were to represent Florentine military successes and were to serve, in effect, as large-scale recruiting posters for the Florentine militia. Both artists must have played a large part in the selection of the episodes they were to depict: Leonardo, a cavalry battle that enabled him to display his mastery of horses and violent movement; Michelangelo, a group of nude infantrymen, who had been bathing, running to battle at the sound of the false alarm. This episode enabled him to revive the nude battle scenes of antiquity, and of Antonio del Pollaiuolo, without absurdity.

Leonardo began his painting, apparently in an encaustic technique rather than true fresco, but only a portion was executed and this seems soon to have deteriorated. Michelangelo never began his fresco, but did complete a cartoon of the central event, comprising some fifteen nude or semi-nude soldiers: it is doubtful if he ever brought subsidiary areas of the composition to this stage. The cartoon, Vasari noted, was revered by young Florentine artists, and numerous drawn copies survive, mostly of single figures, occasionally of twos and threes, but very rarely more. The cartoon seems to have been dismembered before 1520, and pieces of it are recorded in several collections, although all trace of these is now lost. But a copy of, presumably, the whole cartoon was commissioned by Vasari in 1542 from Aristotile da Sangallo, and this is probably the grisaille painting now at Holkham (fig. 78).

Despite Michelangelo's hostility toward Leonardo, the central idea of *Cascina* was, curiously, indebted to the *Last Supper*. In both compositions a group of figures responds to an announcement. In the *Last Supper* it is Christ's to his followers that one of their number will betray him; in the *Battle of Cascina* it is the shout of the veteran soldier Manno Donati, who perceives the danger his comrades are running by unguarded bathing during a hot day, and who shocks them into an awareness of their danger by giving the alarm. In the composition that Michelangelo planned, this episode, which in fact took place the day before the battle proper, was fused with the combat in order to present a unified account of danger faced and overcome. Leonardo's figures are draped and have restricted freedom to maneuver, contained and constrained by the table around which they are placed. Consequently, Leonardo's treatment was an essay in the psychology of facial expressions and limited gesture of a type that a nineteenth-century novelist might have described, or a classic playwright deployed. Michelangelo, although not indifferent to personal psychology, never found it of central interest. His concern was deeper: the revelation of spiritual states. In the *Battle of Cascina*, different degrees of readiness, resolve, energy, action, as well as indices to individual character, assume the nature of moral propositions about the readiness of the spirit when faced with the call to arms. As such, *Cascina* was a test-bed for the *Last Judgment*, in which the dead rise at the sound of the last trumpet; conversely, in its portrayal of action and movement, it also provided a starting point for some of the compositions, full of fast-moving figures, that Michelangelo devised for representations of Christ's Resurrection in drawings of the early 1530s. *Cascina*, in short, opened for Michelangelo possibilities that he exploited for the next fifty years. In this light it is not altogether surprising that Cellini, who saw the cartoon before it was dismembered, thought that it was Michelangelo's best work.

Michelangelo's preparatory drawings for the *Battle of Cascina* are almost all in pen or in black chalk: he employed whichever medium was most effective in establishing the required degree of definition. The compositional sketches are mostly in black chalk, as are individual figure studies, with background figures treated more softly and foreground ones given harder surfaces. Figures that required additional plastic emphasis—largely those on the central axis—were worked up in pen, a practice that Michelangelo reduced in following years. The most dynamic and forward-looking studies were those in chalk.

Although the *Cascina* was never painted, it was enormously influential. Vasari said that it was copied by virtually all Michelangelo's younger contemporaries in Florence, and while only a few among the many surviving copies of parts of the cartoon can as yet be allocated to specific hands, there is no good reason to disbelieve him. No other artist attempted to follow the *Cascina* closely, but without its example, Raphael's conception of the *Resurrection* and the preparatory drawings for it and his and Giulio's *Stoning of Saint Stephen* would have taken a different form.

Shortly before the *Cascina* commission Michelangelo had begun another painting, the *Entombment* (National Gallery, London), which demonstrates a different side of his art: the interest in the isolated and stationary figure. Michelangelo's figures are never fully static of course, but it was inevitable that a sculptor, much of whose work consisted of single freestanding nude statues, like the *David* and the *Risen Christ*, would be profoundly conscious of the values of rhythm and self-containment in the autonomous figure. And this interest in separateness and self-sufficiency led him to another way of organizing multifigure compositions: placing together a series of autonomous figures according to a geometrical pattern, generally a grid system. This method has a source in the compositional construction of antique reliefs and, appropriately, it is first seen in the *Battle of the Centaurs*. Transferred to painting, and somewhat simplified, it was the mode of construction of Michelangelo's *Entombment*. That in turn was the model Michelangelo recalled when he came to prepare his final design for Sebastiano's *Flagellation*, in which the crowded and elaborately contextualized scheme of his preparatory drawing is stripped down and simplified, with all the figures, clothed and unclothed, linked by horizontal and vertical stresses and by the rhythmical relation of contours. Perhaps competition with Raphael at this period alerted Michelangelo to the potential for elegance of such severe geometry, for it is in the late 1510s and the 1520s that Michelangelo designed some of his most graceful nudes.

But elegance was neither the only nor the dominant manner of Michelangelo's treatment of the nude late in the second decade. The *Slaves* (Accademia, Florence), on which he probably worked intermittently for a decade, are colossally powerful, massive in proportions, and are forerunners of the figure style of the *Last Judgment*. Although isolated in the sense that they do not form part of any unified composition, little emphasis is placed on contour and little on those key areas for the expression of pathos: the joints and the shoulders. In the Accademia *Slaves*, stress is on the musculature, which is perceived as continuous, without foci. This totalizing treatment of the body had been anticipated in the figures Michelangelo had devised in the last sections of the Sistine, of which *Haman* is perhaps the best example. Although isolated, he is extraordinarily powerful and although nailed to a tree, explodes from his pendentive. Figures such as *Haman*, and some of the *ignudi* painted during the last phase of work on the ceiling, transcend their apparent roles and seem to become epitomes of humanity. It is significant that, when Michelangelo came later to envisage treatments of the single figure of the *Resurrected Christ*, it was to his work in the last phase of the Sistine that he turned for inspiration.

In his drawings for the second half of the Sistine ceiling, Michelangelo mostly employed red chalk. With its inherent warmth and lighter tone, as well as its capacity to take a sharper point than the black chalk that Michelangelo had used hitherto, red chalk was ideally suited to the necessarily high key of the ceiling fresco, and for the detail of the nude studies, in which the subtle variety of the body's modeling plays a larger role than previously. Red chalk remained Michelangelo's preferred medium for figure studies for the rest of the 1510s, and he employed it also for the *écorché* models that he drew later in the decade (see cats. 41, 42). But the increasing dominance of the *écorché* mode, which fed directly into the Accademia *Slaves* and, subsequently, to the *Last Judgment*, demanded a less sensuous and more generalized technique. Therefore, during the 1520s and later, for his studies of the expressive nude, whether made with sculptural or pictorial intent, Michelangelo once again came predominantly to employ black chalk.

Michelangelo Buonarroti

33a
Standing Male Nude with Proportions Added (RECTO)

33b
Standing Male Nude (VERSO)

c. 1516
red chalk, two hues, over stylus on both sides
28.9 x 18 (11 3/8 x 7 1/16); no watermark
inscribed in Michelangelo's hand
RL 12765

EXHIBITIONS
London 1950–1951, no. 274; London 1953, no. 29; London 1962, no. 67; London 1972–1973, no. 32; London 1975, no. 101; Sydney-Brisbane-Melbourne 1988, no. 15

LITERATURE
Berenson 1903 and 1938, no. 1607; Frey 1909–1911, no. 231; Thode 1913, no. 29; Popham and Wilde 1949, no. 421; De Tolnay 1954, nos. 131, 132; Dussler 1959, no. 716; De Tolnay 1975–1980, I: no. 61

The drawing bears in Michelangelo's hand a number of horizontal lines marking the proportional divisions of the body and appropriate labels. These must be taken together, and they are fully transcribed by Wilde, who also sets them in context: "The figure is marked off in 6 2/3 such units (ie. the superimposed hand and profile at the upper right) extending from the base to the waist. Within the lines delimiting the last unit is inscribed 'una' written from the bottom upwards (the peculiar character of the writing is accounted for by the fact that the paper was not turned round for the purpose). Both to the R. and L. straight lines define certain sections of the body. Their measurements are given thus: R. elbow—'terzo di una testa'; from wrist to the fingers—'terzo di una testa'; upper leg—'dua e u(n) terzo a l a(n)guinaia (= groin)'; L. ankle—'dua terzi.' Measurements are also given of the anatomical sections sketched in the margins: the breadth of the upper arm sketched at upper right—'2 terzi'; the knee sketched at the lower left edge—'(u)na'; the foot sketched in the lower left corner—'una e 3 quarti.'"

In its combination of broadly hatched areas and others densely realized by stumping, this drawing resembles most closely one in the collection of the Ecole des Beaux-Arts in Paris (fig. 75, Inv. 197 recto / c. 62 recto), made in preparation for the *Young Slave*. The date of both drawings is generally put about 1516. Michelangelo's attitude to the physical style of the slaves changed as he was carving them. Compared with the two figures executed for the 1513 project, the *Dying Slave* and *Rebellious Slave*, the scale, musculature, and torsion of the *Young Slave* are much increased, an expansion that cannot be explained solely by its different planned position on the mausoleum of Julius II. The present drawing shows a powerfully muscled type and looks toward the later rather than the earlier slaves.

It is unique to find proportions indicated in Michelangelo's drawings. The system of measurement that Michelangelo employed is indicated by the superimposed hand and profile at the upper right of the drawing. It was described by Wilde: "The unit . . . is the length of the face from the chin to the hair, which corresponds to the length of the hand; the word 'testa' is used in the notes in the sense of 'faccia'. . . . The whole figure is slightly more than 10 units high. This type of figure is called by Lomazzo . . . the Jupiter type." As Wilde notes, a drawing now in the Fitzwilliam Museum, Cambridge (PD 122-1961), by Bartolomeo Passarotti, applies the same proportional system to the famous wax model of a standing male nude in Casa Buonarroti, one of the most copied of all Michelangelo's figures. Therefore, it is evident that this system was associated with Michelangelo.

The recto study seems to have been planned as a self-sufficient image. The proportional labeling and the figure's static pose suggest that the drawing was made not in preparation for a sculpted or painted figure but as a model anatomy with didactic scope. Michelangelo considered the possibility of writing a treatise on figural proportions, Condivi tells us, although no writing by him on the subject survives. But it is probable that the didactic purpose of this drawing was more limited, perhaps to assist his then pupil Pietro Urbano; the *Study of a Left Leg and Other Sketches* at Christ Church (fig. 9) may have had a similar purpose. Little is known of Pietro, but Vasari says that he was talented and at least one copy drawing of reasonable quality, after Michelangelo's Ecole des Beaux-Arts drawing, might be by him (Louvre Inv. 844). Michelangelo trusted Pietro sufficiently to allow him to carry out the finishing touches to the Minerva *Christ*; he did this badly and was expelled from Michelangelo's service, after which he disappears from sight. An alternative hypothesis, suggested by

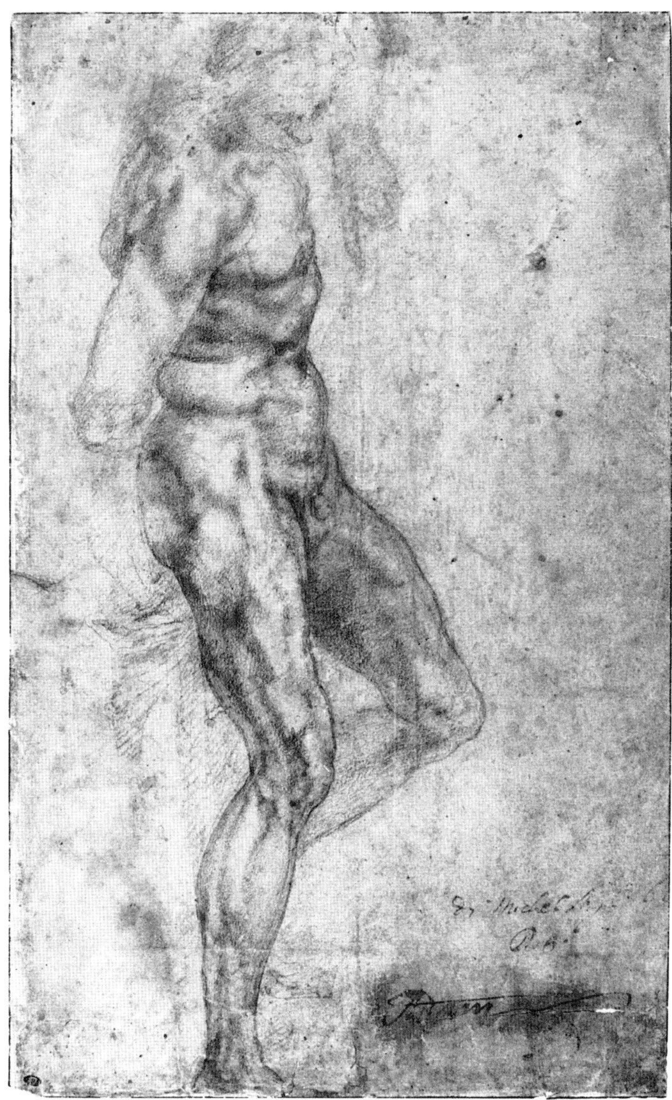

fig. 75. Michelangelo, *Study for the Young Slave*, red chalk, 32.7 x 20 cm. Ecole Nationale Supérieure des Beaux-Arts, Paris

Wilde, is that the drawing was made to instruct Sebastiano del Piombo. If so, it may have been seen in Sebastiano's possession by Giulio Clovio, for, as noted by Wilde, "Una notomia con tutti le misure di Michelangiolo fatta da Dn Giulio" was recorded in Clovio's inventory. Wilde believed this drawing to be identical with a copy of the recto sold with the collection of Sir Edward Poynter, 24 April 1918, lot 82, whose present whereabouts are unknown. But while this may well be correct, the ex-Poynter drawing is not certainly by Clovio, and the "notomia" listed in the inventory might have been the famous crouching figure traditionally connected with Michelangelo, more obviously an anatomy than the present drawing. However, another, partially cut-down, copy of the recto drawing on the present sheet, together with the annotations, is in the Teylers Museum, Haarlem (A. 26): it is of good quality and might be an alternative candidate for Clovio's putative copy. Its provenance would suggest that it was kept among autograph drawings from early on.

That the recto figure is stylistically related to drawings for the slaves finds support in the pose of the verso figure, which is clearly related to the uppermost of sketches of bound figures on the sheet in the Ashmolean Museum (see cat. 30). It was undoubtedly drawn from a live model posed to follow that scheme, but with an easier position of legs, which Michelangelo would certainly have changed in subsequent drawings. Sometimes, when drawing from the live model, Michelangelo included peripheral details such as facial hair: here he shows the model's long hair caught up behind in a knot.

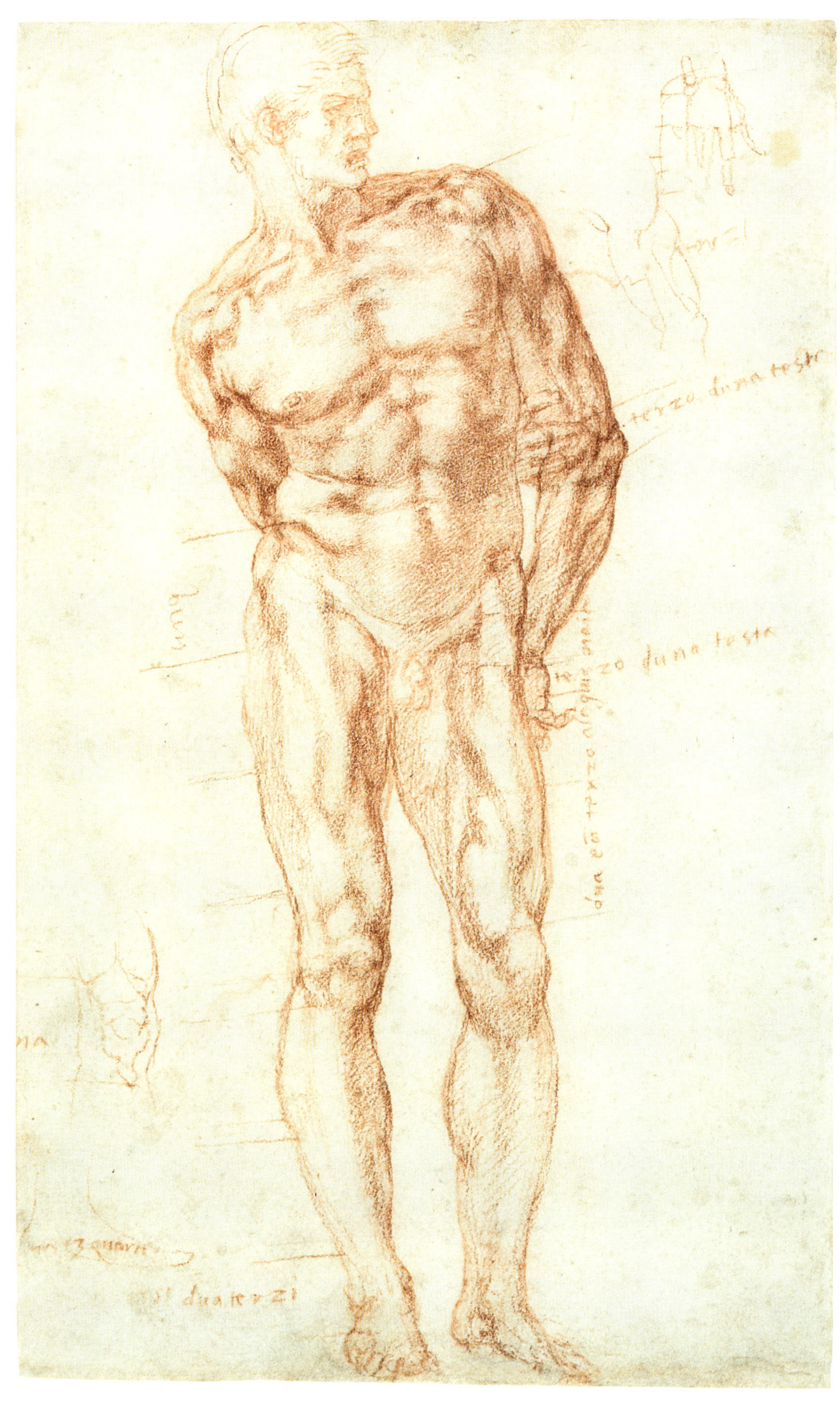

33a

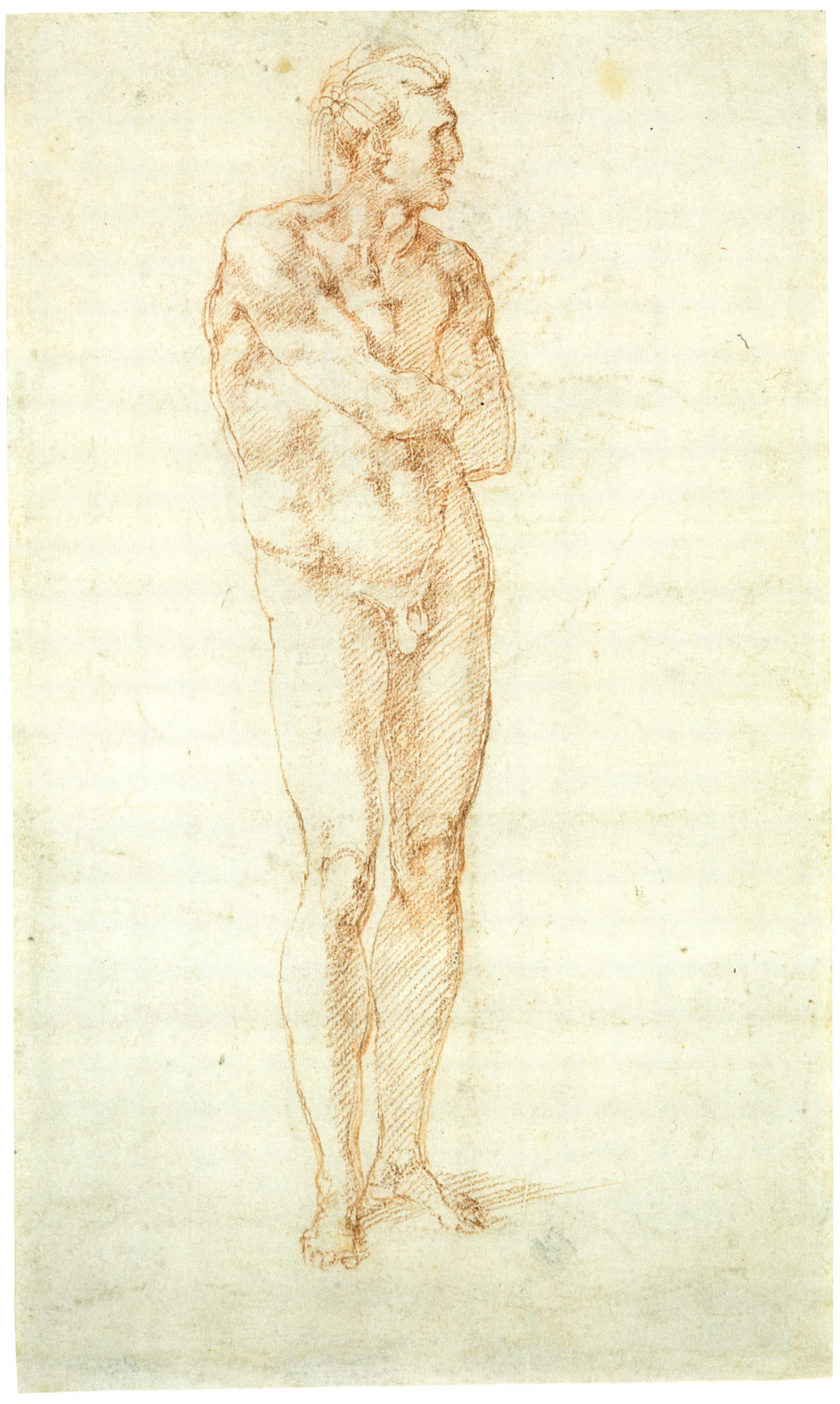

33b

Giulio Clovio after Michelangelo Buonarroti

34
The Flagellation

c. 1545
red chalk over outlining in black chalk
20 x 18.2 (7 7/8 x 7 3/16), the upper corners cut; no watermark
inscribed in pen on the verso by William Gibson: *Julio Clovio da M. Angolo Bon.t /5.2.*
RL 0418

EXHIBITIONS
London 1975, no. 39

LITERATURE
Popham and Wilde 1949, no. 451; Dussler 1959, no. 705; De Tolnay 1975–1980, see 1: no. 73; Hirst 1981, 49–50; Giononi-Visani and Gamulin 1980, 104; Hirst 1988, 46–47

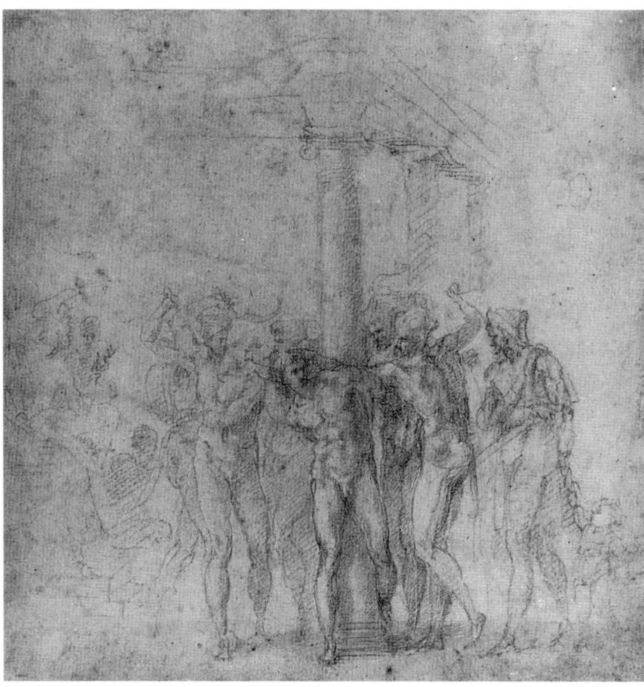

fig. 76. Michelangelo, *The Flagellation of Christ*, red chalk, 23.5 x 23.6 cm. British Museum, London, Department of Prints and Drawings

As pointed out to the compiler by Martin Clayton, the inscription is not of the sixteenth century as Wilde thought, but by the dealer William Gibson. Unlike his similar inscription on *Tityus* (cat. 14), it seems accurate: the tentative contours and the delicate treatment of the feet, for example, are typical of Giulio Clovio. But despite these personal traits, the drawing is fully convincing as a copy of Michelangelo's lost *modello*, made for his friend Sebastiano del Piombo, and prepared in two autograph drawings now in the British Museum (fig. 76, w. 15 / c. 73; Pouncey and Gere 276 / c. 74). As noted by Wilde, further support for the attribution to Clovio is provided by an entry in his inventory: "Un Xpo alla colonna in lapis rosso con tre figure di Michelagniolo fata da D. Giulio." Clovio probably made this copy when the original—about which nothing further is known—was in Sebastiano's possession, for, according to Vasari, the two men were close friends. It must provide a reasonably accurate picture of the original, but the areas of shadow are more even in tone than expected in a drawing by Michelangelo. Also, areas of highlight, such as those on the right-hand flagellator's back, read as though they lie on the surface rather than modeling form in depth. The contours, too, are dully regular.

The commission by the Florentine banker Pierfrancesco Borgherini, a friend of Michelangelo's and a patron of Andrea del Sarto's, to fresco his family chapel in San Pietro in Montorio was probably allocated to Sebastiano on Michelangelo's advice. Michelangelo and Sebastiano had become friends in the years following the latter's arrival in Rome, and Michelangelo had provided him with drawings—indeed, may have devised the whole figure group—for his *Pietà* in Viterbo, of circa 1514. Their friendship was strengthened by shared detestation of Raphael, who had supplanted Sebastiano in the favor of the Maecenas responsible for bringing him to Rome, Agostino Chigi. Combining Michelangelo's powers of design with Sebastiano's richness of surface effect and somber chiaroscuro, the two attempted to combat Raphael's increasing power and reputation. By 1516 conflict between the two camps had reached the point that Cardinal Giulio organized a public competition, commissioning for the cathedral of his diocese of Narbonne two large altarpieces: the *Transfiguration* from Raphael and the *Raising of Lazarus* from Sebastiano. Michelangelo, resident in Florence, sent his protégé drawings for the key figures in the *Lazarus* in 1516. In the same year he also sent drawings for the *Flagellation*, although Sebastiano did not complete the Borgherini chapel until 1524. The outcome of the competition was agreed to be in Raphael's favor. While Sebastiano's painting was sent to Narbonne, the pope decided to keep Raphael's *Transfiguration* in Rome and to commission for Narbonne a replica from Penni. But Raphael's triumph was posthumous, and Sebastiano, in executing the *Flagellation* (fig. 77) and his own *Transfiguration* in the semi-dome above it, had a second chance to vie with Raphael's *Transfiguration*, which the pope had placed in San Pietro in Montorio.

The call to provide a design that would present a further challenge to Raphael came when Michelangelo was planning the façade of the church of San Lorenzo. On it he intended to include, in addition to statuary,

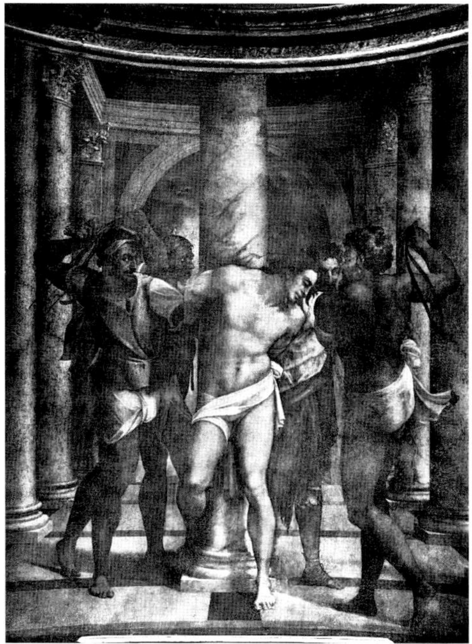

fig. 77. Sebastiano del Piombo, *The Flagellation of Christ*, wall painting in oil. San Pietro in Montorio, Rome [Fratelli Alinari, 1995]

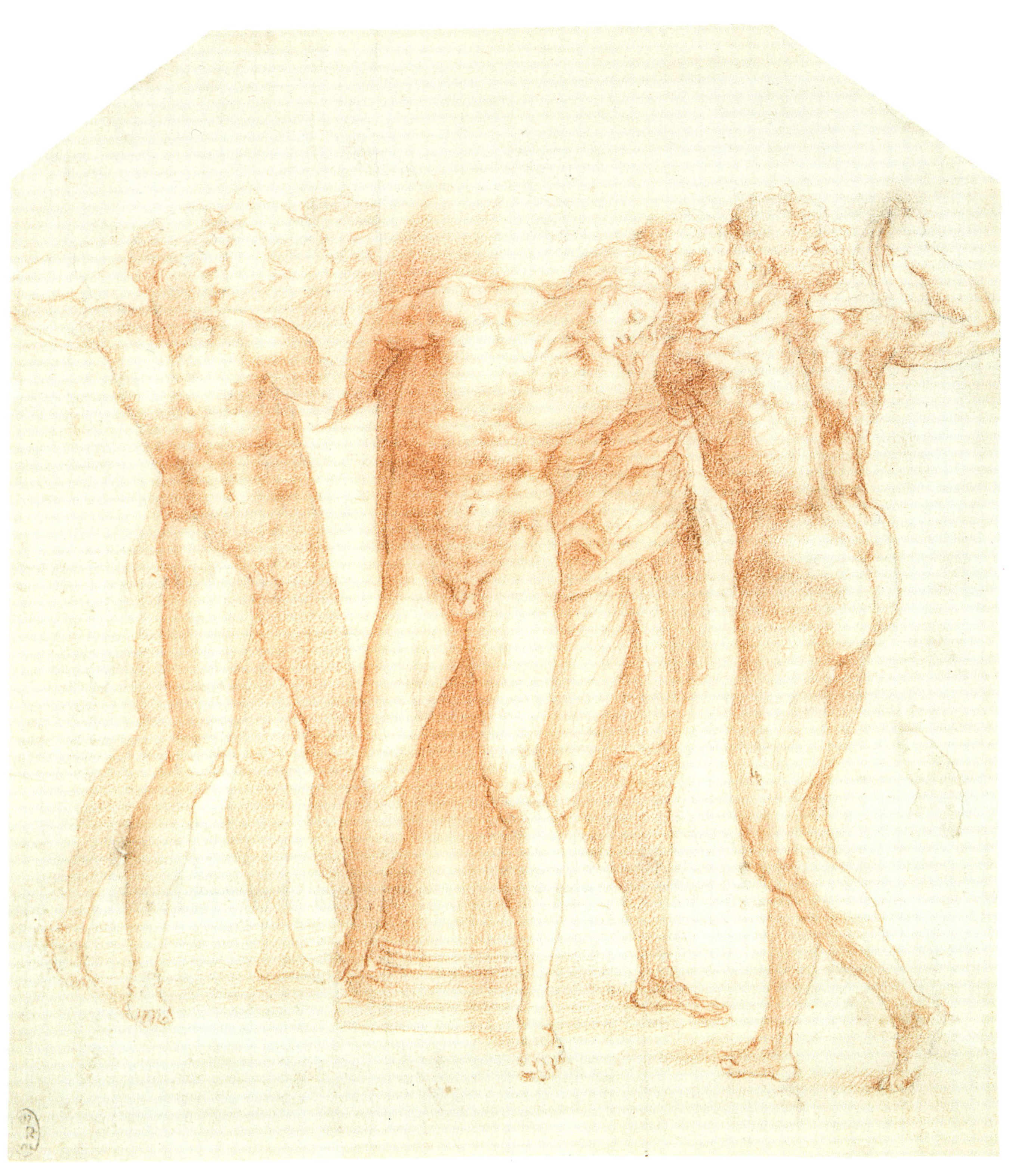

large reliefs of subjects from the lives of Saint Lawrence and Saints Cosmas and Damian. He was also working, perhaps in a more concentrated way than at any other period of his life, on the representation of relatively conventional narratives. In his few surviving drawings for the project, he seems to have experimented with more elongated and elegant forms than he had hitherto employed and he was obviously concerned with severity and clarity. His *modello* for Sebastiano may have been influenced by these current preoccupations, for the pictorial British Museum sketch, with its many figures placed in an obliquely viewed setting, has been reduced to Christ flanked by his four tormentors seen directly from the front, a composition that could have been executed as a high relief.

Michelangelo's composition was intended to be clear, simple, and immediately memorable. In its unrelenting frontality, it develops the scheme of the unfinished *Entombment*: both are presentational images calculated for public display (fig. 77). The *Flagellation*'s influence was great and few later treatments of the subject entirely escaped it. Even Caravaggio's great *Flagellation* in Naples is in its debt. It also elicited a riposte from the Raphael camp. The *Flagellation* in Santa Prassede of around 1520—which seems to have been designed by Giulio and executed by Penni—clearly reveals their meditation on Michelangelo's design, of which they must have been aware.

It may be that the smoothness and streamlined effect of the figures in Michelangelo's *modello* were planned to be appropriate to Sebastiano's inherently geometrical sense of form. But the effect of elegance rather than force is not merely a surrender to Raphaelesque fashion: the Apollonian figure of Christ, in his physical beauty and perfection, triumphs over the efforts of the flagellators, whose impotence to affect his spirit is expressed in their ugliness and confusion.

Giulio Romano (?) after Michelangelo Buonarroti

35
The Central Figure from the Battle of Cascina

c. 1524 (?)
red chalk
16.5 x 19.2 (6 1/2 x 7 9/16); no watermark
inscribed on verso in pen (effaced): *di Raffaello da Urbino*
RL 5317

EXHIBITIONS
London 1975, no. 11

LITERATURE
Popham and Wilde 1949, no. 448

Although Michelangelo's cartoon for *Battle of Cascina* was drawn in charcoal, many of the copies after it are in sanguine. The present drawing is a good early copy of the central and pivotal figure in Michelangelo's design, the older soldier, Manno Donati. Seeing the danger his comrades are running by bathing, he gives a false alarm to alert them to their peril (compare fig. 78). The copyist has not been identified but was clearly accurate, efficient, and, in his rapidity of drawing, self-confident. The old inscription on the verso may have been intended to identify the copyist. However, although Raphael certainly made copies after the cartoon, at least one of which survives (Vatican Lat. 13391 f. 1 verso), the present drawing does not correspond to his drawing style in his Florentine years. It is closer to that of his later Roman period, during which he remembered *Cascina* and quoted from it at least once. While the present drawing can hardly be by him, the treatment of the figure's hair, the chalk lines placed over the fast hatching to indicate the musculature, and the changes of hatching direction point to an artist working within Raphael's circle, and it is tempting to suggest that it is by Giulio Romano. Giulio may have gone to Florence, although no visit is documented, but a portion of the cartoon was recorded in Mantua, where he transferred in 1524, and it may have contained this figure. However, it must be admitted that this attribution is speculative and that the handling of the present drawing is freer than that of any surviving red-chalk drawing securely by Giulio.

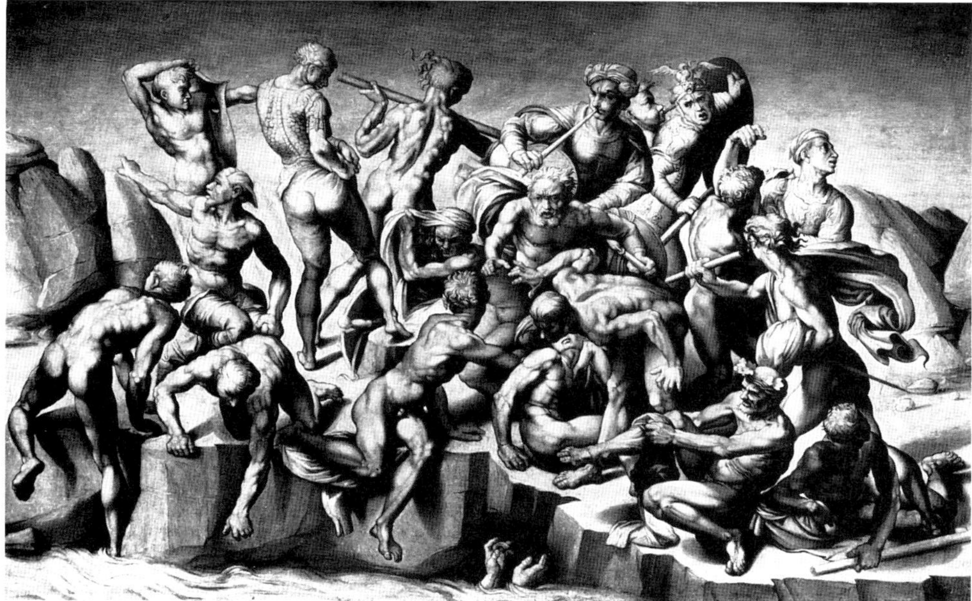

fig. 78. Aristotile da Sangallo after Michelangelo, *The Battle of Cascina*, oil on panel, 78.7 x 129 cm. Collection of the Earl of Leicester, Holkham Hall, Norfolk [Courtauld Institute of Art]

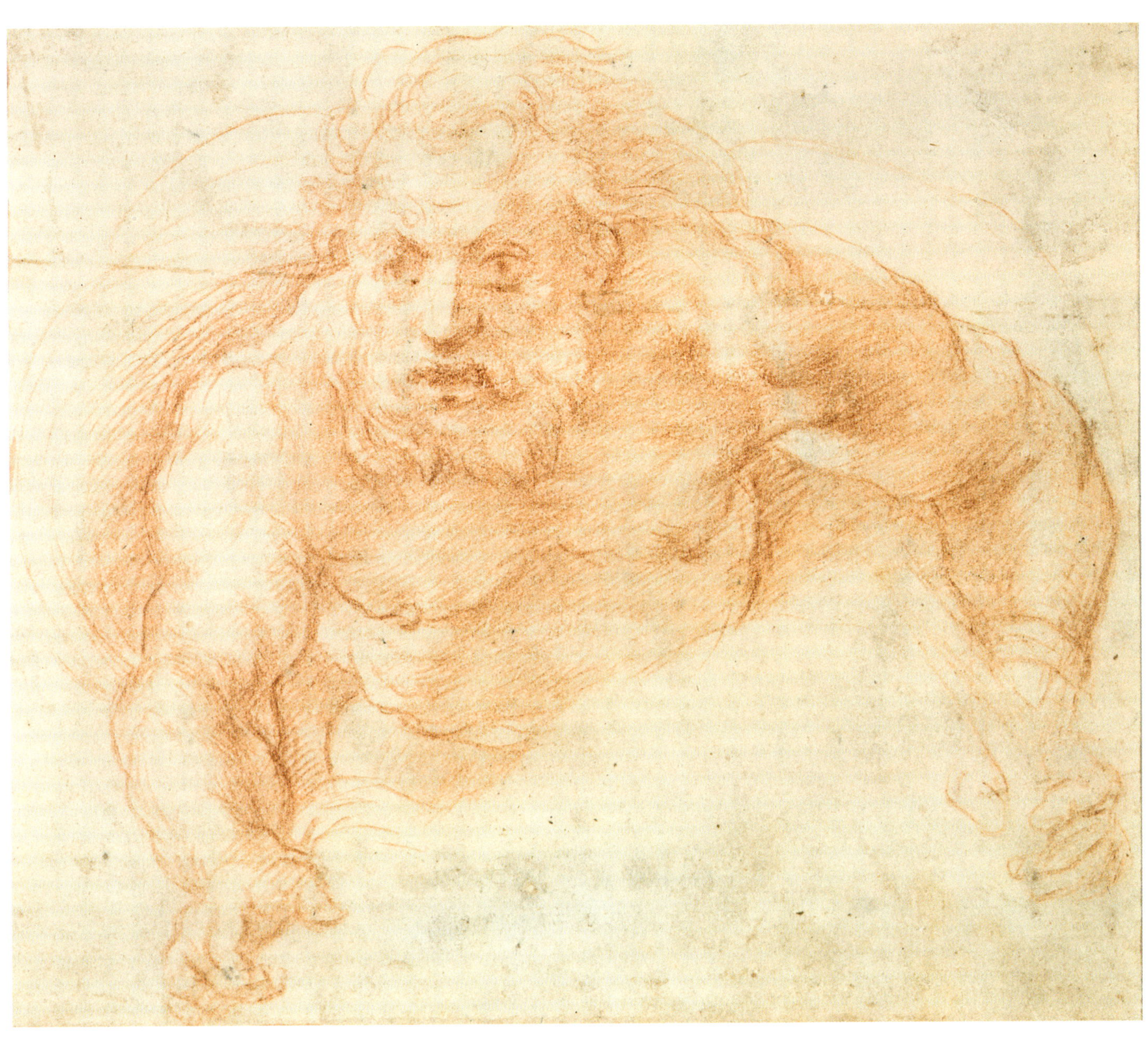

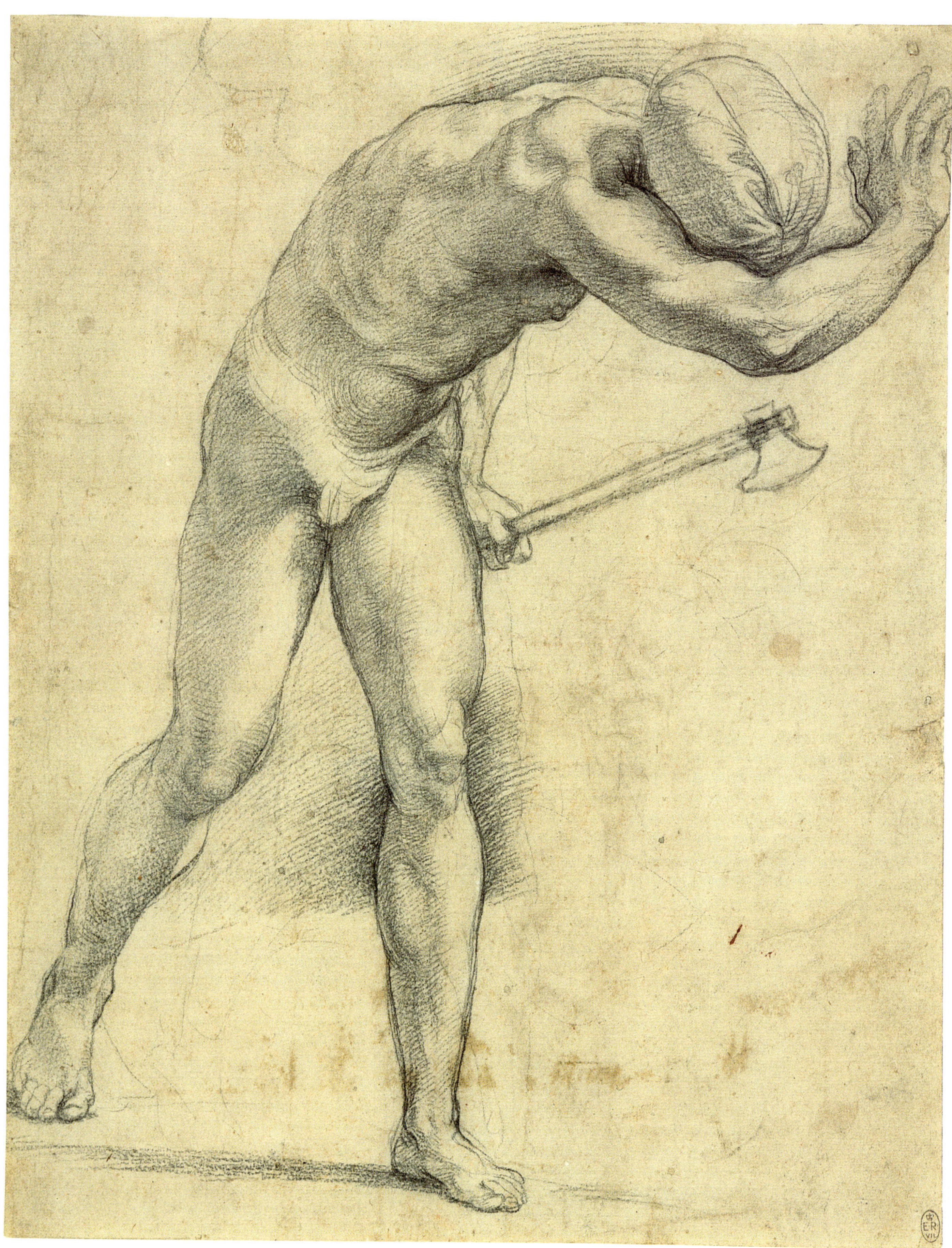

Raphael

36
A Nude Man with an Axe Fleeing to the Right

c. 1512
black chalk
32 x 25.5 (12 5/8 x 10 1/16); watermark: crossbow in circle, not in Briquet
RL 12735

EXHIBITIONS
London 1972–1973, no. 56; London 1983, no. 170; Sydney-Brisbane-Melbourne 1988, no. 18

LITERATURE
Fischel 1898, no. 179; Fischel 1913–1941, 8: no. 393; Fischel 1948, 96–98; Popham and Wilde 1949, no. 799 (recto); Hirst 1961, 171–174; Joannides 1983, no. 307; Knab et al. 1983, no. 476

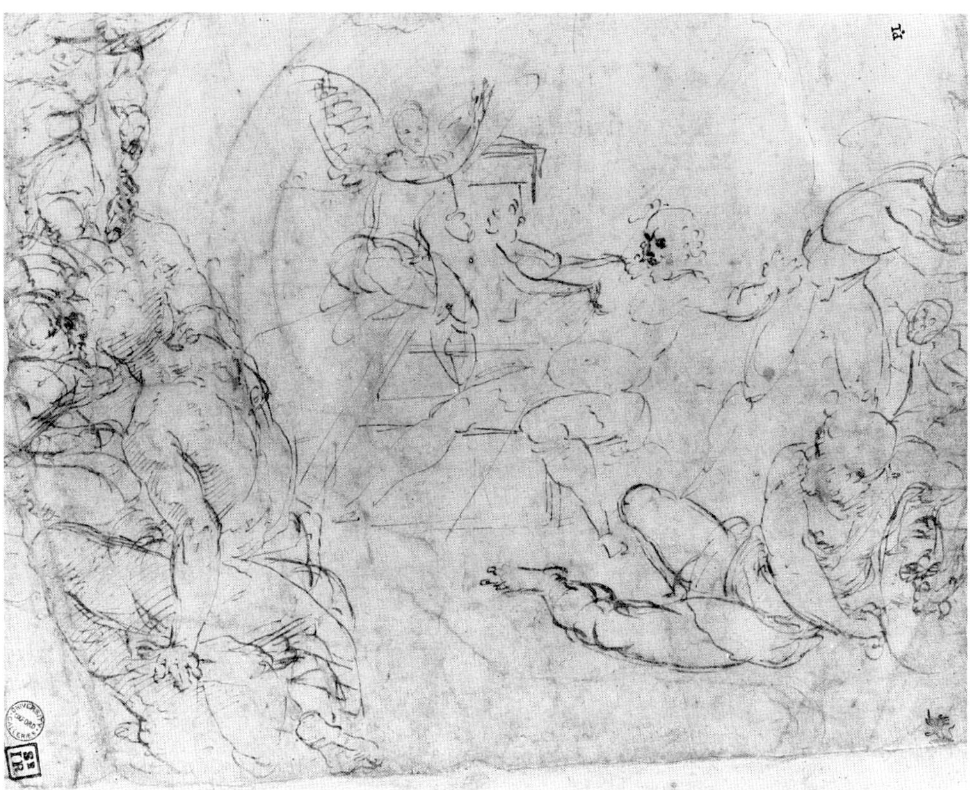

fig. 79. Raphael, *The Resurrection of Christ* (lower section), pen and ink, 20.8 x 26.2 cm. Ashmolean Museum, Oxford

This figure, drawn on the recto of the sheet, was made in preparation for one of Raphael's boldest compositions, an altarpiece of the *Resurrection of Christ* designed around 1512. It is generally believed to have been intended for Agostino Chigi's chapel in Santa Maria della Pace, as a pair to an *Assumption of the Virgin* planned contemporaneously by Raphael for Chigi's chapel in Santa Maria del Popolo. Both altarpieces remained unexecuted. The *Resurrection*'s connection with the Pace, first indicated by Fischel, was argued in detail by Hirst (1961). However, Gould (1992) posed certain objections to this reconstruction on the grounds of the, presumably, large size of the planned *Resurrection* and the rather small space available in the chapel in the Pace. It remains a possibility that the *Resurrection* was intended for the other site, the Popolo chapel, for which a much larger altarpiece was planned.

Compositional sketches for the *Resurrection* survive in Bayonne (Bean 132) and Oxford (fig. 79, p. 558). The former shows the whole composition, but the latter, confined to the lower half, shows a more advanced arrangement of the guards, for whom Raphael made several highly finished nude studies in black chalk. No drawings of them wearing armor are known, and since these would have followed the nude studies, it may be that the project was soon shelved. The figure studied in the present drawing was employed in reverse for a guard in the *Release of Saint Peter* in the Stanza d'Eliodoro, probably painted in 1513. Therefore, it is likely that the *Resurrection* scheme or, at least, the version of it seen in the Oxford and Bayonne drawings, had by then been abandoned. Some support for this dating is found in the watermark, which is identical to that on Popham and Wilde 797, which contains studies for two scenes in the window embrasure of the *Justice* wall of the Stanza della Segnatura, executed in 1511.

The *Resurrection* was Raphael's most elaborate altarpiece composition up to that time. Its double level and dramatic light effects anticipate the *Transfiguration*. In that painting, however, movement is reduced and the final effect of the lower section is contemplative, displaying the apostles' emotional and spiritual reactions to the distress of the possessed boy. The *Resurrection* was Raphael's attempt to equal *Cascina*, to show a group of soldiers responding to a dramatic apparition. In Raphael's case the use of black chalk was probably to strengthen contrasts of chiaroscuro, unlike Michelangelo, who probably employed black chalk for *Cascina* mainly because he had not yet appreciated the potential of red chalk.

Raphael's guards are thrown into a series of complicated poses, some clearly reflecting specific Michelangelesque models as well as general Michelangelesque ambitions. The guard on the left, seen from the rear, reworks one of Michelangelo's *ignudi*; another, lying on the ground, adopts the pose of the man at the right-hand side of the *Cascina*. The *Resurrection* was designed at a period when Raphael had come strongly under the influence of the Sistine ceiling and what he knew of the Julius Tomb. It was this phase that produced the personifications in the upper part of the *Justice* wall in the Stanza della Segnatura, and the *Isaiah* in San Agostino. It was soon to pass, as Raphael abandoned the attempt to imitate Michelangelo and turned to models of a less emphatic Hellenism.

A completely unrelated subject, cattle in a pasture, was sketched by Raphael on the verso of this sheet.

Giulio Romano

37
Figure Study for the Stoning of Saint Stephen

c. 1519
black chalk on buff paper
39 x 12.4 (15 3/8 x 4 7/8), torn and made up on the lower right side; no watermark
RL 0339

EXHIBITIONS
Mantua 1989, 255

LITERATURE
Popham and Wilde 1949, no. 348; Hartt 1958, no. 41; Ferino Pagden 1984, 70–72

Popham's suggestion that this figure was made in preparation for Giulio's great altarpiece of the *Stoning of Saint Stephen*, painted for the church of Santo Stefano in Genoa, was vindicated by Ferino Pagden's discovery of a copy of a lost *modello* for the painting in the Ecole des Beaux-Arts in Paris (fig. 80, Inv. 334), which contains a figure in the same pose.

The *Stoning* is undocumented. It has generally been dated 1522–1523, but an inscription on the now-lost frame is recorded as reading: *Leoni X P.M. Fratrisqu. Julii Card. Medices Beneficio, Templo Praef.* This proves that it was completed before Cardinal Giulio became pope, as Clement VII, in December 1523, but it also suggests that it was completed within the lifetime of Leo X, who died in December 1521. It was painted for the papal councillor, Gianmatteo Ghiberti, who later commissioned the design of the apse of Verona cathedral from Giulio, but it seems more likely than not that it was ordered from Raphael toward the end of his life and that the present drawing, although by Giulio, was made under Raphael's instructions. In late projects, such as the *Transfiguration* and the *Battle of the Milvian Bridge* in the Sala di Costantino, Raphael seems to have worked side by side with his most talented pupil, both making drawings with the same function in the design process. Their respective contributions are distinguished by personal style, not purpose, and Raphael's trust in Giulio was clearly great. The composition of the *Stoning* both in the *modello* and as completed is similar to that of the *Transfiguration*, but in the painting, movement is accelerated and intensified, and the effort of balance recorded in the Ecole des Beaux-Arts drawing is replaced by an emphasis on violence and cruelty. That detachment from the specific, that urge to generalization, always present in Raphael's work, is jettisoned by Giulio in favor of the unbalanced and the aggressive.

The treatment of the figure in a soft broad style, with chalk used as though it were charcoal, is also found in Raphael's late figure drawings in black chalk. In an autograph drawing such as that in the Ashmolean Museum for the *Battle of the Milvian Bridge* (P. 569), the forms seem to be modeled in soft clay. The linearity that characterizes even *Nude Man* (cat. 36) has been superseded by an application in masses, soft but simultaneously highly sculptural. Raphael was probably reflecting anew on Michelangelo's drawing style of the *Cascina* period, such as the Albertina study of the man seen from the back (SR 157 / C. 53 verso), and Giulio was following his master's lead.

The dramatic situation of the *Stoning* is comparable to those of the *Cascina* and Raphael's *Resurrection*; however, the movement is centripetal rather than centrifugal or scattered, in toward Saint Stephen rather than away from a source of alarm.

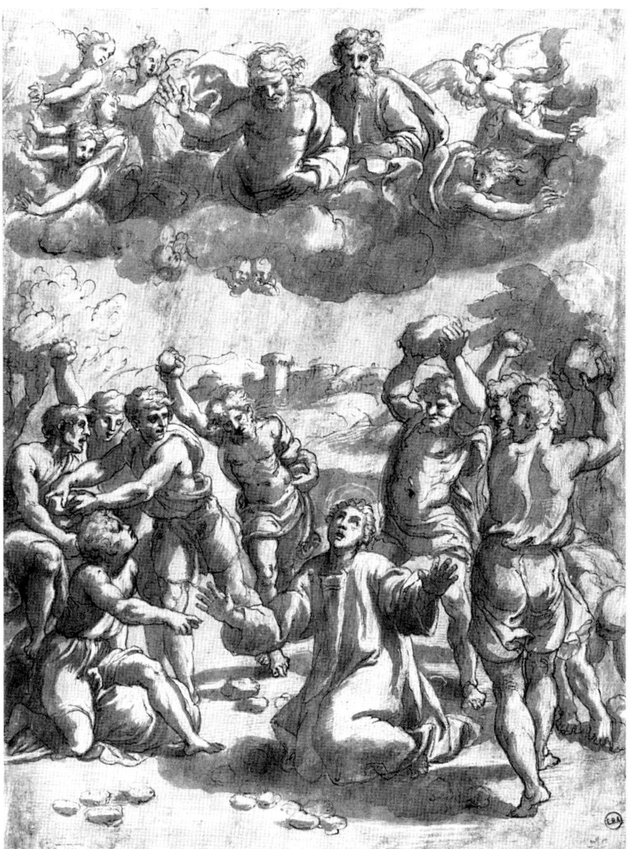

fig. 80. After Raphael or Giulio Romano, *The Stoning of Saint Stephen*, pen and ink and wash over black chalk, 30.2 x 27.2 cm. Ecole Nationale Supérieure des Beaux-Arts, Paris

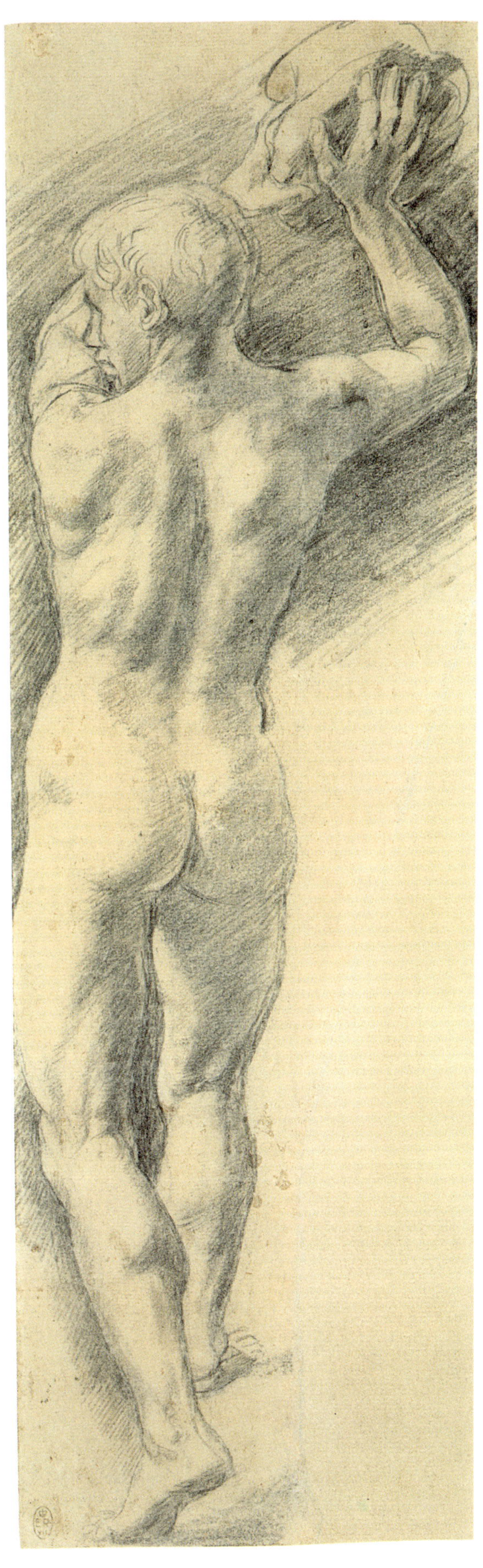

Michelangelo Buonarroti

38
The Resurrection

c. 1532
black chalk, with some red chalk offsetting, over stylus indications
24 x 34.7 (9 7/16 x 13 11/16); no watermark
inscribed in pen on the verso: *D Giulio Clovio* in same hand as the inscription on cat. 16
RL 12767

EXHIBITIONS
London 1930, no. 512; London 1950–1951, 270; London 1953, no. 88; London 1962, no. 76; London 1972–1973, no. 38; London 1975, no. 46; London 1986, no. 25; Washington 1987, no. 23; Montreal 1992, no. 101

LITERATURE
Berenson 1903 and 1938, no. 1612; Frey 1909–1911, nos. 19, 244; Thode 1913, no. 537; De Tolnay 1948, no. 109; Popham and Wilde 1949, no. 427; Goldscheider 1951, no. 78; Dussler 1959, no. 239; Hirst 1961, 178–183; Berti 1965, 452, no. 147; Goldscheider 1966, no. 81; Hartt 1971, no. 256; De Tolnay 1975–1980, 2: no. 255; Hirst 1988, 15; Perrig 1991, 5–7, 42

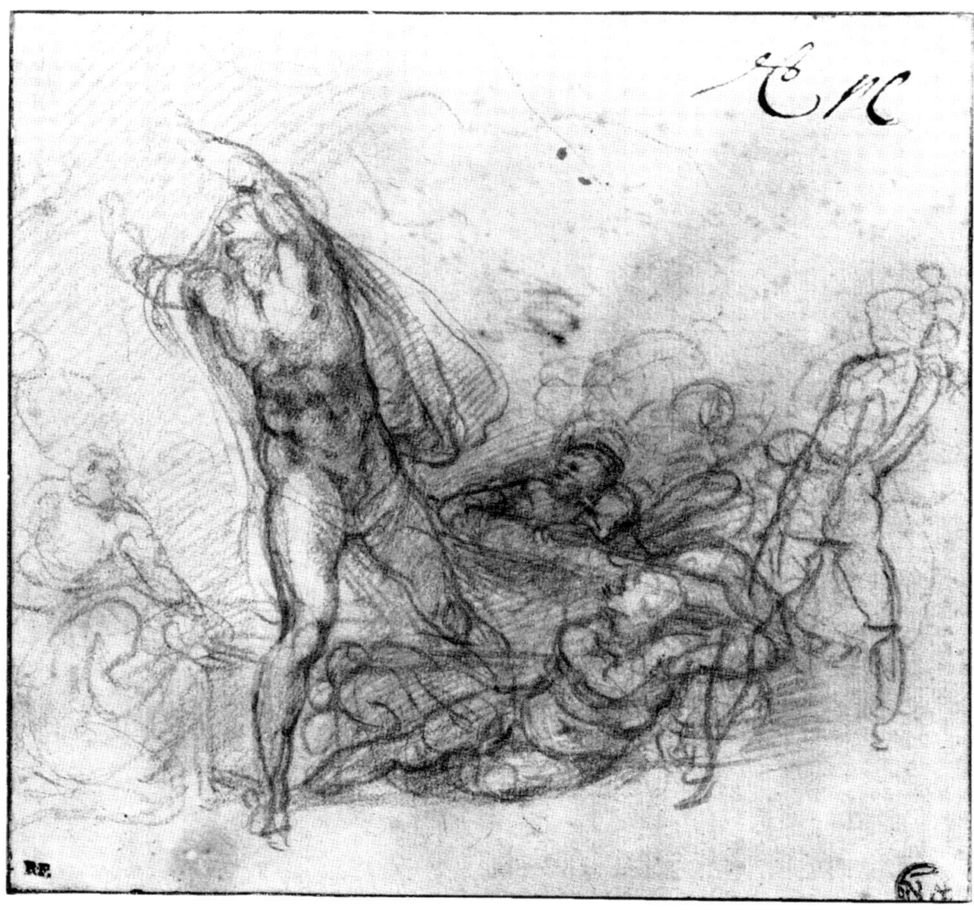

fig. 81. Michelangelo, *The Resurrection of Christ*, red chalk, 15.5 x 17.1 cm. Musée du Louvre, Paris, Département des Arts Graphiques [Photo RMN]

There has been virtual unanimity about this drawing's attribution, approximate date, and relation to a smaller red-chalk sketch of the same composition in the Louvre (fig. 81, Inv. 691bis / c. 253). But no agreement has been reached about the purpose of the two drawings and fourteen others of the same period depicting Christ's *Resurrection*. The problem is too complicated to investigate here, but, in general, the drawings divide into two groups. One comprises multifigure compositions, in which guards scatter in alarm as Christ rises from the tomb; the other consists of single-figure compositions, showing Christ alone, isolated at his moment of triumph over death. It seems to the compiler highly improbable that both groups were intended for the same scheme (for a discussion of the single-figure scenes see cat. 39).

Taking the present drawing, on the recto of the sheet, and the Louvre sketch as one, there exist three multifigure *Resurrections*, all relatively fully worked-out. The present composition is horizontal in emphasis and lit from the left. Of the other two, both in the British Museum, one (w. 52 / c. 258) is broadly horizontal in format, but could be seen as lunette-shaped, and is lit from the right; the other (w. 53 / c. 264) is emphatically vertical and lit from the left. Given such discrepancies in proportion and illumination, it is scarcely credible that all three could have been intended for the same project.

It is unknown whether all or some of these three were made for projects to be executed by Michelangelo himself, by another artist, or by other artists. Various suggestions have been advanced concerning their purpose. Popp suggested that the present drawing and British Museum w. 52 were alternative schemes for a fresco to be executed in the lunette above the Magnifici tomb in the New Sacristy; De Tolnay and Hartt (1971) agreed with this view of some of the drawings but detached others. Hartt considered w. 53 to be for a relief for the Julius Tomb in 1516, which is entirely improbable, while De Tolnay thought it was for an altarpiece for the Sistine Chapel of circa 1534, which is equally improbable. Hirst (1961) suggested that Michelangelo made all the *Resurrection* drawings, including Louvre 691bis, to assist Sebastiano with his altarpiece of the Resurrection for the Chigi chapel in Santa Maria della Pace. First contracted for in 1520, the commission was renewed in 1530, and Sebastiano might well have requested Michelangelo's aid thereafter.

In the compiler's view, the present drawing, for which Michelangelo separately sketched the guard sprawled on the sarcophagus lid (Casa Buonarroti 32F / c. 254), and Louvre 691bis can be separated from the other drawings. He finds most convincing Gamba's suggestion (1945), generally dismissed, that they were made in preparation for a *Resurrection* to be frescoed on the entrance wall of the Sistine Chapel, where the version by Michelangelo's master, Ghirlandaio, had been irreparably damaged in a fall of masonry on Christmas Eve, 1522. Subject, lighting direction, and proportions are appropriate for the location, and both the fresco that had to be replaced and the fresco that finally replaced it were and are multifigure scenes. Gamba's view was also accepted by Perrig, although he believed the present drawing to be a copy by Giulio Clovio after a lost Michelangelo.

Michelangelo's Windsor drawing differs

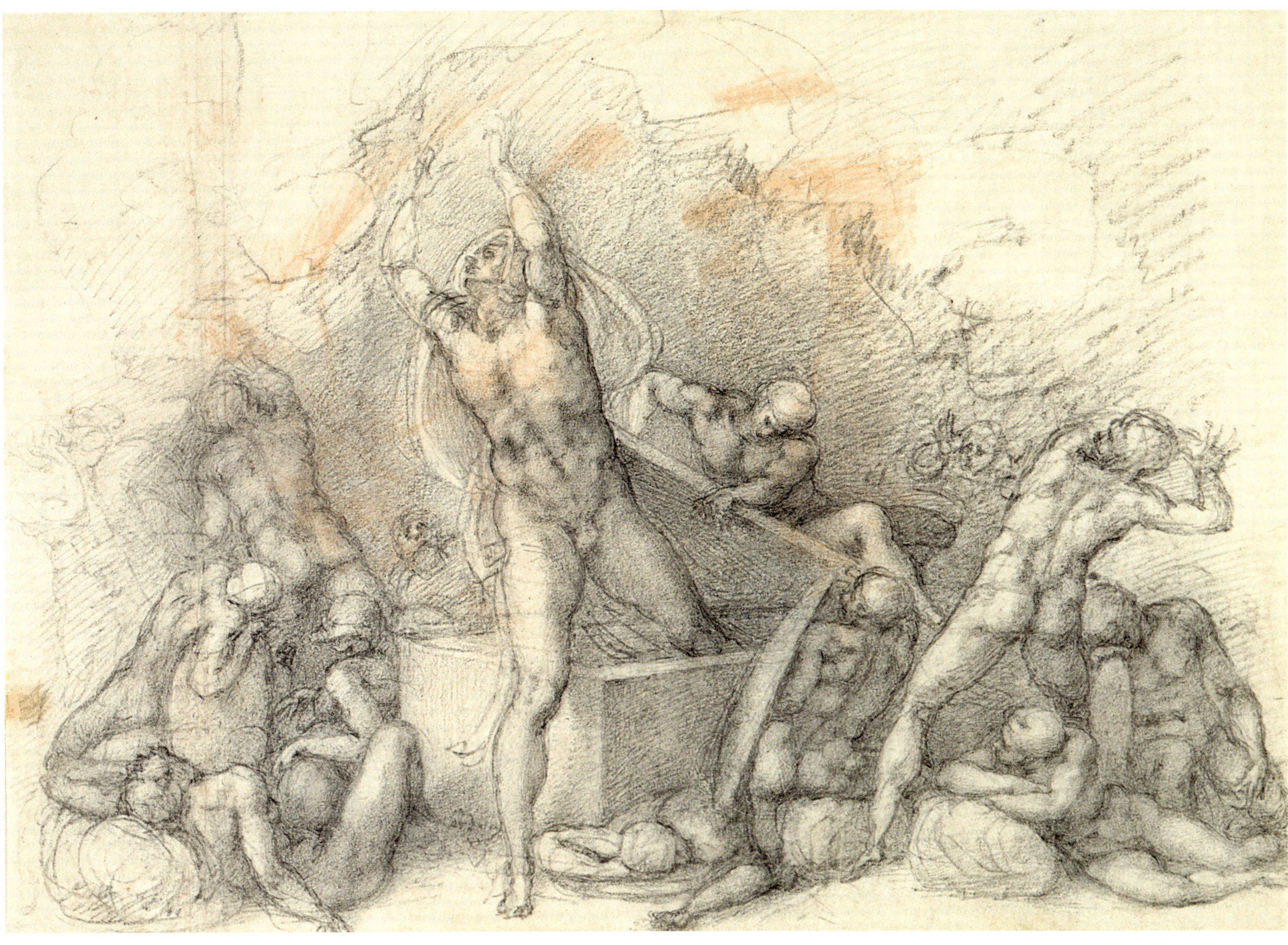

from the Louvre sketch in a number of particulars, especially in the inclusion of more elaborately posed figures of guards and, as pointed out by G. Passavant (1983), Michelangelo obviously alluded to Schongauer's *Resurrection* print. Michelangelo's first recorded work was a colored copy of Schongauer's *Saint Anthony*, and he must have known his engravings well. The adoption of such ideas here, as well as the formula of Christ stepping out from the tomb, which is much commoner in northern Europe than in Italy, is perhaps both a covert acknowledgment of his admiration of the German artist's inventiveness and an effort to revitalize his own ideas.

Monbeig Goguel (1978) had previously linked Giulio Romano's drawing of the *Resurrection* (Staatliche Museen, Berlin KdZ 26368) with Schongauer's print, and the similarity between Giulio's drawing and Michelangelo's Windsor drawing seems too close for coincidence. It is, however, a matter for conjecture what their relation might be. It could be argued that the present drawing, or a copy of it, was sent to Federico Gonzaga—for whom, in 1537, Michelangelo designed a saltcellar and a model for a horse to be cast in bronze—as a *modello* for a painting to be executed by another artist, but no documentary evidence of such a transaction survives. However, Giulio Clovio is a possibility as the intermediary between Michelangelo and Giulio Romano, particularly given the inscription on the verso.

The studies of shoulders on the verso are in the style of drawings for the *Last Judgment*, and were probably made in connection with that fresco, circa 1534. Their placing on the sheet suggests that when they were made they occupied a page in an album. The sketches do not cross the fold and stitching holes can be seen at the right, which suggests that when they were made the album was still bound. This page must have been half the verso of the central sheet in an album and the *Resurrection* on the recto would have been drawn by Michelangelo across the album's central spread, either before or after the album had been disbound. The whole sheet, a double spread, would subsequently have been trimmed to the recto image.

Michelangelo Buonarroti

39
The Risen Christ

c. 1532
black chalk
37.3 x 22.1 (14 11/16 x 8 11/16); watermark: ladder in shield with star, Roberts Ladder G / Briquet 5926
RL 12768

EXHIBITIONS
London 1930, no. 514; Edinburgh 1947, no. 143; London 1950–1951, no. 271; London 1953, no. 86; London 1962, no. 75; London 1972–1973, no. 36; London 1975, no. 44; Washington-Paris 1988–1989, no. 41

LITERATURE
Berenson 1903 and 1938, no. 1616; Frey 1909–1911, no. 8; Thode 1913, no. 541; Popham and Wilde 1949, no. 428; Dussler 1959, no. 363; De Tolnay 1960, no. 167; Hirst 1961, 178–183; Berti 1965, 452, no. 149; Hartt 1971, no. 125; De Tolnay 1975–1980, 2: no. 265; Wilde 1978, 157; Perrig 1991, 45

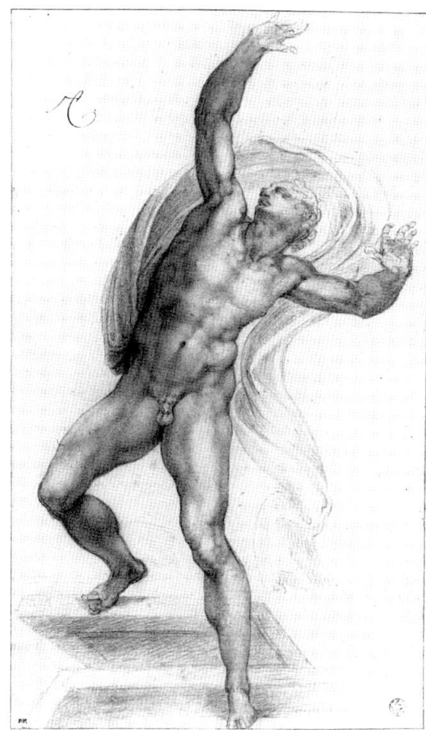

fig. 82. Alessandro Allori after Michelangelo, *The Risen Christ*, black chalk, 37.2 x 22.4 cm. Musée du Louvre, Paris, Département des Arts Graphiques [Photo RMN]

The present drawing is one of four highly worked variants of the single figure of Christ emerging from the tomb. The other three are British Museum W. 54 / C. 263; Casa Buonarroti 65F verso / C. 347 verso; and a lost drawing known in copies in the Museum Boymans-van Beuningen, Rotterdam (I. 20, attributed by Wilde to Giulio Clovio) and in the Uffizi (1450S, as by Alessandro Allori). Casa Buonarroti 65F is more loosely handled than the others, but counts among them. All these figures are lit from the right.

Also, seven rough sketches on six sheets concentrate on the single figure of Christ: five of them seem to prepare various of the developed studies; two were probably made in preparation for comparable drawings that were either never executed or that have been lost. As far as can be seen, all these figures are lit from the left.

It is highly unlikely that the single-figure *Resurrections* were planned for the same projects as any of the group compositions (see cat. 38). To believe otherwise would be to accept an extraordinary freedom in the commission, independent of any constraints of space, proportion, or iconography. Few scholars have suggested specific purposes for the single figures and the most elaborate proposal, by Hartt, who believed both the group and single-figure designs to have been done at different dates over a period of about twenty years for different projects, has found no acceptance and seems wholly unconvincing. All other scholars, including the compiler, date all the *Resurrection* drawings to the early 1530s. No evidence exists for any of Hartt's suggested locations for the single-figure drawings, let alone that the present one was made in 1512 as a study for an altarpiece for the Sistine Chapel. Another explanation was attempted by Perrig, who suggested that at least some of the single figures were made by Michelangelo to assist Sebastiano with the *Descent into Limbo* (Prado, Madrid). However, it is likely that this painting was completed well before the early 1530s. Furthermore, Hirst pointed out (in Washington-Paris 1988) that in the drawing that might most readily be interpreted as a *Descent into Limbo* (British Museum W. 54 recto / C. 263 recto), Christ stands on a lightly indicated, but clearly recognizable sarcophagus. Perrig's suggestion is, in general, improbable because all the single figures show Christ barely touching the ground, apparently ascending rather than descending.

To the compiler the most likely explanation is a modified version of the hypothesis of Hirst, who linked all the *Resurrection* drawings—which, as previously noted, he did not subdivide into different groups—with Sebastiano's commission to paint a *Resurrection* in the Chigi chapel in Santa Maria della Pace. Sebastiano's projected painting, for which no drawings by Sebastiano himself are known, would, like Raphael's sibyls and prophets frescoed above, have been lit from the right. In theory, any of the single-figure compositions could have fitted. Such figures, inappropriate for a large altarpiece, would be fine for a small one.

However, there are two caveats. One is that the payment Sebastiano was to receive was 1200 ducats, only 300 less than for the very large altarpiece in Santa Maria del Popolo, so that the size of the altarpiece is likely in principle to have been comparable. The second is that drawings such as the present one would have put considerable strain on Sebastiano's capacities as a painter of the nude, and it is notable that, in a drawing certainly made for his friend at about the same time (Louvre Inv. 716 / C. 92, for the Ubeda *Pietà*), Michelangelo deliberately simplified the modeling.

It may be that the explanation is a mixed one and that the drawings, although prompted by Sebastiano's putative request, developed an independent existence. Some of them, including the present one, may have been presentation drawings, as Wilde suggested (1953a). In Michelangelo's work, *modelli* and presentation drawings are categories that merge, and it remains a possibility, which the provenance would not oppose, that the present drawing was made for Cavalieri. He possessed a sketch for the *Resurrected Christ* on the verso of the *Tityus*, and since that sketch has a reasonable claim to have been the starting point of the present design, Michelangelo may have developed it as a further gift for his friend. The present drawing was copied, probably by Alessandro Allori, in a drawing now in the Louvre (fig. 82, Inv. 1505), but Allori certainly had access to drawings by Michelangelo other than those owned by Cavalieri.

The figure of Christ in this drawing is one of the most potent in Michelangelo's art. It possesses an unequaled splendor of movement and glory in the body, an uninhibited power and joyousness, as Christ welcomes the light after his forty hours in the tomb. The shroud floats outward, extending like a pennant of victory. Only when representing the divine could Michelangelo feel wholly at liberty, and here he has infused the figure not only with unrivaled energy but with spiritual power. Christ's pose echoes that of *God the Father Separating Light from Darkness* on the Sistine vault. He bursts from the tomb describing an arc of triumph, an all-encompassing embrace.

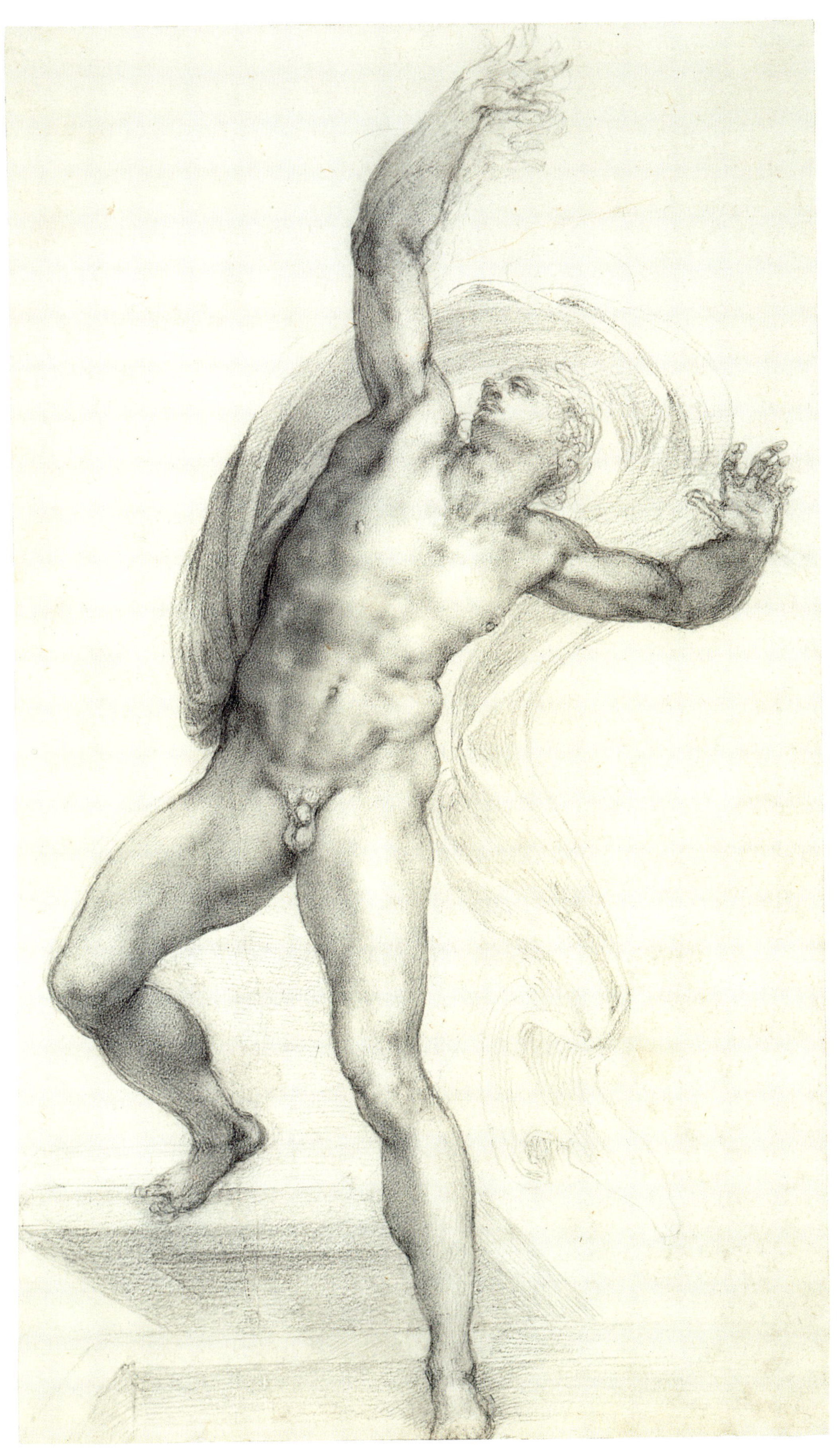

Unidentified French Artist after Michelangelo Buonarroti

40
Study for Haman

c. 1600 (?)
red chalk
39 x 22.2 (15 3/8 x 8 3/4); watermark: three lilies in a shield, not in Briquet
RL 0435

EXHIBITIONS
None

LITERATURE
Popham and Wilde 1949, no. 450; Perrig 1991, 51–52

The crucified Haman in the lunette at the left of the altar wall of the Sistine chapel is one of the most remarkable figures in Michelangelo's oeuvre. It demonstrates that at the end of his crippling labor Michelangelo's energies were still expanding. Indeed, he narrowed the pendentive's frame to make more space for the figures. In the *Crucifixion of Haman*, he juxtaposed three scenes within the same field with the utmost boldness and unconcern, subordinating all to the single figure. This is in part the result of the explosion of energy that characterizes the latest part of the vault, but it was also inspired by the figure's import. At the center of the west end is the prophet Jonah, a prototype of Christ, whose incarceration in the whale prefigures Christ's incarceration in the tomb. The flanking pendentives depict the *Elevation of the Brazen Serpent in the Wilderness*, and the *Crucifixion of Haman*. The *Brazen Serpent* is a well-known prototype of Christ's Crucifixion but it is, on the face of it, strange that a serpent should signify Christ. It contains, in fact, the further dimension that the scene also signifies the crucifixion of sin, in the form of the serpent, showing that the Crucifixion is also the downfall of Satan.

Michelangelo seems to have tried to achieve a comparable superimposition of ideas in the Haman pendentive. Haman, in the Old Testament, attempts to destroy the Jewish people by traducing them to King Ahasuerus. His plot exposed, he is hanged; he is very rarely represented as crucified. So Michelangelo devised a combinatory image, of good and evil overlaid, in which Haman should also signify Christ. Michelangelo achieved this by presenting Haman as a figure of astonishing power,

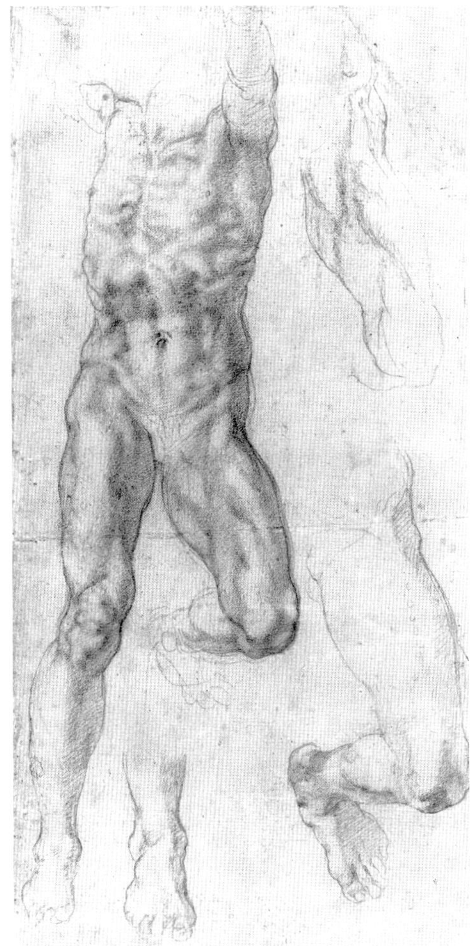

fig. 83. Michelangelo, *Study for Haman*, red chalk, 40.6 x 20.7 cm. British Museum, London, Department of Prints and Drawings

imbuing him with such energy and drive that he seems to leap from the cross. Michelangelo's intention may have been to evoke Christ's Resurrection, and certain aspects of the *Haman* were employed by him twenty years later in a *Resurrection* drawing that survives only in copies (Museum Boymans-van Beuningen, Rotterdam I. 20).

The *Haman* has roots in earlier work by Michelangelo. Around 1506 he seems to have worked on a *Martyrdom of the Ten Thousand*, for which he made a drawing of two men crucified on the same tree, one dead, one still alive (British Museum W. 12 / C. 162). The point of such a representation was not simply to enumerate the agonies of the martyrs but to demonstrate their conquest of pain and transcendence of suffering. The martyr triumphs over his executioners whose cruelty redounds only upon themselves. It is this quality that Michelangelo achieved in the *Haman*.

The figure of Haman on the recto of the present sheet is a same-size copy of Michelangelo's original now in the British Museum (fig. 83, W. 13 recto / C. 163 recto). Textures are sleeker than in the original, and local variety is diminished, but it is accurate in form, even though the *mise-en-page* is not identical. Another copy, still closer to the original, is in the Isabella Stewart Gardner Museum, Boston (B. 400). The British Museum drawing has a provenance from Casa Buonarroti but whether it remained in Michelangelo's studio to be inherited by his family, or whether it was acquired later is unknown. If the former, then the Windsor and Boston copyists must have studied the original while it was in Buonarroti possession, since their accuracy of detail does not suggest that either was made from an intermediate copy. The verso of the present drawing shows the same figure in outline, traced through from the recto.

Wilde thought the Windsor copyist might be a Dutch artist working in the late sixteenth century to whom he also gave another copy, a drawing in the Uffizi (2318F) after Michelangelo's Metropolitan study for the *Libyan Sibyl* (24.197.2 recto / C. 156 recto). The Metropolitan drawing, however, cannot be shown to have a Buonarroti provenance; Wilde may have been thinking of Calvaert. However, the French watermark in the present sheet would suggest that this copy at least is by a French artist. Toussaint Dubreuil is claimed to have made deceptive copies after Michelangelo drawings, but for the present, no attribution to him of any such copies can be more than speculative.

The *Haman* was one of the most influential of Michelangelo's figures, and echoes of it are found throughout the cinquecento: it was referred to by Titian in his *Death of Saint Peter Martyr* and it inspired numerous figures by El Greco.

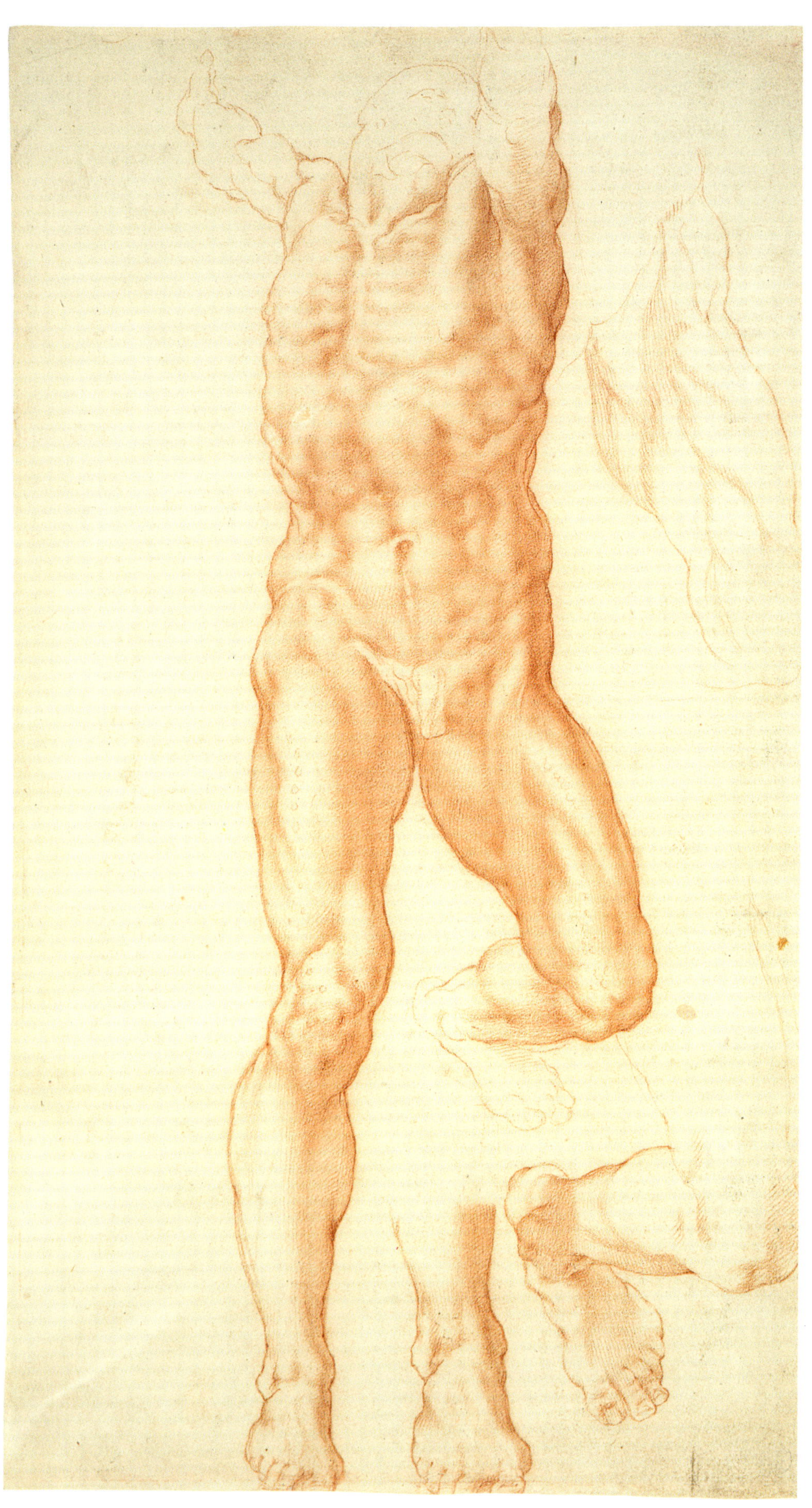

Michelangelo Buonarroti

41
Ecorché Study

c. 1518
red chalk
28.1 x 20.8 (11 1/16 x 8 3/16); no watermark
inscribed by the artist in red chalk at upper right: *braco*; and at lower right: *culo*; inscribed by another hand in pen at upper left *f*; at upper right *26*; inscribed in pen on the verso: *di Michel Angolo Buona Roti*
RL 0624

EXHIBITIONS
London 1953, no. 119; London 1975, no. 81

LITERATURE
Popham and Wilde 1949, no. 439; Wilde 1954, 16; Dussler 1959, no. 711; Blunt 1971, 99; De Tolnay 1975–1980, 1: no. 112; Hirst 1988, 14

The same *écorché* figure, studied from the back rather than the left side, is found on a second sheet at Windsor, drawn in the same technique and evidently en suite (cat. 42). The identity of pose and detail demonstrates that both were made from a wax or clay model exposing the musculature of a male figure, rather than that both were graphic inventions based upon Michelangelo's dissections. It is unlikely that Michelangelo was copying a model by another artist or anatomist, and probable that the model was also his work. This model seems to have possessed only a right leg: studies of this seen from the left side, continuous with the present drawing, and from the rear, continuous with cat. 42, in the same red-chalk technique, are found on a third sheet also in the Royal Collection (RL 0803 / Popham and Wilde 441 / C. 114). This bears the watermark Roberts Char B found in paper used by Michelangelo in the decade following circa 1518.

It may be that other such models were made by Michelangelo. An *écorché*, which had vast circulation in plaster casts, of a crouching figure in a complex pose is traditionally known as *Michelangelo's Anatomy*, and, indeed, its pose is similar to that of a figure drawn by Michelangelo on a sheet in the British Museum (W. 8 verso / C. 139 verso). Another drawing in the present exhibition (cat. 68) demonstrates that the pose of the arms at least was known in the later sixteenth century. It is probable that Michelangelo also made models of parts of figures: indeed, some of his *écorché* studies in pen, of legs, knees, and arms, were probably made from models designed to investigate and record particularly expressive features (see cat. 27). A group of wax models of this type, traditionally believed to be by Michelangelo, was acquired from the Gherardini Collection for the South Kensington Museum in 1854. Although this attribution is now, surely rightly, discounted, it was not unreasonable. Wilde tellingly quotes Sebastiano's request to Michelangelo, made in a letter of 15 July 1532: "Please remember to bring me something: figures or legs or bodies or arms; I have wanted them for so long, as you know."

Wilde connected the pose of the model copied in the present drawings with a figure by Michelangelo that is found, on different scales and reversed, in two drawings now in the Louvre (Inv. 727 recto / C. 34 recto) and the Albertina (Sc. R. 152 recto / C. 22 recto). However, these were made around 1505–1506 and are not *écorchés*. It is likely that the resemblance is due to consistency of motif in Michelangelo's work rather than to any common purpose, for the technique of the present drawings would suggest that they are later by a decade or more. However, whether the model from which the present drawing was copied was made as a demonstration piece, or whether it was prepared for a particular work of sculpture is impossible to say. In the second case, the obvious connections, at this date, would be with the tomb of Julius II, or with the figurative complement of the façade of San Lorenzo, but in neither can such a figure be found. Even if the model were presumed to be simply a demonstration piece, it remains to be explained why Michelangelo should have copied his own work. His drawings could have been intended to aid a pupil like Pietro Urbano, who might have had difficulty in copying the model directly. But, they might also have been made, as Wilde implies, in preparation for a treatise on artistic anatomy that Michelangelo contemplated but never wrote. In their clarity and precision, the red-chalk drawings would have made excellent models for engraving.

The present drawings show how, for Michelangelo, even a "scientific" project is highly expressive. He criticized Albrecht Dürer's anatomical treatise for its static figures; Michelangelo's figure is mobile, stretching his right arm upward and his left down as though braced to restrain: there may be more than a link with the antique horse-tamer motif. The drawing seems to represent a figure who has divested himself of skin in order to operate more freely his muscular structure. The effect is to enhance the action and the action's import, while removing from it all sensual contingency. It was the stripped manner, seen here in embryo, that was to become the defining mode of the Accademia *Slaves*, with their hard, convex modeling, and of the *Last Judgment*.

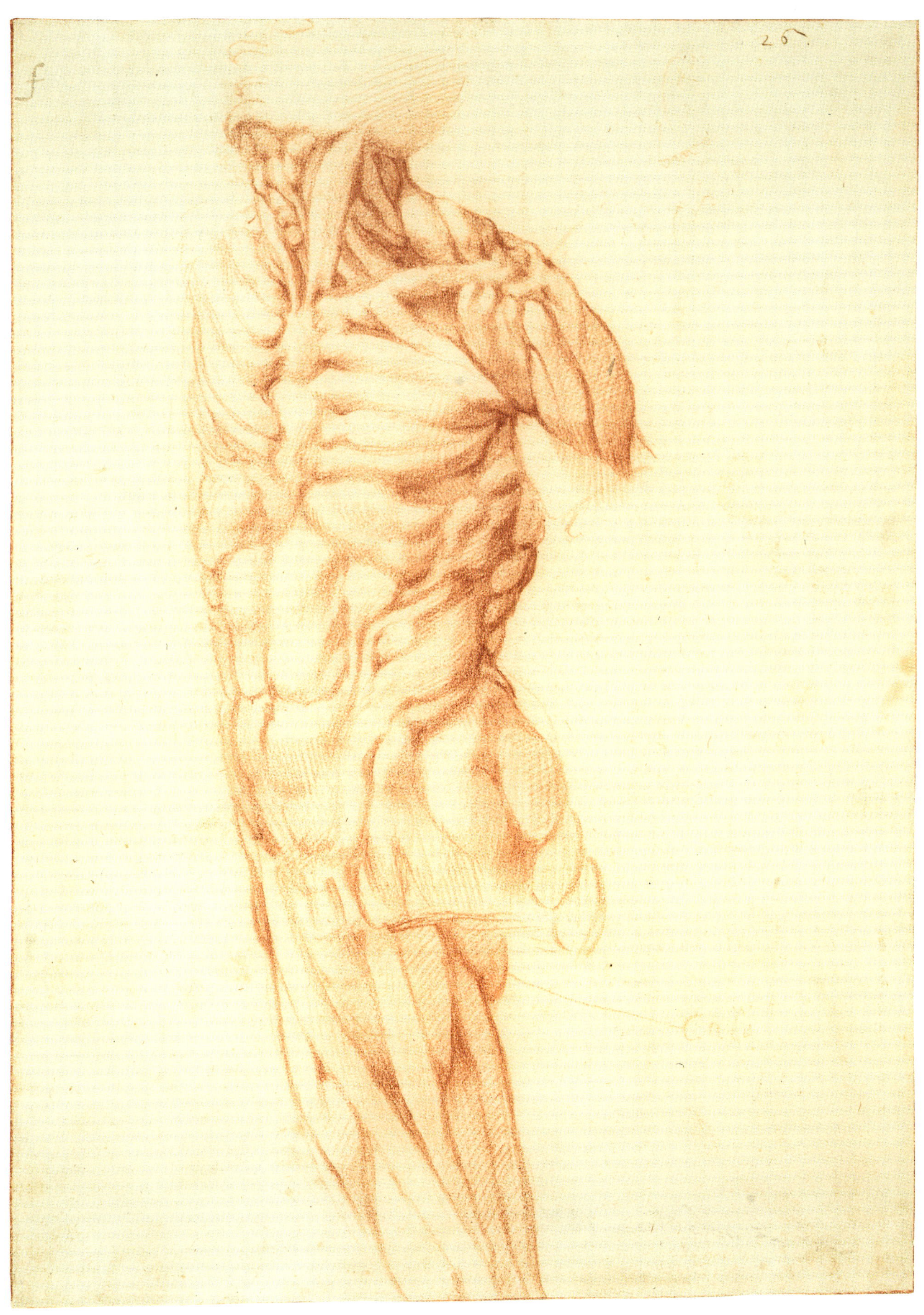

Michelangelo Buonarroti

42
Ecorché Study

c. 1518
red chalk
28.2 x 20.6 (11 1/8 x 8 1/8); no watermark
inscribed in pen at upper left: *M*; at the upper right: *28*; at bottom left: *di Michel Angelo buona Roti*; and, above this: *no. 45*
RL 0802

EXHIBITIONS
London 1953, no. 116; London 1975, no. 79

LITERATURE
Popham and Wilde 1949, no. 440; Wilde 1954, 16; Dussler 1959, no. 710; Blunt 1971, 99; De Tolnay 1975–1980, 1: no. 113

See cat. 41.

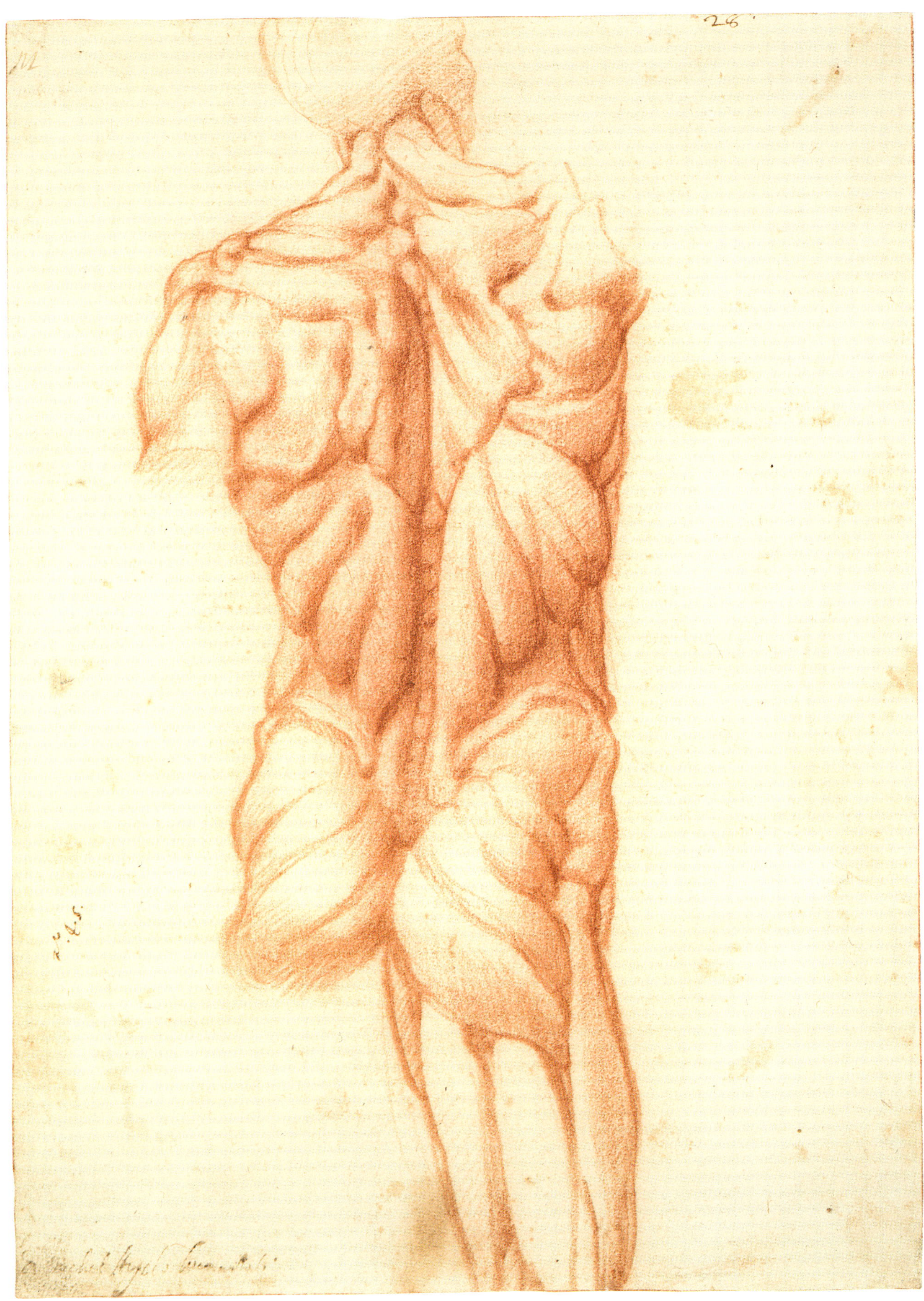

Studies after Michelangelo's Sculpture

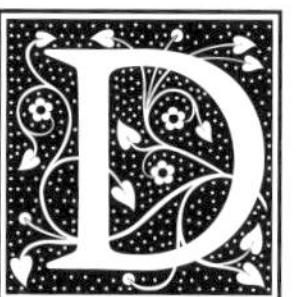

Drawn copies of Michelangelo's sculpture survive in much smaller numbers than copies of his paintings. There were many fewer sculpted than painted figures by Michelangelo, but since some were both famous and accessible, it is surprising that more copies are not known. A complementary paradox is that some three-dimensional works that are peripheral in his oeuvre aroused greater interest than others more central. There are, for example, very many copies after the small model made by Michelangelo, perhaps for the marble *David*, of which a wax replica survives in the Casa Buonarroti (fig. 11), but there are very few after the *David* itself, a statue that could hardly have been more prominent. It seems likely that later-sixteenth-century sculptors made few drawings—virtually none are known by Giambologna, for example—and that they probably preferred to make copies of Michelangelo's figures in wax or clay rather than on paper. Such models were fragile and liable to disintegration, and even when they survive, their authorship is difficult to establish. Painters, on the other hand, might be assumed to be less interested in Michelangelo's sculpted figures than his painted ones, but it had been a cliché ever since Leon Battista Alberti that artists could learn more from drawing after sculpture than after painting, and it is difficult to understand why there are no more than one or two sixteenth-century drawings of the *Slaves* now in the Accademia. Part of the explanation, in this case, may be that these figures were not publicly available until they were installed in Buontalenti's grotto in the Pitti gardens, and were then difficult to see. Only a single drawn copy—by Cherubino Alberti in the Gabinetto delle Stampe, Rome (F.N. 2955), pointed out by Raphael Rosenberg—and a single sixteenth-century bronze reduction (Residenzmuseum, Munich) seem to be known after Michelangelo's *Victory*, installed in the Palazzo Vecchio in the 1560s, even though it was massively influential on sculpture in Florence. By contrast, there are many drawn copies after Michelangelo's *Samson and the Two Philistines*, which was never executed on a large scale, although, as Rosenberg notes, among Central Italian artists these come mainly from the workshops of Battista Naldini and Cristoforo Roncalli.

This discrepancy alerts us to the fact that no sixteenth-century three-dimensional reductions of the four massive Accademia *Slaves* in their final form are known, for it is probable that most drawings after Michelangelo's sculpture were made not directly from the originals but from plaster or wax reductions. Those statues not replicated tended to be overlooked. Conversely, the circulation of reduced versions meant that artists could imbibe at least some of what Michelangelo's sculpture had to teach without ever seeing the originals. Thus Tintoretto, who did not visit Florence, and his shop made numerous drawings after figures from the New Sacristy. He also copied the *Samson*, which was much reproduced in bronze probably, initially, by Michelangelo's friend Daniele da Volterra, who would have been acting as the master's agent. Daniele is further recorded as making reductions of the New Sacristy figures and supplying examples to Tintoretto, but this seems to have occurred only in the later 1550s, and Tintoretto certainly knew Michelangelo's figures well before then. But precisely when and by whom the earliest reductions were made is unknown.

The most famous works of sculpture left by Michelangelo in Rome dated from the early part of his career. These attained canonical status. Several full-size copies in marble, only slightly modified, were made within Michelangelo's lifetime both of the Saint Peter's *Pietà* and the *Risen Christ*: Titian owned a plaster version of the latter. The *Moses* was a major source for artists and plastic reductions of the figure certainly circulated in the final third of the century and probably did so earlier. The influence of all these statues can be found in paintings and other sculpture. Although sixteenth-century drawn copies of them are far from legion, they exist in reasonable numbers. Of the later autograph statues, the *Rachel* certainly and the *Leah* probably were soon available in reductions: one is shown in the portrait of *Ortensia de' Bardi da Montauto* painted in Rome in 1559 by Alessandro Allori (Uffizi, Florence). The *Rachel* and the *Leah*, with their severity and somber mood, exerted a great effect on later-sixteenth-century Roman sculpture, but they were little copied in drawings: a few are known after the *Rachel*, notably by Figino, but none, according to Rosenberg, after the *Leah*. Michelangelo's unfinished four-figure *Pietà*, which is now in Florence, on which he worked during the late 1540s and early 1550s, had a considerable effect. Once again, few drawings after it are known, but it was several times engraved, was copied in three-dimensional models, and was frequently employed as a model by painters, including El Greco.

Nevertheless, in the light of the known evidence, it is clear that the main exception to the general impression of relatively limited graphic copying of Michelangelo's sculptural work is the New Sacristy. Although furnished with only part of the vast complement of statuary Michelangelo planned, it houses nevertheless the most extensive ensemble of his autograph sculpture—the two *Dukes*, the four *Times of Day* and the *Virgin and Child*—plus two of the most impressive works by Michelangelo's studio, *Saint Cosmas* and *Saint Damian*. However, with the exception of the *Dukes*, the figures were not put in place before Michelangelo abandoned Florence for Rome in September 1534, and it is probable that only a limited number of artists had access to the Sacristy during the 1530s. Among them were those sculptors who had worked with Michelangelo, Montorsoli, Montelupo—by whom several drawings after Michelangelo's figures are known—and Tribolo; the adventurous Ammanati and a few painters seem also to have gained entrance. Among the latter was Vasari, who was allowed entrance to the chapel by Alessandro de' Medici as early as 1532 and who borrowed the pose of *Lorenzo* for his 1535 portrait of Alessandro. Vasari's close friend Salviati also made a few hastily drawn copies at an early date (such as British Museum w. 99, 100), but he seems only to have studied Michelangelo's figures with real care about a decade later. Around 1537–1538, Battista Franco worked in the Sacristy: his pen copy of the *Day* (Louvre, Paris Inv. 751) seems, from its style, to be datable at this time. Benvenuto Cellini, too, was certainly aware of Michelangelo's statues before he returned to France in 1540, for he quoted the *Day* and the *Evening* verbatim in the saltcellar that he made for Francis I. Strangely, the artist closest to Michelangelo, both personally and temperamentally, in the early 1530s, Jacopo Pontormo, left no known copies after any of Michelangelo's statues.

It is probable that from circa 1540 the momentum of copying increased, especially after Tribolo placed the *Times of Day* on the sarcophagi in 1546. Naturally, copies are hard to date, and until a more extensive corpus is assembled it will not be possible to chart precisely progress of interest in the Sacristy. But by the 1570s, when Federico Zuccaro made a pair of drawings of the interior, the Sacristy was filled with draftsmen, even though it had still not been fully cleared of marbles for which there was no longer a place. Thus the trophies designed to stand above the ducal tombs, which Michelangelo had decided to exclude from the tombs before he left Florence, were still in the Sacristy, one on the floor, the other perched quite inappropriately on a throne in the attic above the tomb of Lorenzo. The Sacristy had by then become an artistic academy, and this was probably the result of the formation of the Florentine Academy, largely by the exertions of Giorgio Vasari, the great propagandist for Michelangelo: the octogenarian master accepted its honorary presidency. Although no documentation survives, it may be that young artists were specifically set to draw in the Sacristy, in order to enlarge their capacity for difficult foreshortenings and to deepen their awareness of the range of emotion conveyed by Michelangelo's figures.

However, it was mainly second-rate artists who quoted the statues most obviously in their paintings. Bacchiacca borrowed the figure of Giuliano for his *Martyrdom of the Ten Thousand*; Michele di Ridolfo made a series of decorative paintings based on Michelangelo's *Times of Day*, which he succeeded in turning virtually into boudoir pieces. Indeed, there are comparatively few signs in later-sixteenth-century Florentine painting of deep or intelligent interest in Michelangelo's figures. It may have been the very fact that young artists were set to draw from Michelangelo's statues that encouraged them to move in different directions after they attained maturity.

Battista Franco after Michelangelo Buonarroti

43
Dawn

c. 1540
black chalk, over stylus indentation; contours subsequently indented
26.5 x 38.1 (10 7/16 x 15); no watermark
RL 0428

EXHIBITIONS
None

LITERATURE
Popham and Wilde 1949, no. 508

This drawing, which seems to have been made directly from the statue and not from a replica, is obviously by the same hand as, and en suite with, three other black chalk drawings of similar dimensions made after three of Michelangelo's allegories of the *Times of Day*. All four exhibit the same use of hard black chalk; an employment of sharp outlining within the figures in order to demarcate musculature, a device that has the effect of sectioning their forms and reducing internal continuities; and lighter and more evocative treatment of the faces, in which the draftsman displays a certain fantasy in interpreting areas that in some cases Michelangelo did not complete. These drawings are obviously by a very able draftsman who was concerned to produce highly finished images.

Two of the other three drawings are in the Louvre, Inv. 749 (fig. 84) after the *Night* and Inv. 750 after the *Day*; both are squared. They are currently attributed to Giulio Clovio and dated to his Florentine period, 1551–1553. Formerly they were classed simply as after Michelangelo, although Delacre (1938) had proposed for them the name of Bronzino. The fourth drawing, another study of the *Day*, seen from a different angle is in the Uffizi (14778F) as by Bronzino.

To the compiler, the modeling seems harder and the registration of volume more convincingly sculpturesque than anything to be found in Clovio's work. The sharp lines defining the muscular divisions, the tight crosshatching to create the appearance of a stony surface, and the precision with which saliences are defined sits ill with most of what we know of Clovio's style. The attribution to Bronzino can be supported by comparison with his *Joseph Recounting his Dream of the Sun, Moon, and Stars* of the later 1540s (Ashmolean Museum, Oxford; Macandrew 128-1), which shows a similar combination of precision and finish in the bodies, and a wiry sketchiness in some of the heads that is very similar in treatment to that of the head of *Day* in the Uffizi and Louvre copies. Bronzino's most intense engagement with Michelangelo came in the 1550s, but in that decade it was the figure style of the *Last Judgment* that overwhelmed him, and if the chalk copies are by him, it is likely that they date somewhat earlier.

However, Bronzino's authorship is far from secure. His certain drawings generally display a use of stumped areas of chalk and lightly hatched relatively broad strokes of chalk for the midtones. They are usually more sleek and open in feel than these and without such dense local shading. Nevertheless, heavier types of drawing by Bronzino have been identified: a study for the head in his *Portrait of a Young Man* in the Nelson-Atkins Museum of Art, Kansas City, painted in the first half of the 1550s, appeared at Sotheby's on 3 July 1989, lot 64, and the J. Paul Getty Museum, Malibu, owns a study of a hand that was probably made by Bronzino for his Besançon *Pietà*. Bronzino could well have made unhabitually "stony" drawings when copying sculpture since he was an artist supremely aware of texture and one, furthermore, who frequently included representations of sculpture in his portraits. Michelangelo's Medici chapel figures are not reproduced in Bronzino's paintings, so no definite connection can be cited, but Bronzino's interest in the allegories was established by Cox-Rearick (1964), who noted that a sheet of drawings by Bronzino in Dresden (Staatliche Kunstsammlungen, Kupferstich-Kabinett C. 85) contains on its verso—which she dates circa 1540—sketches after both the *Day* and the *Night*.

A different, but related view is expressed by Raphael Rosenberg in recent letters to the compiler. Rosenberg connects the four chalk drawings with two pen copies after the *Day* (Louvre 751 and Budapest K.67.34), remarking that in plastic and characterizational emphases both are close to Louvre 750 and that the Budapest drawing shows the statue from a virtually identical viewpoint. Louvre 751 bears an old inscription, which seems clearly correct, to Battista Franco, and the Budapest drawing, which the compiler has seen only in reproduction, is probably also by him. Louvre 751 is datable circa 1540, when Battista Franco was in Florence and making stylistically comparable drawings; the Budapest drawing would be contemporary. Rosenberg extends the attribution to Franco to the four chalk drawings,

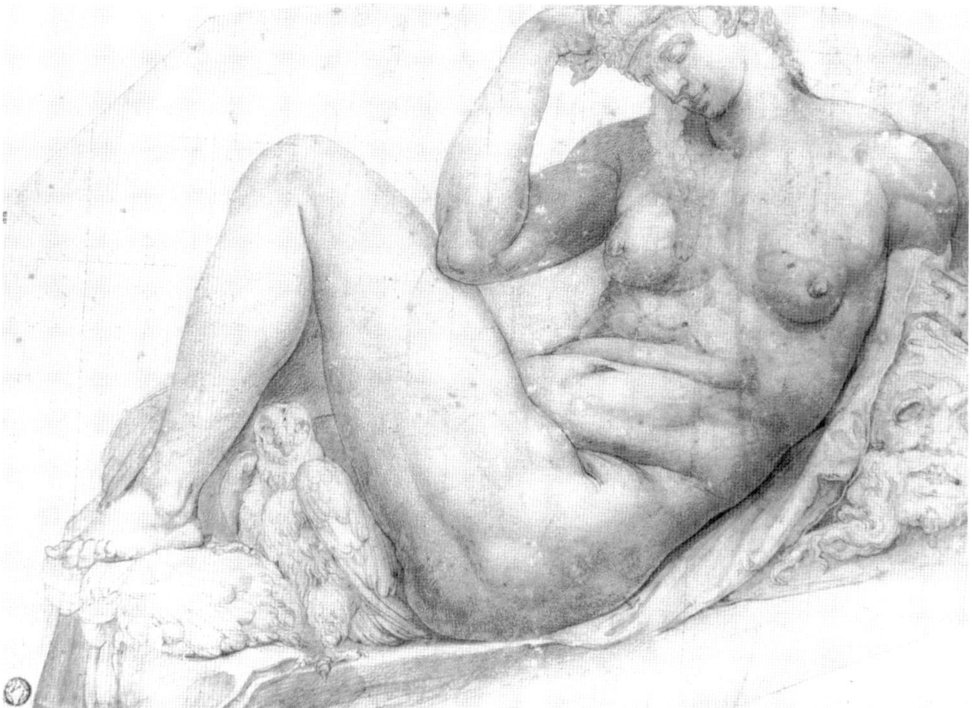

fig. 84. Battista Franco after Michelangelo, *Study of Night*, black chalk, 40.6 x 20.7 cm. Musée du Louvre, Paris, Département des Arts Graphiques [Photo RMN]

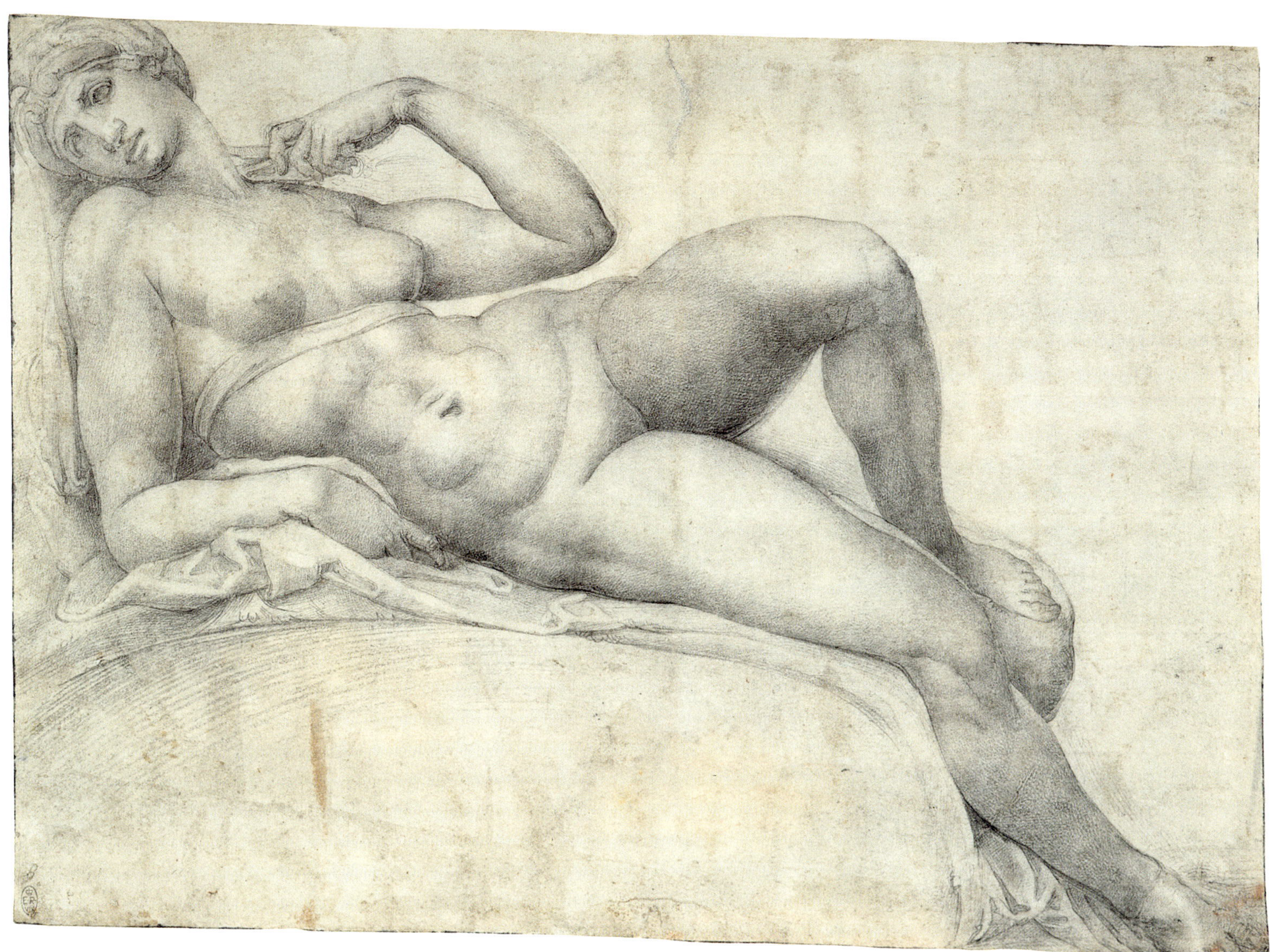

which is obviously logical. Initially the compiler resisted this attribution: the drawings seeming more effortful and less idiosyncratic than other known chalk drawings by the artist. However, as Rosenberg points out, Franco and Bronzino worked together in 1539 on the marriage decorations for Cosimo I and Eleanora of Aragon; at this moment the drawing style of one artist might well have affected that of the other—Vasari specifically says of this episode that Franco's drawings were more labored than Bronzino's. Furthermore, as Anne V. Lauder, who is preparing a dissertation on Franco, very recently pointed out to the compiler, the facial types in Louvre 749 and 750 are highly characteristic of the artist. Faced with the choice between a Francesque Bronzino or a Bronzinesque Franco, the compiler would now feel compelled to opt for the latter.

Unidentified Florentine Artist after Michelangelo Buonarroti

44
Dawn

c. 1550 (?)
black chalk
23.8 x 37.8 (9 3/8 x 14 7/8); watermark: anvil and hammer in a circle, close to Briquet 5964
inscribed in chalk at the lower left (faint): *Del Buonarota*
RL 0429

EXHIBITIONS
None

LITERATURE
Popham and Wilde 1949, no. 509

In this drawing, Michelangelo's reclining allegory of *Dawn* (fig. 85) is observed from a slightly higher viewpoint than in the other drawing of this subject (cat. 43). Such a viewpoint can be obtained in the chapel only from a raised position, and the artist could have drawn the figure from a ladder. As Federico Zuccaro's sketches of artists working in the New Sacristy demonstrate (Louvre Inv. 4554, 4555), they attempted to draw Michelangelo's figures from many different angles. Alternatively, the present drawing could have been made before the statues were set in place in 1546. However, this drawing conveys little sense of the statue's weight and texture, and it seems to miniaturize and, as it were, domesticate Michelangelo's grand figure. The compiler feels it probable, and Raphael Rosenberg concurs, that the drawing was made not from the original statue but from a reduction, in which subsidiary parts like the drapery and headdress were brought to the same level of finish as the body and slightly modified: the eyes are widened and the mouth narrowed in relation to the original (compare the treatment of the face in cat. 43). In the present drawing the figure acquires a quasi-anecdotal immediacy and a demureness, which suggests a character in a narrative composition rather than Michelangelo's majestic allegory of *Dawn*'s reluctant and regretful awakening.

The draftsman, who was surely not a major artist, seems to have been broadly under the influence of Pontormo, as the facial type and linear emphasis suggest, although the line work is scratchy in a way alien to Pontormo's manner. Wilde remarked that the drawing was in the manner of Bronzino, but the stress on contour, shape, and pattern rather than surface qualities or weight does not suggest very close connection with his work. It might nevertheless be by one of his pupils or by an artist influenced by him: Rosenberg's suggestion that it should be placed in the vicinity of Michele di Ridolfo (1503–1577) seems inherently plausible and deserves serious consideration. Michele di Ridolfo, whose drawing style has hardly been identified, made several paintings after Michelangelo's figures and was also interested in his ideal heads.

Of the four *Times of Day* in the New Sacristy, the *Dawn* was probably the most influential. With its elongated proportions, appearance of languor, and slowly spiraling rhythm, it proved an irresistible model for artists and was adapted both for male and female figures. The elongation of Michelangelo's figure, in particular, made it readily assimilable by artists who were attracted by Parmigianino's forms. A fusion of the ideas of the two artists formed a major component of the art of Primaticcio, whose female nudes both in painting and stucco are deeply in their debt.

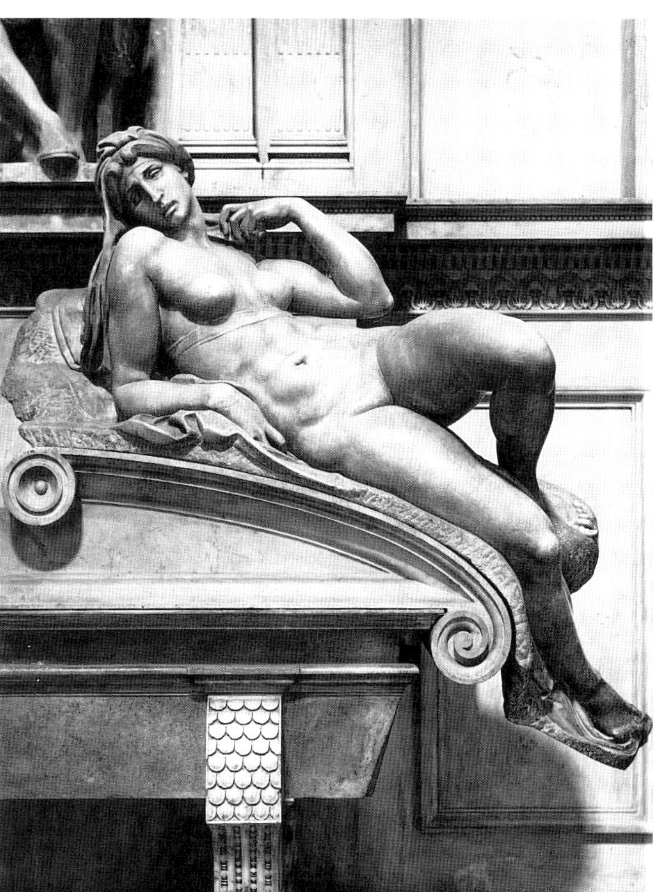

fig. 85. Michelangelo, *Dawn*, marble, length 203 cm. San Lorenzo, Florence

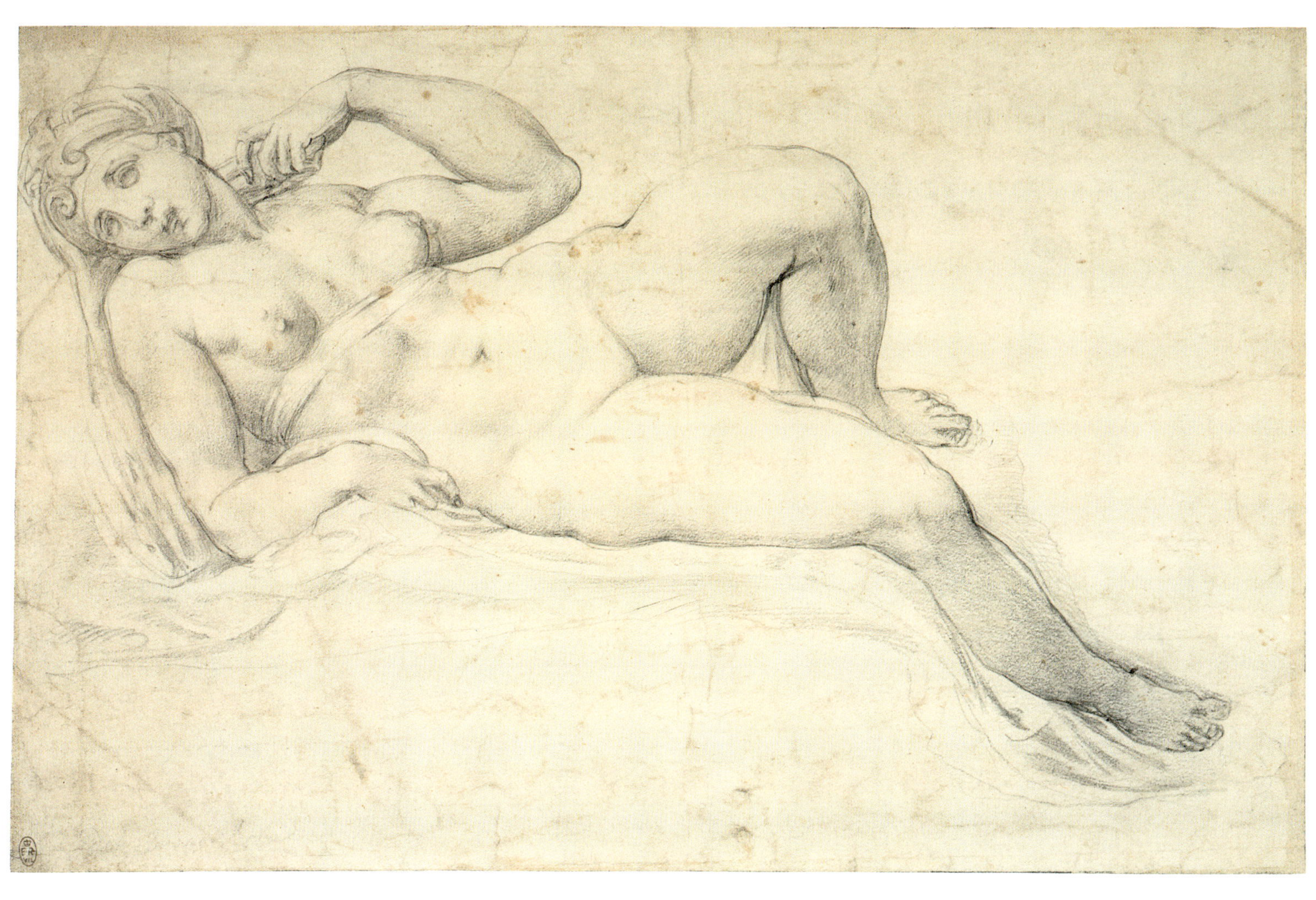

Battista Naldini (?) after Michelangelo Buonarroti

45
Night

c. 1565
black chalk with erasures
27.6 x 39.7 (10 7/8 x 15 5/8); no watermark
RL 0430

EXHIBITIONS
None

LITERATURE
Popham and Wilde 1949, no. 510

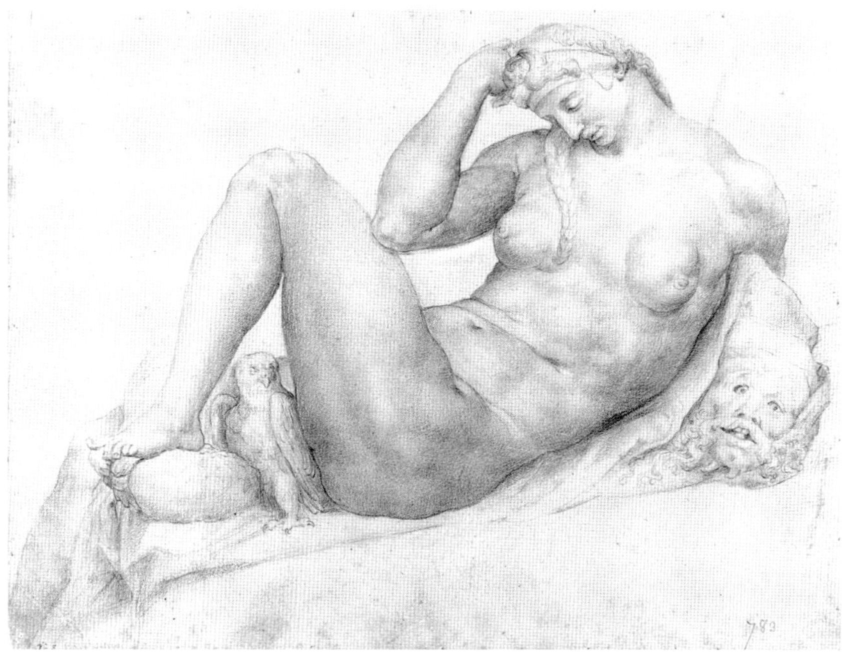

fig. 86. Unidentified Florentine Artist after Battista Naldini after Michelangelo, *Study of Night*, black chalk, 26.5 x 35.8 cm. Musée des Beaux-Arts, Lille

This drawing, more sleekly and smoothly executed than the other copies after Michelangelo's sculpture in the Royal Collection, is probably by Battista Naldini, still relatively little known as a draftsman. Naldini enjoyed a successful career as a painter of altarpieces in Florence and the smaller towns of Tuscany, but never fulfilled the potential he displayed in his paintings of the 1560s and 1570s. Their soft focus, painterly execution, and sensuous color reveal an allegiance to Andrea del Sarto. He might have figured among the "reformers" of Tuscan painting in the later cinquecento like his exact contemporary, Santi di Tito, but perhaps lacked sufficient energy and confidence to make significant changes in Tuscan art.

Although Naldini was a pupil of Pontormo and the inheritor of his drawings, which Naldini was compelled to relinquish, most of his graphic work—apart from a few copies after his master's sketches—does not show close dependence from Pontormo. Naldini's treatment of form was always fuller and more solid. It is evident that he was a varied and at times brilliant draftsman, something of a virtuoso, able to draw in a number of different styles: capable of the greatest freedom and energy in pen drawings, of vaporous form in his chalk drawings, and of pen and wash drawings with white heightening that equal the most beautiful examples by Taddeo Zuccaro.

The present copy shows little similarity to Naldini's compositional drawings, but it links clearly with two others, now in Princeton (Gibbons 1977, nos. 453, 454), after the *Dukes* in the New Sacristy. They are studied from the low viewpoint of a visitor to the chapel. These drawings are given to Naldini primarily on the strength of old inscriptions on the lower corner left of both, although Pilliod (1994) has drawn attention particularly to the splintered contour of Duke Giuliano's left foot, which is often found in Naldini's work, and Raphael Rosenberg accepts the drawings firmly as his. However, his authorship of the Princeton drawings is questioned by Rick Scorza, who compares them with a copy of *Duke Lorenzo* sold as Naldini at Sotheby's, London, 21 November 1974, lot 17. Scorza believes that the Princeton pair are by Allori (personal communication, 1995), but the compiler finds this view hard to accept.

The Princeton drawings are made in the same distinctive technique as the present drawing, richly modeled, with the chalk strokes largely fused to present a dense, continuous surface. Highlights are obtained not by the addition of white body color or white chalk but by erasure, probably with bread, which contributes still further to the effect of continuity. The impression conveyed both by the Princeton drawings and the present copy is of weight and density: they would have been made at the same time, probably in the mid-1560s. Such a date would fit well with the observation of Rosenberg that the Princeton drawings were the models from which Cornelius Cort made engravings in 1570.

There is an unexplained link between the Princeton and Windsor drawings and a group of copies in black chalk with some white heightening from a disbound sketchbook after Michelangelo's New Sacristy figures now in the Musée des Beaux-Arts in Lille, at one time attributed to Francesco Salviati but clearly not by him. Three of these copies (Inv. 2360 [fig. 86], 2356, 2357), although drier in technique than the present drawing and the two in Princeton, are virtually identical to them in viewpoint. Both trios display minor *pentimenti* and neither seems obviously copied from the other. Nevertheless, that the three statues should be drawn from exactly the same viewpoint by two different artists is hard to credit, unless one were to postulate a deliberate and closely controlled competition. In their treatment of light, texture, and form, the three drawings in the Princeton-Windsor group convey the impression of being made directly from the statues; furthermore, since they are more precise and detailed in their description of Michelangelo's statues than their counterparts in Lille, it seems unlikely that the former could be worked-up versions of the latter. On balance it seems more probable, and in this the compiler's tentative opinion is comforted by Raphael Rosenberg's firmly stated view, that the drawings in the Lille sketchbook are copies after a series of drawings—now known only in three examples—by Naldini, perhaps made by a pupil or an associate.

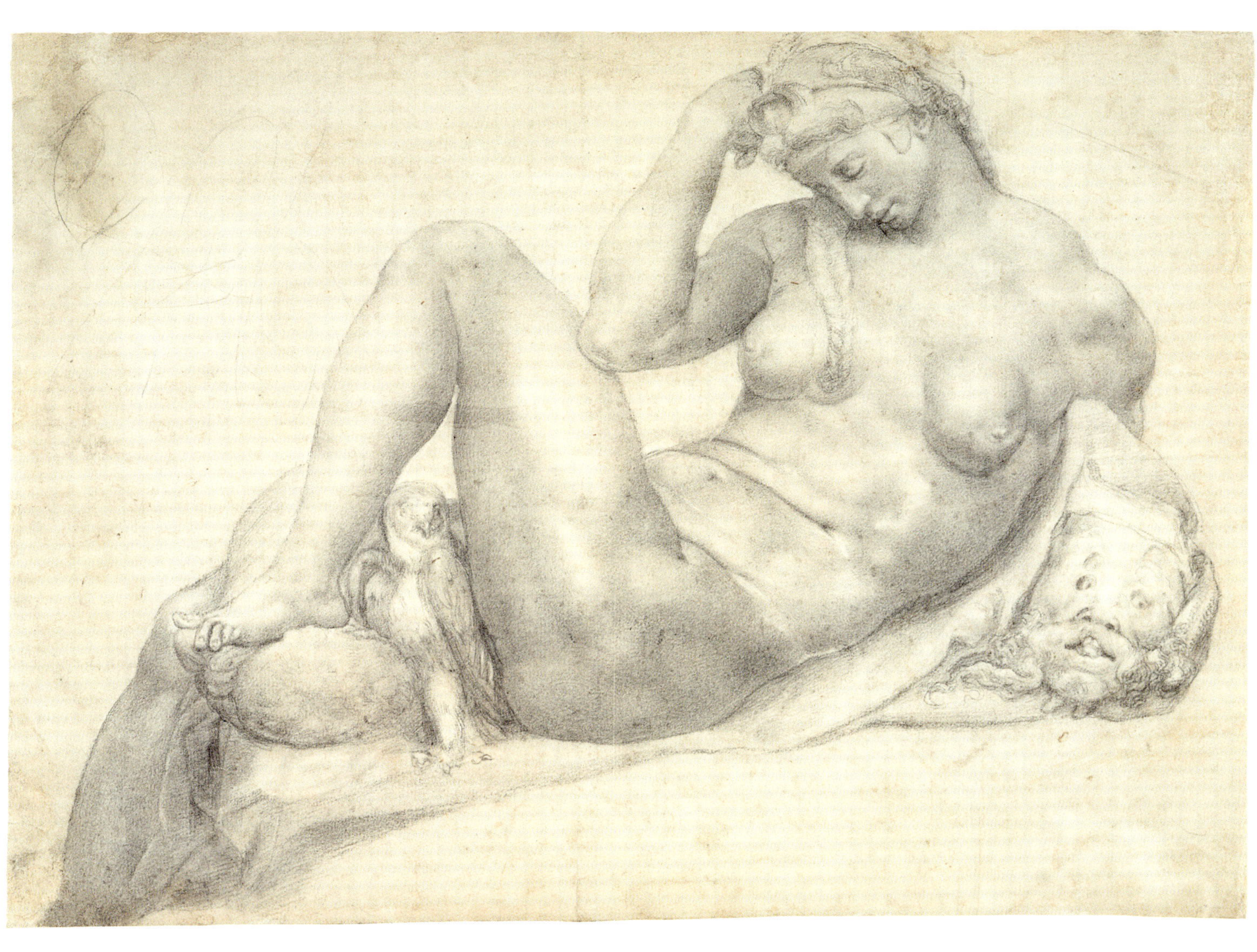

The Effect of the Sistine Ceiling

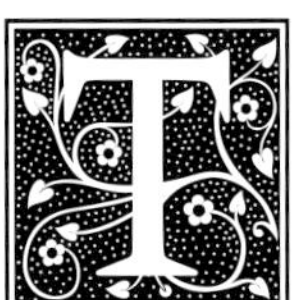he Sistine Chapel had been fully frescoed in the early 1480s by a team of Florentine and Umbrian artists, including Ghirlandaio and Botticelli, on the commission of Pope Sixtus IV. It is likely that Sixtus' nephew, Cardinal Giulio della Rovere, oversaw the project. The scheme was divided into four levels. The vault was decorated with a heaven of gold stars on a blue ground; at the level of the clerestory was frescoed Christ and his lineal successors, the pre-Constantinian popes, embodying the direct transmission of divine authority; the middle story contained two facing series of narrative frescoes paralleling the lives of Christ and his greatest Old Testament forerunner, Moses; on the lowest level were a series of simulated gold and silver hangings. The altarpiece, also a fresco rather than a separate panel, showed the *Assumption of the Virgin.*

In the summer of 1506, three years after Cardinal Giulio had become pope, as Julius II, he decided to have the vault repainted. Michelangelo, then working on the gigantic project of the pope's tomb, was proposed for the task, but this was opposed by Bramante, who argued that Michelangelo was not experienced in vault painting and its problems of foreshortening. However, following Michelangelo's sojourn in Bologna to model and cast a bronze statue of the pope, in the summer of 1508 he received the commission for the Sistine ceiling.

The vault contains twelve pendentives and, according to Michelangelo's later statement, which surviving drawings support, the initial proposal was to decorate it with twelve seated apostles; the rest of the ceiling would be filled with geometrical decoration. If Michelangelo is to be believed, it was at his prompting that the scheme was massively enlarged and Julius allowed him to do what he wanted. Although it is certain that Michelangelo had theological advice, it is likely that his version of events is broadly true. The final scheme, heavily affected by Michelangelo's designs for the now-postponed tomb, was an ingenious thematic and visual extension of the existing decoration.

Although not in any sense illusionistic, the simulated architectural framework of the fresco appears to rise directly from the side walls and to extend, by a number of concealed changes of direction, across the vault. This fictive structure carries a vast complement of figuration. In the center of the vault are nine narratives, five small and four large, from Genesis. These recount the history of creation from the *Separation of Light from Darkness* through the *Creation of Adam* and the *Fall* to the *Drunkenness of Noah.* Thus Christ's two other major Old Testament forerunners are included and his Passion is foreshadowed in Noah's disgrace. Each small narrative is surrounded by four nude youths, probably wingless angels, draped with garlands of oak leaves, the pope's heraldic symbol, and supporting roundels containing apocryphal narratives of particular relevance to the pope. Below these sit, not evangelists, but seven prophets, the Jewish seers who predicted the advent of Christ, and five sibyls, their gentile female counterparts. These figures emphasized the universality of the church's mission. Between these figures and the sequence of popes on window level, in the lunettes of the walls and the triangular groins above them, were painted the ancestors of Christ, the bloodline listed at the beginning of Saint Matthew's Gospel. In the corners of the vault are four Old Testament scenes that, in various ways, display the triumph of the Israelites over their enemies.

Michelangelo began painting the vault, with a group of Florentine assistants, in late 1508. He soon found he could not work with them and resolved to complete the vault single-handed, which he did, with the aid of one or two assistants to execute minor tasks. He completed the scheme, after two lengthy interruptions, in October 1512. He later said that the painting had taken twenty months, which may not be much of an exaggeration.

As a physical as well as an artistic effort, it has remained unequaled.

Since its recent cleaning the vault is more legible than at any period since the mid-sixteenth century, but to look at it for the length of time required to become familiar with its wealth of figures and scenes, its repertoire of roles and types, makes severe physical demands on the spectator. It is also extremely difficult to copy, and for sixteenth-century artists, entrance to the chapel would not necessarily have been easy. So, difficult of access and hard to draw, it is not surprising that most of the surviving copies were made not from the originals but from intermediary copies, and, quite frequently, from engravings. Furthermore, impressive though Michelangelo's work on the ceiling undoubtedly was, its relevance for other artists was limited, for it provided little assistance for most of the tasks they had to perform. Thus the narratives, especially those of the Creation, the grandest and most powerful, could be imitated but not easily assimilated, and it took decades of collective effort to tame them to domestic use.

It was probably the single figures that were most productively influential. Michelangelo's art always had a tendency to concentrate on the individual figure as the vehicle of spiritual expression, and in the vault the *ignudi*, for example, increased in size and expanded in energy as work proceeded. Their influence can be seen, directly or indirectly, virtually wherever seated nudes are portrayed later in the century. A comparable but more dramatic effect can be found in some of the nude or seminude figures painted toward the end of the project. Some of the figures from the corner vaults, especially the nude Haman (see cat. 40), recur again and again in later art.

Somewhat surprisingly, given their relatively marginal position, the ancestors of Christ provided a number of models for Virgin and child groups and Holy Families. But it was probably Michelangelo's treatment of the massive seated figure that proved the greatest revelation to his contemporaries and followers. Ghirlandaio and Filippino Lippi, both of whom Michelangelo studied with care, had created massively imposing seated figures of evangelists and prophets for the vaults of their respective fresco schemes, such as those in Santa Maria Novella. But Michelangelo's designs for the seated figures on the first story of the tomb of Julius II and for the closely related prophets and sibyls on the Sistine ceiling imbued the seated forms with an unprecedented range of emotion as well as physical strength. Michelangelo made enormous play with the possibilities of constraint and movement: Ezekiel looks out, gesturing to his neighbor, anxious to communicate; Jeremiah is slumped in thought, depressed and withdrawn but immovable in his concentration; the Cumaean Sibyl, who seems to have experienced every aspect of suffering, embodies compassion. It was probably the prophets and sibyls, as personifications of moral and spiritual elevation, that proved to be the most influential legacy of the Sistine ceiling.

Unidentified Artist after Michelangelo Buonarroti

46
Study for the Ignudo at the Right above Persica and Other Studies

c. 1630 (?)
red chalk
39 x 23.5 (15 3/8 x 9 1/4); watermark: Pascal lamb in circle, not in Briquet
inscribed below in red chalk: *Del Buona Rota*; on the verso in pen by William Gibson: *Michol Angilo. 3.3.*
RL 0441

EXHIBITIONS
None

LITERATURE
Popham and Wilde 1949, no. 449

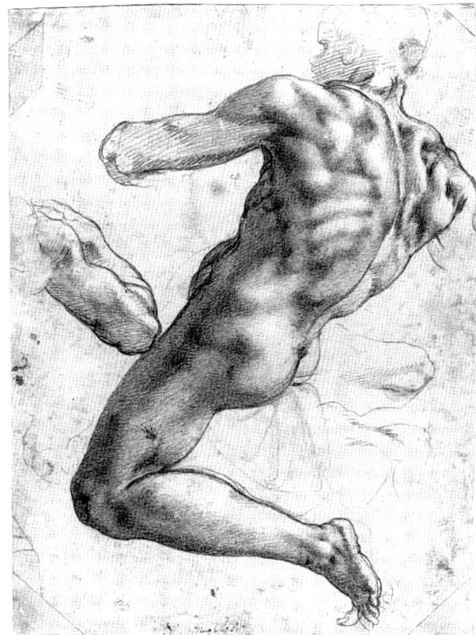

fig. 87. Michelangelo, *Study for the Ignudo at the Right above the Persian Sibyl*, red chalk, 27.9 x 21.4 cm. Teylers Museum, Haarlem

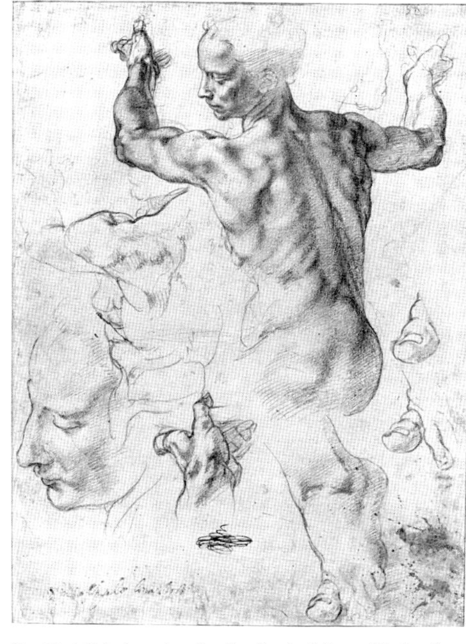

fig. 88. Michelangelo, *Studies for the Libyan Sibyl*, red chalk, 28.8 x 21.3 cm. The Metropolitan Museum of Art, New York, Joseph P. Pulitzer Bequest

Sadly, no autograph drawings by Michelangelo for the Sistine ceiling are in the Royal Collection. The lack is particularly grave since it was at this period that Michelangelo's use of red chalk in nude figure studies reached an unsurpassed level of vitality and precision. His life drawings in this medium have remained models for all subsequent figure drawing, and they retained their fascination for artists even in periods when Michelangelo's other work had become unfashionable.

The figures in this drawing are copied from studies on the rectos and versos of two sheets by Michelangelo, now in the Teylers Museum, Haarlem (fig. 87, A. 27 / C. 135 and A. 20 / C. 136). These two sheets were originally parts of the same large page that the present copyist may have known before it was divided. The Haarlem collection contains a large proportion of Michelangelo's surviving red-chalk studies for figures in the later part of the Sistine ceiling, which rank among the most beautiful of all figure drawings. It seems likely that a group was either given away by Michelangelo or was abstracted from his studio very early. The Michelangelo drawings in the Teylers Museum can be traced to Joachim von Sandrart, who probably acquired them piecemeal or in small groups in Italy between 1629 and 1637. Sandrart's collection was acquired en bloc in 1651 by Queen Christina's ambassador in the Hague. They went with her to Rome and, at her death in 1689, they were bequeathed with the rest of her collection to Cardinal Decio Azzolini. The drawings were subsequently sold by his nephew to the duke of Bracciano, Don Livio Odescalchi, who disposed of many but not all of them. Some of those that he sold probably entered the Royal Collection: it is likely, for example, that Michelangelo's *écorché* drawings in pen and ink and red chalk (see cats. 26, 27, 41, 42) came from this source. The remains of the Odescalchi collection was acquired for the Teylers Museum in Haarlem in the 1790s.

The inscription was probably made by the copyist. Drawings of this sort are difficult to attribute and date but it was probably made in the early to mid-seventeenth century, perhaps while the originals were in Sandrart's collection. The artist has imitated Michelangelo's style in a general way, but did not attempt to replicate Michelangelo's handling: the master's combination of local vitality with idealizing clarity entirely eluded his softening touch.

Although Michelangelo's influence in the seventeenth century was limited, the immediacy of his red-chalk figure drawings continued to exert its spell. The Italian seventeenth century, indeed, might be described as the century of academic life studies in red chalk: many thousands of such drawings survive, mostly unattributed. It was only natural that their sixteenth-century forerunners should have been collected and copied.

The original of the main study on the present sheet was made in preparation for the *ignudo* to the right above the *Persian Sibyl*. The other copies on the sheet are after studies for the complementary *ignudo* and for details in the *Creation of Adam*. All the studies, therefore, were for the penultimate group of *ignudi* and the immediately adjacent large narrative scene. The fact that figures from proximate areas of the ceiling were studied on the same sheets suggests that Michelangelo made considerable efforts to coordinate figure types across compartments. It also supports the view that he determined the final figural arrangements for, at least, the later sections of the ceiling only shortly before he painted them: this ensured freshness of inspiration and renewed vitality.

In the absence of autograph studies for the Sistine ceiling in the Royal Collection, the present sheet and *Study for Haman* (cat. 40) must serve as representatives of Michelangelo's method. His original studies, despite their superhuman beauty (fig. 88 is perhaps the most dramatic example of this), must have been based on the life: it seems clear that Michelangelo chose models of exceptional physical beauty, but, in drawing them, altered their proportions to conform to his ideal types and emphasized different aspects of their anatomy according to his expressive purposes.

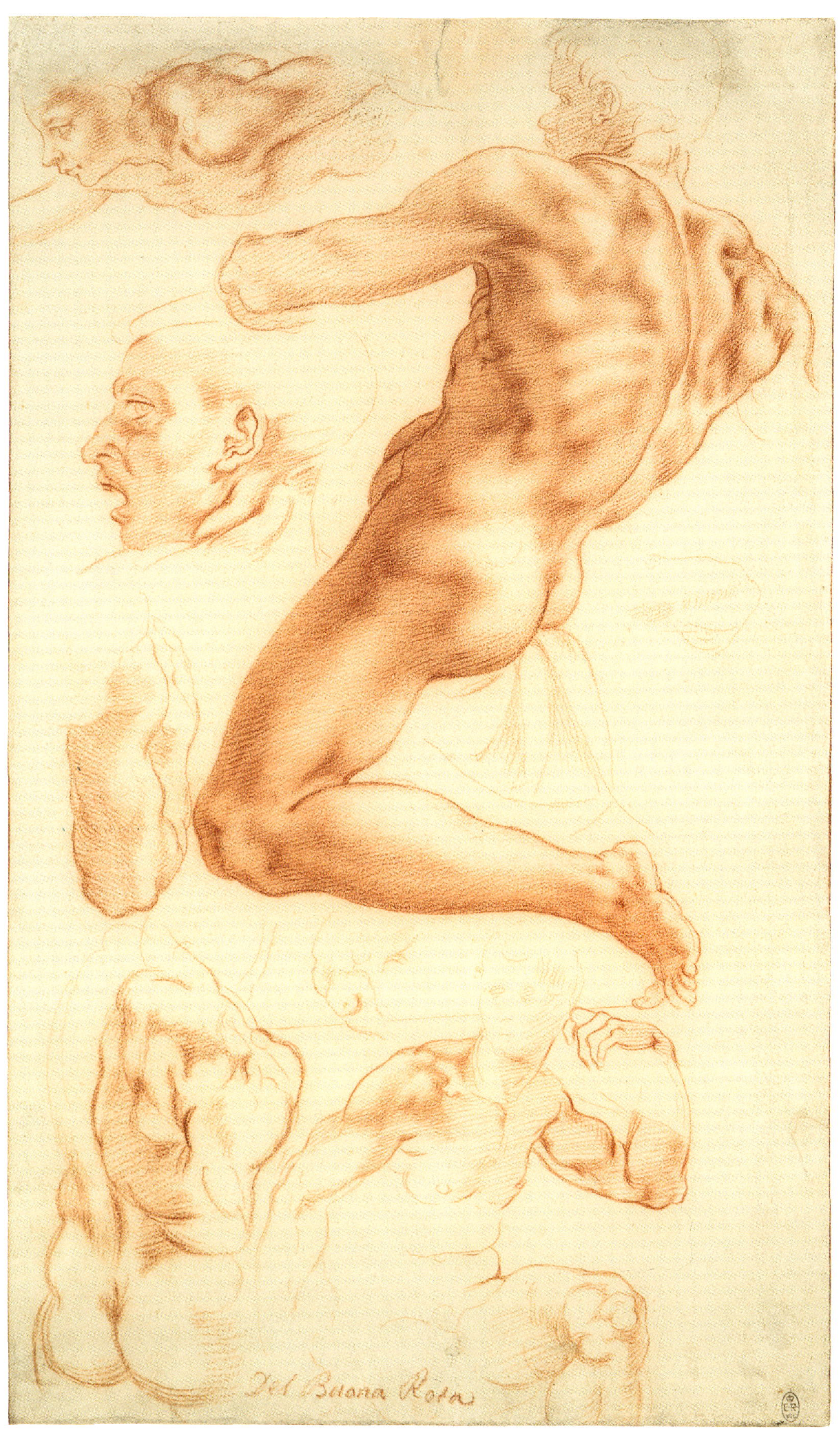
Del Buona Rota

Annibale Carracci

47
Ignudo

c. 1597
black chalk with white chalk on blue paper
52.9 x 35.8 (20 13/16 x 14 1/8); laid down
RL 2358

EXHIBITIONS
None

LITERATURE
Wittkower 1952, no. 325

Although in his earliest work Annibale Carracci rejected the superficial Michelangelism practiced by the leading Bolognese masters in favor of Venetian modes of paint handling and naturalistic observation of figures, he was a powerful advocate of life study and, in particular, chalk study from the nude. Thus his own creative procedures paralleled in a fundamental way those of Michelangelo. On arrival in Rome in 1596, experiencing Michelangelo's work directly and not through the medium of graphic copies, his response was strong. Knowledge of Michelangelo's painting may have been supplemented by awareness of his drawings, for Annibale produced two of his most important schemes for the Palazzo Farnese, which Michelangelo had part constructed and which contained a superb collection of his drawings (see cat. 17). Michelangelo would have been a revered memory in the palace of the family of Pope Paul III, who had commissioned the *Last Judgment* and the Pauline Chapel frescoes and who had given Michelangelo the superintendency of Saint Peter's.

The gallery Annibale painted in the Palazzo Farnese between 1597 and 1604—partly to celebrate a wedding and partly as a setting for the display of the Farnese's collection of sculpture—made obvious reference to the work of Michelangelo, and in particular to the Sistine *ignudi*. It seems likely that Annibale at first planned poses that were not self-consciously allusive and only as he worked resolved to make reference to Michelangelo's figures. But Annibale kept his distance from the master and employed humor as a means of defense. The *ignudi* in the Farnese gallery are witty and alert, unlike Michelangelo's preoccupied and distant figures. Paradoxically, and at a much higher level of intelligence, Annibale here rejoins his Bolognese predecessors, draining Michelangelo's forms of spiritual content and employing them for decorative and sensuous effect. Although the present figure was not demonstrably made in preparation for the gallery and is not included in the catalogue of the drawings for the scheme by Martin (1965), it was pointed out by Wittkower that its pose is close to the *ignudo* that Annibale painted to the right of his *Venus and Anchises*.

Some of Annibale's more developed drawings for the *ignudi* in the Farnese gallery seem plausibly related to the drawing style of Michelangelo. Although the present sheet with its broad handling seems at first sight Venetian in inspiration, it is possible that Annibale knew some of the soft black chalk drawings, with which Michelangelo laid out the basic poses of his Sistine figures—especially the *ignudi* (for example, Louvre Inv. 860 verso / c. 143 verso). Such drawings have often been considered formless by Michelangelo scholars, and it is an interesting parallel that the present drawing was felt by Wittkower to have "certain weaknesses." But it is the function that this type of drawing performs in both Annibale's and Michelangelo's oeuvres that creates this impression.

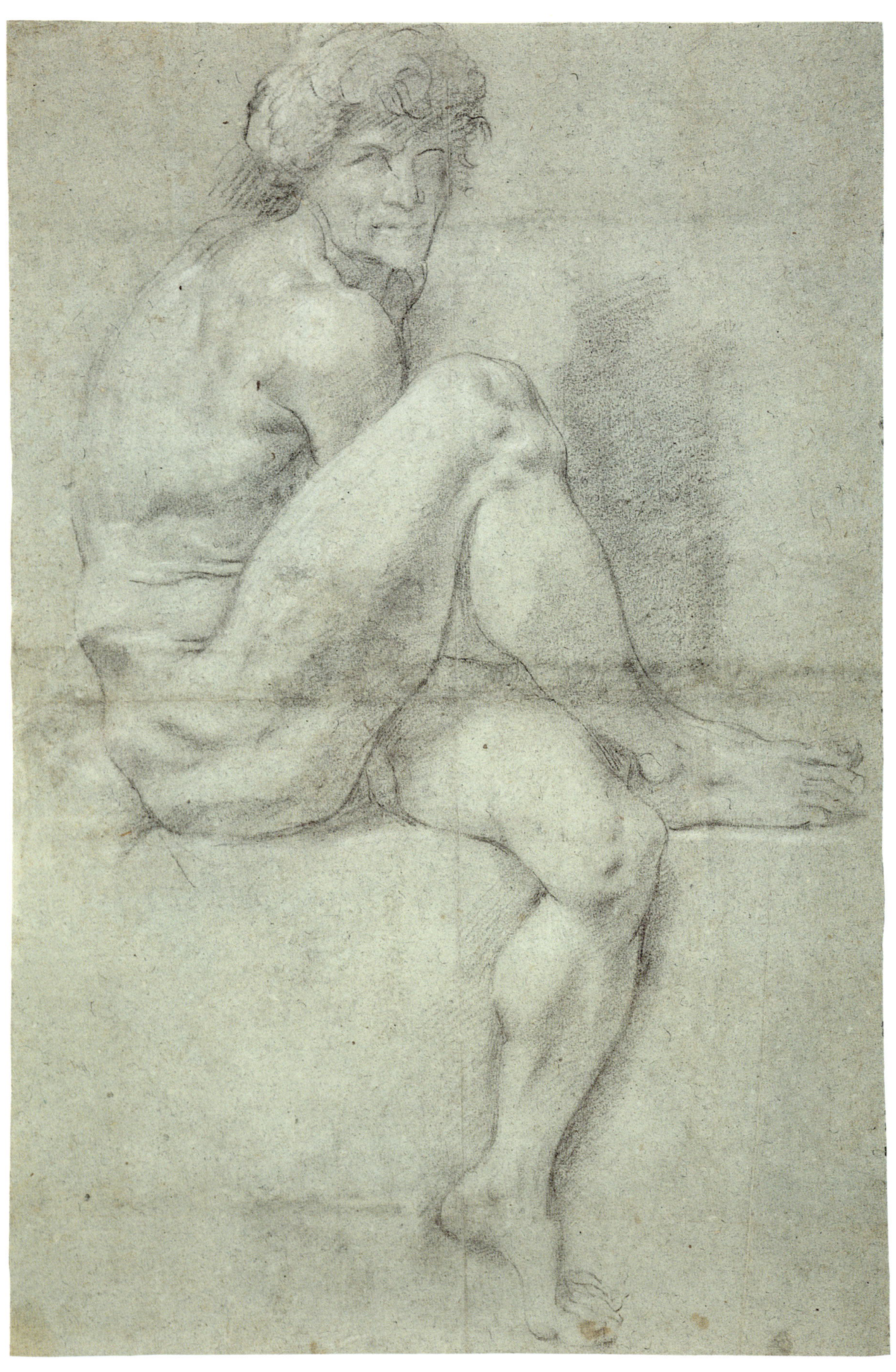

Perino del Vaga

48
Saints Mark and John

1525
red chalk over squaring in stylus at 30 mm
31.7 x 40.3 (12 1/2 x 15 7/8), traces of stitching down the center of the sheet; watermark: anchor in circle with star, not in Briquet
RL 01218

EXHIBITIONS
London 1986, no. 37

LITERATURE
Popham and Wilde 1949, no. 974; Parma Armani 1986, 262

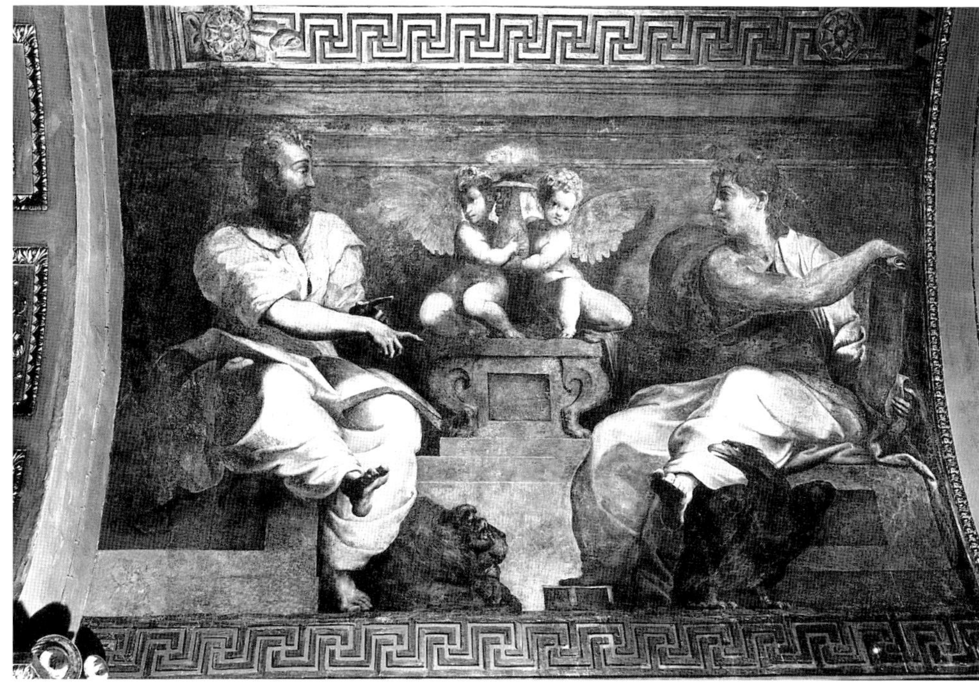

fig. 89. Perino del Vaga, *The Evangelists Mark and John*, fresco. San Marcello al Corso, Rome [Ministero per i beni culturali e ambientali, Rome]

Between Raphael's death and the Sack of Rome in 1527, Perino was one of the most prominent painters in the city, his position enhanced by Giulio Romano's departure to Mantua in 1524. He was not without competitors, but he carried out several prestigious commissions during these years.

This large sheet is a preparatory study for one side of the barrel vault of the Cappella del Crocefisso in the Roman church of San Marcello al Corso (fig. 89). On 6 February 1525, Perino signed a contract to decorate the whole chapel, which he was supposed to complete by 20 March 1526. He had painted only two thirds of the vault before the Sack of 1527. The vault was completed to Perino's designs by Daniele da Volterra circa 1543. It is not known what was envisaged for the side walls and the altarpiece of the chapel, but further decoration was clearly abandoned.

Perino had spent some time in Florence in 1523 but he reveals no interest in Michelangelo's latest style, referring directly to the Sistine ceiling. A drawing by Perino of circa 1522 (Louvre Inv. 631 verso), demonstrates his interest in the layout of the ceiling, and the vault of the Cappella del Crocefisso is in essence a reworking of one of Michelangelo's smaller Genesis bays. Perino's earlier *modello* for the vault (Kupferstichkabinett, Berlin 22004) shows God the Father, of Raphaelesque type, in the central compartment rather than the *Creation of Eve*, but when the subject was changed, Michelangelo became the source for the narrative (fig. 90) as well as for the four evangelists: they are inspired both by the *ignudi* and the prophets; their draperies, however, are lighter and more lyrical versions. The two putti holding the candelabrum in the center of the sheet also pursue the Michelangelesque theme, for these make lighthearted allusion to the paired putti in the arms of the thrones of Michelangelo's prophets and sibyls. Even the block on which Saint Mark sits is derived from those of Michelangelo's *ignudi*. Perino's efforts to combine the grandeur and vitality of Michelangelo's figures with Raphael's fluency are similar to contemporary endeavors by Parmigianino, who had arrived in Rome in 1524: the two artists seem to have watched each other closely.

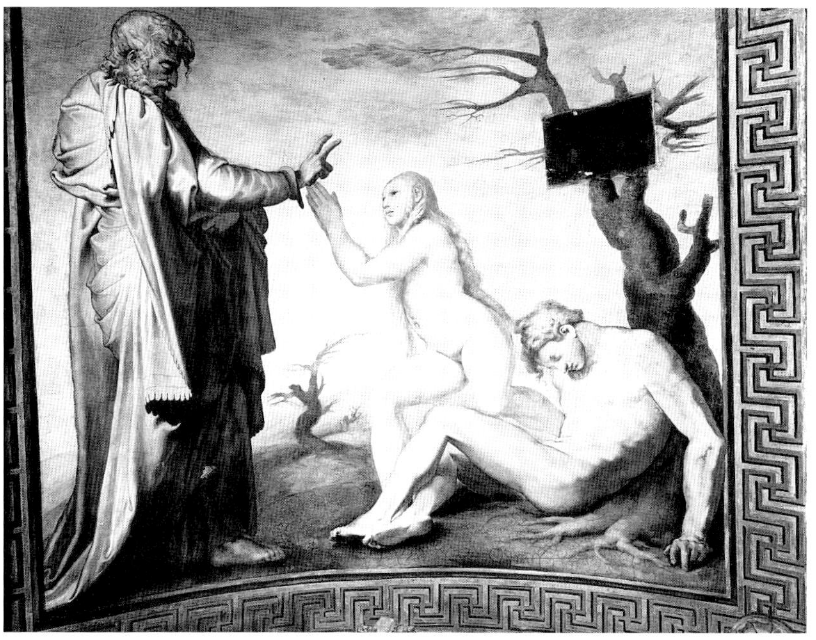

fig. 90. Perino del Vaga, *The Creation of Eve*, fresco. San Marcello al Corso, Rome [Ministero per i beni culturali e ambientali, Rome]

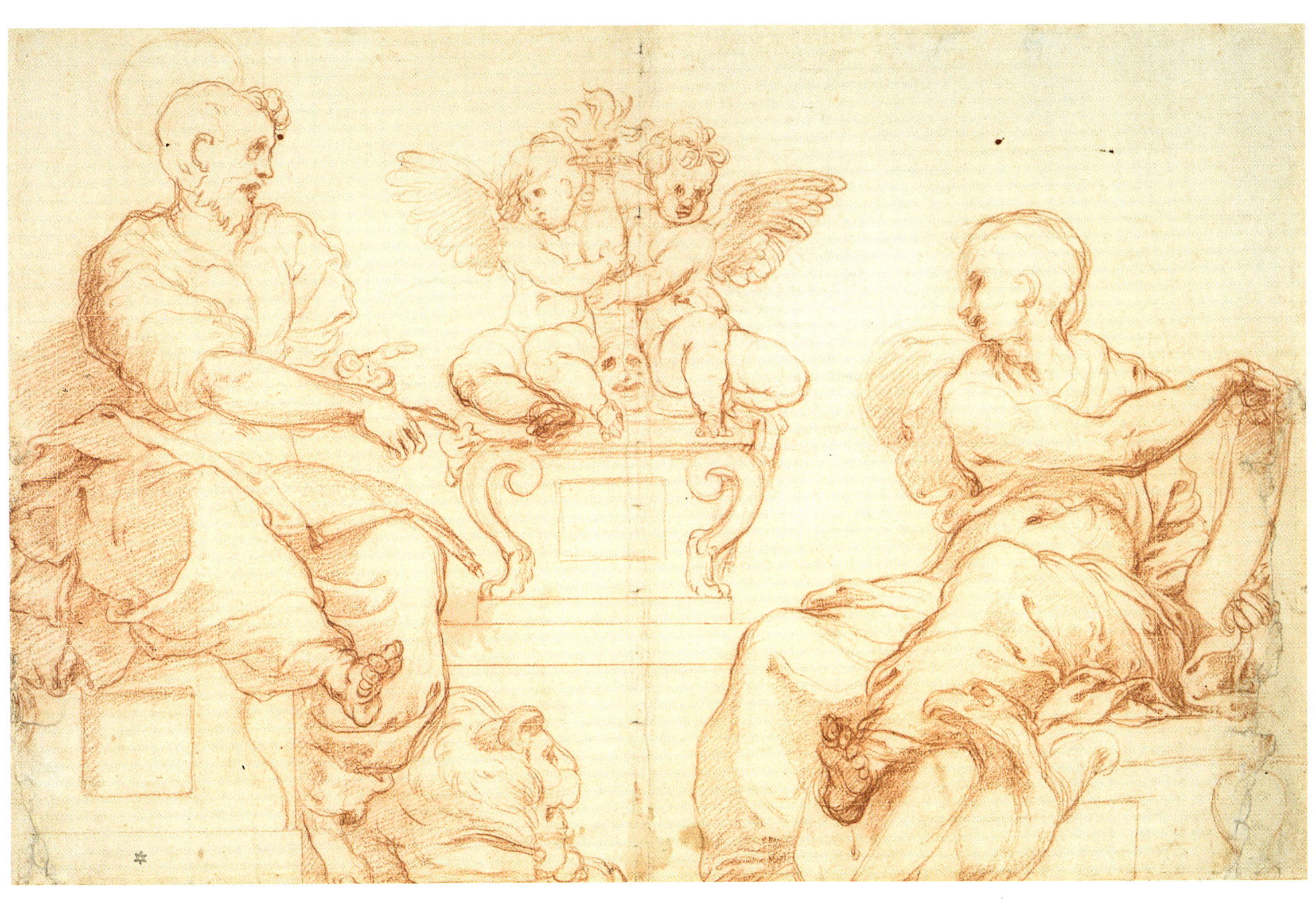

Girolamo Muziano

49
Saint Jerome

c. 1584
red chalk, washed over in the lower part of the draperies
39 x 27.6 (15 3/8 x 10 7/8); watermark: crossed keys surmounted by a lily, in a shield surmounted by a star, close to Briquet 1158
RL 0440

EXHIBITIONS
None

LITERATURE
Popham and Wilde 1949, no. 518

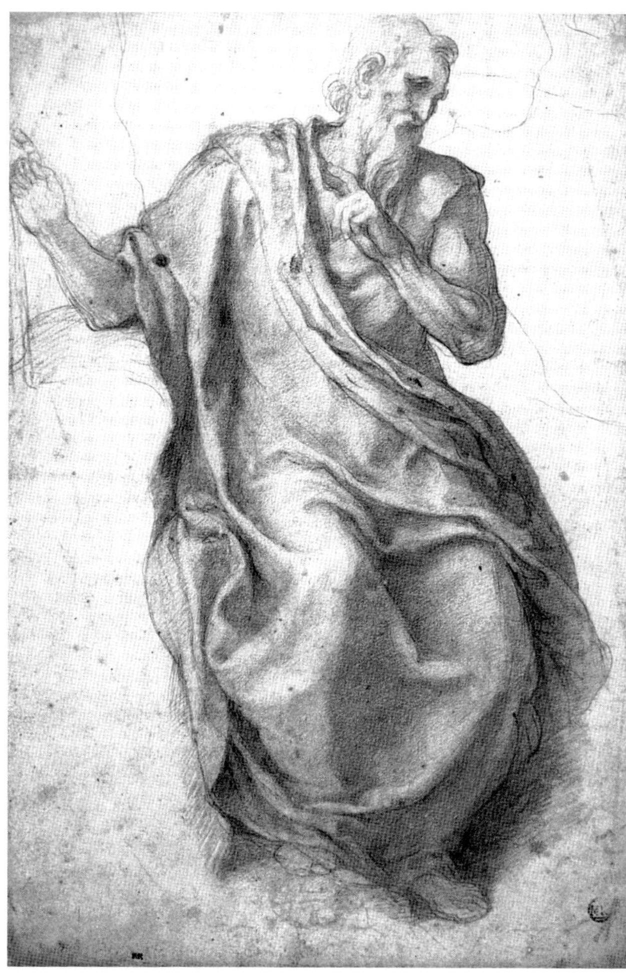

fig. 91. Girolamo Muziano, *Saint Jerome*, red chalk, 40 x 27.5 cm. Musée du Louvre, Paris, Département des Arts Graphiques [Photo RMN]

This drawing was made in preparation for the large altarpiece, begun before 1584 but still unfinished at Muziano's death in 1592, of *Saint Jerome and Saint Romuald*, made for Saint Peter's but subsequently transferred to Santa Maria degli Angeli. A very similar study, witness to the care with which Muziano prepared his paintings, is in the Louvre (fig. 91, Inv. 5109) together with a compositional draft for the altarpiece (Inv. 5105). The pose of Saint Jerome is loosely based on Michelangelo's Sistine *Ezekiel*, modified in the light of Muziano's knowledge of Michelangelo's later style. The areas of drapery lying smoothly over much of the figure, which run into and are articulated by pipelike folds, are developed from works like Michelangelo's Pauline frescoes or his even later *modelli* for Marcello Venusti, such as the *Saint Jerome Contemplating the Crucifix*, now known only in a print and a copy drawing in Rotterdam (De Tolnay 1960, no. 238, fig. 251). Muziano's drawing exemplifies the way in which different periods in Michelangelo's stylistic development could be fused by his successors.

Despite Muziano's Venetian background, it is difficult to discern here much trace of Venice. The combination of smoothly stumped areas and rather loose vaporous lines seems entirely Roman and reminiscent of Taddeo Zuccaro, also much inspired by Michelangelo's last phase as a painter. In the present exhibition, Muziano's drawing can be compared with Taddeo Zuccaro's study for the *Agony in the Garden* (cat. 67). However, Muziano was a much more restrained artist than Taddeo, and he strove in his compositions for clarity and grandeur of statement, with minimal indulgence in virtuosity of pose or arrangement. His great canvas of the *Raising of Lazarus*, signed and dated 1555 (Vatican Museums), earned Michelangelo's praise, and Muziano remained one of the most eminent exponents of the severe style in Roman painting in the second half of the century. His debt to Sebastiano del Piombo extended to his manner of drawing, and in the Louvre drawing for this figure, the application of chalk in tight regular strokes to build up dense masses shows a clear response to Sebastiano's drawing style.

Although Muziano was not an executant on Sebastiano's level, the unwavering seriousness of his work and his refusal of extravagance either of form or of color make him one of the most significant figures of the later cinquecento. He is now best known for his dense and detailed landscape drawings, but his achievements as a figure painter deserve a fresh evaluation. Muziano's art was rapidly eclipsed after his death by the new developments brought about by the Carracci and Caravaggio, but some response to it can be seen in the later work of the most imposing painter of the next generation: Domenichino.

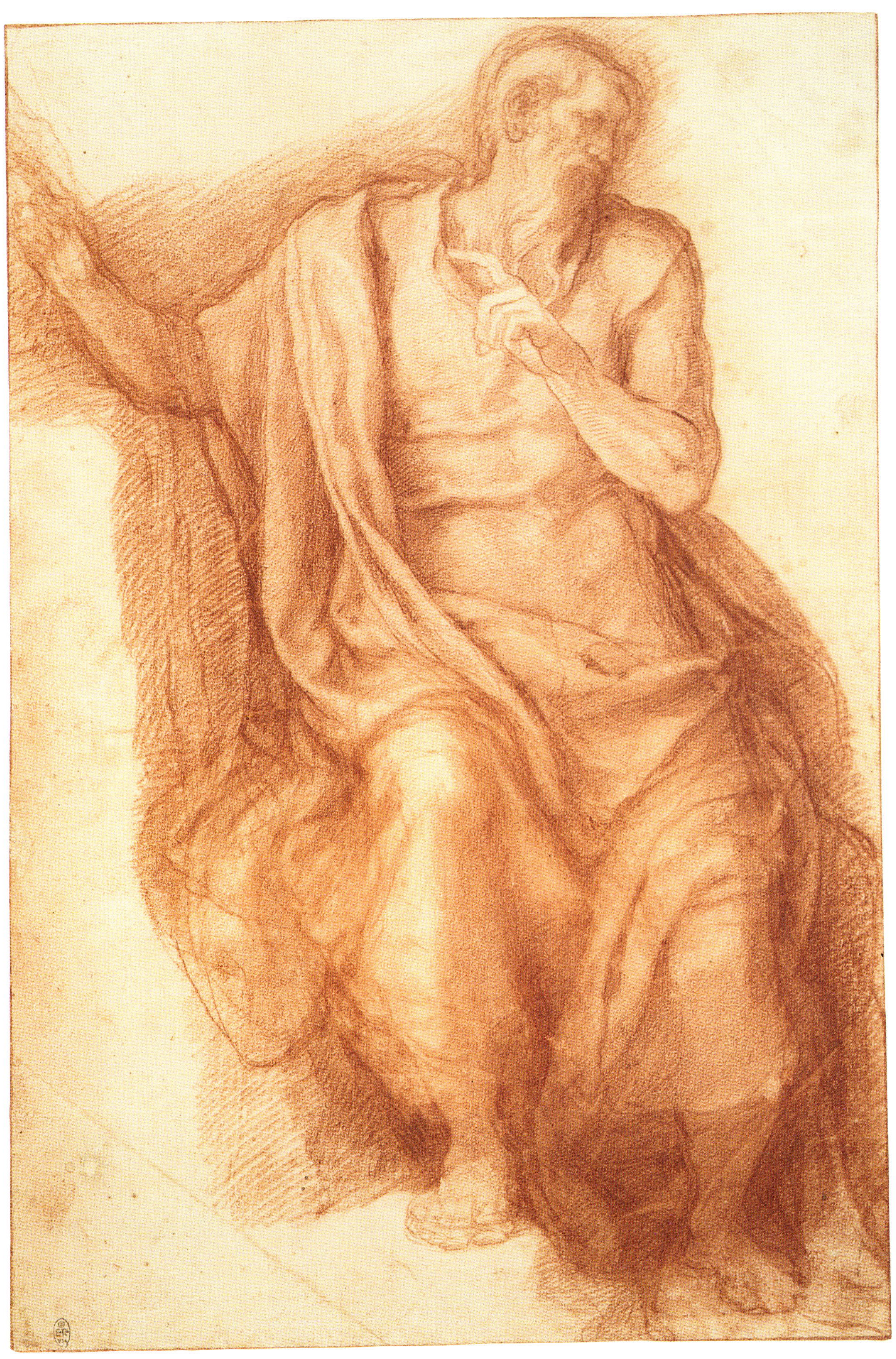

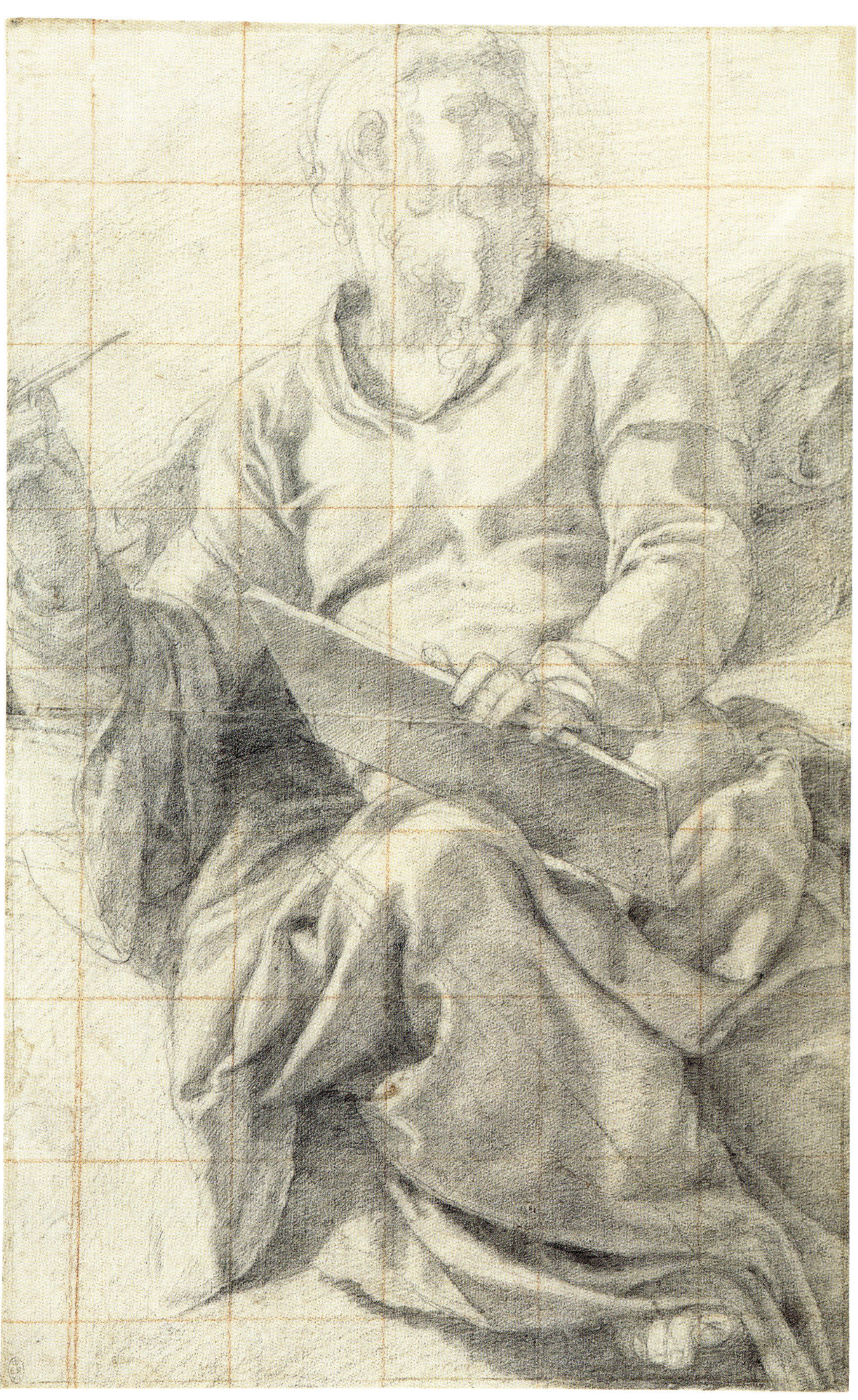

Unidentified Roman Artist

50
A Seated Prophet or Evangelist

c. 1570 (?)
black chalk, squared in red chalk at 48 mm
42.9 x 27.3 (16 7/8 x 10 3/4); watermark: crown with fleur de lys, not in Briquet
RL 0439

EXHIBITIONS
None

LITERATURE
Popham and Wilde 1949, no. 520

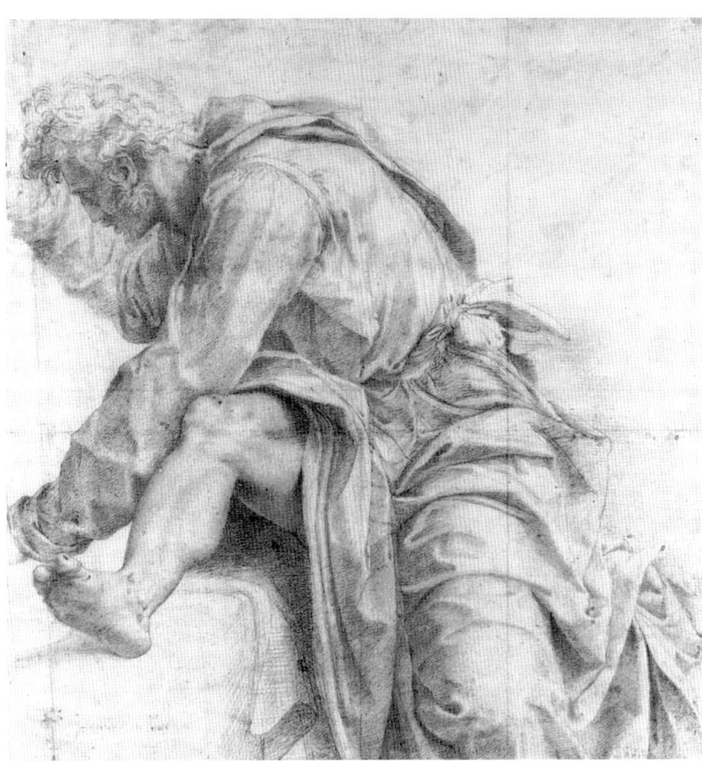

fig. 92. Daniele da Volterra, *A Seated Man*, black chalk, squared, 36.4 x 34.7 cm. The Royal Collection, Windsor Castle

Although this drawing was accepted by Popham as the work of Muziano, its authorship is uncertain. Taco Dibbits, who is preparing a study of the artist's drawings, has also expressed doubts about Muziano's authorship. It has not been linked with any painting, and the technique is not very close to other drawings certainly by Muziano—although his red-chalk study in the Louvre of *Christ Carrying the Cross* (Inv. 5101), a drawing retouched by Rubens, is probably least dissimilar.

The careful and painstaking method of the present drawing, with separate and regular strokes of the chalk applied one after another, seems to the compiler reminiscent of the handling of Daniele da Volterra, for whom this time-consuming and slightly dry method served the functions of restraining an excessive facility and producing forms that, while powerful and volumetric, were subtly generalized. But Daniele's figure studies, such as one in the Royal Collection (fig. 92), are invariably more solid and heavy than this, and more fully worked in the shadows. Nor does an attribution to Girolamo Siciolante da Sermoneta, whose drawings have sometimes been confused with those of Daniele, seem plausible, since his application of chalk is denser than that in the present drawing, and he makes less use of individually distinguishable lines. But on balance, an artist in Daniele's circle is a more likely candidate than Muziano.

None of these three artists—Muziano, Daniele, or Siciolante—employed such freely voluminous drapery as the draftsman who made this drawing: he obviously delighted in playing full and mobile folds against the swinging movement of the body. Indeed, a fold of cloak blows free of his left shoulder as though to convey the breath of inspiration flowing through this evangelist or prophet. Also, his forms are grander and more confident than those of most drawings of the mid-century. They display a strong response to the Sistine ceiling and are broadly based on those of the prophet *Daniel*. The figure is clearly self-sufficient and, while the gaze is upward and outward, seems not to be participating in a scene of any sort. The drawing was probably made for a figure to be painted, in a formula very popular in Rome in the second half of the cinquecento, in the right-hand spandrel of the entrance arch to a chapel. The curved line lower left strongly suggests this, as does the low angle from which the figure is foreshortened: it is probable that the drawing once extended further to the right, where the figure's left leg would have extended down, filling the lower section of the spandrel. It is also possible, but less likely, that the figure could have been intended for a pendentive, but the center of gravity of the figure would seem too far to the left for this to be likely. Muziano designed four evangelists for the pendentives of the Cappella Gregoriana in Saint Peter's in the late 1570s, but not one corresponds in pose to this figure.

Michelangelo's sense of urgency and internal moral complexity is lacking in this figure, but the artist has caught something of his massiveness and grandeur, especially in the play of planes of drapery over the chest. He has also demonstrated considerable intelligence in playing the rumpled folds that lie over the figure's lap and calves, which create a varied range of shadows, against the relative smoothness of the chest, upper arms, and head, which are much more brightly lit by the light reflected upward from the pages of the book. The image provides a forceful representation of conviction and security, with the outward gaze invoking divine guidance.

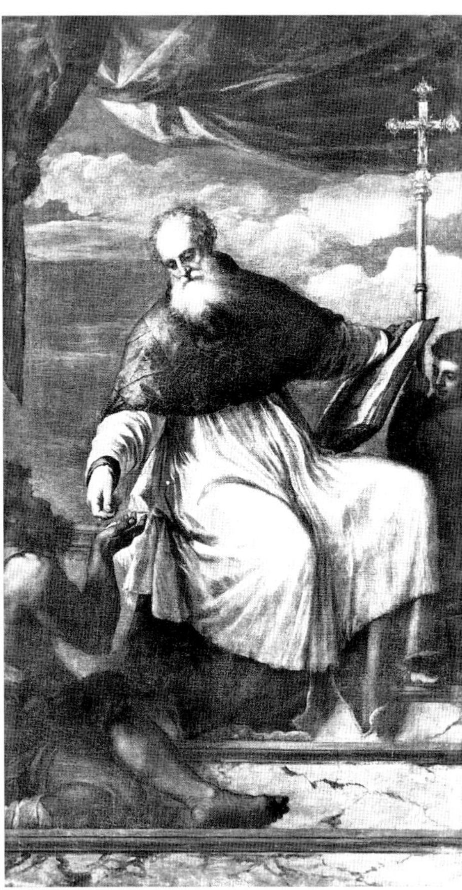

fig. 93. Titian, *San Giovanni Elemosinario*, oil on canvas, 264 x 148 cm. San Giovanni Elemosinario, Venice [Fratelli Alinari, Florence]

Giovanni Antonio da Pordenone

51
Saint Augustine

c. 1528–1530
brush and wash heightened with white on blue-green paper
24.6 x 19.4 (9 11/16 x 7 5/8); laid down
inscribed with an indication of perspective in stylus in lower part, consisting of two diagonal indentations running into the horizontal ruled at the level of the step; two further stylus horizontals ruled at the level of the head
RL 5458

EXHIBITIONS
London 1972–1973, no. 101; Pordenone 1984, no. 4.15; London 1986, no. 39

LITERATURE
Von Hadeln 1925, 37; Fiocco 1939, 155; Tietze and Tietze-Conrat 1944, no. 1361; Popham and Wilde 1949, no. 741; Cohen 1980, 126; Furlan 1988, D.24

This *modello*, for which a preparatory *concetto* survives in the Ashmolean Museum (Macandrew 1980, no. 490A), was connected by Von Hadeln, followed by Popham, with Pordenone's fresco of *Saint Augustine* in the church of the Madonna di Campagna, Piacenza, which was probably executed in the early 1530s. The Tietzes' view, followed by Cohen, was, rather, that the drawing was made a little earlier, in preparation for one of probably four frescoes of the church fathers recorded by Marco Boschini in San Giovanni Elemosinario in Venice, a figure that Pordenone would then have reworked—as was his custom—for Piacenza. Cohen remarks on the "dynamic, Michelangelesque, luministic" features of the drawing, "all the qualities he tried to stress in Venice, especially in his first works in the city in the late 1520s." However, according to Furlan (1988) those fresco fragments so far recovered in San Giovanni do not include a representation of Saint Augustine and seem not to be by Pordenone. But Furlan does point to a similarity between the saint's head in the present drawing and a fragmentary fresco by Pordenone's associate Pomponio Amalteo formerly in the Palazzo del Consiglio dei Nobili at Belluno, which was painted in 1529, in support of the view that the present drawing was made for a lost painting by Pordenone antedating that year. Furlan also remarks that Pordenone painted a fresco of the saint, now lost, in the Convent of San Agostino in Cremona in 1523, but she doubts that the present drawing could be so early.

In the Windsor sheet—"one of Pordenone's finest, fully pictorial, chiaroscuro designs" (Cohen 1980)—in which the forms are energized by the fast application of the wash and white gouache in striated strokes, the bishop saint, whose intellectual energy is conveyed by the vigor with which he compares codices, is clearly inspired by Michelangelo's Sistine prophets, without repeating any of them. The saint's communicative zeal comes closest to that of *Ezekiel*, but his pose is perhaps closer to *Joel*.

Pordenone probably traveled to Rome more than once, although no sojourns are documented. While relatively few of his figures are direct quotations, Michelangelo's influence pervades his work, and among his North Italian contemporaries Pordenone was most impressed by the energy that characterizes the last phase of the Sistine. He seems also to have known some drawings by Michelangelo: a figure designed by him for the frontispiece of Ludovico Dolce's *Il primo libro di Sacripante*, published in 1536 (the original drawing is in Biblioteca Ambrosiana, Milan, Cod. F269 inf. no. 36bis; Cohen 1980, fig. 129), depends directly from one of Michelangelo's *Resurrection* studies. It was partly in response to Pordenone—who, Vasari indicates, was felt by Titian in the later 1520s and 1530s to be a dangerous competitor—that Titian attempted to aggrandize his style. Titian had long been aware of Michelangelo's work, and his knowledge of it was extensive and his understanding subtle. Indeed, Pordenone's *modello* for the *Death of Saint Peter Martyr* of circa 1526 borrows from Titian's earlier interpretation of Michelangelo in his Padua fresco of 1511, the *Jealous Husband*. But Pordenone founded his work on a supercharged vigor and energy, a response to Michelangelo that might be called brutalist; Pordenone's extremism was designed for maximum impact. It was this type of Michelangelism that challenged Titian and it was in response to Pordenone that Titian produced two of his most energetic works, both destroyed: the *Death of Saint Peter Martyr*, with its heavily Michelangelesque figures, and the *Battle of Spoleto*. His surviving altarpiece of *San Giovanni Elemosinario*, probably of 1533 (fig. 93), might well reflect awareness of the present design.

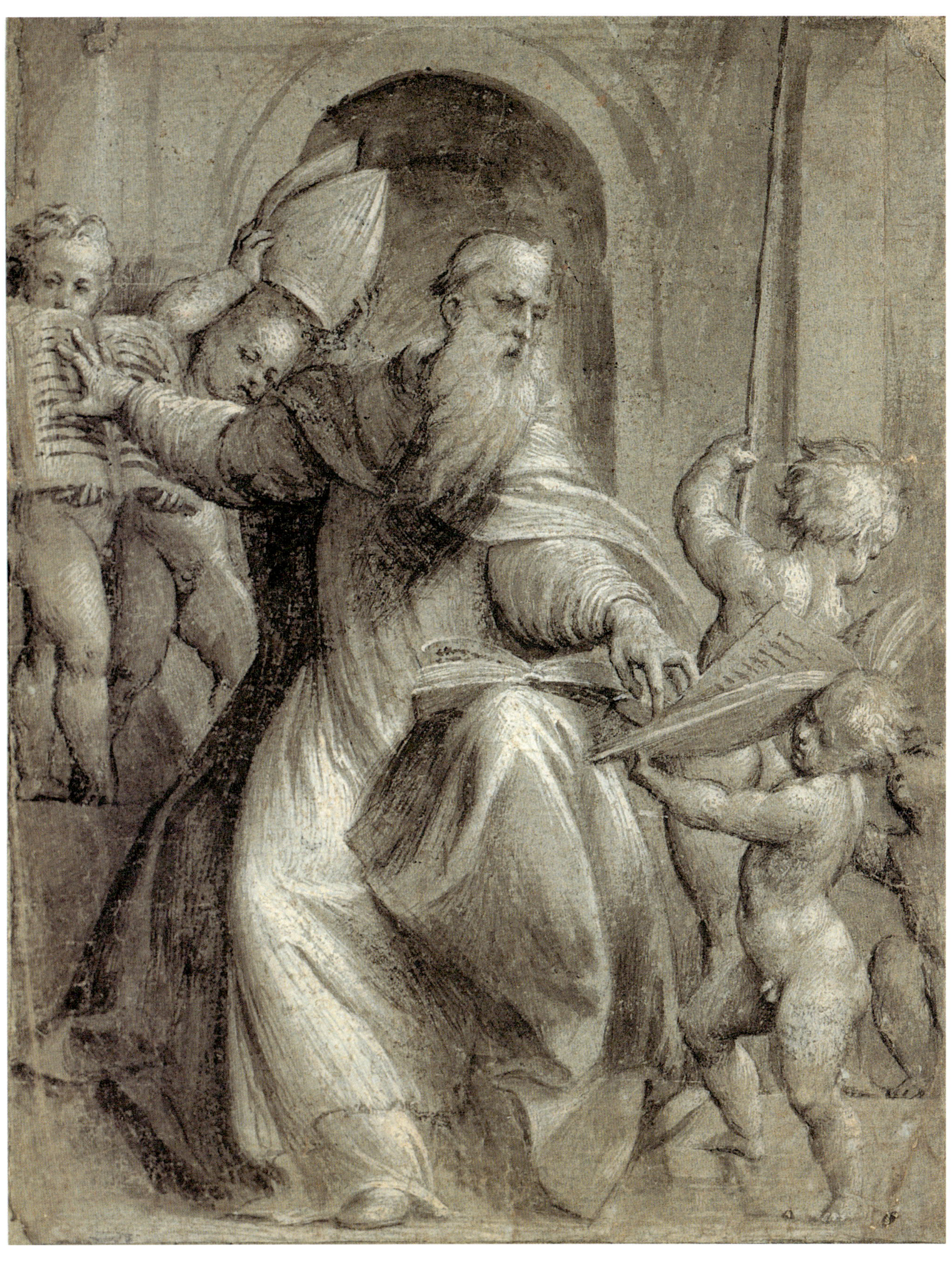

Annibale Carracci after Michelangelo Buonarroti

52
Azor

c. 1604
pen and ink
18.1 x 22.1 (7 1/8 x 8 11/16); laid down
RL 1997

EXHIBITIONS
None

LITERATURE
Wittkower 1952, no. 420

It is difficult to know whether Annibale's copy of *Azor* was made directly from the original (fig. 94) or from some intermediate copy. Although the ancestors of Christ are mostly posed in profile, which diminishes for a copyist problems of foreshortening, they can only be seen from a difficult low angle. This figure is so well adjusted that it seems to have been

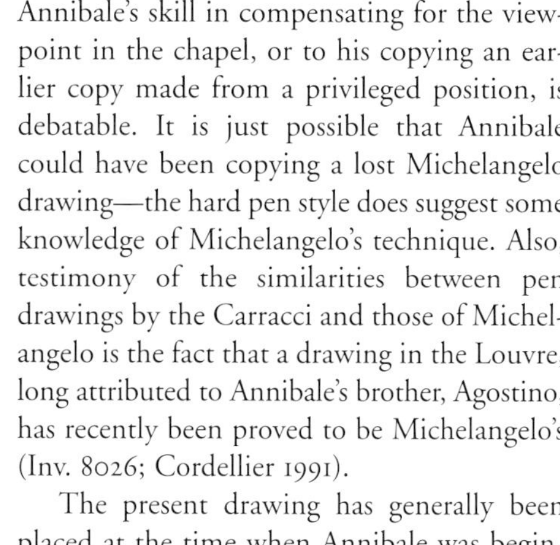

made from eye level. Whether this is due to Annibale's skill in compensating for the viewpoint in the chapel, or to his copying an earlier copy made from a privileged position, is debatable. It is just possible that Annibale could have been copying a lost Michelangelo drawing—the hard pen style does suggest some knowledge of Michelangelo's technique. Also, testimony of the similarities between pen drawings by the Carracci and those of Michelangelo is the fact that a drawing in the Louvre, long attributed to Annibale's brother, Agostino, has recently been proved to be Michelangelo's (Inv. 8026; Cordellier 1991).

The present drawing has generally been placed at the time when Annibale was beginning work on the Farnese gallery, circa 1597. It was then that Annibale began to tighten his style and to aim for greater clarity of organization and meaning. However, in the Farnese gallery Annibale's Michelangelism is vivacious and lighthearted. The strength and simplicity of the present drawing and the fact that Annibale chose to copy one of Michelangelo's more restrained and withdrawn figures suggest rather that it dates from after the completion of the scheme, perhaps around 1604, when Annibale's style was developing a greater solidity and more powerful relief. It would be appropriate if, in approaching the heavier and more somber manner that characterizes his late work, Annibale, himself in a state of profound depression, should have looked closely at the most restrained and rhythmically contained of Michelangelo's forms.

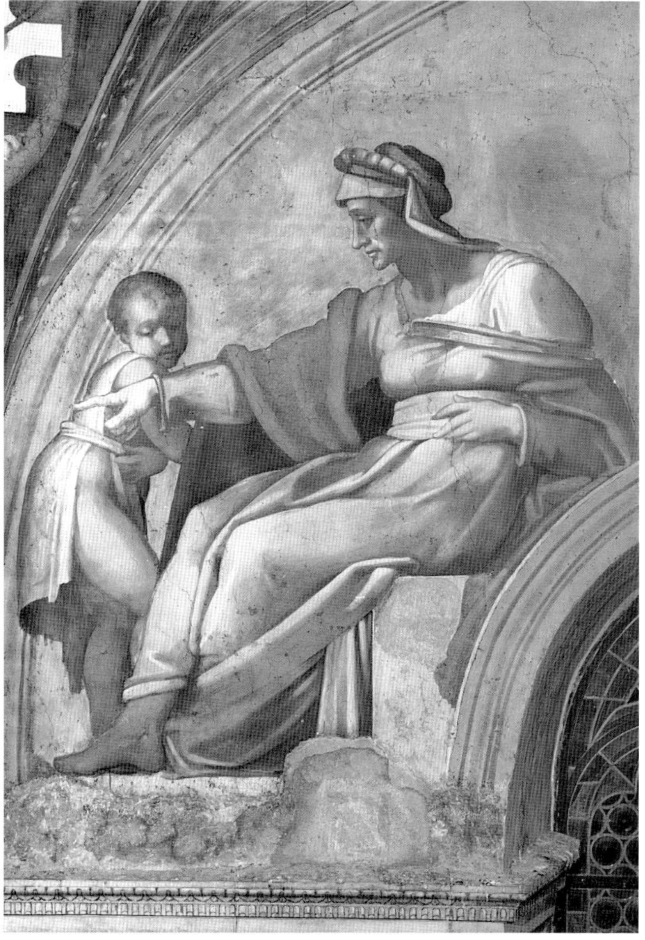

fig. 94. Michelangelo, *Azor*, fresco. The Sistine Chapel, Vatican Museums

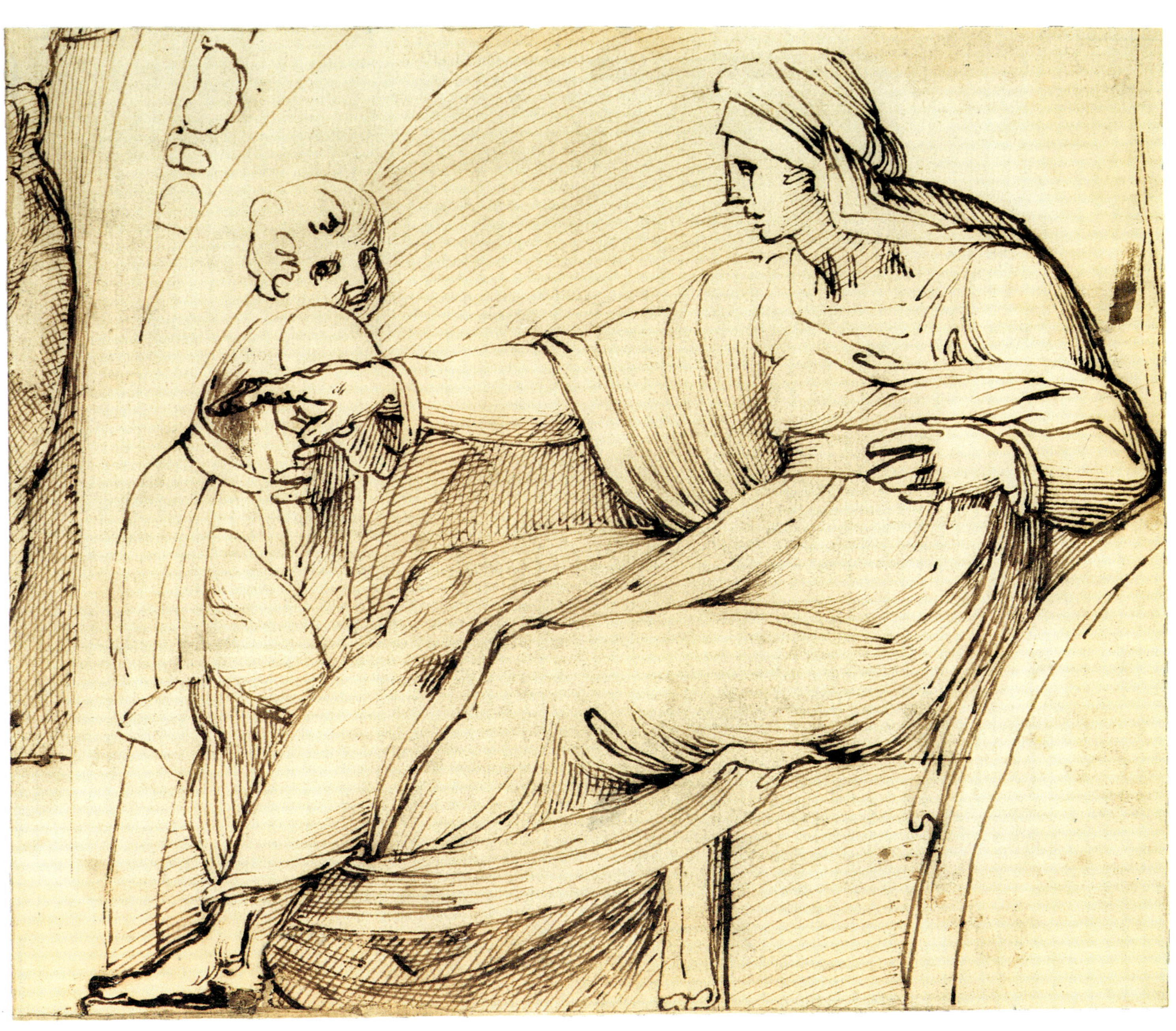

Sebastiano del Piombo

53
God the Father

c. 1532
black chalk heightened with white
30.1 x 23.7 (11 7/8 x 9 5/16); no watermark
inscribed in pen and ink, lower right: *Sebastiano del Piombo.*
RL 4815

EXHIBITIONS
London 1972–1973, no. 97

LITERATURE
Berenson 1938, no. 2505B; Popham and Wilde 1949, no. 924; Hirst 1981, 130; Perrig 1991, 85

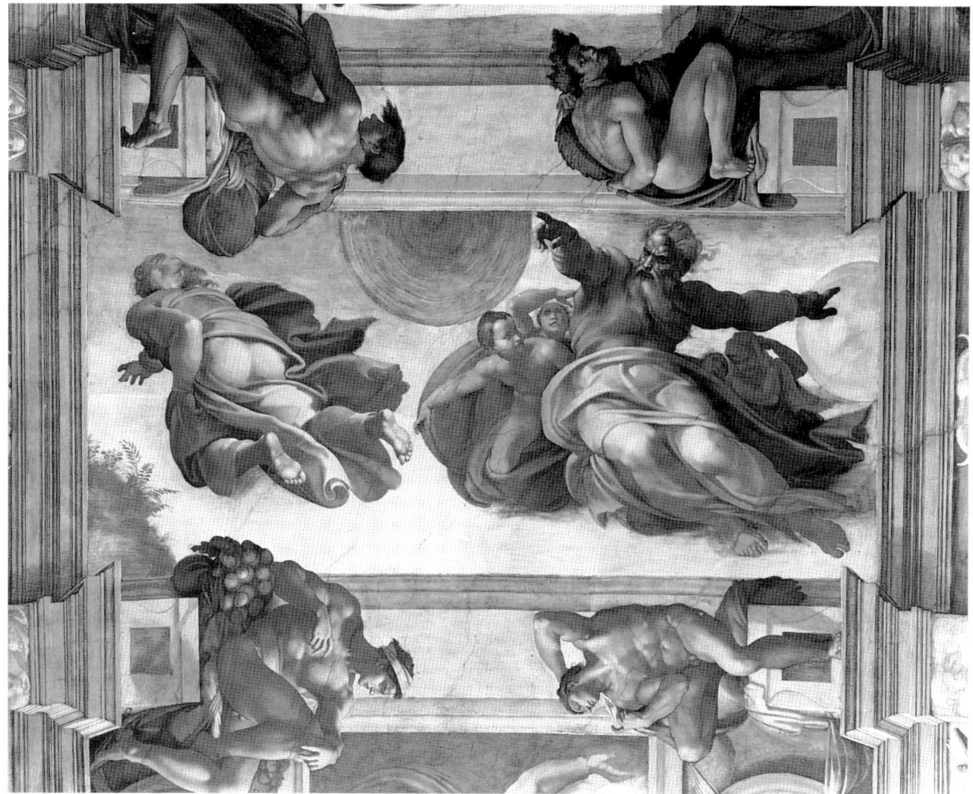

fig. 95. Michelangelo, *God the Father Creating the Sun and the Moon; God the Father Creating Vegetation*, fresco. The Sistine Chapel, Vatican Museums

This was identified by Popham as a study for one of the scenes from Genesis planned for the drum of the Chigi chapel in Santa Maria del Popolo. These paintings were part of a commission that seems initially to have been given to Sebastiano in the 1520s, but that was renewed in the early 1530s. Sebastiano requested Michelangelo's graphic aid, in a letter of 25 March 1532, with a "Nativity with God the Father in the midst of angels" and probably received it. He executed most of the altarpiece, but it was completed, probably according to his intentions, by Francesco Salviati only in 1554. Sebastiano seems not to have begun the drum frescoes, and Salviati also executed these, entirely to his own design.

It is likely that two lightly executed drawings of the *Separation of Light from Darkness* and the *Creation of the Sun and the Moon* (Louvre Inv. RF 34.504 recto and verso) were made by Sebastiano for the drum: the latter drawing includes an indication of framing that would fit this location. Although the present sheet could well show the Father in one of the acts of creation, it seems less suitable for such a location or such a purpose. The figure is vertical in orientation, whereas the drum spaces are square, and it is so grand and majestic that it would have overpowered the available space. It is also worked out much more fully than the Louvre drawings. It is therefore more likely, if it really is connected with the Chigi chapel, that it was intended for the upper section of the altarpiece that contains a similarly posed figure of God the Father. Although the Father's action in this drawing does not seem particularly appropriate to a *Birth of the Virgin*, this is true also of his role as finally painted, in which his gestures are not readily explicable in relation to the scene.

In pose and gesture God the Father here is based on Michelangelo's *God the Father Creating the Sun and the Moon* (fig. 95) on the Sistine ceiling, but Sebastiano's elongation of the figure, and the sense of weightlessness that he imparts to it, would seem also to reveal a response to the *Resurrection* drawings that Michelangelo was making at this period, some of which may have been made for Sebastiano himself. But in contrast to Michelangelo's vitality of modeling with every muscle and sinew of the body deployed for expressive meaning, Sebastiano imposes a geometrical simplification on the body and creates a quasi-mechanical articulation, as if it were a jointed lay figure. In execution the present figure would have been more fully draped, and there was, perhaps, no need here to describe the physique in detail. But this type of stylization, idealizing but of great severity, was increasingly to become Sebastiano's preferred mode, and this severity may, in turn, have affected the late pictorial ideas of Michelangelo.

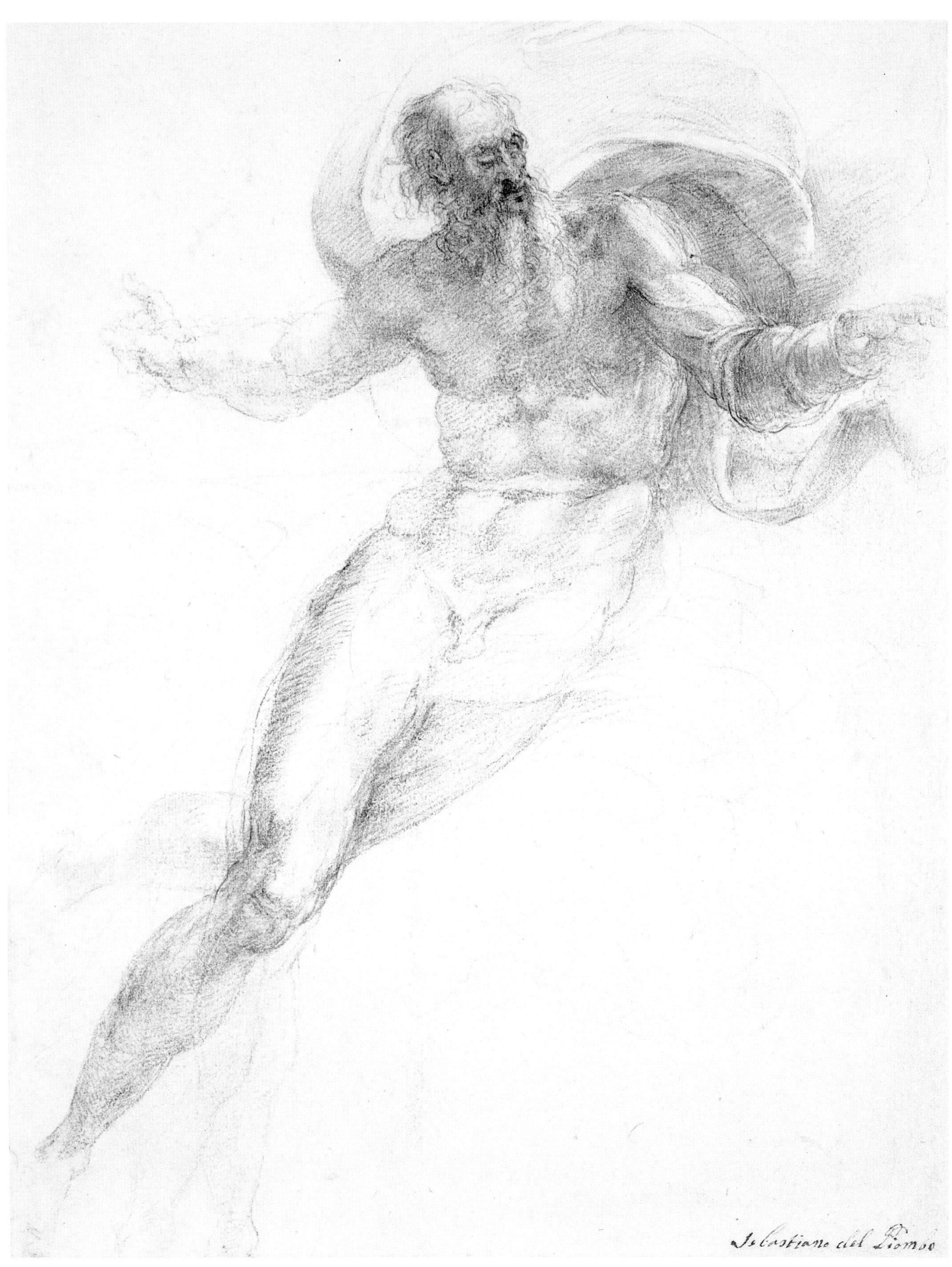
Sebastiano del Piombo

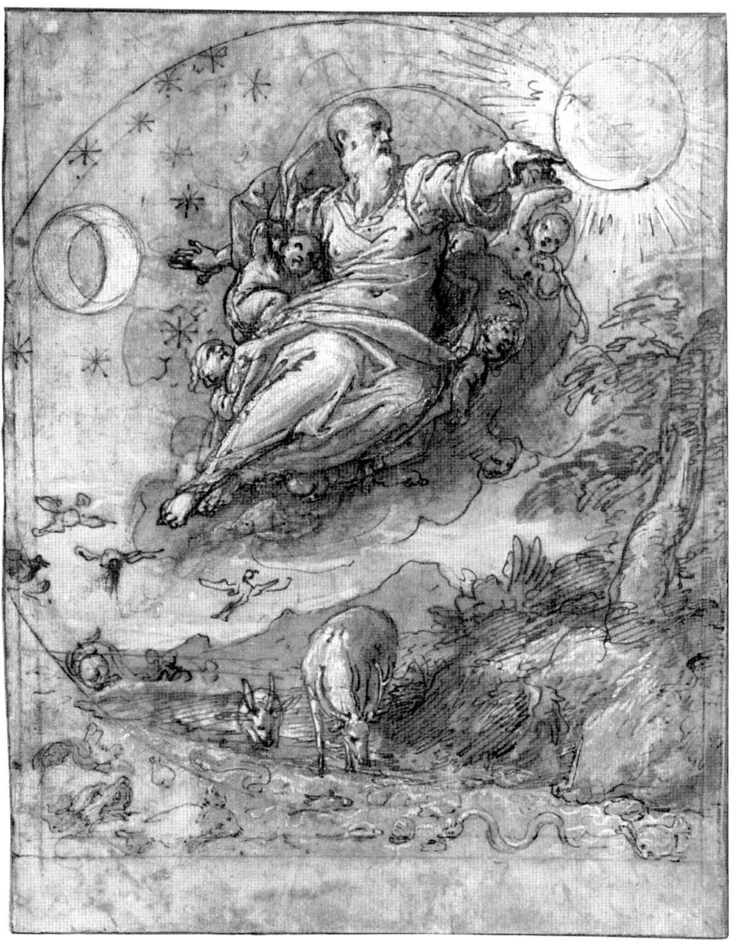

fig. 96. Federico Zuccaro, *God the Father Creating the Sun and the Moon,* pen and ink heightened with white, 32.5 x 26 cm. Allen Memorial Art Museum, Oberlin College, Ohio, Gift of Robert Lehman

Federico Zuccaro

54
The Creation of the Sun and the Moon

c. 1566–1568
pen and ink and wash, heightened with white, over black chalk on blue paper
27.8 x 23 (10 15/16 x 9 1/16); no watermark
RL 5976

EXHIBITIONS
None

LITERATURE
Popham and Wilde 1949, no. 1056

The design, as Popham observed, is for the tondo in the center of the vault of the chapel at Caprarola, decorated by Federico in 1566–1568. As Popham also noted, this drawing is based upon another by Federico, formerly at Wilton and now at Oberlin (fig. 96; see Milwaukee-New York 1989–1990, no. 41). Popham assumed that the present drawing was a copy by another artist, but Federico often made versions of his own drawings, perhaps for sale or gift. Indeed, the quality of the present drawing—the birds, for example, are very lively—justifies an attribution to Federico himself.

In employing one of the most popular and widely copied of Michelangelo's Sistine ceiling figures—Giulio Clovio, for example, produced a version of it in the Farnese *Book of Hours*—Federico was making no attempt to disguise his model, for he surely intended it to be seen as a conscious echo of Michelangelo's invention. Although Federico's reputation has recently suffered by comparison with the livelier and wilder work of his elder bother Taddeo, he was a highly intellectual and very well-informed artist, who was also an indefatigable copyist with a wide range of interests. The present drawing shows Federico's proclivity for neatness and sharpness of focus. The sublime, immeasurable aspect of Michelangelo's figure—or that of Sebastiano's drawing (cat. 53)—is suppressed and what Federico provides is a clearly legible image. In a sense, Federico Zuccaro is a dry artist, but dryness is in part a function of a desire for clarity. His selective use of references and quotations is that of an artist of great visual education and deep self-knowledge.

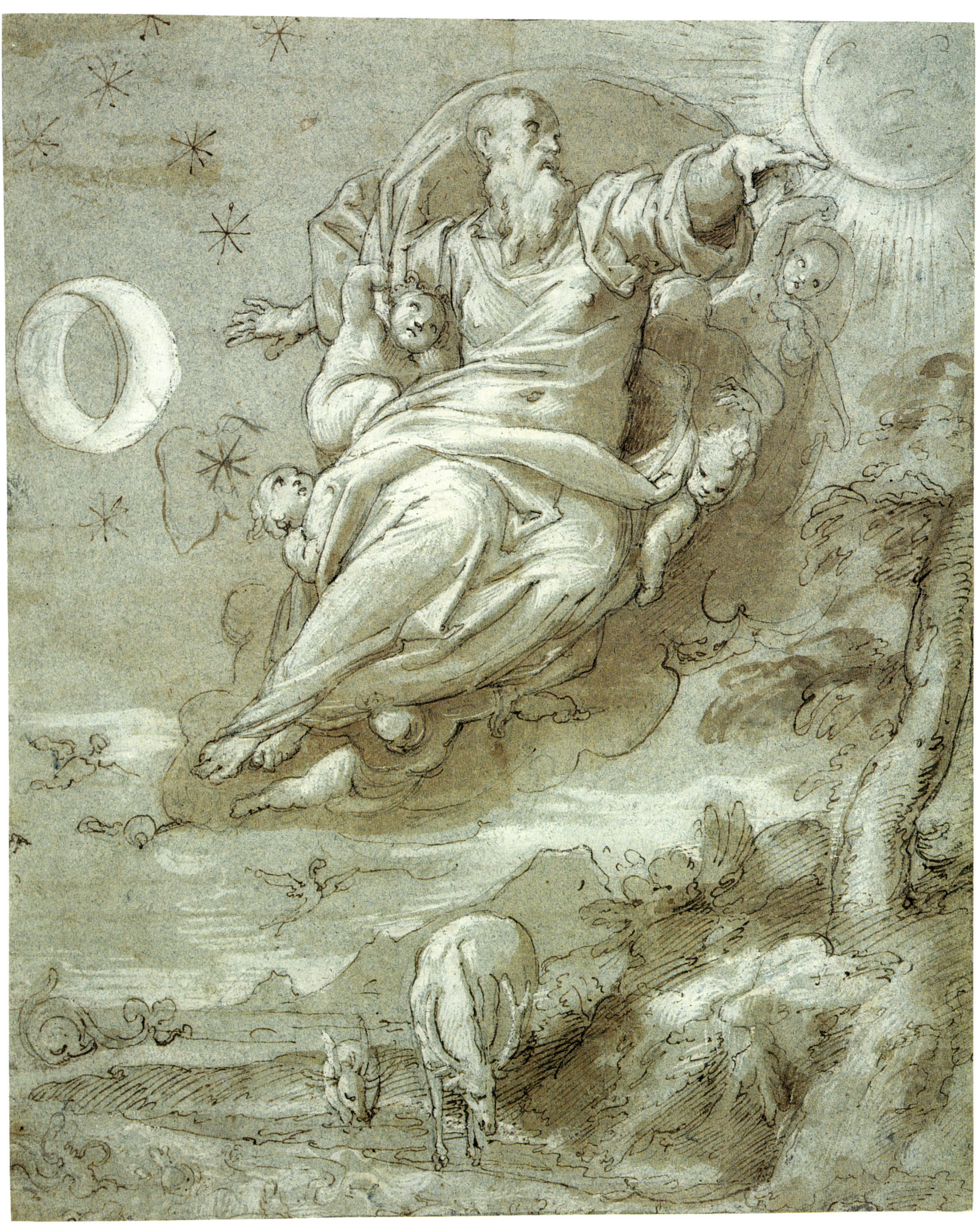

The Last Judgment and Its Impact

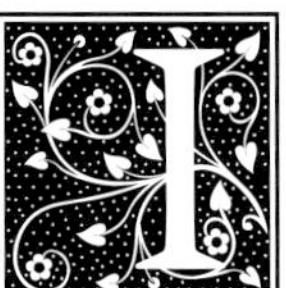

It is likely that preliminary discussions between Pope Clement VII and Michelangelo about a major modification to the pictorial decoration of the Sistine Chapel took place during their meeting in 1533. The chapel's pictorial decoration was then complete, with Michelangelo's ceiling, the series of popes, and the paired historical cycles of the lives of Moses and Christ dating from the 1480s. The single noteworthy addition to the decoration since 1512 was confined to the lowest level, where the simulated hangings, also of the 1480s, were in part, and on special occasions, covered by the sequence of tapestries of the parallel ministries of Peter and Paul designed by Raphael around 1515. A loss had also been suffered: on Christmas Eve 1522 a section of the architrave above the entrance to the chapel had fallen, irreparably damaging the last two frescoes of the Christ and Moses cycles, the *Resurrection* and the *Death of Moses*.

In 1533 the altar wall was entirely frescoed and was the most densely decorated and thematically loaded area of the chapel. It comprised two lunettes of the ancestors of Christ by Michelangelo; a row of figures, with Christ in the center, possibly Mary and Saint John the Baptist on either side of him, between the windows; and the figures of Saints Peter and Paul at the edges of the wall, between the windows and the side walls. Below them were placed the *Nativity of Christ* and the *Finding of Moses* and, probably rising between them, Perugino's frescoed altarpiece of the *Assumption of the Virgin* (or the *Immaculate Conception*). At either side of the altarpiece, on the lowest level, hung the first two of Raphael's tapestries, the *Miraculous Draft* and the *Stoning of Saint Stephen.* Thus any new decoration would radically disrupt the old. The fact that Clement VII and then Paul III, who insisted on continuing with the project when he succeeded to the papacy, were prepared to accept such disruption argues strongly that it was deemed of great importance. According to Vasari, it grew from a project to place above the Castel Sant'Angelo a vast bronze group of *Saint Michael Casting Down the Seven Deadly Sins.* This became transmuted into a pictorial *Last Judgment*, which retained the motif of the casting down of sin. While the scheme may have included an element of penitent self-criticism, it was primarily defiant, threatening God's punishment upon sinners and, implicitly, heretics.

Relatively few preparatory drawings survive for the *Last Judgment* from the hundreds, perhaps thousands, that Michelangelo made. Most, presumably, were consumed in one or other of his periodic bonfires. But from those that are known it seems that the project went through at least two, possibly three, stages. Initially, the existing lunettes and the altarpiece were to be retained. The final fresco, characteristically for Michelangelo, came to occupy the whole wall. But Clement's scheme was still more ambitious, for Vasari tells us that he wanted Michelangelo to paint a facing fresco on the entrance wall, the *Fall of the Rebel Angels.* Nothing seems to have been done about this, and no surviving drawings can securely be connected with it. But such a project would inevitably have eliminated any idea of replacing the damaged frescoes of the *Resurrection* and the *Death of Moses* (see cat. 38).

Clement died before work began on the cartoon of the *Last Judgment*, but it seems that the design was already far advanced. A letter of 2 March 1534 refers to a *Risurretione* planned for the Sistine Chapel, and this is sometimes taken to indicate that Michelangelo intended to paint Christ's Resurrection for the altar wall. But the reference is undoubtedly to the general Resurrection, that of Christ's second coming, which is part of the events of the last day and which is, indeed, shown prominently in the finished fresco. It may be because the scheme was so far advanced that Cardinal Alessandro Farnese insisted that Michelangelo continue with it when he was elected pope, as

Paul III, on 13 October 1534.

It seems that Sebastiano del Piombo undertook the preparation of the wall in 1535, while Michelangelo was making cartoons, but he assumed that Michelangelo was to paint the *Last Judgment* in Sebastiano's own technique of oil on wall. Michelangelo, a believer in *buon fresco*, was furious, broke with Sebastiano, and ordered the preparation to be replaced. He seems to have begun the physical task of painting in 1536. The *Last Judgment* was unveiled in October 1541 to universal acclaim. Michelangelo was then sixty-six years old.

Although Michelangelo had rejected oil, the style of the *Last Judgment* is much heavier than the ceiling fresco. It is the defining example, according to Lomazzo, of Michelangelo's second style. Following the recent cleaning, it has frequently been remarked that the painting now resembles the work of Bronzino: in detail the fresco is indeed executed with great precision and refinement. Michelangelo did not attempt to generate an effect of power through loose execution and his forms are very densely painted, stony in quality, and extremely solid. It marks a radical change from the ceiling in form, texture, and color, which is now more restricted, with rather leaden flesh tones and deep ultramarine for the surrounding sky.

The closest precedent for the *Last Judgment*'s scheme is Giotto's fresco in the Arena chapel in Padua. Whether or not Michelangelo knew this, it is evident that he aimed in his fresco for the rigidity and severity of medieval Last Judgments, as well as recalling Luca Signorelli's great apocalyptic cycle at Orvieto. Unlike Fra Bartolommeo's unfinished *Last Judgment* of 1498–1500, the most recent ambitious attempt to treat the subject, Michelangelo eliminated perspective from his fresco. Although he included small figures who are obviously set well behind the foreground plane, space is not measurable. Michelangelo wished to present an unrelenting and inescapable picture of Christ's power both to damn and to save. The result is a wall of figures that allows the viewer no escape. Michelangelo's painting, by presenting so unrelenting and sustained a vision of divine power and divine justice, forces the viewer to turn inward and to confront his own sins.

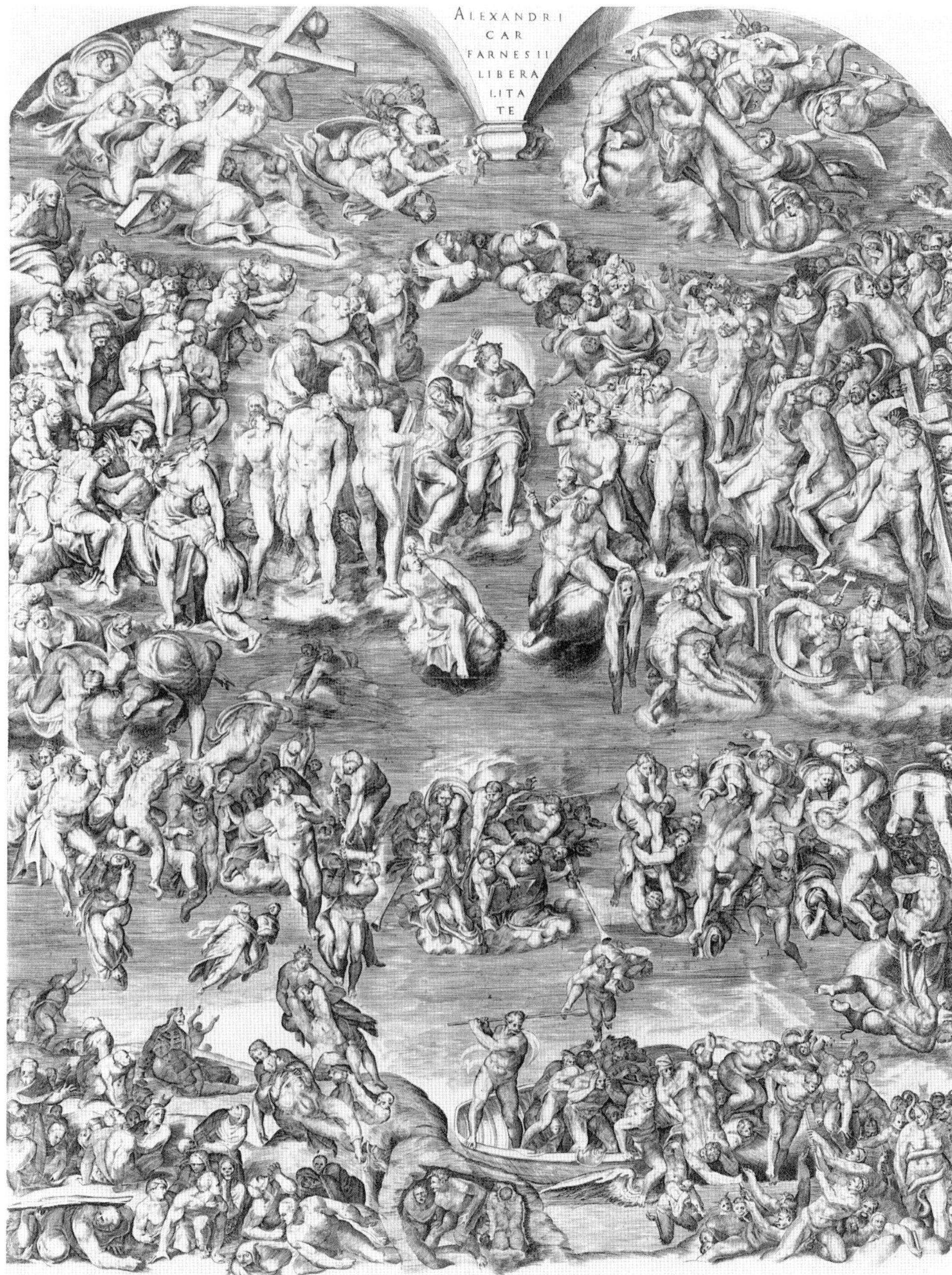

fig. 97. Giulio Bonasone after Michelangelo, *The Last Judgment*, engraving, 58.3 x 44.7 cm. The Royal Collection, Windsor Castle

Apart from his innate preference for the nude as his primary expressive vehicle, Michelangelo was compelled for several reasons to depict his figures entirely or largely nude. It was only through presenting musculature that he could convey fully the sense of physical and thus spiritual power that he required. Clothing would inevitably have undermined the timeless effect that he sought—any artist wishing to show the resurrection of the dead would obviously encounter difficulties if he wished to show the dead clothed—and only the nude could effectively embody the spiritual. But, in employing the nude, Michelangelo faced the obvious problem of sensuality: a wall of nude bodies would inevitably run the risk of being misinterpreted. Michelangelo attempted to avoid this by re-creating the human body, both male and female. He intended that the forms he created should not be elegant. His aim was for emotional effect—terror, pity, and catharsis.

He produced a type—thick-waisted, rubber-muscled, a pulsating mass of gristle—of overwhelming power and energy but lacking in any of those delicacies of internal articulation that make for sensual interest. He undermined beauty by irregularity and inflation. Thus Christ's head is based on that of the *Apollo Belvedere*, but thickened and simplified so that it becomes a mask of haughty intransigence rather than refinement. The group of the younger and older female saints at the left, presumably a mother and child, are adapted from an antique group of Niobe sheltering one of her daughters against the wrath of Apollo, but the proportions of the classical originals are changed, and all grace discarded. Michelangelo carefully devised this figure type in his drawings, in which he composed them out of deliberately hard, geometrical lines. It seems doubtful whether he actually worked from models, but if so, they must have been men accustomed to the heaviest possible labor, whose forms were further simplified by Michelangelo into superhuman engines. As a result, Michelangelo was able to include the most simple and apparently banal actions—an angel or a martyr striking down a vice with his fist; Christ himself, his mighty right arm raised to damn the sinners—with conviction.

The first reaction to the *Last Judgment* was wonderment. It was soon engraved (fig. 97) and was very much copied. Its effect, both on artists with direct knowledge and on those who knew it only from engravings, was enormous. As a grid composition built up entirely of figures, whose only controlling elements were the vertical and horizontal divisions of the chapel's architecture, it provided little inspiration as an overall composition. But the grid allowed maximum freedom to individual figures, and these were seized upon. The great majority of copies from the fresco are after single figures or small groups, sometimes drawn in such a way as to isolate them further. It is probably true to say that all of the most ambitious of Michelangelo's younger contemporaries registered the effect of the *Last Judgment.* But it took about a decade for the fresco to develop its most impressive progeny, in the work of Bronzino, Salviati, Allori, and even Jan van Scorel.

However, Michelangelo's method had an unexpected consequence. For the first time, his work came under serious attack, orchestrated by a man who had become an unscrupulous and vicious enemy: Pietro Aretino. Aretino's attack on the fresco, which he never saw, was leveled at the work's supposed indecency, its nudes. Strangely, this attack was not extended retrospectively to the ceiling, some of whose forms might well have been found unnecessarily sensual. Aretino's criticism, soon taken up by other writers, was never supported by sustained arguments; it rested solely upon the assumption that the exposed body was indecent, to which, on occasion, were attached various covert comments about the fresco's Lutheranism. Nevertheless, the attack was effective to the extent that one later pope even thought about destroying the fresco, and just within Michelangelo's lifetime, his friend and follower Daniele da Volterra was commissioned to cover some of the more obvious nudities.

Michelangelo Buonarroti

55a
Study for a Soul Being Saved by an Angel (VERSO)

55b
Sketch for the Lower Left-Hand Corner of the Last Judgment (RECTO)

c. 1535
black chalk
27.7 x 41.9 (10 7/8 x 16 1/2); no watermark
inscribed on verso in pen and ink: *di Bona Roti*
RL 12776

EXHIBITIONS
London 1950–1951, no. 268; London 1953, no. 67; London 1962, no. 77; London 1972–1973, no. 37; London 1975, no. 136; Washington-Paris 1988–1989, no. 52

LITERATURE
Berenson 1903 and 1938, no. 1620; Frey 1909–1911, no. 188; Thode 1913, no. 545; Popham and Wilde 1949, no. 432; Dussler 1959, no. 364; De Tolnay 1960, no. 180, 181; Berti 1965, 471, no. 173; Hartt 1971, no. 376 (recto), 388 (verso); De Tolnay 1975–1980, 3: no. 351 (recto only); Hirst 1988, 38; Perrig 1991, 80–82

The recto of this sheet, which was drawn first, depicts the lower left-hand corner of the *Last Judgment*, the area of the resurrected. It is one of very few surviving thumbnail sketches of figure groups made in preparation for the fresco. As in comparable sketches made thirty years earlier for the *Battle of Cascina*, Michelangelo employed black chalk rather than pen in the initial stages of his work, to define forms in mass and volume rather than contour. But, in the *Battle of Cascina* the bulky figures of the initial sketches were modified in subsequent studies, whereas in the *Last Judgment*, massive figural types remain a constant presence throughout all stages of the preparation and execution.

The drawing shows a variety of figures in the process of emerging from the ground: one with his back turned three-quarters to the spectator, another pushing himself out of his tomb on his forearm, a third clambering out of his tomb with one lower leg already on the soil outside, a fourth, emerging sideways, crablike. But all these—who are retained in similar form, although with variations in position, in the finished fresco—are subsidiary to the most dramatic group. This is the figure who is placed closest, among the saved, to the hell-mouth that dominates the lower center. He is the subject of dispute between an angel and devil, an equivocal soul stretched between salvation and damnation. Occasionally, in earlier Last Judgments, satanic-angelic conflicts over particular souls were depicted. But Michelangelo made the situation a major motif, rendering it in the most literal way, as a tug of war, with the disputed soul racked into an X, head-down. In this group, which from any other artist would have appeared crude and absurd, Michelangelo has realized with unsurpassed directness the energy of the struggle between good and evil, two angels competing against a single devil.

In the Windsor drawing this group is tried in whole or in part at least eight times; it is evident that it was of supreme importance for him. No further drawings for it are known. But just to the left of this group in the fresco (fig. 98) is a less extreme version of a similar theme, with an angel lifting another sinner, whose legs are entangled by a snake, a motif reminiscent of Michelangelo's *Slaves* as well as of the *Laocoön*. In this figure Michelangelo was particularly concerned with stomach and leg muscles, and it is the latter that are tried on the verso of the sheet, where Michelangelo depicted the legs as they come under tension from the snake. This drawing, although for only part of the figure, shows Michelangelo's concern with exact characterization of the action and the response to it. It is clear that the legs, powerful as they are, are not capable of disentangling themselves under their own strength: Michelangelo has expressed simultaneously power and impotence. The right arm with forefinger bent seems also to be a study for the saved soul and shows a similar lack of energy.

The roles of the other drawings on this page are uncertain. The outline figure, drawn before the leg study, may have been an idea for a soul higher in the fresco. However, it is surprising that he appears to be clothed, and he may therefore have been made for some other, unidentified, project. The right hand holding the loop is presumably a sketch for the angel pulling up a couple by their rosary; the arm, although similar to that in the figure pushing himself out of the ground, cannot be for it since the arm is in reverse and the figure's orientation had already been determined in the recto sketch. And the figure, drawn upside down in relation to the others, who walks to the left while looking over his shoulder to the right is mysterious. Wilde's attempt to link it with the recto is implausible, as is Bruce Sutherland's ingenious suggestion, in a letter to the compiler, that it might be related to Michelangelo's later fresco of the *Conversion of Paul*, which its placing on the sheet would render unlikely. It is probably for some project yet to be identified.

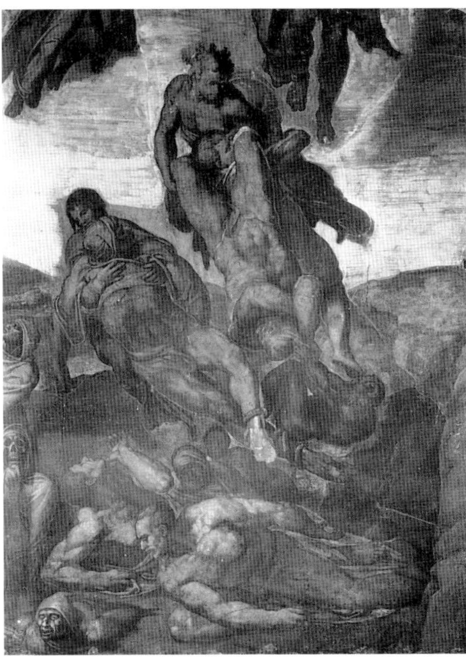

fig. 98. Michelangelo, *The Last Judgment* (detail), fresco. The Sistine Chapel, Vatican Museums

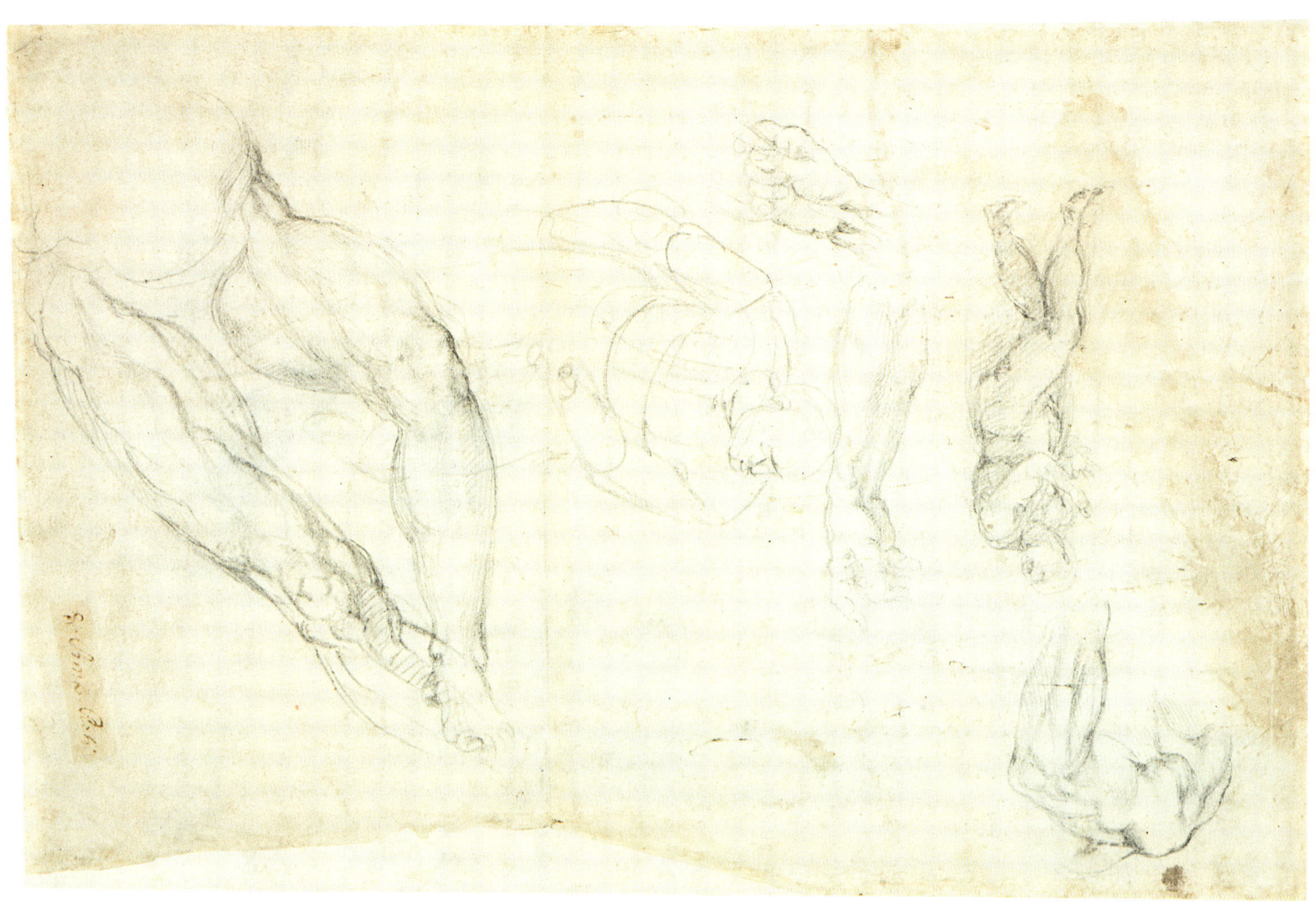

55a

55b

Unidentified Artist after Michelangelo Buonarotti

56
A Soul Saved by an Angel

c. 1545 (?)
black chalk
40.2 x 24.6 (15 13/16 x 9 11/16); watermark: unidentifiable object in a shield
RL 0436

EXHIBITIONS
None

LITERATURE
Popham and Wilde 1949, no. 500

Made in hard black chalk, with sharp, clearly defined individual lines, the technique is relatively unusual in a copy after the *Last Judgment*. The draftsman has attempted to reproduce Michelangelo's musculature accurately, although without the finesse of cat. 57, but has avoided the concentration on light and shade that evokes tension in the body as painted (fig. 98). At the same time the body is stiffened in relation to the original, without the telling curve by which it registers the tension between the lifting angel and the snake wound round the lower legs. The drawing is a highly competent but not particularly sensitive response to Michelangelo's work, and is, perhaps, by an artist past his first youth, who observes Michelangelo with interest, but without empathy.

However, the sheet is of greater interest than it might at first sight appear, because it seems that the draftsman was not limited simply to knowledge of the fresco. In the main figure, for example, the hatching on the left calf is not dissimilar to that found on the same part in cat. 55. This might be simply coincidence were it not for the fact that two other drawings appear on the sheet. One, upside down in relation to the main study—a reversal of the orientation of the sheet frequently found in Michelangelo's own drawings—is of the profile of John the Baptist, who stands to Christ's right in the fresco. There are, however, no differences between the profile in the drawing and that in the fresco as executed, which may, therefore, have been its source. But the third sketch, the extended right arm again drawn in a different orientation, is not to be found in the *Last Judgment* or in the Sistine ceiling—although it is not far from that of the fleeing Adam in the *Expulsion*. It does, however, seem convincingly Michelangelesque. The inference would be that the draftsman, probably directly rather than through an intermediary copy, had access to some of Michelangelo's preparatory drawings for the fresco as well as to the fresco itself, or possibly fragments of the cartoons for it. This conjecture can be supported by the observation that the main figure's left calf was lightly drawn somewhat to the viewer's right of its final position.

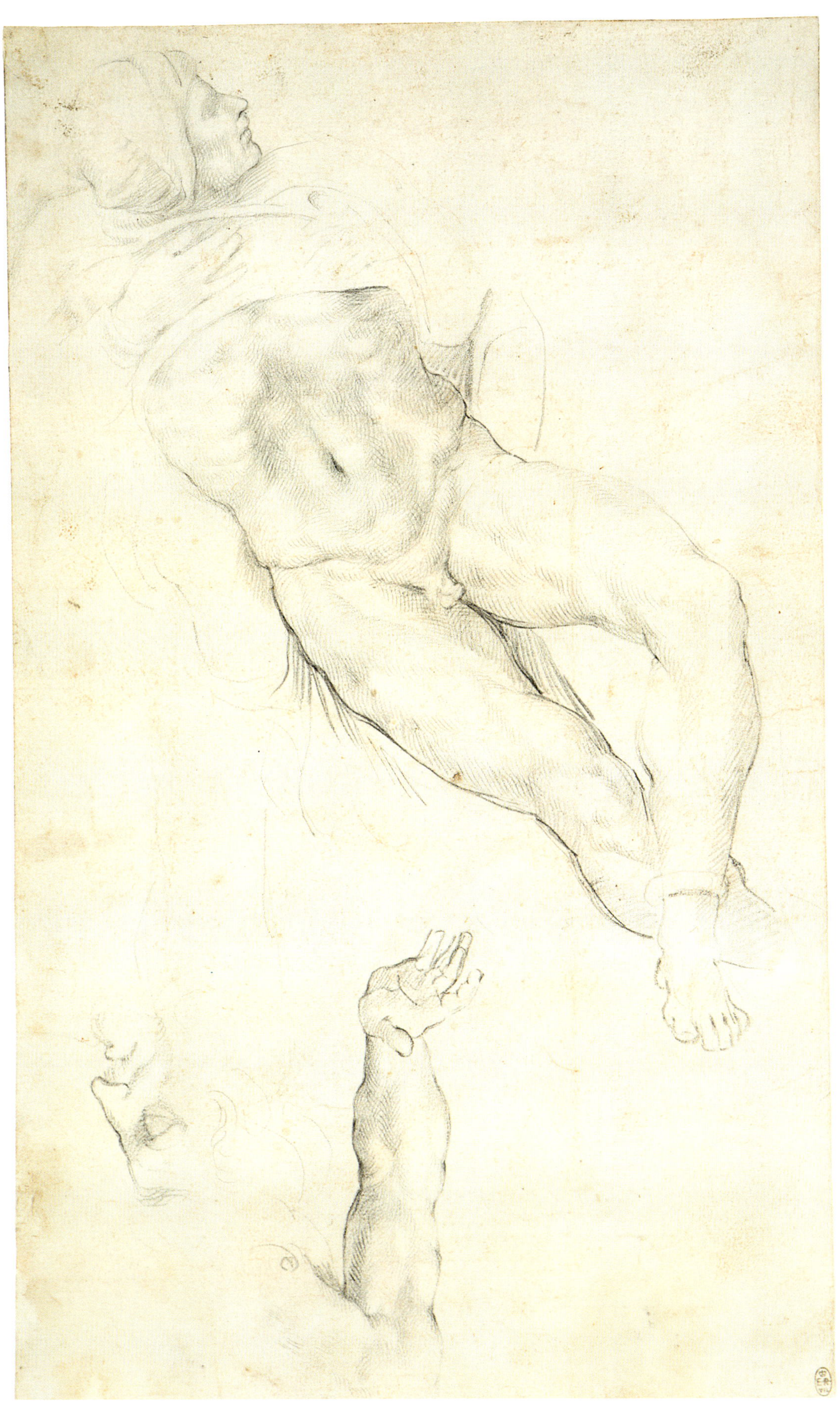

Unidentified Artist after Michelangelo Buonarroti

57
A Soul Saved by an Angel

c. 1545 (?)
black chalk with stumping
30.5 x 24.2 (12 x 9 1/2); watermark: Paschal Lamb within double circle, close to Briquet 58
inscribed in pen on verso: *Bonaroti 154[1?]*
RL 01364

EXHIBITIONS
None

LITERATURE
Popham and Wilde 1949, no. 499

This drawing, on the recto of the sheet, is an unusually sensitive and very finely finished copy of the same group, made directly from the fresco (fig. 98). The draftsman has tried to convey the sleekness of the fresco's surface by washing over some areas of the black chalk with a wet brush, as well as by the direct use of the chalk. The artist was clearly interested in the most subtle chiaroscuro and enjoyed working in a dark register. Such is the delicacy of the handling that it is possible that the drawing was made for sale rather than simply a record for the artist's own portfolio. As well as producing an accurate copy and a visually impressive image, the artist has contemplated the fresco with great sympathy, and has understood Michelangelo's message. The soul being rescued by the angel, despite himself being subject to tension, nevertheless gazes, with an expression that seems to be that of compassion, at the more dramatic struggle going on to his left. This detail, not registered with particular appreciation in cat. 56, demonstrates this draftsman's awareness of Michelangelo's subtleties. Likewise, his treatment of the head of the angel, gazing down at another resurrected soul while he carries his own burden upward, reveals a comparable detachment and compassion. These features convey to the viewer why it is that one of these figures is angelic, and why the other is being saved.

On the verso, the group of resurrected souls on the second level is outlined, with only one figure, that still partly wound in its shroud, at the extreme left edge of the fresco, defined in detail. The artist has once again responded to the larval emergence of the figure from the shroud's cocoon, in a way that demonstrates real understanding of Michelangelo's poetics. Whereas other artists generally concentrated upon the forms, this artist was alert to the animating spirit. So far, however, no clue has emerged concerning his identity.

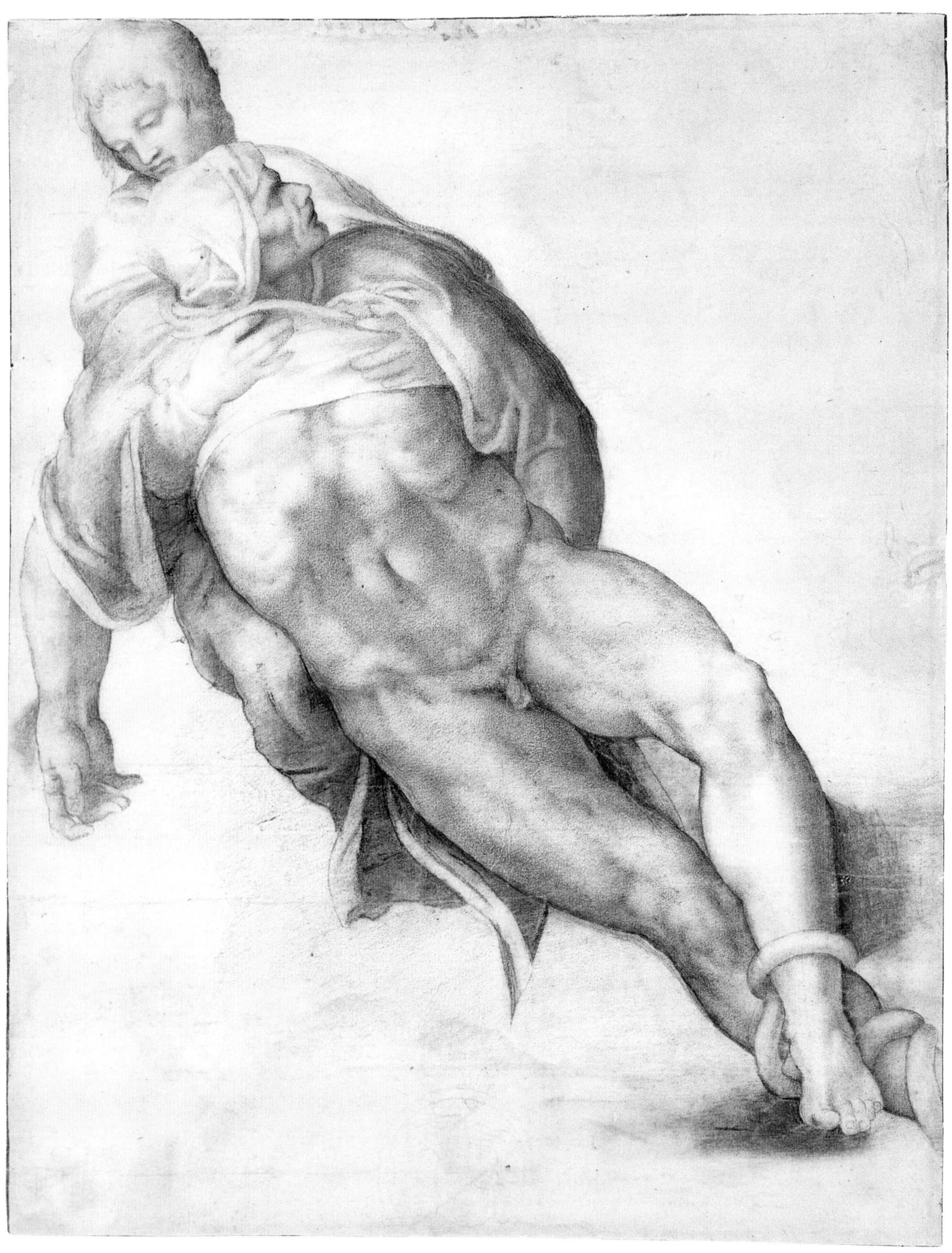

Bartolomeo Passarotti after Michelangelo Buonarroti

58
Two Seated Figures of the Saved

c. 1570
pen and ink over black chalk
44 x 28 (17 5/16 x 11), lower right corner made up; no watermark
inscribed in pen and ink, lower right: *Del Passerotto*
RL 6040

EXHIBITIONS
None

LITERATURE
Popham and Wilde 1949, no. 666; Höper 1987, no. A360

Demonstrating a crosshatching rather closer to Michelangelo's own than most other drawings by Passarotti, this drawing, on the recto of the sheet, suggests that he was copying the *Last Judgment* in a style influenced by his knowledge of the master's earlier draftsmanship. Here, copying rather than inventing, Passarotti uses a handling less self-consciously wild than usual. Although the group is left incomplete, the artist's intention was clearly to produce a self-contained image, since he has hatched in offsetting shadow around the figures on the left. Despite a slight awkwardness in the contour of the main figure's right inner thigh, the definition of forms, especially in the detached leg, is well controlled. The drawing demonstrates the high level of sensitivity to local modulations of form that Passarotti could attain in his more careful pen studies. While it should be noted that the present drawing is not considered autograph by Höper, the compiler sees no good reason to doubt the attribution.

This pair of figures proved particularly popular with copyists: another example is in the Royal Collection (RL 0451 / Popham and Wilde 496). Despite the expressive bulk of the main figure, and Michelangelo's characteristically abrupt foreshortening, he is arranged in a particularly graceful pose, with the right arm and the right leg describing a stretched S, imparting an elegant movement to the chest. It is a pose that can easily be adapted to a supporting figure for a coat of arms, for example, and its decorative legacy was great. However, despite this drawing's intelligent response to Michelangelo's group, it was probably not made directly from the fresco (fig. 99) but from an intermediate copy, most likely one by Passarotti himself. The figures in the fresco have been modified by the omission of the right-hand figure's right arm, which stretches across the chest of the turning figure, and the area of chest covered by the arm in the original has carefully been supplied, with no trace of *pentimenti*. Although little direct influence from the *Last Judgment* is in Passarotti's paintings, references to it do sometimes occur. But in the present drawing there was evidently a conscious intention to regularize Michelangelo's forms, and it may have been made with didactic intent some years after Passarotti's Roman sojourn, perhaps as late as 1570. Passarotti studied Michelangelo's works assiduously, and his copies and adaptations would have been available to Agostino Carracci when he was working with Passarotti in the 1570s.

The chalk sketch on the verso, revealed when the drawing was lifted for this exhibition, is too faint to reproduce. However, it clearly prepares a lofty round-topped altarpiece and what can be descried of the slight figural indications suggests that it may be for Passarotti's altarpiece of the *Presentation of the Virgin* (Pinacoteca Nazionale, Bologna), which he contracted to paint in 1583.

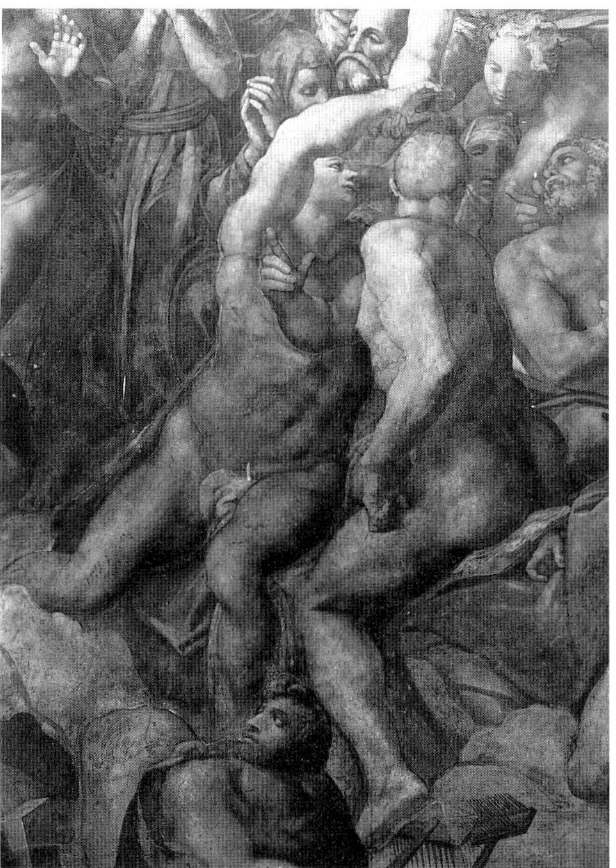

fig. 99. Michelangelo, *The Last Judgment* (detail), fresco. The Sistine Chapel, Vatican Museums

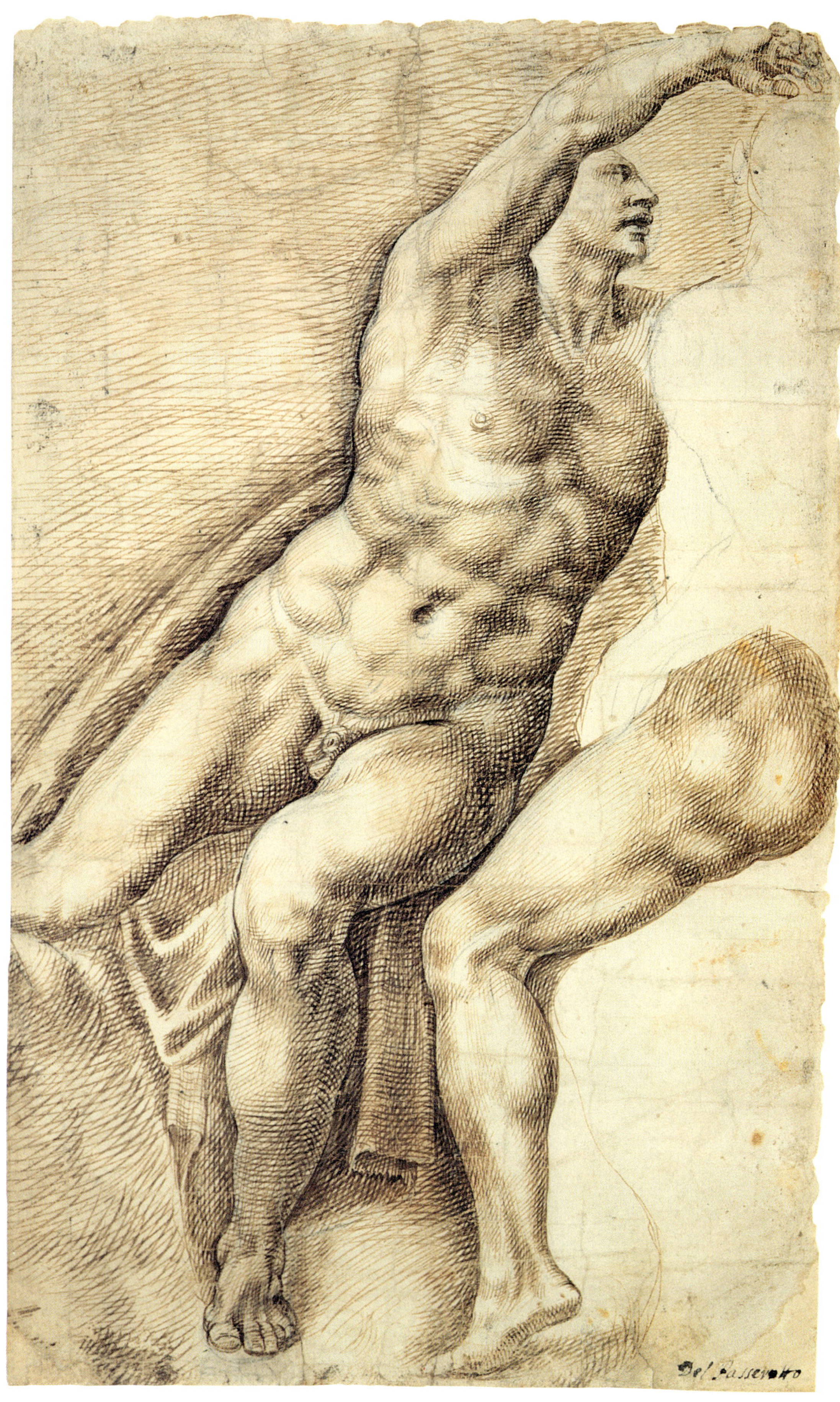
Del Passerotto

Orazio Samacchini (?) after Michelangelo Buonarroti

59
Group of Martyred Saints

c. 1563
black chalk
39.7 x 27.6 (15 5/8 x 10 7/8); no watermark
RL 0422

EXHIBITIONS
None

LITERATURE
Popham and Wilde 1949, no. 497

This group of saints at the upper left, while not directly engaged in combating the vices, displays to them the instruments of their martyrdoms (fig. 100); in this the saints imitate Christ, the instruments of whose Passion are held by the angels in the upper left and right lunettes of the fresco.

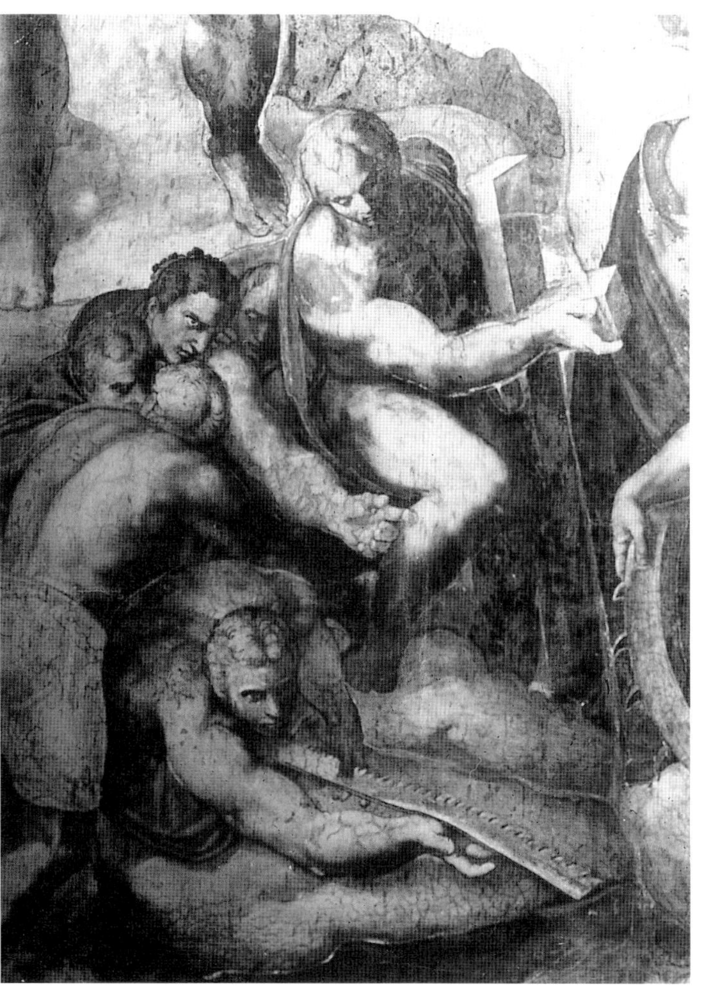

fig. 100. Michelangelo, *The Last Judgment* (detail), fresco. The Sistine Chapel, Vatican Museums

The draftsman who made the present drawing has hitherto remained unidentified, but the compiler is tempted to propose, with due caution, an attribution to the Bolognese artist who worked with Vasari in Rome in the early 1560s, Orazio Samacchini. This suggestion is based on a comparison of the present drawing with one representing the *Miracle of the Serpents* formerly on the New York art market as by Giulio Clovio, and reproduced as such in Giononi-Visani and Gamulin (1980, 97). This drawing, which was transferred to Samacchini by Philip Pouncey (information kindly provided by Julien Stock), shows both a handling of chalk and an interpretation of Michelangelo very similar to those of the present copy. The ex-New York drawing also takes over, with only minimal alterations, the left-hand figure from the present drawing.

The application of chalk is refined and elegant, but the artist has simplified Michelangelo's modeling and imposed upon his figures a lumbering heaviness by shaping them into a thicker geometry, rendering them still more blocklike. This brings them closer to the mood of the figures in the *Crucifixion of Saint Peter* in the Pauline Chapel, knowledge of which surely influenced this drawing's interpretation of the earlier fresco. The cuboid emphasis in Michelangelo's late work (see Calí 1980) is here enthusiastically adopted.

Most copies after the *Last Judgment* concentrate on single figures or, occasionally, pairs of figures. Some were made after sections of the composition, but copies of isolated groups of figures are relatively uncommon and, when they occur, were usually taken from the more dynamic areas of the fresco. However, the group copied in this drawing, plus three additional nearby figures, was also drawn by Figino in a drawing now in the Accademia, Venice (Inv. 1086 / Perissa Torrini 23).

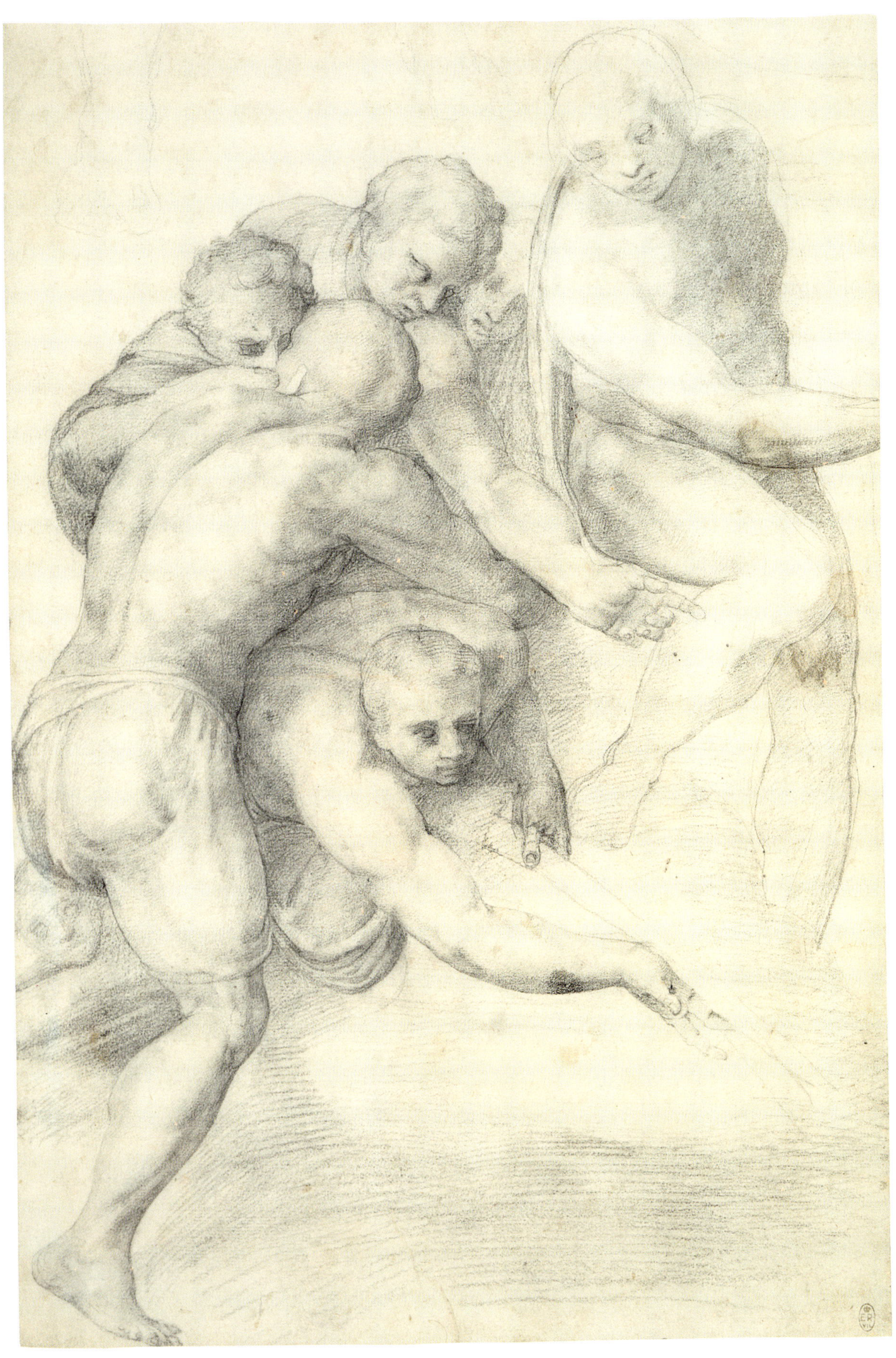

Giovan Ambrogio Figino

60
Climbing Figure

c. 1576 (?)
black chalk on blue paper
42.3 x 27.1 (16 5/8 x 10 11/16); no watermark
inscribed on the recto, lower left, in pen and ink:
No. 41
RL 6912

EXHIBITIONS
None

LITERATURE
Popham and Wilde 1949, no. 326/44; Ciardi 1968, no. 68

The Milanese artist Ambrogio Figino was an exceptionally accomplished and lively draftsman. His drawings divide into two main types: sheets containing multiple thumbnail pen studies of small figures in action; and larger elaborate figure studies, in pen or chalk, the latter often on blue paper, and including numerous copies after a limited range of antique and modern sculpture and sculpturesque painting. A large group of his drawings is in the Royal Collection, and an even larger one in the Accademia in Venice, analyzed in Ciardi's monograph and the catalogues of Popham and Perissa Torrini (1987).

Figino's drawings include many copies after Michelangelo. Most are after the *Last Judgment*, but some are copies of parts of the Sistine ceiling, a few after the Pauline Chapel, and others after Michelangelo's statues on the tomb of Julius II. However, it is clear that Figino's copies of the prophets and sibyls were made not from the frescoes but either from engraved versions or from intermediary copies. Indeed, few of his Sistine ceiling copies have any claim to be direct nor, for the most part, are they among Figino's liveliest drawings. The same is true of his relatively few copies of Raphael's Roman works. But those after the *Last Judgment* are another matter. Their number, precision, and often very high quality strongly suggest direct experience and considerable excitement. A comparable excitement is found in his copies from the *Laocoön*, for which he chose unusual angles in a way that would seem to indicate an artist moving round the original, or a cast of it (fig. 101).

Little is recorded of Figino's movements, and the date of his presumed sojourn in Rome is conjectural: Perissa Torrini (1987) places it before 1577, Ciardi between 1577 and 1581. But there is a puzzle. Figino could not have known Michelangelo's *Last Judgment* before the additions applied by Daniele da Volterra and others to cover the genitals of the nudes, but his copies after Michelangelo's fresco invariably show the figures in their original undraped state. It remains an open question whether Figino cleverly "restored" the figures that he copied, or whether his drawings might have been made not after the fresco but after a copy of an earlier date. The relative freedom with which figures from different areas of the fresco are juxtaposed in his drawings, and the absence of any of the difficulties that confront a draftsman in the chapel when trying to draw figures placed well above eye level, could also suggest that Figino was working after a painted replica, such as that by Marcello Venusti (commissioned by the Farnese and now in the Museo Nazionale di Capodimonte, Naples). Given the surface subtlety of Figino's copies, it seems highly unlikely that they could have been made from engravings. He could, in theory, have been working from earlier drawn copies—such as those that his master Lomazzo would presumably have made during his Roman sojourn between 1559 and 1565—perhaps executed from a scaffolding, but if so, they must themselves have been of exceptional beauty.

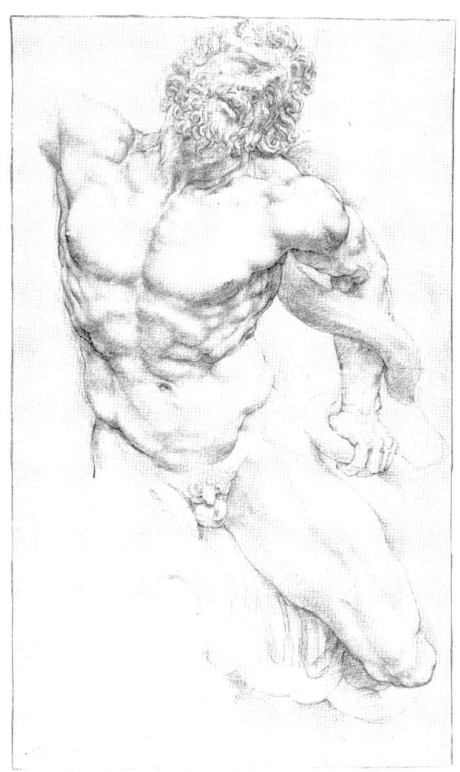

fig. 101. Ambrogio Figino, *Copy after the Laocoön*, black chalk on blue paper, 42 x 25.3 cm. The Royal Collection, Windsor Castle

Figino's taste in the antique seems also to have been influenced by Michelangelo, for he copied two of the master's most revered models, the *Laocoön* and the *Belvedere Torso*. However, Figino's own paintings demonstrate little direct borrowing from Michelangelo or from Hellenistic sculpture, and it might be reasonable to explain his copying as—following the precepts of his master Lomazzo—simply an educational process, an attempt to take possession of the idea that they embody without any intention of employing their forms directly. Yet the number and intensity of his copies contradicts such a view and suggests that Figino responded to Michelangelo in an emotional and intense way.

The present copy, on the recto of the sheet, displays Figino at his most effective. Power and energy are convincingly conveyed, and the modeling is faithful to Michelangelo's fresco. But Figino's figure is sleeker, with a sharper contour; this is a result of a chalk application that, made up of small regular touches moving in the same direction and of smoothly stumped areas, tends to regularize and streamline the form. This aspect of Figino's drawing style is a more robust variant of that practiced by the late Leonardo and, still more, his immediate followers, with which Figino would have been familiar: Lomazzo and Figino himself both owned drawings attributed to Leonardo.

Another copy of this figure, with a smaller part of that immediately above it, is in the Accademia, Venice (Inv. 1054 / Perissa Torrini 24). The Venice drawing is very similar in technique to the present drawing, but Figino has added touches of white chalk, and the main figure is on a slightly larger scale.

The Windsor sheet was recently lifted to reveal on the verso an outline drawing of a seated male figure with outstretched arms accompanied by a standing female figure, both apparently nude.

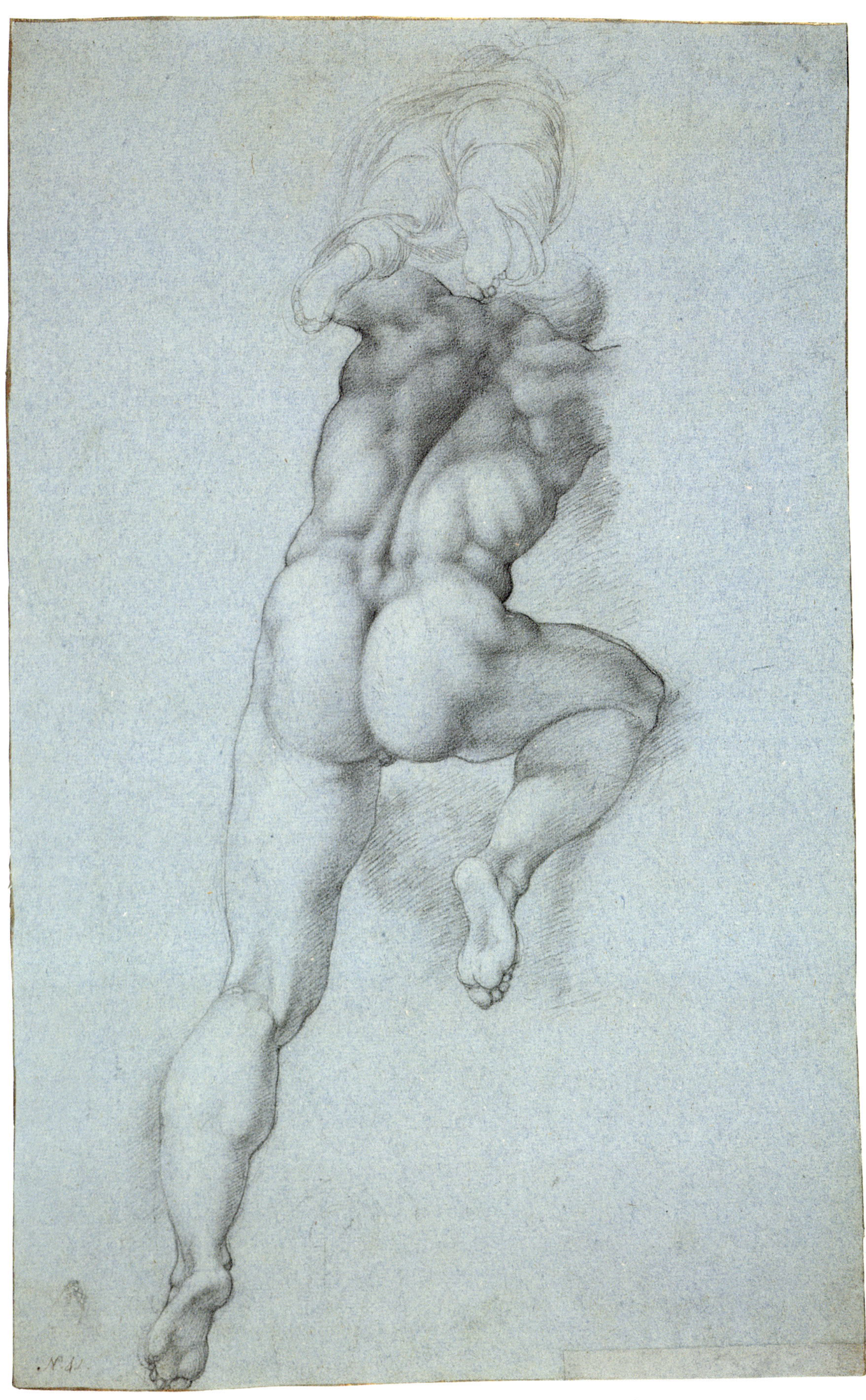

Agnolo Bronzino (?)

61
Nude Man

c. 1552
gray chalk
22 x 38.9 (8 5/8 x 15 5/16); no watermark
inscribed, upper left, in pen and ink: *Daniel da Volterra*
RL 0447

EXHIBITIONS
None

LITERATURE
Popham and Wilde 1949, no. 143; Smyth 1971, 44; Schaefer 1976, 39–43; Lecchini Giovannoni 1991, no. 4; Pilliod 1992, 728–729

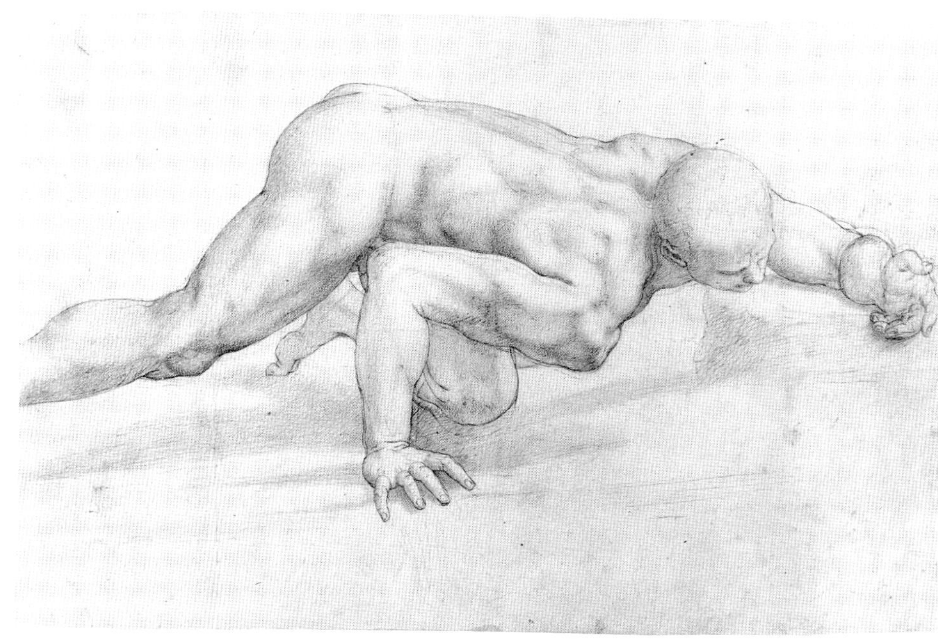

fig. 103. Agnolo Bronzino (?), *Study for Descent into Limbo*, black chalk, 22.3 x 35.5 cm. Staatliche Kunstsammlungen Dresden, Kupferstich-Kabinett

There exists another version of this drawing, made in preparation for Bronzino's altarpiece of the *Descent into Limbo* (fig. 102) in the Florentine church of Santa Croce, signed and dated 1552, in the Kupferstich-Kabinett in Dresden (fig. 103, c. 1967-390). According to Schaefer, who first published it, the Dresden drawing is the original and the present one a copy of it by Bronzino's favorite pupil, Alessandro Allori, who was aged sixteen or seventeen in 1552. Allori's authorship of the present drawing had already been suggested by Smyth in 1971 and Lecchini Giovannoni agreed with this view; in 1992, however, Elizabeth Pilliod returned it to Bronzino.

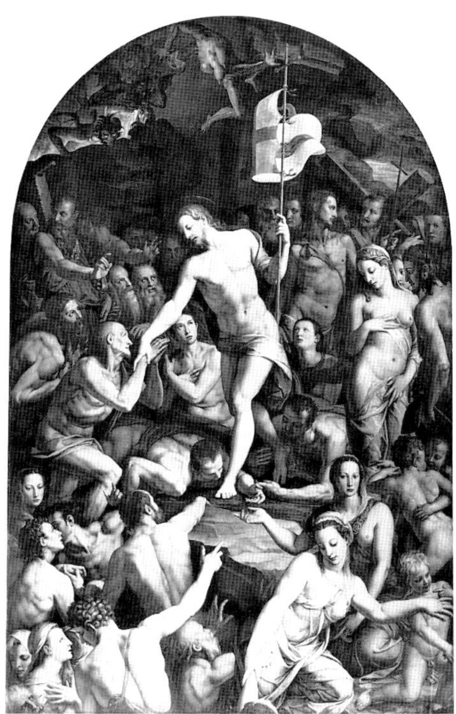

fig. 102. Agnolo Bronzino, *The Descent into Limbo*, oil on panel, 443 x 291 cm. Santa Croce, Florence [Fratelli Alinari, Florence]

The compiler has not seen the Dresden drawing in the original, but from a photograph of it placed side-by-side with the drawing in Windsor it seems to him that strong arguments can be mounted on behalf of both. The Windsor drawing combines stumped and rather scratchily worked parts in a way that seems characteristic of Bronzino; on the other hand the Dresden version, which is more laboriously handled, shows a sharper definition of forms and what appear to be more extensive *pentimenti*. Pilliod has emphasized to the compiler "the erased and redrawn fingers and leg" of the present drawing, which she is surely correct to find "entirely characteristic" (letter of 26 December 1995). So little is certain about Bronzino's drawing style and its development and the artist's graphic practices that any suggestion must be tentative. Nevertheless the compiler is inclined to think both drawings autograph and that in the present sheet Bronzino was making adjustments to his Dresden drawing—changing the movement of the shoulder, opening slightly the space between the legs—which to the viewer might seem trivial but which to so refined an artist as Bronzino would have been significant.

The form is based on the figure types of the *Last Judgment*. Surprisingly for an artist trained by Pontormo, Bronzino's early work displays only slight interest in Michelangelo, although he does seem to have been affected by his portrait drawing of *Andrea Quaratesi*. In his subject paintings of the 1530s, Bronzino aimed for clear, neatly structured compositions that look back to painting of the turn of the century. In his frescoes in the chapel of Eleanora of Toledo, aside from certain coloristic links, Michelangelo's presence is minimal, although a little later, in the National Gallery *Allegory*, Bronzino artfully borrowed from Michelangelo both in theme and arrangement: it is in part a teasing variant of the *Doni Tondo*. But around 1550, Bronzino began to manifest a strong interest in Michelangelo's later style. This was increased after Pontormo's death in 1557 by his undertaking to complete his master's unfinished fresco scheme in the choir of San Lorenzo, which was heavily influenced by Michelangelesque ideas. Bronzino showed an increasing obsession with Michelangelo's forms and finally, in his *Martyrdom of Saint Lawrence* of 1569, produced a composition where the influence of Michelangelo's most inflated figure style is such that his figures become painfully muscle bound. The present figure, however, is more streamlined in form than the contorted actors in the *Saint Lawrence*, and shows Bronzino at a moment when Michelangelo inspired rather than overwhelmed him.

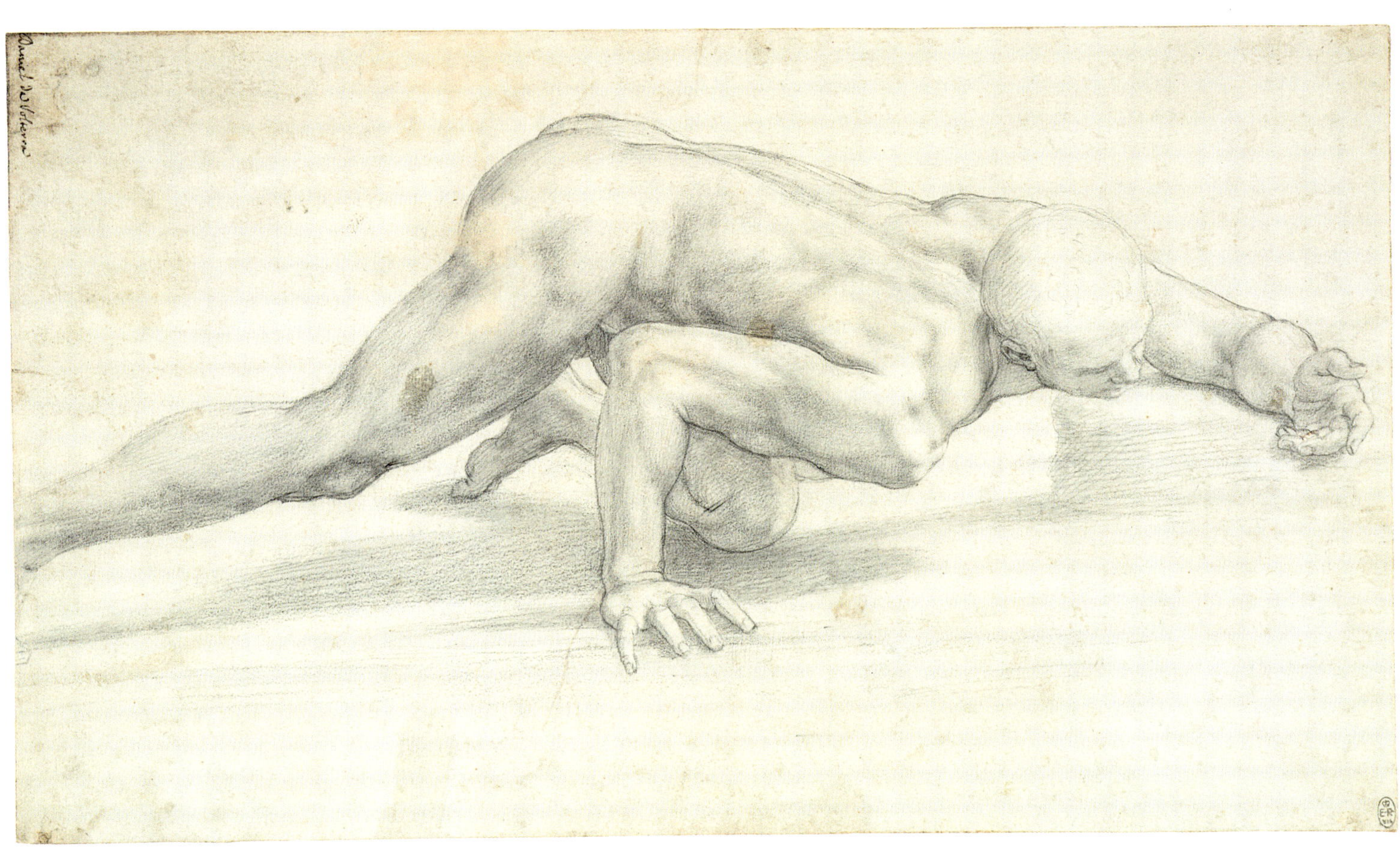

The Effect of the Pauline Chapel

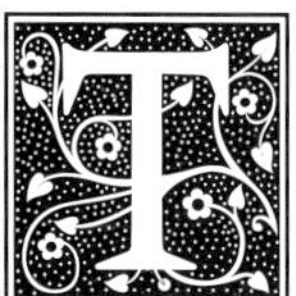

he decoration of the Pauline Chapel, a narrow chapel in the Vatican opening off the Sala Regia and intended for the pope's private ceremonies, was commissioned from Michelangelo by Paul III in 1542. Designed by Antonio da Sangallo the Younger, its construction had been completed that year. Its side walls comprise a large central bay flanked by two equal narrower bays, and all six compartments are frescoed.

Michelangelo was reluctant to accept the commission, saying that fresco painting was work best suited for young men: he was then sixty-seven. It might be supposed that the pope wished him to fresco the whole of each wall, but there is no evidence, visual or documentary, to clarify this. In any event, Michelangelo painted the two central bays, while the flanking bays, which are all frescoed in Michelangelesque style and which treat complementary episodes, were executed much later, between 1573 and 1583. Three of the frescoes were executed, on Vasari's recommendation, by the Bolognese artist Lorenzo Sabbatini. Following his death in 1577, the fourth bay and the vault were painted by Federico Zuccaro. No Michelangelo designs are known that would be appropriate for the subsidiary wall spaces, and Vasari would surely have said so had he been aware of any. It has been suggested that an *Expulsion of the Money Changers from the Temple*, prepared by Michelangelo in several drawings, was to be executed in the lunette above the chapel's entrance, but it is doubtful if the composition would have been suitable for this space, even had the subject been appropriate. The scene finally painted by Federico Zuccaro above the entrance was the highly appropriate *Release of Saint Peter*.

It took Michelangelo until 1550, the year after the death of Paul III, to complete his two frescoes. He inevitably worked more slowly than in the past, but the project was also interrupted for a period by the final act of the tragedy of the Julius Tomb. The heirs of Julius II were once again exerting pressure on Michelangelo to complete the project, which had been under way since 1505, and Michelangelo knew that his financial transactions with them were not above reproach. To protect his name and, perhaps, to clear an uneasy conscience, Michelangelo, as well as enlisting the collaboration of Raffaello da Montelupo, resolved to carve personally two of the statues to be placed on the tomb. These were the *Rachel* and the *Leah*, and although they had probably been roughed out some years earlier, their completion must have occupied a good deal of Michelangelo's time between 1542 and the tomb's unveiling in 1545.

Michelangelo had probably not painted much of the Pauline Chapel before 1545 and what he had done would have been confined to the left-hand wall, the *Conversion of Saint Paul*. In the first edition of his *Lives* published in 1550, of which the manuscript was largely complete by 1547, Vasari states that Michelangelo's two frescoes were to show the *Conversion of Saint Paul* and *Christ Giving the Keys to Saint Peter*. These were two of the founding events of the papacy. Christ delegated to Saint Peter, the first pope, the powers to loose and bind, which were to descend to his successors. Through his miraculous conversion, Saul, the persecutor of the Christians, became Paul, the apostle to the gentiles. The two episodes had been treated in the series of tapestries that Raphael had designed for the Sistine Chapel in 1515–1517, and were an obvious pairing. Presumably until 1545–1546, Michelangelo still intended to paint the *Delivery of the Keys* on the right-hand wall. However, the subject was subsequently changed to the *Crucifixion of Saint Peter*. Although this change must have been approved by the pope, it may have been prompted by Michelangelo himself, increasingly preoccupied with death. This final fresco eschews the celestial presences of the *Conversion* and depicts a circle of spectators and executioners turning round the laborious elevation of the apostle on his cross, crucified, at his request, head down to escape comparison with Christ. Michelangelo creates a procession of pilgrimage, as the mourners from the martyr's flock file silently around the slow atrocity.

When Michelangelo was attempting to evade the commission, he said that he was displeased and would paint things displeasing. In any event, the style of these last paintings is, if not actively ugly, consciously different from anything he had painted hitherto. Michelangelo's approach is akin to that of the late Botticelli, who abandoned conventional notions of composition and violated his earlier canons of beauty in order to communicate more profoundly tragedy and divinity. In his last works Botticelli created swollen, lumpy, and dislocated forms; in this he looked back to the late reliefs of Donatello. Michelangelo followed suit. Apart from the angels who revolve in the sky around Christ in the *Conversion*, Michelangelo avoided the nude. He showed no interest in physical beauty, although he still included some complicated poses, and little even in vigor: with the exception of Christ and some subsidiary figures in the *Conversion*, energy is reduced; in the *Crucifixion* even the most powerful figures move in a hopeless and mechanical way. Above all, the compositional rigor found in his other work is violated. In the *Conversion*, the figures do not form coherent groups and their locations are often unclear. In the *Crucifixion*, the movement of the spectators around the raising of the cross is countered by the oblique rotation of the cross, and the composition is unbalanced by the group of mourning women placed at lower right. But it should be emphasized that this awkwardness was due neither to lack of competence nor lack of physical control. The cartoon fragment of two subsidiary figures in the *Crucifixion of Saint Peter* (Museo Nazionale di Capodimonte, Naples) is more detailed and precise than any other surviving sixteenth-century cartoon. It must have taken weeks to execute and days to prick. The style of the Pauline Chapel, then, is deliberate. Michelangelo wished to disrupt the viewer's expectations of pictorial norms in order to convey more fully and immediately the meaning of the scenes represented. He was aiming at a metaphysical style, in which physical disorganization is the visual evidence of spirituality. Thus, in the *Conversion of Saint Paul*, Christ falls like a stone, crushing Saul and scattering those around him, rendering the strongest impotent by the mightiness of his voice. And although the organization of the *Crucifixion* is tighter, the spectators are inconsistent in scale and move without volition. In the two frescoes Michelangelo thus conveys the psychic shock of the Divine's imperious interruption of Saul's mission and the bereft dumbness of Peter's converts, witnessing the last direct link with the Savior destroyed.

Disruption of expectations is extended to the relation of the paintings with the viewer. Michelangelo engineers clashes of form, awkwardness of rhythm, and spatial uncertainty. There is a disjunction between space and the figures placed within it, and their relation evades the spectator's attempt to understand it and to locate himself with reference to the frescoes. Michelangelo was never particularly concerned with perspective space—although he was a highly competent perspectivist when he wished—but here he produces a space at once perspectival and pre-perspectival. There is a deliberate unbalancing, a deliberate refusal of commensuration, and the beholder's experience in the Pauline Chapel is one of physical disorientation. In painting, this corresponds to Michelangelo's very latest development as an architect, a decade later, in the Sforza chapel, which is planned to overturn the worshiper's normal sense of proportion.

The influence of the Pauline Chapel, which was difficult of access, was less than that of either the Sistine ceiling or the *Last Judgment*. But it was nevertheless significant. The inflated figure style had an important effect, releasing artists from established physical norms and allowing them to produce massive figures who, although usually performing subsidiary roles within a narrative scene, pose or move in ways that are so excessive that they become, as it were, metaphoric summations of the images of which they pretend to be a part. The Pauline Chapel also encouraged artists to disrupt spatial expectations, to juggle with scales, although few were able to do so dynamically. One of the cleverest uses of the *Conversion* was made by a passionate admirer of Michelangelo, one who copied his work assiduously, although no drawings by him survive after Michelangelo's paintings. Nevertheless, Tintoretto must have learned of the composition of Michelangelo's fresco within a year or so of its completion for, in his *Miracle of the Slave* of 1548, he transferred the tilted axial link between the fallen Saul and the plunging Christ to the floored slave and the hovering Saint Mark. Unlike Michelangelo, Tintoretto, employing one of his key dramatic devices, shows both slave and saint in vertiginous foreshortening, but the source of his idea is clear.

Giulio Clovio after Michelangelo Buonarroti (?)

62
The Delivery of the Keys

c. 1555
brush and wash over outlines in black chalk, damaged by damp
38.2 x 28.5 (15 1/16 x 11 1/4); laid down
RL 4814

EXHIBITIONS
None

LITERATURE
Popham and Wilde 1949, no. 244; Steinberg 1975, 45; Giononi-Visani and Gamulin 1980, 106–107

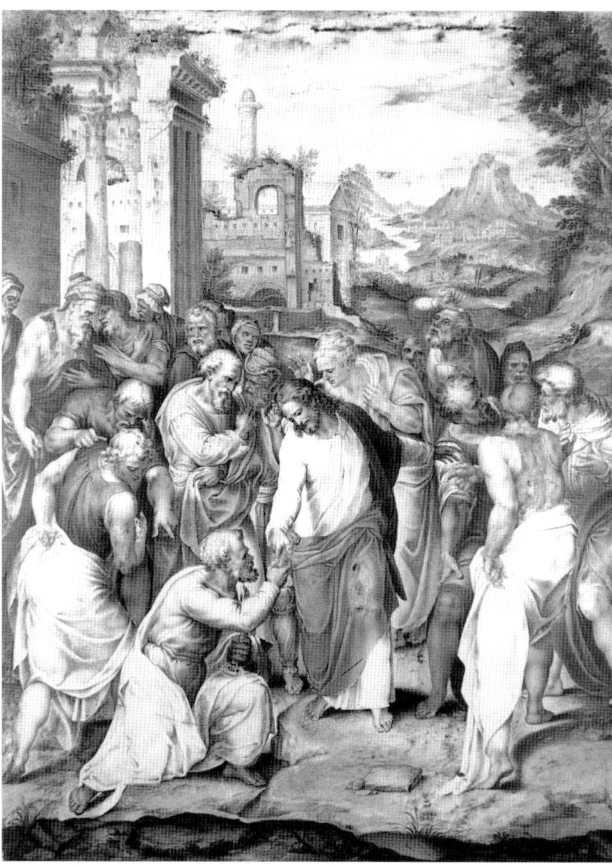

fig. 104. Giulio Clovio, *The Delivery of the Keys*, tempera on vellum, 37.5 x 29 cm. Musée du Louvre, Paris, Département des Arts Graphiques [Photo RMN]

Another version of this composition is in the Louvre (fig. 104, Inv. 3044), a miniature painting on parchment, identical with the present drawing in size and figural arrangement. The Louvre miniature is described in Charles Lebrun's 1671 inventory of the French Royal Collection as by Giulio Clovio after Michelangelo. The current attribution of the present drawing, which was listed in the inventory of George III as by Sebastiano, follows from that in Paris; however, its poor condition renders any stylistic judgment insecure. It may be that both images record the figure composition and, in the case of the Windsor drawing, even the landscape of a design by Michelangelo, a *modello* for the *Delivery of the Keys*, the subject initially to be painted on the right wall of the Pauline Chapel. Several arguments support this. The figures are clearly Michelangelesque and in bulk and mass are consistent with his style of the mid-1540s. The solemnity and grandeur of the treatment are appropriate, and the overall arrangement is not dissimilar to the *Crucifixion of Saint Peter* as it was finally executed. And, finally, the ratio of height to width is roughly the same as that of the frescoes.

Doubts remain, however. That no autograph drawings by Michelangelo can be connected with this composition is not a serious objection, for very few by him survive from this period. But not one of the figures is completely convincing in itself as of Michelangelo's invention: his executed Pauline Chapel figures are not so neat as these. The present composition also seems unduly compact, and if expanded to the scale of the space to be filled in the chapel, its figures would be very much larger than those in the *Conversion of Saint Paul*. Of course, many of these problems could be resolved by assuming that Michelangelo's putative *modello* for the *Delivery of the Keys* was made in 1542 when the scheme was first broached, and that figure-scale and composition were subsequently changed before the subject was abandoned. Alternatively, one might argue that Clovio somewhat compressed Michelangelo's design, which might have spread wider. But such hypotheses are inherently unsatisfactory and inevitably ad hoc. At present, the matter can only be left in suspension.

If not after Michelangelo, Muziano, a previous attribution for the present drawing, is a not implausible candidate. His taste for grand compositions is compatible with the present image and he was capable of designing figures in complicated Michelangelesque poses. The *Delivery* also has more than an echo of Sebastiano's *Raising of Lazarus*, and Muziano's admiration for Sebastiano was great. The *Lazarus*, of course, was largely designed by Michelangelo, who might have referred back to it but, on balance, this would seem more plausible from another artist.

Whereas the landscape in the present drawing is spare and empty, as one would expect from Michelangelo, that in Clovio's Louvre miniature is crowded. Bacou (1972–1973) noted that the artist had grouped together real and invented elements: on the left is shown the temple of Minerva in the Forum of Nerva; behind, a somewhat modified version of the so-called Ark of Noah, demolished in 1611; and behind that the column of Trajan. The Bruegelian features of the landscape, observed by Bacou, would suggest a terminus post quem for the miniature of 1553, when Pieter Bruegel the Elder and Clovio met, exchanged drawings, and collaborated.

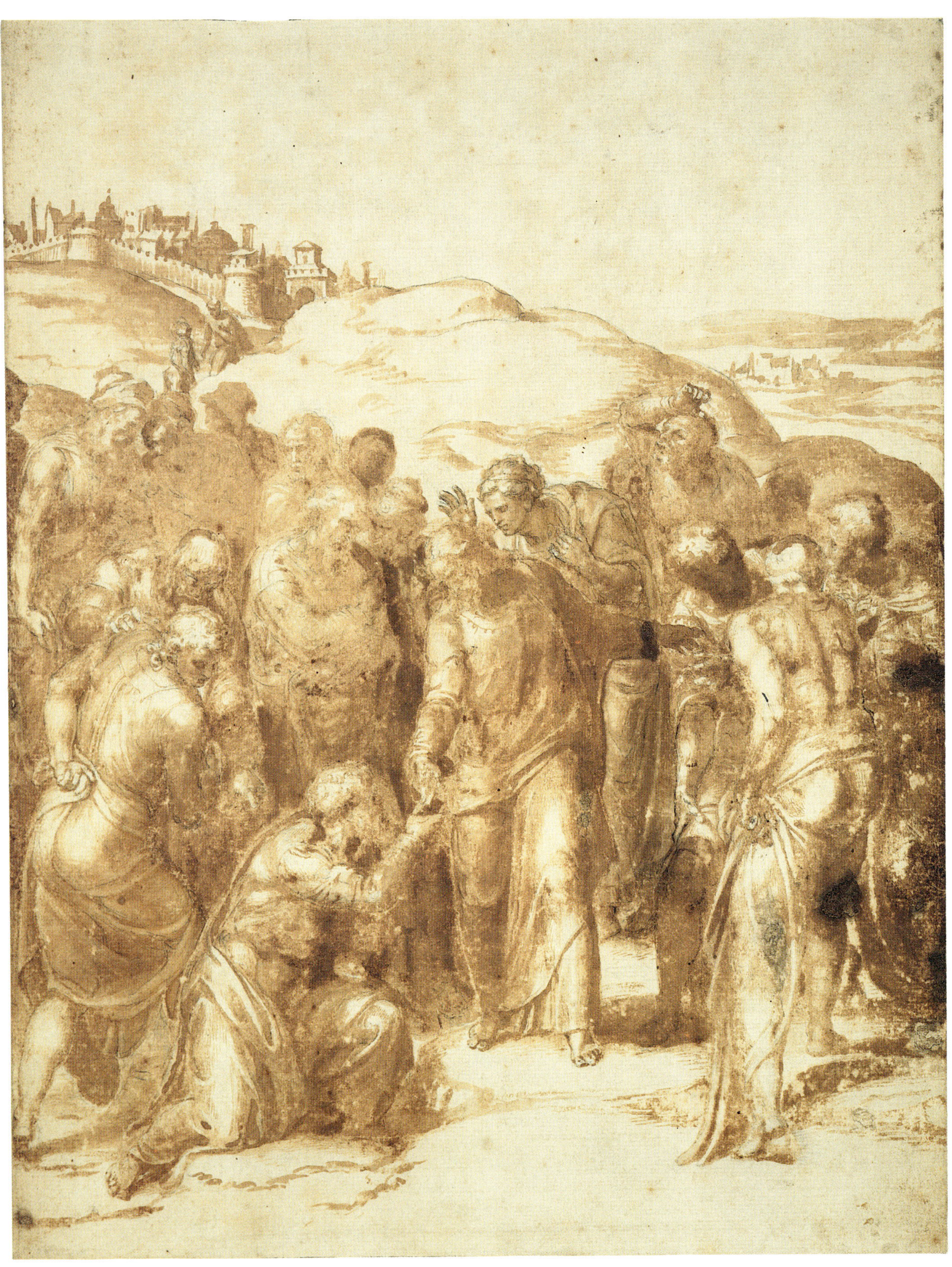

Unidentified Artist after Michelangelo Buonarroti

63
Detail of the Conversion of Saint Paul

c. 1560
black chalk
41.3 x 33 (16 1/4 x 13), on three pieces of paper, two large and one small, initially joined by sealing wax, made up at the left corners; watermark (right-hand sheet): blacksmith with anvil, close to Heawood 1360/1361
inscribed in pen on the lower right corner of the recto: *Studi di Michelangelo*
RL 0647

EXHIBITIONS
None

LITERATURE
Popham and Wilde 1949, no. 505

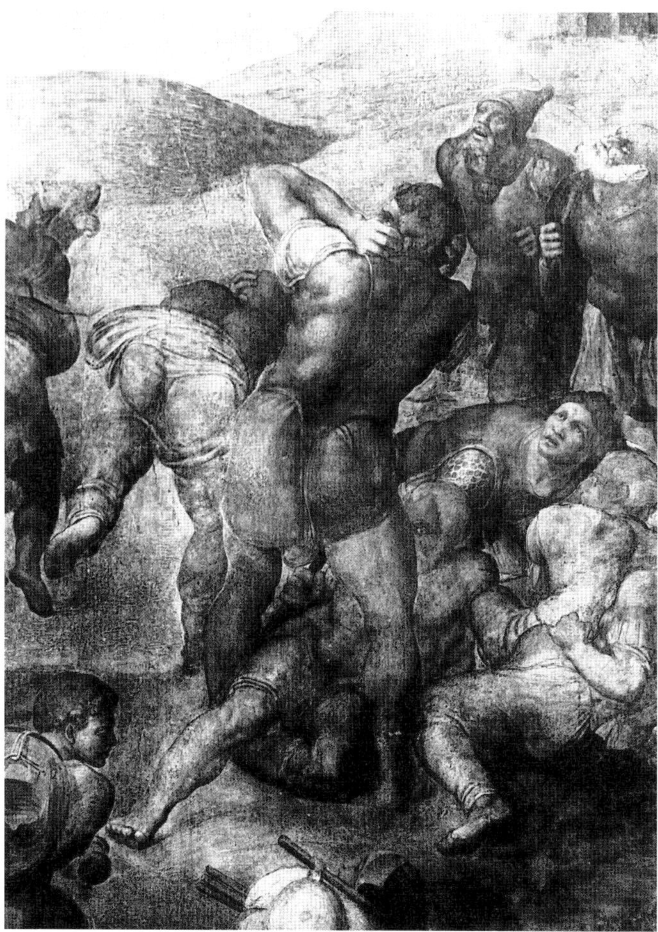

fig. 105. Michelangelo, *The Conversion of Paul* (detail), fresco. The Pauline Chapel, Vatican Museums

Although superficially unattractive, the present partial and unfinished copy is of considerable interest. The fact that it is composed of three pieces of paper, which the draftsman attached by sealing wax, suggests that it was made under difficult conditions, probably before the fresco itself, and not, like so many copies, from some intermediate copy. The same is true of its companion (RL 01362 / Popham and Wilde 504), which is made up of four pieces of paper, irregularly cut. The difficulties of copying a large fresco situated in a narrow space, where the copyist could not retreat far enough to survey the image as a whole, were considerable. Given the size of the present copy and of RL 01362, a complete copy would have been very large and may have been aimed at producing a painted version or, conceivably, a large engraving, perhaps in sections, like some of those made after the *Last Judgment.* However, the treatment seems unusually broad to be the basis of an engraving. The watermark is Roman, datable around 1560.

The draftsman seems to have adopted the procedure of copying a section of the fresco (fig. 105) and then, perhaps when he encountered difficulties, cutting his sheet and joining another to it, on which the forms begun on the first were continued. In the present example, the recto of the right-hand fragment of this composite sheet, which was drawn first, contains the standing soldier clasping his ears and another soldier sprawled beneath him. The outlines of the standing figure, but not of the sprawled one, were then traced through to the verso and squared. The reason for this can only be conjectured. The draftsman then silhouetted the left-hand edge of the standing figure and added a separate piece of paper torn to parallel the now irregular edge of the first sheet, on which he drew the figure of the fleeing soldier. Then the left-hand side of this second sheet was cut to a curve, perhaps to fit with a further section.

The fleeing soldier is more fluently executed than the main figure, and this might suggest that the copy is collaborative. But since no such qualitative discrepancies can be detected in the companion drawing, this possibility should probably be dismissed. Nevertheless, the draftsman was clearly capable of vivacity, even if only in a part of his drawing. The way in which this figure is executed, with softer shadows and more emphatic realization of drapery folds than in the standing soldier, is reminiscent of the painterly manner of some of the chalk drawings of Taddeo Zuccaro. A drawing for the Frangipani chapel in San Marcello al Corso in Rome, begun circa 1558 (Uffizi, Florence 13598F / Gere 1969, no. 77, pl. 92), although in red rather than black chalk, shows distinct similarities. In fact, Michelangelo's fleeing figure was of particular interest to Taddeo Zuccaro, who produced a magnificent variant upon it in a drawing now in the National Gallery of Art (fig. 25), and it may be that the present drawing was made in Taddeo's circle: he seems to have had numerous assistants, but little is known about them.

The massive figure in the foreground protecting his ears is a potent image of physical strength reduced to impotence by divine intervention, one of the few occasions in painting where an effort is made to represent the effect of sound.

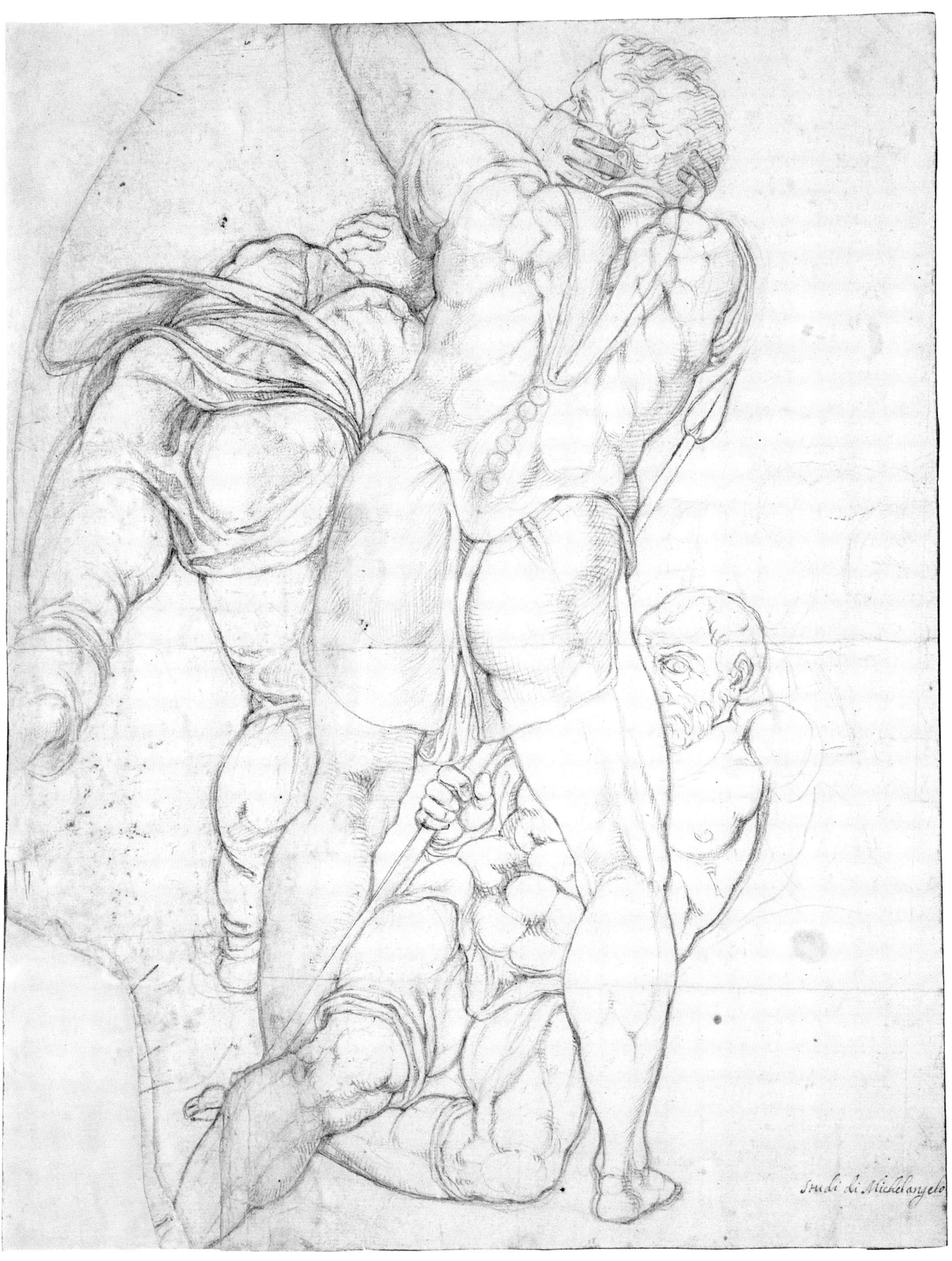
Studi di Michelangelo

Francesco Salviati

64
Angel Striking Idolaters (?) or a Plague of Egypt (?)

c. 1555
pen and ink with wash and white heightening
39.6 x 27.9 (15 9/16 x 11); watermark: shield with double bend and a half-length unicorn; close to Briquet 1884
RL 5958

EXHIBITIONS
None

LITERATURE
Popham and Wilde 1949, no. 949; Blunt 1971, no. 430; Mortari 1992, no. 580

This drawing was given by Bodmer and Popham to Pellegrino Tibaldi by analogy with the *Conception of the Baptist* (cat. 65) and with the composition of the fresco for which the drawing was made. But, as the late John Gere (Blunt 1971) observed, its style is unmistakably that of the brilliant but erratic Florentine artist, Vasari's friend and contemporary, Francesco Salviati. The long looping rhythms, very free outlining, and the loose handling of wash are characteristic of drawings made by Salviati in the 1550s, and the dependence of the design from Michelangelo's *Conversion* would support such a date. However, the link with Tibaldi is also strong, and since he and Salviati both worked in the Palazzo Sacchetti in Rome in 1553, reciprocal influence is likely. In the present case Tibaldi may have been the prime mover, since the composition is unusually dramatic and dynamic for Salviati.

It was pointed out by Hirst (1979) that some of the decorative motifs employed by Salviati in his Palazzo Sacchetti frescoes evince knowledge of Chinese painted scrolls, and it is tempting to extend this observation. The loose application of wash in the present sheet, and in Salviati's *Seated Woman* in the Louvre (Inv. 18375), may owe something to Chinese brush drawing. Thus, although the fundamental compositional idea of Michelangelo's fresco, its "dive-bombing" device, is taken up here, Salviati's drawing style is here radically unlike either Michelangelo's or Tibaldi's.

Both the subject and the purpose of this composition are unknown. The shape of field and complexity of action would suggest a fresco, perhaps a scene from the Old Testament, and perhaps one of a cycle, its narrative clarified by its companions. But no other drawings are known that could confirm this intuition. The sphinx sketched on the left suggests that the scene takes place in Egypt, and Popham identified it tentatively as the *Angel of the Lord Smiting the First Born of Egypt.* However, the arrangement does not immediately suggest this episode, and it is not inconceivable that the scene might be secular. The freedom and vivacity of this drawing may seem to run counter to received ideas about cinquecento draftsmanship: the pen lines in loops look like the work of Picasso at his most playful, the looseness of the wash might recall Honoré Daumier. But this is simply another facet of the artist who was probably the most inventive, experimental, and unpredictable draftsman of his generation, the scope of whose achievements is still far from fully appreciated.

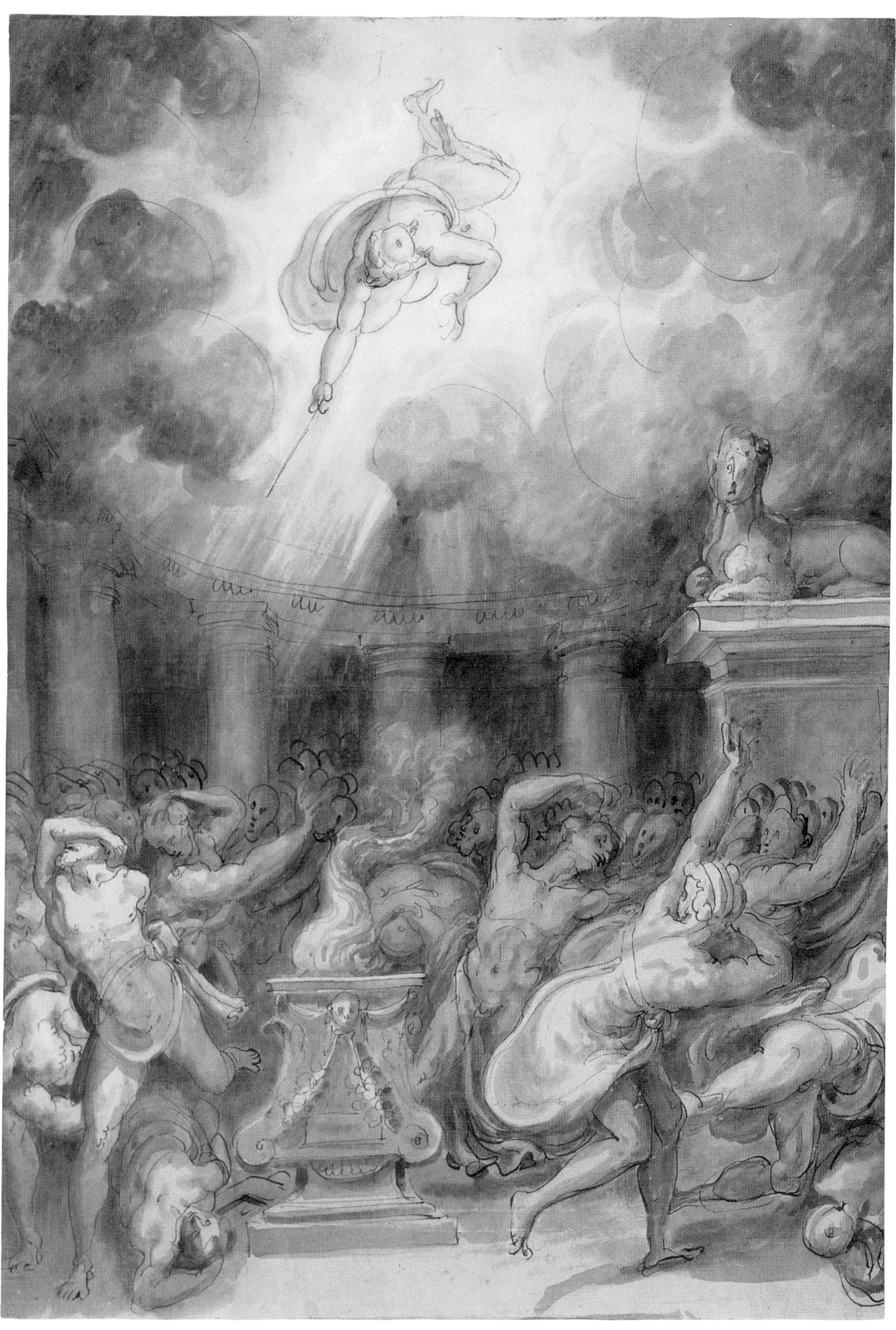

Pellegrino Tibaldi

65
The Conception of the Baptist

c. 1555 (?)
pen and ink and brush and wash with white heightening over red chalk
42.3 x 28.6 (16 5/8 x 11 1/4), arched; no watermark
RL 5965

EXHIBITIONS
London 1972–1973, no. 135; Washington-Parma 1984, no. 104; London 1992, no. 60

LITERATURE
Popham and Wilde 1949, no. 947; Winkelmann 1986, 527

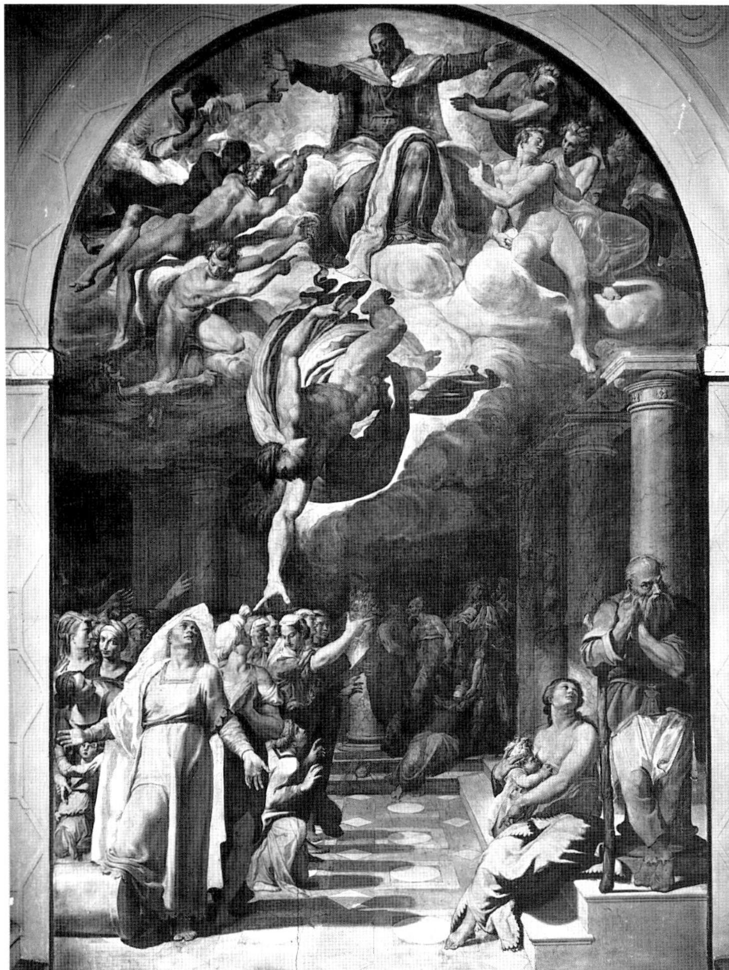

fig. 106. Pellegrino Tibaldi, *The Conception of the Baptist*, fresco. The Poggi Chapel, San Giacomo Maggiore, Bologna [Fratelli Alinari, Florence]

This drawing is a preliminary design for the fresco on the right wall of the Poggi chapel in the church of San Giacomo Maggiore in Bologna (fig. 106); a separate study for Saint Elizabeth is in the Musée Atger, Montpellier. The *Conception* is faced by the *Baptism of the Multitude*, which also, unusually for such a scene, contains in its upper part a dramatic apparition: a heavenly conflict, in which devils are overthrown by angels. Both frescoes, with great intelligence and efficacy, adapt Michelangelo's device from the *Conversion of Saint Paul* of the precipitate fall of Christ, who crushes Paul beneath the weight of his will. Tibaldi registers the violence of the angel's appearance in the void that runs orthogonally into the fresco's center, swept clear by the shock wave of his descent. But unlike Paul in the *Conversion*, Saint Elizabeth is not crushed by the angel's arrival: she is rather transfixed and ravished, still more so in the fresco than in this drawing, where Tibaldi gave her a rising movement akin to Michelangelo's *Rachel* on the tomb of Julius II. This kinesis makes manifest both the divinity of the Baptist's conception and the inevitable overthrow of sin in the *Baptism*.

Although Tibaldi's fresco is obviously Michelangelesque, with extreme foreshortenings and heavily muscled figures, as well as the adoption of smooth drapery articulated with pipelike folds, his drawing, with its loosely sketched pen lines and vivacious, atmospheric application of wash and white heightening, is radically different from anything by Michelangelo and reflects knowledge of Correggio. Combinations of Michelangelesque and Correggesque influence in different strands and in different proportions form a leitmotif of Bolognese art in the later cinquecento. This drawing seems to be an early example of this fusion.

On the right can be seen an early idea for the huge standing figure in the fresco who, as finally painted, seems to be a brother of the swollen and powerful figures employed by Tibaldi's lesser-known Bolognese contemporary, Giovanni Francesco Bezzi, called Il Nosadella. Nosadella's and Tibaldi's works have frequently been confused: the relations between these two painters, their reciprocal influence, and the possibility that they collaborated have begun to be investigated, but much remains uncertain.

Tibaldi was one of the few artists who appreciated the possibilities opened by Michelangelo's disjunction of space and figures in the Pauline Chapel, and he sometimes exploited space and figures as independently expressive vehicles. On occasion, in narrative scenes, he deployed quite startling contrasts between dense figures and empty space. Tibaldi also looked to the earlier work of Michelangelo both for color and for thinner, harder figures. Thus in the ceiling of the Palazzo Poggi, for example, he plays witty variations on Michelangelo's Sistine *ignudi*, setting figures in poses reminiscent of Michelangelo's in sharp *di-sotto-in-su* foreshortening.

Tibaldi's work in the Poggi chapel, like that in the Palazzo Poggi, is not documented, and its dating is controversial. Tibaldi was peripatetic, and his chronology during much of the 1550s is far from clear. He is sometimes thought to have returned from Rome to Bologna around 1550, but as he is documented in Rome, painting a frieze in the Palazzo Sacchetti in 1553, he may have remained there until then. Between 1553 and 1561 Tibaldi worked concurrently in Bologna, Loreto, and Ancona; his Poggi chapel frescoes were probably completed circa 1560.

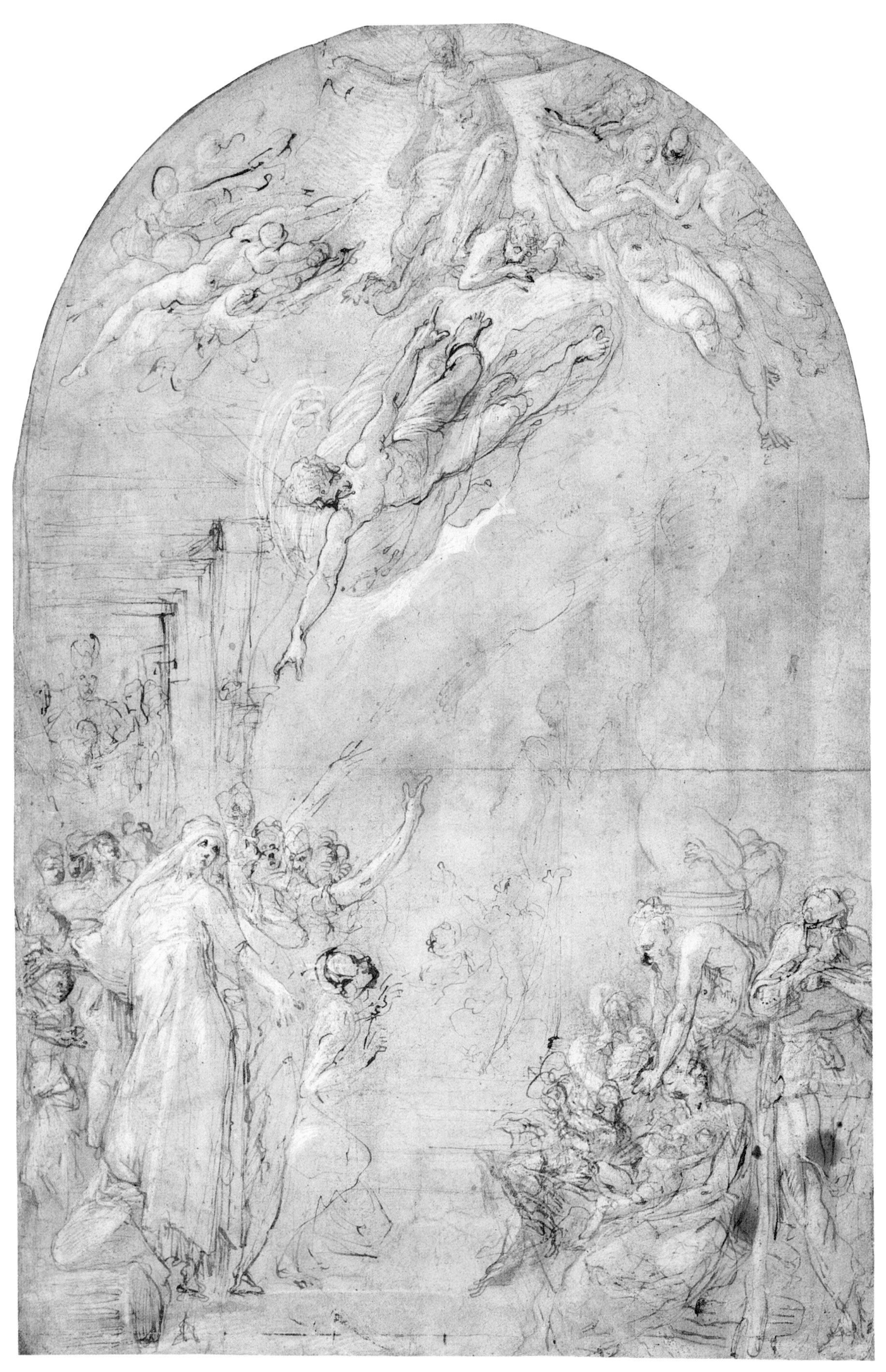

Pellegrino Tibaldi

66
Figure Study for the Castel Sant'Angelo

1548 (?)
pen and ink and brown wash heightened with white over black chalk on blue paper
31 x 14.2 (12 3/16 x 5 9/16); no watermark
RL 5488

EXHIBITIONS
Rome 1981–1982, no. 106; London 1986, no. 36

LITERATURE
Popham and Wilde 1949, no. 943; Winkelmann 1986, 500; Romani 1990, 39

This drawing, on the recto of the sheet, was made for the trompe-l'oeil figure of a servant opening a curtain in a false doorway in the right-hand corner of the Sala Paolina in the Castel Sant'Angelo (fig. 107). As Roberts noted (London 1986, 57), the verso study "is a view of the actual doorway on the left-hand side of the same wall . . . Tibaldi traced the outlines in reverse on to the recto in order to achieve an exactly symmetrical background for the two figures in his trompe l'oeil doorway."

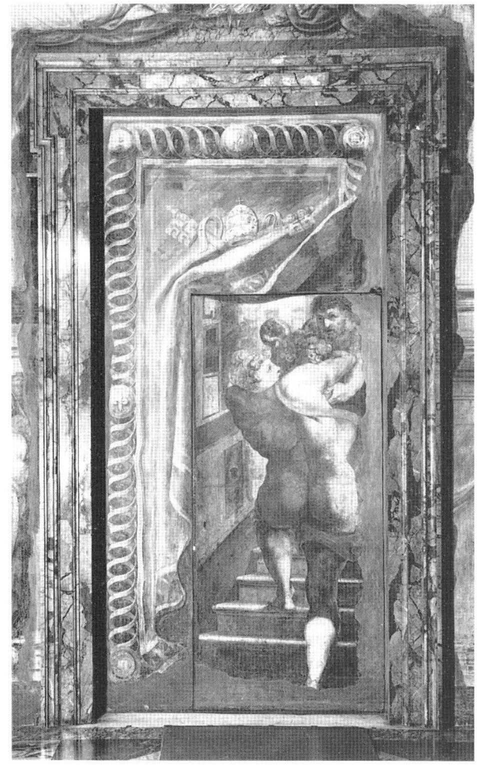
fig. 107. Pellegrino Tibaldi, *Man Opening Door in Sala Paolina* (detail), fresco. Museo Nazionale di Castel Sant' Angelo, Rome

This scheme of the Sala Paolina, which parallels the life of Alexander the Great with that of Saint Paul, was a double homage to Alessandro Farnese, Pope Paul III. The decoration was probably begun on the pope's commission in 1545 with Perino del Vaga supervising the work. Perino, more active as a designer and entrepreneur than an executant, made extensive use of assistants, some of whom seem to have been permitted a design and not solely executive role. The vault seems to have been completed by late 1546, but, at Perino's death on 20 October 1547, the walls may still have been incomplete, as suggested by some elements of their decoration that seem to diverge from Perino's ideas. If not, then he allowed his assistants extraordinary latitude. The enhanced massiveness of figures in the later examples of the large fictive reliefs of Alexandrian scenes that constitute the room's primary narrative scheme, and which were mostly executed by others to Perino's design, suggests a pressure toward a heavier style among the artists who worked with him, and this seems to have increased following his death. Romani (1990) argues that the *Family of Darius before Alexander* is entirely due to Tibaldi, and it seems certain that numerous subsidiary elements in the *basamento* are also his. It is likely that the trompe-l'oeil motif, prepared in the present drawing, of an attendant opening a curtain onto a fictional flight of stairs matching the real ones in the opposite corner of the room, was an idea of Tibaldi's own since it does not seem to correspond to Perino's patterns of thought.

In the present figure, the slow-moving massiveness of the forms is notable, and the link with Michelangelo—the *Crucifixion of Saint Peter* rather than the *Conversion of Saint Paul*—clear. However, the emotional weight and spiritual solemnity with which Michelangelo's figures were imbued is entirely absent here, and while Tibaldi has made a highly successful essay in Michelangelesque form, the figure has been drained of content and has become little more than an occasion for virtuoso display. A figure by Salviati similar in type and pose, one that equally drains Michelangelesque form of Michelangelesque content, is also known (fig. 108). The comparative playfulness of the present figure design would imply Tibaldi's interest in Salviati, the most active and inventive painter in Rome in the second half of the 1540s.

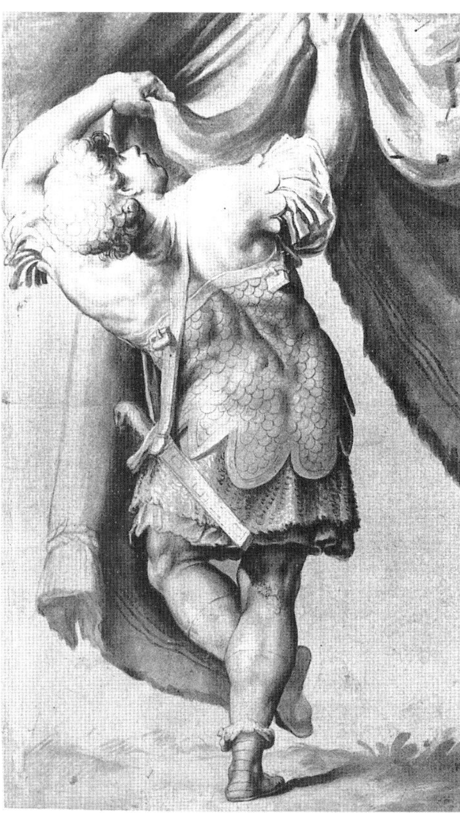
fig. 108. Francesco Salviati, *Standing Soldier Lifting a Curtain*, brush, brown and gray wash with white heightening, 42.6 x 25.8 cm. Collection of Jeffrey E. Horvitz [Colnaghi Drawings, London]

The somnambulistic movement of the main figure in the present drawing was to become an important component of Bolognese style on Tibaldi's return, but it is generally more evident in the work of Nosadella than in his own. In his later painting, Tibaldi maintains a strong interest in Michelangelo, but it was rather to the Sistine ceiling that he turned, both for its iridescent colors and more wiry form, than to the master's late work.

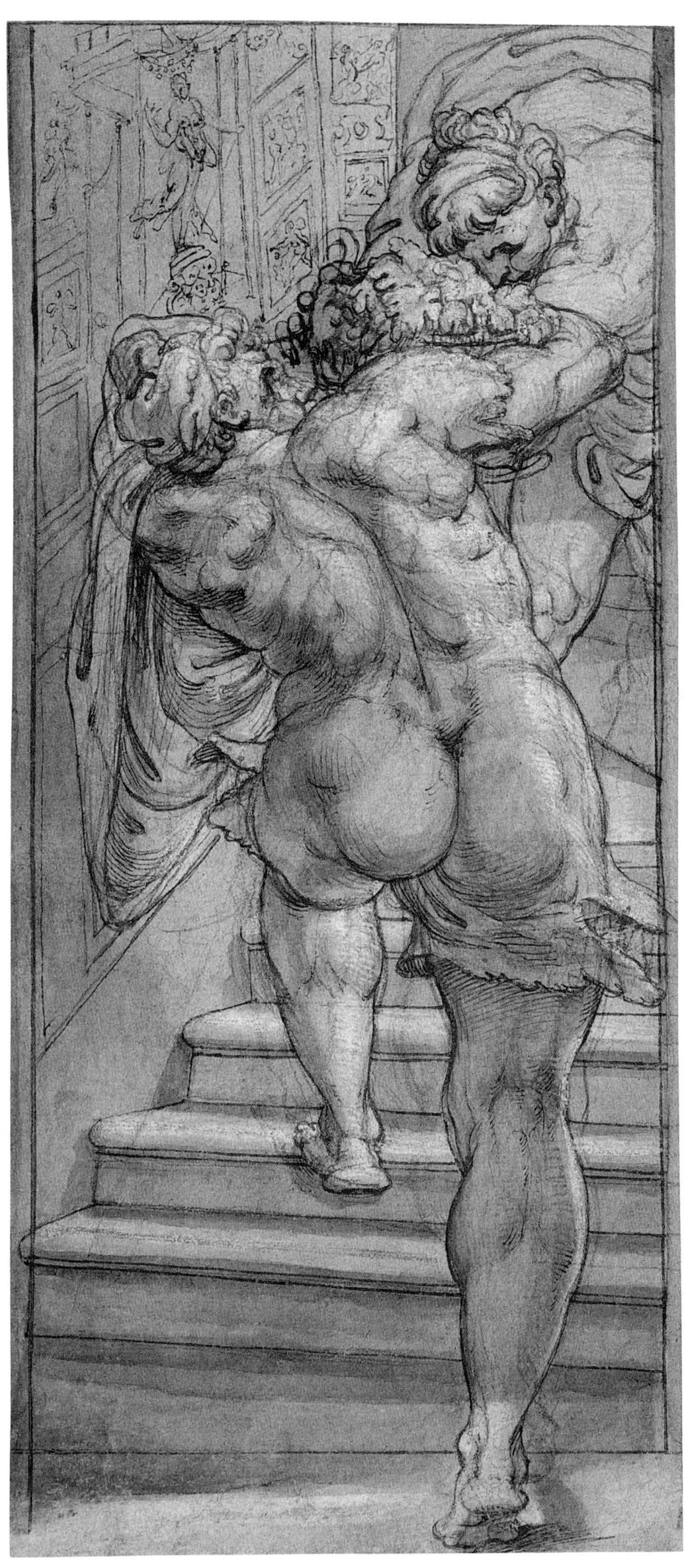

Taddeo Zuccaro

67
Two Apostles for an Agony in the Garden

c. 1555
brush and wash over black chalk
25.7 x 39.1 (10 1/8 x 15 3/8), upper corners cut; no watermark
inscribed on the verso, in pen and ink, by William Gibson: *Taddeo Zuccaro 8.1.*
RL 6024

EXHIBITIONS
None

LITERATURE
Popham and Wilde 1949, no. 887; Gere 1969, no. 259; Blunt 1971, no. 521, 128

This study for the apostles in an *Agony in the Garden*, previously attributed to Salviati, was identified as by Taddeo Zuccaro by the late John Gere. Taddeo Zuccaro is known to have treated the subject of the *Agony* twice in painting, on a small panel, in the Strossmayer Gallery in Zagreb, and in a fresco on the vault of the Mattei chapel in Santa Maria della Consolazione in Rome, of the early 1550s. At least three other drawings are known of this subject (Gere 1969, nos. 117, 132, 261) and all four are closer to the Strossmayer panel than to the Mattei fresco. However, the execution of the panel is so loose that it is more likely to be a *modello* for an altarpiece than self-sufficient. Polidoro da Caravaggio, whom Taddeo much admired, had made such *modelli*. It furthermore seems improbable that so small a painting would have required such extensive graphic preparation, and it may be that the present drawing is not a study for the Strossmayer panel but a development of it, made in preparation for something larger. Taddeo's concentration on the figures and on the powerful relief with which he has imbued them suggests forms to be executed on a large scale.

The drawing shows Taddeo's interest in the massiveness of Michelangelo's forms in the Pauline Chapel frescoes and, unlike Tibaldi's drawing (cat. 66), an appreciation of their inherent seriousness. The pipelike folds that run over the draperies of the figures are quintessentially Michelangelesque and evoke the paradox of very powerful figures trapped by their draperies—that is to say, their environments. It is probable that this formulation in Michelangelo's work is, consciously or unconsciously, an equivalent of the cords that bound his slaves, and the motif of struggle against constraint that is so central to Michelangelo's work was appreciated also by Taddeo. A more obvious homage to Michelangelo was paid by Taddeo in his own *Conversion of Saint Paul*, the altarpiece of the Frangipani chapel in San Marcello al Corso, which he finished in the year of Michelangelo's death, 1564. Taddeo's earlier work is supposed to have been admired by Michelangelo himself, and a scene of the aged Michelangelo watching the young Taddeo frescoing a palace was included by Federico Zuccaro in his pictorial biography of his brother.

The richness of handling in the present drawing reveals some of the qualities brought by Taddeo to Rome. With his background in Urbino, his knowledge of the work of Barocci, who influenced the style of the present drawing, and a colorism imbibed from stays in Venice and Parma, his expansiveness of form combined with a fluid pictorialism is very like the synthesis achieved by Salviati, also much impressed by the art of Parma and Venice.

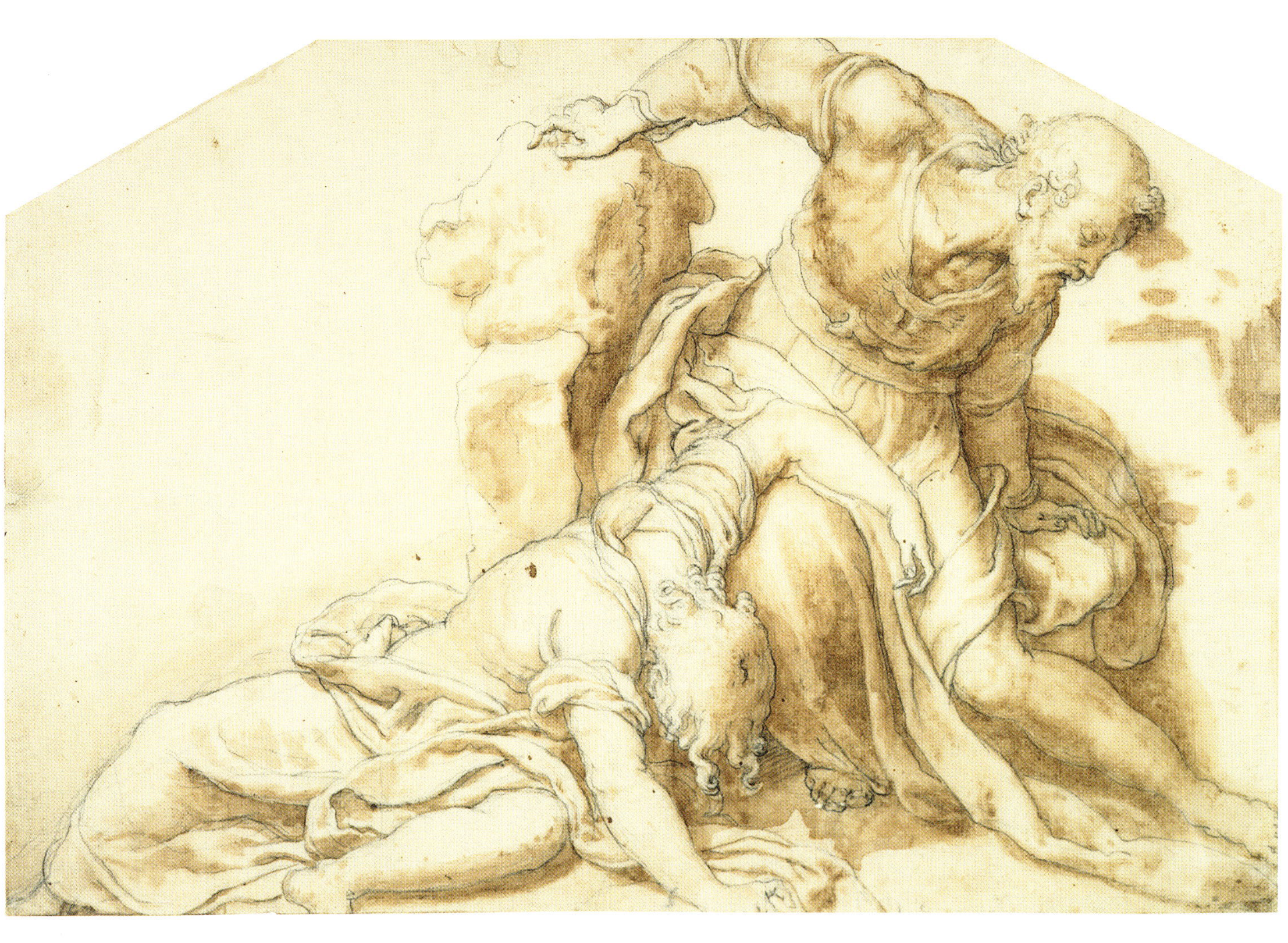

Attributed to Camillo Procaccini

68
Fleeing Soldier

c. 1610 (?)
red chalk
24.9 x 13 (9 13/16 x 5 1/8); no watermark
inscribed on the recto, lower right, in pen and ink: *Cristofolo Storis*; on the verso, in pen and ink: *L3*; *Cristofolo Storis*; and brush and ink: *NI33*
RL 5216

EXHIBITIONS
None

LITERATURE
Popham and Wilde 1949, no. 1161

This drawing was attributed to Camillo Procaccini by Mario di Giampaolo in an annotation on the mount; Popham had thought of either this artist or the Cavaliere d'Arpino. The same old inscription is found on another drawing in the Royal Collection (RL 3816), which Blunt (1971, no. 379) records was recognized in 1966 by Philip Pouncey as a study for an altarpiece of the *Adoration of the Shepherds*, now in the Pinacoteca di Brera, Milan, painted by Camillo in 1615. The inscription, as pointed out to the compiler by Clayton, presumably refers to the Swiss painter, mainly active in Milan, Johann Christophorus Storer (c. 1611–1671), who was a pupil of Ercole Procaccini, Camillo's nephew.

The present drawing cannot be connected with a known composition by Camillo, but it was undoubtedly intended for a fleeing soldier in a Conversion of Saint Paul rather than the other obvious subject, a Resurrection. Like the standing figure in Michelangelo's fresco (see cat. 63), he clasps his hands over his ears: great noise accompanies the Conversion but not the Resurrection. Camillo Procaccini is not, in general, a strongly Michelangelesque artist but is indebted to the Michelangelo of the Pauline phase, together with, perhaps, awareness of the great figures of fleeing guards painted by Marco Pino in his fresco of the *Resurrection* in the Oratorio del Gonfalone, Rome, or his closely related panel of the same subject now in the Galleria Borghese, Rome. Camillo's figure demonstrates a critical approach to Michelangelo's later style, with which it seems to combine inspiration from earlier periods of Michelangelo's work. The elegant proportions, with long tapering legs, are rather those of Michelangelo's *Resurrection* drawings of the early 1530s, and, consciously or unconsciously, the arrangement of the soldier's arms echoes an earlier work by Michelangelo: the model of a seated *écorché*, the so-called *Anatomia di Michelangelo*. Camillo's drawing represents the practical utilization of motifs derived from Michelangelo rather than an attempt to work within his style.

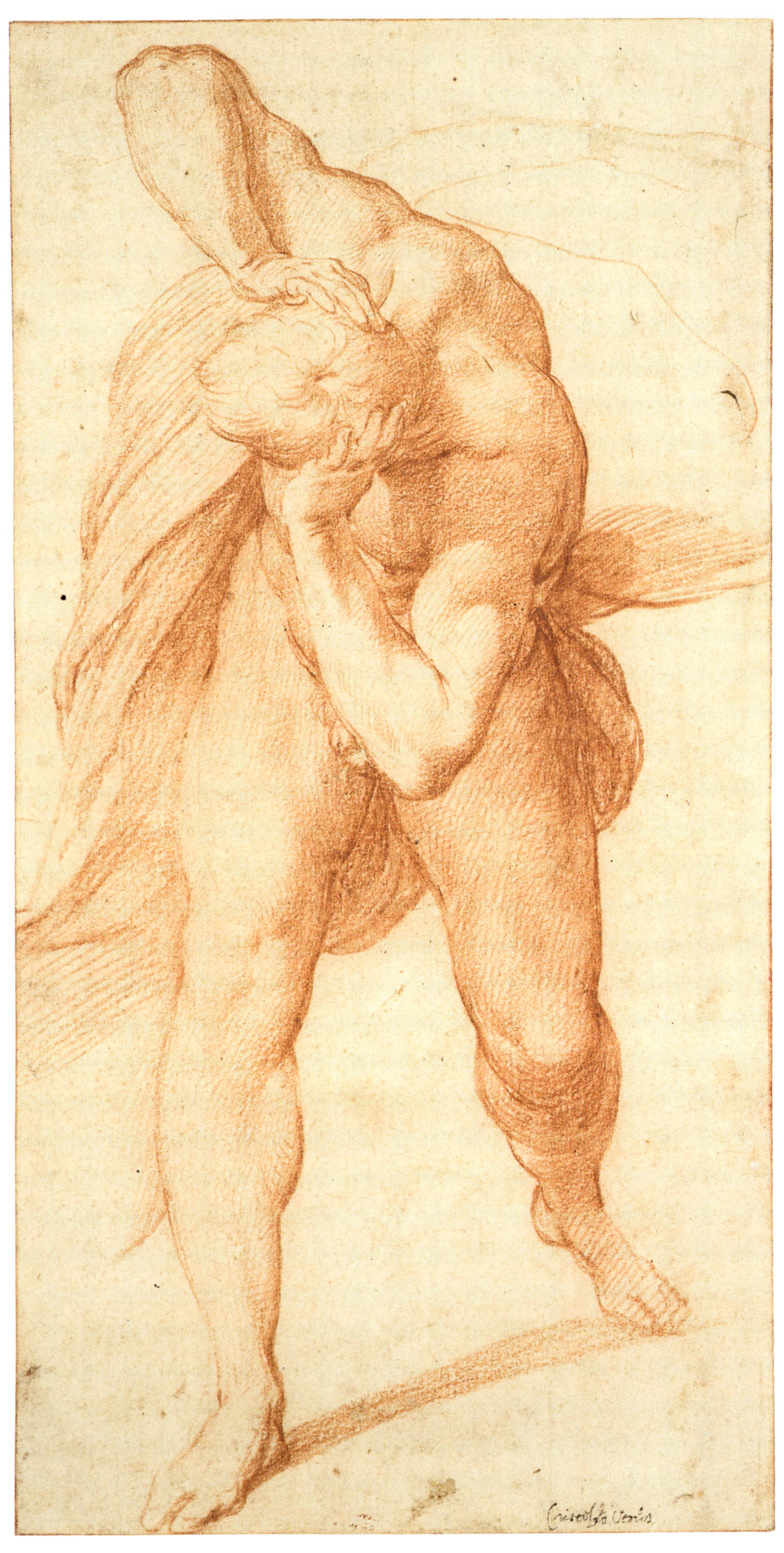

Biographies

With catalogue numbers listed for each artist

Alessandro Allori
Florence 1535–1607 Florence
Allori was trained by Bronzino and proclaimed his loyalty to his master until nearly the end of his life by incorporating Bronzino's name in his signature. But he was never as concerned with surface perfection and formal exactness as Bronzino. From 1554 to 1560 Allori resided in Rome and came strongly under the influence of Michelangelo. For a period after his return to Florence, he produced Michelangelesque designs and figures, but his innate preference was for calm statement, crowded compositions, and decorative surfaces. Allori was probably the most prominent and productive Florentine painter of the last forty years of the cinquecento, working in every medium and executing every type of picture. In his late years, in part influenced by his son, Cristoforo, Allori experimented with less complex forms and with richer but more restricted colors; he was the only Florentine artist of his generation to develop in this way. See cat. 4.

Bartolommeo Ammanati
Florence 1511–1592 Florence
Ammanati was one of the most important and ambitious Florentine sculptors of the cinquecento. After initial training with Bandinelli, and a raid on Michelangelo's Via Mozza studio to purloin designs, he worked with Jacopo Sansovino in Venice. Back in Florence he collaborated with Montorsoli on the tomb of Jacopo Sannazaro (Santa Maria del Parto, Naples) and executed the tomb, never unveiled, of Bartolommeo Nasi. The latter is highly Michelangelesque in design but Sansovinesque in anatomy and surface texture. He worked again in Venice and Padua during the 1540s, executing decorative sculpture for Sansovino, and both a tomb and a colossal *Hercules* for the humanist Marco Benavides in Padua. Reconciled with Michelangelo, he worked on the Del Monte chapel in San Pietro in Vincoli in the 1550s and co-designed the Villa Giulia. In the later 1550s he returned to Florence, where he was active both as a sculptor and an architect. He executed the stairs of the Laurenziana to Michelangelo's design and the Ponte Santa Trinita. His colossal *Neptune* fountain in the Piazza della Signoria, a commission won against competition from Giambologna, is a failure. But his now-disassembled indoor fountain for the Palazzo della Signoria is one of the most elegant sculptural groups of the later cinquecento, developing the most graceful aspects of the New Sacristy *Allegories*. Ammanati underwent a late religious crisis in which he repudiated portrayal of the nude, and may have destroyed his own drawings. Ammanati, also an architectural theorist, is a major figure; the full dimensions of his achievement have still to be appreciated. See cat. 11.

Baccio Bandinelli
Florence 1493–1560 Florence
Bandinelli had early contact with Leonardo and, perhaps, Raphael, before producing a statue of *Saint Peter* for the Cathedral of Florence. He then moved to Loreto where, under the supervision of Andrea Sansovino, he carved a large-scale relief for the Santa Casa. In 1516 Michelangelo intended to employ him on the San Lorenzo façade, but the project was shelved. Later, the two sculptors were estranged after Bandinelli accepted a commission, which dated back to 1508 and which Michelangelo regarded as his own, for the *Hercules* to stand as a pair to the *David* in the Piazza della Signoria. The statue that resulted, Bandinelli's *Hercules and Cacus*, attacked by contemporaries and reviled by modern critics, is nevertheless a major and impressive work.

Bandinelli was probably the most disliked artist of his time, but he was an expert intriguer and very successful in attracting patronage. His attempted emulation of Michelangelo was less in the realm of style, for there is little visual similarity between their works. Rather, it was on the level of ambition, and Bandinelli's overwhelming ambition outstretched his real abilities. Like Michelangelo he left many projects incomplete but with less reason. Although he was mostly active in marble, it is arguable that his best sculptural work is in bronze and on a small scale in which his hyper-classical stylization seems seductive rather than bland. Bandinelli was a virtuoso draftsman with a large graphic oeuvre: some of his drawings were widely copied. See cat. 31.

Agnolo Bronzino
Florence 1503–1572 Florence
Although trained by, and a loyal friend to, Pontormo, whose frescoes in San Lorenzo he completed after his death, Bronzino is an artist of different stamp, concerned with solid, sharply focused, enamel-finish forms. Most famed for his portraits, which re-create for posterity the court of Cosimo I, he also executed highly wrought mythologies and

allegories, and designed tapestries. After 1550 his production of altarpieces and frescoes expanded, and simultaneously he came heavily under the influence of Michelangelo's later style. But Bronzino's large-scale paintings become progressively less refined in color and texture, and his later figure style, although expressive, is strangely boneless, appearing eccentric rather than emotive. Vasari says that Bronzino was a fine draftsman, but his surviving drawings are rare and the subject of much scholarly debate. See cats. 13, 61.

Annibale Carracci
Bologna 1560–1609 Rome
Annibale was the most important Italian painter of his generation. Together with his cousin Lodovico and his brother Agostino, he reacted against prevailing styles in Bologna and turned to the example of Venice and Parma. A devotee of life drawing, he extended his interest in naturalism to landscapes and to genre scenes, which in Annibale's hands are imbued with a deep human sympathy that eschews the grotesqueries of Passarotti's examples. Through the 1580s and early 1590s he produced a series of great altarpieces with dynamic and vigorous compositions. A move to Rome in 1595 led to a clarification of form, increased interest in antique sculpture, and enhanced appreciation of Michelangelo. Tragically disappointed by his patrons' response to the Farnese Gallery, he fell into a profound depression, and the few paintings he made in his last years are severe and withdrawn. He was a great teacher: Domenichino, Guido Reni, and Giovanni Lanfranco among others were his pupils and collaborators. See cats. 47, 52.

Bernardino Cesari
Arpino 1571–1622 Rome
Bernardino Cesari was the younger brother of Giuseppe, called the Cavaliere d'Arpino (1568–1640). His date of birth, previously unknown, was discovered by Röttgen (1973), who also corrected his death date, previously given as 1614. Bernardino is a little-known artist, and although several paintings have been attributed to him by Röttgen, they were all produced within the orbit of his brother, to whom he acted as assistant. See cat. 17.

Giulio Clovio
Grisone 1498–1578 Rome
Croatian by birth, Giorgio Glovicic was persuaded to become a miniaturist by Giulio Romano before 1524; later, when he took holy orders, he adopted Giulio's name. According to Vasari he had already begun to copy Michelangelo by the mid-1520s. He worked for some years in Padua and Perugia, but seems to have returned to Rome by 1537, when he began his masterpiece, the *Book of Hours* for Cardinal Alessandro Farnese (The Pierpont Morgan Library, New York). He remained in Farnese service, mostly in Rome, until the end of his life, also acting as an artistic adviser. He befriended and assisted several foreign artists, including Pieter Bruegel the Elder and El Greco, who painted his portrait, but it is unclear how much personal contact he had with Michelangelo. It remains to be elucidated how much of his work is derivative and how much inventive: his execution shows great surface refinement, but he was neither a solid figure draftsman, nor a fluent composer. See cats. 5, 15, 22, 25, 34, 62.

Giovan Ambrogio Figino
Milan 1548–1608 Milan
Figino was a prolific draftsman, but his paintings are relatively few in number and, while formally competent and, on occasion, iconographically inventive, are rarely of the highest quality. Figino trained with Lomazzo and therefore had the benefit of deep theoretical as well as practical study. His earliest certain work is a portrait (present location unknown) and, indeed, portraiture seems to have been his staple. He is recorded as traveling to Corsica in 1575 and may have included a visit to Rome on this trip or subsequently. He was certainly back in Milan by 1577 and further travels by him are unrecorded. His known oeuvre consists largely of religious paintings, and he worked for a number of churches in and around Milan in a confident and vigorous, if somewhat overblown, manner. Occasional reminiscences of Michelangelo occur in his work, but he was in no sense a Michelangelesque painter. The high point of his career was probably the commission he received in 1590 to paint the organ shutters of the Duomo in Milan. See cat. 60.

Battista Franco, called Semolei
Venice c. 1510–1561 Venice
Although Venetian by birth, Battista Franco passed his formative years in Rome—where he was closely associated with followers of Michelangelo, in particular Raffaello da Montelupo, whom he assisted on the triumphal entry for Charles V in 1536—and in Florence—where he worked with both Vasari and Bronzino. In 1538 or 1539 he painted the famous panel celebrating the victory of Cosimo I at the Battle of Montmurlo. He spent most of the following decade in Rome, where he executed the *Capture of the Baptist* in San Giovanni Decollato as well as chapel decorations in other churches. He also frescoed the choir of Urbino cathedral, a vast scheme destroyed in the collapse of the church in 1789. By 1554, he was back in Venice, where he was much employed as a leading representative of Central Italian *disegno* until his death. Battista Franco's paintings, criticized by Vasari, can be of fine quality, although comparatively few are known today. But he was a prolific and highly inventive draftsman whose work is to be found in many public collections. See cat. 43.

Michelangelo Buonarroti
Caprese 1475–1564 Rome
See introduction and cats. 1, 7, 9a, 12, 16, 18, 19, 21, 23, 24, 26, 27, 33, 38, 39, 41, 42, 55.

Antonio Mini
Florence 1506–1534/1535 France
Little is known about Antonio. He joined Michelangelo as a pupil assistant in 1522 and remained with him until late 1531 when, partly to escape a fruitless passion for a girl of higher social class, he traveled to France hoping to make his fortune. Michelangelo was fond of him and gave him his painting of *Leda* and a large number of models and drawings, but Mini was swindled out of the *Leda* and seems to have made no use of the models and drawings. He found an early and obscure death. Mini was a weak artist and the drawings attributed to him are feeble. But most of these probably date from his earliest years with Michelangelo, and he may have developed more than is commonly thought; by the time he went to France he had surely attained a basic competence. Of models and drawings that he took to France, the former are entirely lost; but some surviving drawings by Michelangelo were already known to Primaticcio in the 1540s and the most likely source of these is Mini. See cat. 9 (verso).

Girolamo Muziano
Brescia 1528–1592 Rome
Muziano studied in Padua with Domenico Campagnola and in Venice before arriving in Rome in 1549; Venetian-style landscape remained one of his great interests, and a series of engravings of penitent saints in landscapes after Muziano was published in the early 1570s. Muziano made an imposing debut as a figure painter in Rome with his *Raising of Lazarus* of 1555 and, thereafter, was ceaselessly active, mostly in Rome and Orvieto, painting altarpieces, designing mosaics, and supervising fresco schemes. His severe, at times brutal, pictorial style was primarily based on the later work of Sebastiano, but he rejected any emphasis on surface beauty. Muziano was a dominant figure in later cinquecento Rome and his achievement is much underrated. See cat. 49.

Battista Naldini
Florence 1535–1591 Florence
Although Naldini's birth date has always been given as 1537, it has now been discovered by Elizabeth Pilliod that he was born in 1535 (this information will be published in Pilliod's forthcoming study of Pontormo, Bronzino, and Naldini, *Masters and Pupils* [Yale University Press], which she has generously allowed the compiler to anticipate here). Although Naldini was a pupil of Pontormo and a copyist of his drawings, Naldini's work does not reflect closely that of his master, except in some peripheral features. Naldini spent some time in Rome after 1560, where he made numerous copies of antique remains and sketches of sites in and around the city in vigorous pen drawings. He may have come into contact with Taddeo Zuccaro in this period. He had returned to Florence by 1564 and spent the remainder of his career in Tuscany, where he was active as a

painter of altarpieces. Looking to the example of Andrea del Sarto, Naldini was one of the earliest Florentine painters to react against the preceding generation's focus on local color, and to attempt to revive Andrea's tonal approach. See cat. 45.

Bartolomeo Passarotti
Bologna 1529–1592 Bologna
Passarotti is supposed to have spent some years in the 1550s working in Rome, first with Jacopo Barozzi da Vignola, then with Taddeo Zuccaro, after whose drawings he made prints, but whose art did not much influence him. He had returned to Bologna by 1560 and passed the rest of his career there, becoming one of the city's most prominent artists. He was a prolific portraitist, and produced many altarpieces. He practiced a coarse, exaggerated, and hyper-dramatic art, with large surface-dominating figures, plunging depths, and violent movement; he also executed a number of genre paintings of unusually aggressive ugliness. Michelangelesque citations occur in his paintings, but he was at least as much influenced by Correggio. His pen drawings show an obsession with the techniques and forms of Michelangelo and of Bandinelli. Agostino Carracci trained with him and his early pen drawings can be mistaken for Passarotti's, but in sum Passarotti embodied much of what the Carracci reacted against. See cats. 32, 58.

Perino del Vaga
Florence 1501–1547 Rome
Piero Buonaccorsi, who took the name Vaga from his first master, probably joined Raphael's studio circa 1517, during work on the Vatican Loggia. He was precocious, and seems to have executed independent commissions even before Raphael's death. He formed close associations with both Giovanni da Udine and Gianfrancesco Penni, whose sister he married. Giulio Romano's departure for Mantua and the relative inefficacy of Penni left him as one of the most prominent painters in Rome, and he extended his range by closer study of Michelangelo. After the Sack of Rome in 1527, he worked for Andrea Doria in Genoa for most of the 1530s, returning to Rome at the end of the decade. As a fluent and highly attractive draftsman, he was more a designer than an executant and became very active as an artistic entrepreneur before his unexpected and early death. With Michelangelo's approval, he made the design for a hanging to be placed below the *Last Judgment*. See cat. 48.

Giovanni Antonio de' Sacchis, called Pordenone
Pordenone 1483/1484–1539 Ferrara
Pordenone's earliest years as a painter were spent in the Friuli painting altarpieces and frescoes for local churches. Although relatively coarse in handling, his work was always ambitious and he aimed for large-scale effects. At some time before 1520 he evidently visited Rome. The effects can first be seen in the Malchiostro chapel in Treviso Cathedral of 1520 and his frescoes in Cremona, but other influences also supervene. More specifically Michelangelesque effects are seen in his Spilimbergo organ shutters of 1523–1524 and in his subsequent work. In the second half of the 1520s Pordenone—while remaining peripatetic: he worked in Piacenza, Genoa, Udine, and elsewhere—made Venice a particular focus of his activity, and, for a period in the 1530s, he was regarded by Titian as a serious threat. See cat. 51.

Camillo Procaccini
Bologna 1555/1560–1621 Milan
Trained in Bologna by his father Ercole, Camillo worked in the city until his transfer to Milan in 1587, where he lived and worked very productively for the rest of his life. Camillo's earliest work shows the influence of his father and of Bartolomeo Passarotti. But since his *Assumption of the Virgin* in Santi Gregorio e Siro in Bologna, variously dated but probably commissioned in 1582, demonstrates Camillo's interest in Daniele da Volterra's *Assumption* in Santa Trinità al Monte, an early trip to Rome seems likely. There are in fact a number of formal connections between his works and those of artists active in Rome like Raffaellino da Reggio. Although Michelangelo did not play a large part in Camillo's work, he is an intermittent presence. See cat. 68.

Biagio Pupini
Documented in Bologna from 1511 to 1551
Pupini was working with Bagnacavallo senior in 1511, but no work by him survives that can securely be dated before the 1520s. One signed painting, however, a seated *Saint Petronius* (formerly Salina Collection, Bologna), is strongly Peruginesque in style and certainly early. Pupini became acquainted with the workshop of Raphael, Perugino's former pupil, but the date of his visit to Rome is uncertain, placed both before and after Raphael's death. He may have made more than one visit. He knew well both Raphael's work and that of his followers, and was particularly interested in the art of Polidoro da Caravaggio. Many drawings by Pupini survive, although relatively few can be connected with his paintings. They demonstrate that he had access to drawings and *modelli* by a number of painters, above all by Raphael and his followers, but also by Parmigianino and Michelangelo. How he obtained this is an open question. Pupini's greatest claim to interest, in fact, lies in his drawings, for his known pictorial output, while competent, is not particularly distinctive. See cat. 30.

Raphael Sanzio
Urbino 1483–1520 Rome
The youngest of the great triumvirate of Italian High Renaissance artists, Raphael, in his short life, was active as painter, architect, designer, theorist, and archaeologist. Trained in Umbria and Florence, he dominated the Roman artistic scene from 1509 until his premature death, despite powerful competition from Michelangelo and Sebastiano. He was involved in an enormous range of projects, affecting fundamentally every area that he touched. The possessor of one of the clearest and best-organized of all artistic minds, he ran an extremely successful studio, and the roll call of his pupils and associates is unmatched. Raphael was the first artist fully to appreciate the importance of printmaking to enhance his fame. After his death, it was rumored that Pope Leo X had intended to make him a cardinal. Raphael is probably the single most influential European painter. See cats. 29, 36.

Raffaello da Montelupo
Florence 1504/1505– 1566/1567 Orvieto
Raffaello is one of the few artists of the cinquecento to have left an autobiography, albeit limited and fragmentary, from which a happy-go-lucky character emerges. Unfortunately, his story stops short of his collaboration with Michelangelo. Raffaello was the son of the sculptor Baccio da Montelupo, who seems to have been a friendly acquaintance of Michelangelo's, and, against his father's wishes, himself became a sculptor. He displayed some talent in his early years, but he usually worked in collaboration and never became a top-level master in his own right. He worked for Michelangelo in the New Sacristy in 1533–1534, carving the *Saint Damian*, but his later failure with the Julius Tomb effectively prevented him from gaining further important sculptural commissions. He subsequently became architect to Orvieto Cathedral. See cats. 3, 10.

Giulio Romano
Rome 1492/1499–1546 Mantua
Giulio Pippi, called Giulio Romano (because he was born in Rome), was Raphael's most important and most favored pupil. In his youth he was a miraculously fine executant of high-finish paintings who sometimes worked side-by-side with Raphael on the same picture and who sometimes produced paintings in Raphael's name. But Giulio never fully attained Raphael's mastery of the human figure and, after his death, relied on his fluent imagination rather than life drawing. Giulio was active as a painter—fascinated by chiaroscuro effects—and as an architect in Rome, and his success led to a call from Mantua in 1524. There he practiced mostly as an architect and designer of decorative schemes, which he did not generally execute himself. He was a prolific and extraordinarily fluent draftsman in pen and wash, and his capacity to work in the style of antique reliefs was prodigious. His designs had considerable influence on Rubens, who seems to have collected them avidly. Giulio was about to succeed Antonio da Sangallo as architect of Saint Peter's when his own early death opened the way to Michelangelo. See cats. 35, 37.

Francesco Salviati
Florence 1510–1563 Rome
The neurotic and difficult Francesco de' Rossi, who took the name Salviati from his first major patron, was a close friend of Vasari's, who left a memorable account of his character. Like Vasari he was peripatetic, but unlike him, Salviati never found secure patronage. Both as an executant and as an inventor, he was an artist of higher quality than Vasari, with a virtually unbridled imagination. He was perhaps the most talented and various draftsman of his generation, the full range of whose graphic activity has yet to be elucidated. He is not, on the whole, a creator of great dramatic power or psychological insight, although he could create moving religious images, but his capacity for inventive scenography is extraordinary. Salviati, like Rosso by whom he was influenced, often seems to have taken a quasi-parodic attitude toward his sources, and this may account for the evident coolness toward him of Michelangelo, who favored Daniele da Volterra's concentration and sobriety above Salviati's extravagance. See cats. 6, 64.

Orazio Samacchini
Bologna 1532–1577 Bologna
Although Samacchini's whereabouts before 1563–1564 are unrecorded, it may be that, although Bolognese-born, he was Florentine-trained. When first documented, Orazio was working with Vasari in the Vatican, executing a fresco in the Sala Regia, the great hall situated between the Sistine and Pauline Chapels. He was back in Bologna by 1568 and executed a number of paintings and frescoes in that city, and in Parma and in Cremona over the next decade. He was closely associated with his friend Lorenzo Sabbatini and even early writers remarked on the difficulty of distinguishing their work. At his premature death he left some 1,500 drawings and prints, as well as several unfinished paintings. See cat. 59.

Sebastiano del Piombo
Venice c. 1485–1547 Rome
According to Vasari, Sebastiano and the probably slightly younger Titian were the "creati" and then rivals of Giorgione. But, of the three, Sebastiano's work in his Venetian period is the most confidently composed, strongly modeled, and densely painted, displaying a love of crepuscular lighting. Taken to Rome by Agostino Chigi in 1511, he spent the rest of his life in the metropolis, working for the highest level of patrons and closely connected with the papal court. He became the rival of Raphael and a close friend of Michelangelo's, who assisted him with drawings. After Raphael's death, he obtained some of his commissions. He was less active in later years as a painter of walls and altarpieces and, after their friendship ended, was criticized by Michelangelo for laziness. But the physical refinement and spiritual profundity of his religious images had no peers among his contemporaries. The fact that he liked to rework the same images should not be seen as a weakness, but as an indication of their richness and intensity. His effect on Counter-Reformation art was immense. See cats. 20, 53.

Pellegrino Tibaldi
Puria in Vasolda 1527–1596 Milan
Tibaldi is documented in Rome in 1549; he was probably there at least from 1547. He was powerfully influenced by Michelangelo's latest style in his *Adoration of Shepherds* (Galleria Borghese, Rome), dated 1549. He produced a number of major frescoes in Bologna and elsewhere during the 1550s, in which he also drew inspiration from the Sistine ceiling. In 1561 Tibaldi was appointed city architect in Milan, where he remained, executing occasional paintings and designs for wood reliefs and stained glass, until he was called to Spain in 1585. Over the next decade Tibaldi supervised—and in part executed—the pictorial decoration of the Escorial, with a series of frescoes and altarpieces, in a style that revives his fascination both with late Michelangelo and with the Sistine. He returned to Milan to die. See cats. 65, 66.

Federico Zuccaro
Sant'Angelo in Vado 1540 or 1541–1609 Ancona
Federico was one of the most traveled artists of his time, with a European-wide reputation. He was active in most of the major Italian centers—Rome, Venice, Milan, Florence, where he completed the *Last Judgment* in the Cupola of the Duomo left unfinished at Vasari's death—and worked for the Hapsburgs in Spain and the Netherlands, and in England during the reign of Mary Tudor. Educated and intelligent, Federico was an important art theorist and, to some extent, an art historian in his avid copying of the works of both predecessors and contemporaries. The range of his work is very wide and its quantity enormous; he deserves further study. While he has recently fallen under the shadow of his more artistically vivacious and inventive elder bother Taddeo, it is evident that Federico was among the leading painters of the later cinquecento. See cat. 54.

Taddeo Zuccaro
Sant'Angelo in Vado 1529– 1566 Rome
The short-lived Taddeo Zuccaro was one of the most energetic artists working in Rome in the decade 1555–1565. He was much employed by the Farnese, both in Rome and at Caprarola, and this may have been at Michelangelo's instigation, for he is recorded as admiring the young man's work. Taddeo was a virtuoso draftsman, producing images of extreme vitality in pen—in which his style was strongly influenced by the seductively wandering line of Perino del Vaga—and of richly pictorial images in red chalk. Taddeo, like most artists of his generation, made use of assistants—including his brother Federico—for much of the execution of his works, and his surviving frescoes can disappoint those acquainted with his drawings. However, his rare panel paintings, notably the *Adoration of the Magi* (Fitzwilliam Museum, Cambridge), can combine Correggesque textures and coloring with Raphaelesque composition in an exquisitely beautiful way. See cat. 67.

Unidentified Artists
See cats. 2, 8, 28, 40, 44, 46, 50, 56, 57, 63.

The Provenance of the Drawings by Michelangelo at Windsor Castle

MARTIN CLAYTON

All the drawings by Michelangelo—and, indeed, the great majority of the old master drawings—at Windsor were in the Royal Collection by the reign of King George III (1760–1820). The first reliable reference to drawings by Michelangelo in the collection is the manuscript Inventory A, mostly compiled around 1800 (though partly based on earlier lists) with some later annotations. At this time all but one of the Michelangelo drawings were mounted on the pages of three volumes, together with copies after Michelangelo and other sheets perhaps thought to be by the master, although the lists are usually inexplicit about the supposed authorship. The three volumes had been dismantled, or at least rearranged, by the time that their contents were listed and numbered in a typescript inventory earlier this century. No trace of the old bindings has survived.

The entries in Inventory A for those drawings that can be identified with autograph Michelangelos or other drawings in the present catalogue are as follows:

Mich: Angelo Buonarroti

TOM. I.

2. *Woman's Head*.......... *Black Chalk.*
   [CAT. 1]

3. *Head of a Fury*.......... *Ditto.*
   [CAT. 8]

5. *...of Hannibal*.......... *Red Chalk.*
   [CAT. 6]

6. *Woman's Head; remarkably attired*.......... *Black Chalk.*
   [CAT. 2]

9. *Ganimede*.......... *Black Chalk.*
   [CAT. 15 OR POPHAM AND WILDE (P&W) 265]

11. *Various studies of the naked*.......... *Red Chalk.*
   [CAT. 46]

18, 19. *Promotheus tormented by the Vultur*.......... *Black Chalk.*
   [CATS. 13, 14]

20. *Ganimede on the Eagle of Jupiter*.......... *Black Chalk.*
   [CAT. 15 OR P&W 265]

24. *A figure kneeling in an attitude of Surprize.*
   [P&W 433]

27, 28. *Studies for a Woman, on one of the Monuments of Cosmus; or Lorenzo de Medicis.*
   [CATS. 43, 44]

30. *A Sketch; part with a...Pen...and part in*.......... *Red Chalk.*
   [P&W 422?]

32. *A drawing of part of a Body; and Hip-Bone.*
   [CAT. 28]

33 to 40. *Studies for seperate figures; in his last Day's Judgement, with a...Pen; and in Black...and*.......... *Red Chalk.*
   [PROBABLY INCLUDING CATS. 56, 57, 58]

47. *Christ giving the Keys to Saint Peter.*
   [CAT. 62]

Volume I contained several drawings with an early English provenance. Of those that can be identified, four have the star mark (Lugt 2885–2886) of Nicholas Lanier (1588–1666), eight have the inscriptions and price marks associated with William Gibson (1644/1645–1702?), and a number have had the upper corners chamfered, a common feature among drawings that passed through early English collections. None of the drawings can be traced back to owners earlier than Lanier, who was active as a collector mainly in the 1620s and 1630s, buying paintings and drawings for both King Charles I and the earl of Arundel.

It was stated by the younger Jonathan Richardson (in a marginal annotation to the London Library's proof copy of his father's *Works* of 1728) that Gibson's price mark was "by him put there for the use of his widow, as she told us, and of which my F[ather] bought a large quantity of them but not until the D[uke] of Devon[shire] had taken what he chose." The testimony of Gibson's widow would imply that the prices were added toward the end of his life, that is, after he had bought a large number of drawings at the sale in 1688 of the great collection of Sir Peter Lely. A quick survey of other British collections might support this: of fourteen sheets in the British Museum (in the Raphael, Parmese, and Roman 1550–1640 catalogues) with Gibson inscriptions, nine have a Lely stamp (Lugt 2092–2094); of seven in the Ashmolean (Parker 1956 and Macandrew 1980 catalogues), six have a Lely stamp; of seven at Christ Church (Byam Shaw 1976 catalogue), four have a Lely stamp; of another seven in Edinburgh (Andrews 1971 catalogue), five have a Lely stamp. (It is remarkable, in view of the testimony of Gibson's widow, that no drawing at Chatsworth is known to have a Gibson inscription; however Gibson usually wrote on the verso of his drawings and many of the Chatsworth sheets are laid down.)

Yet of the twenty-six drawings in the Royal Collection with Gibson inscriptions, not one bears a Lely stamp. In fact, surprisingly few drawings in the Royal Collection have a certain Lely provenance: a mere six, one of which (cat. 10) did not enter the collection until 1875; not one was contained in Volume I. There are also occasional revisions of Gibson's price mark in a different ink (for example, Popham and Wilde 661 and 829), which would imply that the price marks were not added in a single session, to pass on to Gibson's widow as Richardson reported, but were in use over an extended period.

All this suggests that many, if not all, of the Royal Collection drawings with a Gibson inscription left his hands before he made his purchases at the Lely sale, that is, before 1688; and, as Blunt surmised (1971, 5), they were probably bought by King Charles II (died 1685). Details concerning both Charles II's activity as a collector of drawings and William Gibson's career are very elusive. According to Horace Walpole, Gibson was a miniaturist, the son and pupil of Richard Gibson (1615–1690), who had connections at court, serving until 1677 as drawing master to the two daughters of the duke of York, the future Queens Mary and Anne; William Gibson may thus have had an introduction to court collectors, including the king, through his father.

Could Volume I have been an album assembled in the time of Charles II? The first inventory of the drawings in the Royal Collection is the summary "List of the Books of Drawings and Prints in the Buroe in His Majestys Great Closset at Kensington," made about 1735. This includes nothing that can be identified with Volume I; the only reference to Michelangelo is "No. 9. Drawings by Julio Romano, M. Angello, Raphaell," which is hardly enlightening. It is possible that there were volumes of drawings elsewhere within the royal residences, and that Volume I was overlooked when the 1735 list was compiled; but George III's bookbinders frequently rearranged and augmented albums in the late eighteenth century, before Inventory A was compiled, and Volume I may just as well have been created at that time from miscellaneous material.

Mich: Angelo Buonaroti.

TOM. II.

1. *Of the Labours of Hercules*..*Red Chalk.*
[CAT. 18]

2. *Men and Women suspended in the Air and shooting Arrows at a Target fixed on a Term. Cupid a sleep and two Boys burning his Arrows.—This Emblematical Subject is painted in the Villa call'd Raphael's near the Walls of Rome*...........*Red Chalk.*
[CAT. 16]

3. *Several Boys carrying a dead Monster, One with a Pig; some boiling a Caldron, others in Groupe in the fore ground drinking; A female Satyr and two Children; one sucking her lank Breast, the other uncovering an Old Man a Sleep—perhaps the Emblem of Night—the subject very obscure, but the Drawing very Capital*...*Red Chalk.*
[P&W 431]

4. *Resurrection of Christ*..*Black Chalk.*
[CAT. 38]

5. *Study for the figure of Christ*..*Do.*
[CAT. 39]

6. *Prometheus*...*Do.*
[CAT. 12]

7. *Fall of Phaeton*...*Do.*
[CAT. 9]

8. *Virgin, Jesus and St John Baptist*..*Do.*
[CAT. 19]

9. *A prophet*...*Red Chalk.*
[CAT. 49?]

12. *Sketch of a River God*..*Black Chalk.*
[CAT. 11]

13. *First thoughts for Various Groupes and single Figures, for the Painting of the last Judgment.*
[CAT. 55]

18. *Sketch of one of the Monumental Figures at Florence.*
[CAT. 45?]

22. [*Womens Heads* corrected to] *Head of a Woman, large as Life*...........[*Pen*]
[CAT. 3?]

This album was quite different in character from Volume I, and contained all the autograph presentation drawings now in the collection, grouped together at the start of the album. Of these, the *Children's Bacchanal* (no. 3), *Tityus* (no. 6), and the *Fall of Phaeton* (no. 7) are known to have been given by Michelangelo to Tommaso de' Cavalieri in 1532–1533. After Cavalieri's death in 1587, his collection of drawings was bought by the Farnese for 500 scudi.

Inscriptions on the versos of the Archers (no. 2) and the *Resurrection* (no. 4) suggest that these two drawings may have belonged to Giulio Clovio. An inventory of Clovio's possessions taken a few days before his death in 1578 describes a drawing as "il saggittario di Michelagniolo fatto da D. Giulio," and Clovio's collection of drawings was bequeathed to Cardinal Alessandro Farnese, who had employed Clovio during his later life. But it is also possible that the inscriptions were added by someone who knew that Clovio had copied the drawings and mistakenly identified the originals with the copies.

Thus three of the drawings in Volume II certainly, and two possibly, were in the Farnese collection by 1600, although Volume II certainly did not contain all the drawings by Michelangelo known to have been in the Farnese collection. Access to the drawings in the Farnese collection seems to have been limited. The Archers was copied (cat. 17) by Bernardino Cesari (died 1622), who presumably had access to the collection through his brother, the Cavaliere d'Arpino; another visitor in the early seventeenth century, possibly the painter Sisto Badalocchio, recorded seeing the *Fall of Phaeton* and a portrait of Cavalieri.

The early provenance of the other drawings in Volume II is unknown. Not one seems to have an early English provenance—no Lely or Lanier stamp, no Gibson inscription, no chamfered top corners. The only candidate is that on page 10: "Study for an Altarpiece, Holy Family with St Francis.....Black chalk." This might conceivably have been the drawing by Sebastiano (cat. 20) that has a Lanier stamp, but the subsidiary figure (possibly Pope Clement VII) is bearded, and his identification as Saint Francis is thus unlikely. If the drawing on page 10 was *not* the Sebastiano, this would allow for the possibility that the whole of Volume II was assembled in Italy.

When this volume (or, at least, its components) might have come to England is unknown. Around 1636 William Petty, an agent of the earl of Arundel, secured five hundred drawings reputedly by Michelangelo from an unnamed Neapolitan collection, which might point to a Farnese link, and an unpublished inventory of the Farnese collection in 1649 does not list any drawings that can be identified with those now at Windsor. But we hear nothing more of this huge collection of drawings, and the Windsor volume (or its contents) was possibly among the many purchases made by George III's agents in Italy in the 1760s and 1770s.

Michael Angelo, Fra: Bartolomeo, And: del Sarto &

TOM. III.

1.... to 4.... } *A Mask Head & three different Studys of the Crucifixtion.*
[CATS. 7, 23, 24, 25]

7... to 15... } *Anatomical Studys.*
[INCLUDING CATS. 26, 27, 41, 42]

16.... *Virgin and Child... All these are by Michael Angelo.*
[CAT. 21]

The volume continues with thirteen pages of drawings attributed to Bandinelli, twelve pages attributed to Fra Bartolommeo, one Bugiardini, and nine pages attributed to Andrea del Sarto. This arrangement by artist is typical of George III's bookbinders, and it is probable that the drawings were assembled from various sources in the later eighteenth century.

Of the drawings in Volume III, the earlier histories of cats. 7, 21, and 23–25 are unknown. But Paul Joannides has noted (and I am indebted to him for all the following information) that cats. 26, 27, 41, and 42 carry an inscription that is found in the same hand, though with variations in spelling, on a relatively large number of drawings by Michelangelo. This is usually *di Michel Angelo bona Roti*, sometimes with the variant *Buona*, and sometimes simply *di Bona Roti*.

Furthermore, sheets with this inscription usually carry numbers in a different hand, in the form *n°. 76*. The numbers and inscriptions are never aligned, and they often appear on opposite faces of the sheet. It is also possible to identify this *n°.* form on other sheets that do not bear the inscription, but as some of the drawings have been cut down, it is not possible to infer anything from this.

These inscriptions or numbers or both are found on the following drawings:

Haarlem, Teylers Museum: Inv. A16 / C. 164, A18 / C. 51, A20 / C. 135, A22 / C. 10, A23 / C. 357, A25 / C. 89, A26, A27 / C. 136, A28 / C. 108, A30 / C. 216, A31, A32 / C. 376, A33a / C. 218, A33b / C. 219, A34 / C. 250, A35 / C. 434, A36 / C. 215, A37 / C. 109, A38 / C. 84, A39 / C. 111, A42 / C. 115, A.11X (copy after Ashmolean Draped Men);

Windsor Castle: P&W 422 / C. 99 (from Volume I), 432 / C. 351 (from Volume II), 439 / C. 112, 440 / C. 113, 441 / C. 114, 442 / C. 106, 443 / C. 107 (from Volume III);

Oxford, Ashmolean Museum: P. 291 / C. 17, 292 / C. 18, 294 / C. 103, 310 / C. 212, 314 / C. 295, 338 / C. 369, 343 / C. 415;

London, British Museum: Wilde 29 / C. 97, 71 / C. 394, 72 / C. 395;

Paris, Musée du Louvre: Inv. 727 / c. 34;

Paris, Ecole des Beaux-Arts: Inv. 197 / c. 62;

Turin, Biblioteca Reale: Inv. 15627 / c. 155;

New York, The Metropolitan Museum of Art: 24.197.2 / c. 156.

The fact that the inscriptions and numbers are not found on all of the Haarlem drawings (and that they are found on drawings in other collections) suggests they predate Joachim von Sandrart, who formed his collection between 1629 and 1637; indeed, the inscriptions appear to be in a sixteenth-century hand. It is virtually certain that the numbers postdate the inscriptions: of two sheets at Haarlem that originally formed a single sheet, only one carries an inscription but both carry (consecutive) numbers.

Not one of these drawings is purely architectural or of presentation type; on the other hand they comprise almost all the anatomical sheets, and some of the finest studies for the Sistine ceiling. Of the forty-three sheets, only two are not by Michelangelo, but these are copies of high quality and might well have come from his studio.

It is thus likely that the collection was formed by somebody with access to Michelangelo's studio (for the drawings do not share a Casa Buonarotti provenance) and was partly dispersed sometime around 1600. Who this collector may have been is not known. Although Michelangelo gave two cases of models and drawings to Antonio Mini, several of the aforementioned drawings date from after Mini's departure to France in 1531; most of Michelangelo's other studio assistants are obscure figures who did not mix in the mainstream of the Roman art world, whereby their collection might have been noted by an acquaintance.

This accounts for all of the autograph Michelangelo drawings now in the collection with the exception of the proportional study (cat. 33); although Wilde identified this with Volume I, page 11, that drawing is probably the *ignudo* copy (cat. 46), and the proportion study may be identified instead with a loose drawing listed on page 146 of Inventory A as "a Figure & anatomical sketches by Michelangelo."

Bibliography

ABBREVIATIONS: C. (De Tolnay 1975–1980), P. (Parker 1956), W. (Wilde 1953)

Andrews 1971: Andrews, K. *Catalogue of Italian Drawings at the National Gallery of Scotland.* Cambridge, 1971.

Annesley and Hirst 1981: Annesley, N. and M. Hirst. "*Christ and the Woman of Samaria* by Michelangelo." *Burlington Magazine* 123 (1981), 608–614.

Bacou 1972–1973: Bacou, R. In *Il paesaggio nel disegno del cinquecento Europeo, Mostra all'Accademia de Francia.* [exh. cat., Villa Medici] (Rome, 1972–1973), no. 107.

Barocchi 1962: Barocchi, P. *Michelangelo e la sua scuola, I disegni di Casa Buonarroti e degli Uffizi.* Florence, 1962.

Barocchi 1964: Barocchi, P. *Michelangelo e la sua scuola, I disegni dell'Archivio Buonarroti.* Florence, 1964.

Barolsky 1979: Barolsky, P. *Daniele da Volterra. A Catalogue Raisonné.* New York and London, 1979.

Bean 1960: Bean, J. *Inventaire général des dessins des Musées de Province. 4. Bayonne, Musée Bonnat. Les dessins italiens de la collection Bonnat.* Paris, 1960.

Berenson 1903: Berenson, B. *The Drawings of the Florentine Painters.* 2 vols. London, 1903.

Berenson 1938: Berenson, B. *The Drawings of the Florentine Painters.* 3 vols. 2d ed. Chicago, 1938.

Berenson 1961: Berenson, B. *I Disegni dei pittori Fiorentini.* 3 vols. 3d ed. Milan, 1961.

Berti 1965: Berti, L. "I Disegni." In Salmi et al. 1965, 389–507.

Birke and Kertesz 1992: Birke, V. and J. Kertesz. *Die Italienischen Zeichnungen der Albertina. Generalverzeichnis. Vol. 1, Inventar 1–1200.* Vienna-Cologne-Weimar, 1992.

Birke and Kertesz 1994: Birke, V. and J. Kertesz. *Die Italienischen Zeichnungen der Albertina. Generalverzeichnis. Vol. 2, Inventar 1201–2400.* Vienna-Cologne-Weimar, 1994.

Blunt 1971: Blunt, A. "Supplements to the Catalogues of Italian and French Drawings." In Schilling and Blunt 1971.

Borea 1991: Borea, E. "Michelangelo e le stampe nel suo tempo." In *La Sistine riprodotta, gli affreschi di Michelangelo dalle stampe del cinquecento alle campagne fotografiche Anderson.* [exh. cat., Calcografia] (Rome, 1991).

Borenius and Wittkower 1938: Borenius, T. and R. Wittkower. *Catalogue of the Collection of Drawings by the Old Masters Formed by Sir Robert Mond.* London, 1938.

Borough Johnson 1908: Borough Johnson, E. *The Drawings of Michelangelo.* London, 1908.

Brinckmann 1925: Brinckmann, A. E. *Michelangelo Zeichnungen.* Munich, 1925.

Briquet: Briquet, C. M. *Les Filigranes.* Paris, 1907.

Brugerolles 1981: Brugerolles, E. *De Michel-Ange à Géricault. Dessins de la collection Armand-Valton.* [exh. cat., Ecole Nationale Supérieure des Beaux-Arts] (Paris, 1981).

Brugerolles 1984: Brugerolles, E. *Les Dessins de la collection Armand-Valton.* Paris, 1984.

Brugnoli 1964: Brugnoli, M. V. *I grandi Maestri del disegno: Michelangelo.* Milan, 1964.

Byam Shaw 1976: Byam Shaw, J. *Drawings by Old Masters at Christ Church Oxford.* Oxford, 1976.

Calì 1980: Calì, M. *Da Michelangelo al Escorial.* Turin, 1980.

Chambers and Quiviger 1995: Chambers, D. S. and F. Quiviger. *Italian Academies of the 16th Century.* London, 1995.

Ciardi 1968: Ciardi, R. P. *Giovan Antonio Figino.* Florence, 1968.

Clark 1956: Clark, K. *The Nude.* London, 1956.

Cohen 1980: Cohen, C. E. *The Drawings of Giovanni Antonio da Pordenone.* Florence, 1980.

Condivi-Gori 1746: Condivi, A. *Vita di Michelangelo Buonarroti pittore scultore architetto e gentiluomo fiorentino.* Ed. A. Gori. 2d ed. Florence, 1746.

Cordellier 1991: Cordellier, D. "Fragments de jeunesse: deux dessins inédites de Michel-Ange au Louvre." *Revue du Louvre et des Musées de France* 41, no. 2 (1991), 43–55.

Costamagna 1991: Costamagna, P. "L'étude d'après les maîtres et le rôle de la copie dans la formation des artistes à Florence au 16e siècle." In Ramade 1991, 51–59.

Costamagna 1992: Costamagna, P. "A propos du séjour florentin de Giulio Clovio." In *Kunst des Cinquecento in der Toskana (Acts of the Congress in Honour of Sylvie Béguin, Florence, 24–27 October, 1989),* 168–175. Munich, 1992.

Cox-Rearick 1964: Cox-Rearick, J. "Some Early Drawings by Bronzino." *Master Drawings* 2, no. 4 (1964), 363–382.

D'Achiardi 1908: D'Achiardi, R. *Sebastiano del Piombo.* Rome, 1908.

De Tolnay 1943a: De Tolnay, C. *Michelangelo I: The Youth of Michelangelo.* Princeton, 1943. (2d ed. 1947).

De Tolnay 1943b: De Tolnay, C. *Michelangelo II: The Sistine Ceiling.* Princeton, 1945.

De Tolnay 1948: De Tolnay, C. *Michelangelo III: The Medici Chapel.* Princeton, 1948.

De Tolnay 1954: De Tolnay, C. *Michelangelo IV: The Tomb of Julius II.* Princeton, 1954.

De Tolnay 1960: De Tolnay, C. *Michelangelo V: The Final Period.* Princeton, 1960.

De Tolnay 1968a: De Tolnay, C. "Une composition de la jeunesse de Michel-Ange, Hercule étouffant le lion de Némée, dessin au Musée du Louvre." *Gazette des Beaux-Arts* 72 (April 1968), 205–212.

De Tolnay 1968b: De Tolnay, C. "Le Madonne di Michelangelo. A proposito di due disegni della Vergine col Bambino al Louvre." *Mitteilungen des Kunsthistorischen Institutes in Florenz* 13 (1968), 343–366.

De Tolnay 1975–1980: De Tolnay, C. *Corpus dei disegni di Michelangelo.* 4 vols. Novara, 1975–1980.

Delacre 1938: Delacre, M. *Le Dessin de Michel-Ange.* Bruxelles, 1938.

Donati 1989: Donati, V. *Pietre dure e medaglie del Rinascimento, Giovanni da Castel Bolognese.* Ferrara, 1989.

Dussler 1942: Dussler, L. *Sebastiano del Piombo.* Basel, 1942.

Dussler 1959: Dussler, L. *Die Zeichnungen des Michelangelo, Kristischer Katalog.* Berlin, 1959.

Dussler 1974: Dussler, L. *Michelangelo—Bibliographie 1927–1970.* Wiesbaden, 1974.

Ekserdjian 1993: Ekserdjian, D. "Parmigianino and Michelangelo." *Master Drawings* 31, no. 4 (1993), 390–394.

Ferino Pagden 1984: Ferino Pagden, S. "Invenzione raffaellesche adombrate nel libretto di venezia: la *Strage degli Innocenti* e la *Lapidazione de S. Stefano* a Genova." In *Studi su Raffaello, atti del congresso di Urbino-Firenze, 6–14 April 1984,* 63–72. Urbino, 1987.

Fiocco 1939: Fiocco, G. *Giovanni Antonio da Pordenone.* Udine, 1939.

Fischel 1898: Fischel, O. *Raphaels Zeichnungen.* Strasbourg, 1898.

Fischel 1913–1941: Fischel, O. *Raphaels Zeichnungen.* 8 vols. Berlin, 1913–1941.

Fischel 1948: Fischel, O. *Raphael.* Trans. B. Rackham. London, 1948.

Forlani Tempesti 1970: Forlani Tempesti, A. *I Disegni di Maestri 1: Capolavori del Rinascimento, il primo cinquecento toscano.* Milan, 1970.

Fortunati Pietrantonio 1986: Fortunati Pietrantonio, V., ed. *Pittura Bolognese del '500.* 2 vols. Bologna, 1986.

Frey 1909–1911: Frey, K. *Die Handzeichnungen Michelangiolos Buonarroti. Herausgegeben und mit kritischem Apparate.* 3 vols. Berlin, 1909–1911.

Frommel 1979: Frommel, C. L. *Michelangelo und Tommaso dei Cavalieri.* Amsterdam, 1979.

Furlan 1988: Furlan, C. *Il Pordenone.* Milan, 1988.

Gamba 1945: Gamba, C. *La pittura di Michelangelo.* Novara, 1945.

Gere 1969: Gere, J. *Taddeo Zuccaro. His Development Studied in His Drawings.* London, 1969.

Gere 1990: Gere, J. *The Life of Taddeo Zuccaro from the Collection of the British Rail Pension Fund.* Sale catalogue. Sotheby's, New York, 11 January 1990.

Gibbons 1977: Gibbons, F. *Catalogue of Italian Drawings in the Art Museum, Princeton University.* Princeton, 1977.

Giononi-Visani and Gamulin 1980: Giononi-Visani, M. and G. Gamulin. *Giorgio Clovio, Miniaturist of the Renaissance.* New York, 1980.

Giovanetti 1991: Giovanetti, A. *Francesco Morandini detti il Poppi: i disegni; i dipinti di Poppi e Castiglion Fiorentino.* [exh. cat., Liceo Scientifico Statale G. Galilei] (Poppi, 1991).

Goldscheider 1951: Goldscheider, L. *Michelangelo Drawings.* London, 1951.

Goldscheider 1966: Goldscheider, L. *Michelangelo Drawings.* 2d ed. London, 1966.

Gombrich 1986: Gombrich, E. "Michelangelo's Cartoon in the British Museum." In *New Light on Old Masters,* 171–178. Oxford, 1986.

Gould 1992: Gould, C. "Raphael at S. Maria della Pace." *Gazette des Beaux-Arts* 120 (September 1992), 78–88.

Griswold and Wolk-Simon 1994: Griswold, W. and L. Wolk-Simon. *16th Century Italian Drawings in New York Collections.* [exh. cat., The Metropolitan Museum of Art] (New York, 1994).

Hartt 1958: Hartt, F. *Giulio Romano.* New Haven, 1958.

Hartt 1971: Hartt, F. *The Drawings of Michelangelo.* London, 1971.

Hirst 1961: Hirst, M. "The Chigi Chapel in S. Maria della Pace." *Journal of the Warburg and Courtauld Institutes* 25 (1961), 161–185.

Hirst 1975: Hirst, M. "A Drawing of the *Rape of Ganymede* by Michelangelo." *Burlington Magazine* 117 (March 1975), 166.

Hirst 1979: Hirst, M. "Salviati's chinoiseries in Palazzo Sacchetti." *Burlington Magazine* 121 (December 1979), 791–792.

Hirst 1981: Hirst, M. *Sebastiano del Piombo.* Oxford, 1981.

Hirst 1988: Hirst, M. *Michelangelo and His Drawings.* London, 1988.

Hirst 1994–1995: Hirst, M. "The Artist in Rome 1496–1501." In *Making and Meaning: The Young Michelangelo.* [exh. cat., The National Gallery] (London, 1994–1995).

Holroyd 1911: Holroyd, C. *Michael Angelo Buonarroti. With Translations of the Life of the Master by His Scholar Ascanio Condivi, and Three Dialogues from the Portuguese by Francisco d'Ollanda.* 2d ed. London, 1911.

Höper 1987: Höper, C. *Bartolomeo Passarotti, 1529–1592.* 2 vols. Worms, 1987.

Jaffé 1977: Jaffé, M. *Rubens and Italy.* Oxford, 1977.

Jaffé 1994a: Jaffé, M. *The Devonshire Collection of Drawings: Tuscan and Umbrian Schools.* London, 1994.

Jaffé 1994b: Jaffé, M. *The Devonshire Collection of Drawings: Venetian and North Italian Schools.* London, 1994.

Joannides 1977: Joannides, P. "Michelangelo's Lost Hercules." *Burlington Magazine* 119 (August 1977), 550–555.

Joannides 1983: Joannides, P. *The Drawings of Raphael.* Oxford, 1983.

Joannides 1992: Joannides, P. "'Primitivism' in the Late Drawings of Michelangelo." In Smyth 1992, 245–261.

Joannides 1994a: Joannides, P. "A propos d'une sanguine nouvellement attribuée à Michel Ange (1475–1564). La connaissance des dessins de l'artiste en France au 16e siècle." *Revue du Louvre et des Musées de France* 43, no. 3 (1994), 15–29.

Joannides 1994b: Joannides, P. "Bodies in the Trees: A Mass Martyrdom by Michelangelo." *Apollo* 140 (November 1994), 3–14.

Kinney 1974: Kinney, P. *The Early Sculpture of Bartolommeo Ammanati.* Ph.D. Diss., New York University, 1974. (Published New York and London, 1976).

Kirschenbaum 1951: Kirschenbaum, B. D. "Reflections on Michelangelo's Drawings for Cavalieri." *Gazette des Beaux-Arts* 38 (March–April 1951), 99–110.

Knab et al. 1983: Knab, E., E. Mitsch, K. Oberhuber, and S. Ferino Pagden. *Raphaels Zeichnungen.* Stuttgart, 1983.

Lanfranc de Panthou and Perronet 1995: Lanfranc de Panthou, C. and B. Perronet. *Dessins italiens du musée Condé à Chantilly, I. Autour de Pérugin, Filippino Lippi et Michel-Ange.* [exh. cat., Musée Condé] (Chantilly, 1995–1996).

Lecchini Giovannoni 1970: Lecchini Giovannoni, S. *Disegni di Alessandro Allori.* [exh. cat., Galleria degli Uffizi] (Florence, 1970).

Lecchini Giovannoni 1991: Lecchini Giovannoni, S. *Alessandro Allori.* Turin, 1991.

Lewis 1992: Lewis, D. "Genius Disseminated: The Influence of Michelangelo's Works on Contemporary Sculpture." In Montreal 1992, 179–199.

Llewellyn and Romalli 1992: Llewellyn, E. and C. Romalli. *Drawing in Bologna 1500–1600.* [exh. cat., Courtauld Institute Galleries] (London, 1992).

Lugt 1921: Lugt, F. *Les Marques de collections de dessins et d'estampes.* Amsterdam, 1921.

Macandrew 1980: Macandrew, H. *Ashmolean Museum, Oxford, Catalogue of the Collection of Drawings.* Vol. 3, *Italian Schools: Supplement.* Oxford, 1980.

Martin 1965: Martin, J. R. *The Farnese Gallery.* Princeton, 1965.

Moltedo 1991: Moltedo, A. "Gli affreschi Sistine di Michelangelo nelle stampe antiche." In *La Sistine riprodotta, gli affreschi di Michelangelo dalle stampe del cinquecento alle campagne fotografiche Anderson.* [exh. cat., Calcografia] (Rome, 1991).

Monbeig Goguel 1978: Monbeig Goguel, C. "Francesco Salviati e il tema della Resurrezione di Cristo." *Prospettiva* 13 (1978), 7–23.

Monbeig Goguel 1988: Monbeig Goguel, C. "Giulio Clovio 'nouveau petit Michel-ange.' A propos des dessins du Louvre." *Revue de l'Art* 80 (1988), 37–47.

Mongan and Sachs 1940: Mongan, A. and P. Sachs. *Drawings in the Fogg Museum of Art.* Cambridge, Massachusetts, 1940.

Mortari 1992: Mortari, L. *Francesco Salviati.* Rome, 1992.

Mundy 1989–1990: Mundy, E. J. *Renaissance into Baroque. Italian Master Drawings by the Zuccari, 1550–1600.* [exh. cat., Milwaukee Art Museum and National Academy of Design] (Milwaukee and New York, 1989–1990).

Oberhuber 1984: Oberhuber, K. "A Drawing by Raphael Mistakenly Attributed to Bandinelli." *Master Drawings* 22, no. 4 (1984), 398–401.

Pallucchini 1944: Pallucchini, R. *Sebastian Viniziano.* Milan, 1944.

Panofsky 1939: Panofsky, E. *Studies in Iconology.* New York, 1939.

Panofsky-Soergel 1984: Panofsky-Soergel, G. "Postscriptum to Tommaso Cavalieri." In *Scritti di storia dell'arte in onore di Roberto Salvini,* 399–405. Florence, 1984.

Parker 1956: Parker, K. T. *Catalogue of the Collection of Drawings in the Ashmolean Museum. Vol. 2, The Italian School.* Oxford, 1956.

Parma Armani 1986: Parma Armani, E. *Perin del Vaga. L'anello mancante.* Genoa, 1986.

Passavant 1983: Passavant, G. "Reflexe nordischer Graphik bei Raffael, Leonardo, Giulio Romano und Michelangelo." *Mitteilungen des Kunsthistorischen Institutes in Florenz* 27 (1983), 193–222.

Perissa Torrini 1987: Perissa Torrini, A. *Galleria dell'Accademia di Venezia, Disegni del Figino.* Milan, 1987.

Perlingieri 1992: Perlingieri, I. S. *Sofonisba Anguissola, The First Great Woman Artist of the Renaissance.* New York, 1992.

Perrig 1991: Perrig, A. *Michelangelo's Drawings, the Science of Attribution.* New Haven and London, 1991.

Pilliod 1992: Pilliod, E. "Review of *Alessandro Allori* by Simona Lecchini Giovannoni." *Burlington Magazine* 124 (November 1992), 728–729.

Pilliod 1994: Pilliod, E. "Review of *From Studio to Studiolo, Florentine Draftsmanship under the First Medici Dukes.* Exhibition catalogue by L. J. Feinberg." *Master Drawings* 32, no. 4 (1994), 387–392.

Pluchart 1889: Pluchart, H. *Musée Wicar. Notice des dessins, cartons, pastels miniatures et grisailles exposés.* Lille, 1889.

Poggi 1965–1983: Poggi, G. *Il Carteggio di Michelangelo.* Eds. P. Barocchi and R. Ristori. 5 vols. Florence, 1965–1983.

Popham 1946: Popham, A. E. *Leonardo's Drawings.* London, 1946.

Popham and Pouncey 1950: Popham, A. E. and P. Pouncey. *Italian Drawings in the Department of Prints and Drawings of the British Museum. The 14th and 15th Centuries.* London, 1950.

Popham and Wilde 1949: Popham, A. E. and J. Wilde. *The Italian Drawings of the 15th and 16th Centuries in the Collection of His Majesty the King at Windsor Castle.* London, 1949. (Reissued in 1984 with appendix by R. Wood).

Popp 1922: Popp, A. E. *Die Medici-Kappelle Michelangelos.* Munich, 1922.

Popp 1925–1926: Popp, A. E. "Bermerkungen zu Einigen Zeichnungen Michelangelos." *Zeitschrift für Bildende Kunst* 59 (1925–1926), 134–146, 169–174.

Pouncey 1963: Pouncey, P. "I Disegni dei Pittori Fiorentini." *Master Drawings* 2, no. 3 (1964), 278–293.

Pouncey 1966: Pouncey, P. "Some Drawings by Camillo Procaccini Connected with Paintings and Choir Stalls." In *Arte in Europa: scritti di storia dell'arte in onore di Eduardo Arslan,* 641–649. Milan, 1966.

Pouncey and Gere 1962: Pouncey, P. and J. Gere. *Italian Drawings in the Department of Prints and Drawings in the British Museum. Raphael and His Circle.* London, 1962.

Price Amerson 1975: Price Amerson Jr., L., ed. *The Fortuna of Michelangelo. Prints, Drawings, and Small Sculpture from California Collections.* [exh. cat., E. B. Crocker Art Gallery and University of California] (Sacramento and Davis, California, 1975).

Ramade 1991: Ramade, P., ed. *Disegno. Actes du Congrès, Rennes, 9–10 octobre, 1990.* Rennes, 1991.

Roberts 1988: Roberts, J. *A Dictionary of Michelangelo's Watermarks.* Milan, 1988.

Robertson 1992: Robertson, C. *'Il Gran Cardinale,' Alessandro Farnese, Patron of the Arts.* New Haven and London, 1992.

Romani 1990: Romani, V. *Tibaldi 'D'Intorno' a Perino.* Padua, 1990.

Röttgen 1973: Röttgen, H. *Il Cavalieri d'Arpino.* [exh. cat., Palazzo Venezia] (Rome, 1973).

Salmi et al. 1965: Salmi, M. et al. *Michelangelo—Artista—Pensatore—Scrittore.* 2 vols. Novara, 1965.

Schaefer 1976: Schaefer, S. "Bronzino Drawings: A Plus and a Minus." *Master Drawings* 14, no. 1 (1976), 39–43.

Schilling and Blunt 1971: Schilling, E. and A. F. Blunt. *The German Drawings in the Collection of Her Majesty the Queen at Windsor Castle and Supplements to the Catalogues of Italian and French Drawings.* London, 1971.

Scorza 1995: Scorza, R. "Borghini and the Florentine Academies." In Chambers and Quiviger 1995, 137–152.

Sensier 1881: Sensier, A. *Jean-François Millet, Peasant and Painter.* Trans. H. De Kay. London, 1881.

Smyth 1971: Smyth, C. H. *Bronzino as Draftsman.* Locust Valley, 1971.

Smyth 1992: Smyth, C. H., ed. *Michelangelo Drawings.* Studies in the History of Art, no. 33. Washington, 1992.

Steinberg 1975: Steinberg, L. *Michelangelo's Last Paintings.* London, 1975.

Steinmann 1903–1905: Steinmann, E. *Die Sixtinische Kapelle.* 2 vols. Munich, 1903–1905.

Sutherland 1964: Sutherland, A. B. "A New Michelangelo Drawing in the Louvre." *Burlington Magazine* 106 (December 1964), 572–575.

Thode 1908: Thode, H. *Michelangelo, Kritische Untersuchungen über Seine Werke.* 2 vols. Berlin, 1908.

Thode 1913: Thode, H. *Michelangelo, Kritische Untersuchungen über Seine Werke. Vol. 3, Verzeichniss der Zeichnungen, Kartons und Modelle.* Berlin, 1913.

Tietze and Tietze-Conrat 1944: Tietze, H. and E. Tietze-Conrat. *The Drawings of the Venetian Painters in the 15th and 16th Centuries.* New York, 1944.

Turner 1986: Turner, N. *Florentine Drawings of the 16th Century.* [exh. cat., British Museum] (London, 1986).

Valenti Rodinò 1989: Valenti Rodinò, S. P. *Galleria dell'Accademia di Venezia, Disegni romani, toscani e napoletani.* Milan, 1989.

Vasari 1568: Vasari, G. *Le Vite dei piu eccelenti pittori, scultori ed architetti.* Florence, 1568.

Vasari-Barocchi 1962: Vasari, G. *La Vita di Michelangelo nelle redazioni del 1550 e del 1568.* Ed. P. Barocchi. 5 vols. Naples, 1962.

Von Hadeln 1925: Von Hadeln, D. *Venezianische Zeichnungen der Hochrenaissance.* Berlin, 1925.

Wallace 1995: Wallace, W. E. "Instruction and Originality in Michelangelo's Drawings." In *The Craft of Art, Originality and Industry in the Italian Renaissance and Baroque Workshop,* 113–133. Eds. A. Ladis and C. Woods. Athens, Georgia, and London, 1995.

Ward 1982: Ward, R. Baccio Bandinelli as a Draughtsman. Thesis submitted for Ph.D., Courtauld Institute of Art, London, 1982.

Wazbinski 1983: Wazbinski, Z. "La Cappella dei Medici e l'origine dell'Accademia del Disegno." *Firenze e la Toscana dei Medici nell'Europa del '500,* 55–69. Florence, 1983.

Wazbinski 1987: Wazbinski, Z. *L'Accademia Medicea del Disegno a Firenze nel Cinquecento, Idea e Istituzione.* 2 vols. Florence, 1987.

Wilde 1953a: Wilde, J. *Italian Drawings in the Department of Prints and Drawings in the British Museum. Michelangelo and His Studio.* London, 1953.

Wilde 1953b: Wilde, J. "Michelangelo and Leonardo." *Burlington Magazine* 95 (March 1953), 65–77.

Wilde 1954: Wilde, J. *Michelangelo, the Group of Victory.* Oxford, 1954.

Wilde 1978: Wilde, J. *Michelangelo, Six Lectures.* Oxford, 1978.

Winkelmann 1986: Winkelmann, J. "Pellegrino Tibaldi." In Fortunati Pietrantonio 1986, 2:475–541.

Wittkower 1937: Wittkower, R. "Physiognomical Experiments by Michelangelo and His Pupils." *Journal of the Warburg and Courtauld Institutes* 1 (1937–1938), 183–184.

Wittkower 1952: Wittkower, R. *The Drawings of the Carracci in the Collection of Her Majesty the Queen at Windsor Castle.* London, 1952.

Woodward 1870: Woodward, B. B. *Specimens of the Drawings of the Masters from the Royal Collection at Windsor Castle.* London, 1870.

Exhibitions

Catalogue authors or editors are given in parentheses

Florence 1964: *Michelangelo, mostra di disegni, manoscritti e documenti.* Casa Buonarroti and Biblioteca Laurenziana (P. Barocchi).

Florence 1980: *Il primato del Disegno.* Palazzo Strozzi (G. G. Bertelà, for no. 25).

Lisbon 1983: *Portuguese Discoveries and Renaissance Europe.* Museo Nacional de Arte Antigua.

London 1950–1951: *Works by Holbein and Other Masters of the 16th and 17th Centuries.* The Royal Academy, Burlington House.

London 1953: *Drawings by Michelangelo from British Collections.* British Museum (J. Wilde).

London 1972–1973: *Drawings by Michelangelo, Raphael, Leonardo and Their Contemporaries.* The Queen's Gallery, Buckingham Palace (A. F. Blunt).

London 1975: *Drawings by Michelangelo.* British Museum (J. A. Gere and N. Turner).

London 1983: *Drawings by Raphael.* British Museum (J. A. Gere and N. Turner).

London 1992: *Drawing in Bologna 1500–1600.* Courtauld Institute Galleries, University of London (E. Llewellyn and C. Romalli).

London, Queen's Gallery 1986: *Master Drawings in the Royal Collection, from Leonardo da Vinci to the Present Day.* The Queen's Gallery, Buckingham Palace (J. Roberts).

Mantua 1989: *Giulio Romano.* Palazzo del Tè and Palazzo Ducale (S. Ferino Pagden).

Montreal 1992: *The Genius of the Sculptor in Michelangelo's Work.* Montreal Museum of Fine Arts (P. C. Marani).

Pordenone 1984: *Il Pordenone.* Comune di Pordenone (C. Cohen).

Rome 1981–1982: *Gli Affreschi di Paolo III a Castel Sant'Angelo, 1543–1548.* Museo Nazionale di Castel Sant'Angelo (F. M. Aliberti Gaudioso and E. Gaudioso).

Washington-Paris 1988–1989: *Michelangelo Draftsman.* National Gallery of Art and Musée du Louvre (M. Hirst).

Washington-Parma 1984: *Correggio and His Legacy.* National Gallery of Art and Galleria Nazionale di Parma (D. De Grazia).

Tables of Concordance

The concordance of numbers from Royal Collection catalogues with numbers from this exhibition catalogue is as follows:

Popham and Wilde 1949	Exhibition
68	6
75	31
143	61
242	22
243	5
244	62
326/44	60
348	37
421	33
423	18
424	16
425	7
426	19
427	38
428	39
429	12
430	9
432	55
434	1
435	21
436	24
437	23
439	41
440	42
442	26
443	27
448	35
449	46
450	40
451	34
453	8
454	4
455	2
456	17
457	15
458	13
459	14
460	25
461	28
497	59
499	57
500	56
505	63
508	43
509	44
510	45
518	49
520	50
662	32
666	58
741	51
785	30
786	3
787	10
791	29
799	36
887	67
923	20
924	53
943	66
947	65
949	64
974	48
1056	54
1090	11
1161	68

Wittkower 1952	Exhibition
325	47
420	52

Blunt 1971	
521	67